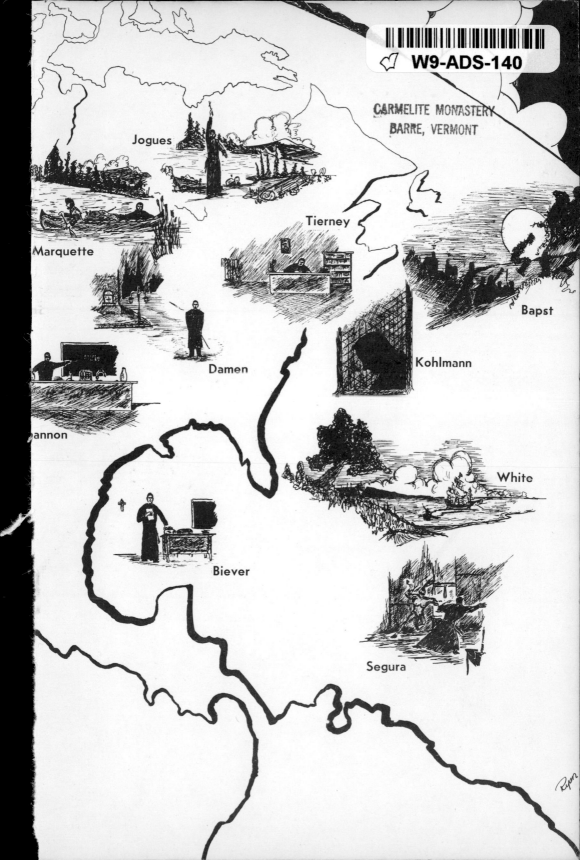

Jogues

Marquette

Tierney

Bapst

Damen

Kohlmann

annon

White

Biever

Segura

Ryan

I Lift My Lamp

I Lift My Lamp

JESUITS IN AMERICA

Edited by John P. Leary, S.J.

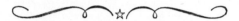

Keep, ancient lands, your storied pomp.
Give me your tired, your poor,
Your huddled masses yearning to
  breathe free.
The wretched refuse of your teeming
  shore,
Send these, the homeless, tempest-tost
  to me,
I lift my lamp beside the golden door.
(Inscription from the base of the Statue of Liberty)

The Newman Press • *1955* • *Westminster, Maryland*

To the Virgin Mary
Immaculately Conceived,
Chosen Patroness
of the United States of America
by the First Plenary Council of Baltimore
in the year 1846

Contents

Introduction

This story has wanted telling for a long time. It is about a company of brave men who came here four hundred years ago to challenge the wilderness of America. Before anyone had ever dreamt of Jamestown or Plymouth Rock, these men in black soutanes had pushed their way into Georgia. They had settled on five different spots in Florida, had ventured into the Carolinas, and had reddened the soil of Virginia with their blood.

We never read very much about these men in our history books when we were children. They scarcely seemed to be of even passing significance in the swift and mercenary calculations of many American historians.

Actually the Jesuits were a foundation only fifteen years old when they sent their men to the New World. They have been in America ever since. No one, no group of individuals has better right to feel at home in this bountiful land.

First they came to reclaim the savages, to teach them of God, give them the sacraments, offer the Mass. The Indians broke the hearts of the blackrobes; the tomahawk found its way into the head of many a brave man who gladly gave up his dearest possession that God's kingdom might move forward.

The annals of history show that the first efforts of the Order met only with failure, a dismal pattern closely approximating that of Christianity itself and its Founder who culminated an unspectacular life on a bitter Friday afternoon. It was the old, old story of the seed falling into the ground and dying and bringing forth, in time, God's time, much fruit.

Jesuits came with the French, with the Spanish, with the English to Maryland. They won the grudging admiration of the Dutch in New York. They sailed along the Great Lakes and down the Mississippi through the heart of the future United States.

They rode horseback over the hot sands of Arizona and Southern California. They pushed their way into Missouri, out over the Rockies to Montana and Idaho. Many of the places they saw, the rivers, the mountains, the strange tribes of Indians, looked perhaps for the first time on a white man, dressed in black with his crucifix and rosary at his side.

The Jesuits helped build the cities of America, dot the landscape with churches where the human spirit might drink deeply of the ideals needed to build this new empire. They built schools and universities to transmit their cultural heritage, to help clarify the vision of her people and deepen their grasp of the need for the spiritual in human outlook.

These men helped cement the loyalties of heartsick immigrants, weld all the varied and dissident factors into a new unity. Her preachers stormed up and down the land begging the faithful to be true and those who had fallen to come back. In a land gone wild over material enhancement they stoutly stood their ground. Eternal values came first.

You cannot think of anything fundamentally American without eventually thinking also of the sons of the Society of Jesus. They were at the Chesapeake, the Wabash, the Colorado, rode into Abilene on the saddle and into Cheyenne, came up against the Adirondacks and the Cascades, crossed the Oregon Trail and the Sante Fe; they pushed up through the Yukon and the Chilkoot Pass.

They purchased the ground for St. Patrick's Cathedral, told Brigham Young how to get to Salt Lake, were among the first white men to hit the Palouse.

And there was bigotry to be wrestled with; some of their members were tarred and feathered; they were criticized and threatened. But they persevered as part of the national scene. Their contribution to the life blood of America is incalculable. But both naturally and in the order of grace it has undoubtedly been in God's eyes a wonderful contribution.

The Fathers and Brothers of the Company charted new

paths from all corners of the country. As the historian Bancroft says in one of his books, "Not a cape was turned, not a river entered, but a Jesuit led the way." And all of this at the price of unbelievable hardship, sacrifices they would not make for all the treasures of the Klondike or California.

The ardor and enterprise of America flowed in their veins. Their mission was to help channel this great river of progress moving forward tumultuously into new, unexplored phases of human destiny. Men have cried out always for betterment, a decent living, a just social order, opportunity for the underprivileged, peace under law, as an extension and fulfillment of the life which Christ came to give. It was the task of the Order to help as much as possible in achieving these ideals. Its flexibility and respect for the views of others equipped it well for work among peoples of such various backgrounds and conflicting points of view. The Jesuits aimed to be before all else apostles; they wanted to be Christ walking through America at evening, offering the Great Prayer at dawn each day for the souls entrusted to their care. Like St. Paul, they tried to make themselves liked and esteemed by their fellow men, so to gain audience and win favor for their principles.

There are not many lands left now for conquest. The terrain of physical effort is visibly hemmed in and confined. In our day the process of deepening and solidification has already begun. It shall never end, for there are no limits to the human potential.

So there is work for all of the Company, for her missionaries and explorers, for her builders, founders of schools, her writers and preachers, retreat masters, chaplains and teachers, saints and martyrs. We younger Jesuits, who have written here about a few of our great brother priests, are proud to take the mantle from the august shoulders of our forebears. Though we feel dwarfed walking in the shadow of past glories, still everyone knows that God will provide help for the emergencies and crises which lie in store for us who are to follow in their footsteps.

The Society today braces itself for the new tasks which must be accomplished. A whole nation is waiting to be Christianized: people in her mills and factories, her mines and industries, the farms and cities must be helped to share in the vision for which they crave so earnestly even in their errors, their sins, and disbelief. The people of the United States are actually looking for God, looking for Him in the theaters, in TV sets, on the radio, in books and magazines and automobiles, in escape from futility. And since He is looking for them too, they are bound to meet somewhere, sometime, if only someone will bring them together. Jesuits aspire to help achieve that mission.

We keep in mind, of course, that our Founding Father called his Order "this least Society of Jesus." We are glad that God wills to use these least instruments in His plans for world reclamation. All of us realize very well that we are only one movement in the great vitalizing process, one small part of the leaven at work patiently, at times darkly in the mass.

Where its works have abounded, it would be unthinkable for the Society to glory in a sort of isolated splendor. It has not worked alone. And furthermore all real glory, a sense of homage, men's labor and love . . . all accrue to the Church, and hence to Christ, Our Lord, and hence to His Divine Father, the Source and Fountainhead of all good.

For it was the Church which gave birth to the Society. And it has been the Church, out of its infinite fecundity, that has nourished and sustained our Order down the years. Even before the Jesuits were thought of, forces were at work which would converge in time of crisis to help shape the outlook and the way of life peculiar to the Society. It has always been so. That same inspired pattern of wisdom and foresight has repeated itself with every Religious Order and Congregation and Confraternity, and indeed, with every single human vocation, so manifold are the hidden designs of Providence.

Fitting the Society of Jesus into this fuller and far more resplendent life of the Catholic Church in which she abides and moves and has her being, we can only cry out that indeed God is wonderful in His variety.

And so more and more it seems now that a wise Providence has precious designs upon America. Her eminent position in world affairs, her bounteous resources, her idealism and gener-

Introduction

osity, her sense of freedom and fair play mark the country for leadership in the long process of man's historic development. We Jesuits are happy to take our place, as our forefathers did, in the vanguard of progress. We want to stand in spirit by the Statue of Liberty in New York harbor. What is inscribed on the base of that statue has been for centuries the cry of the Church and of the Order. It is a symbol of America's destiny and our own. We cannot work separately. People who are confused look to us from the darkness for light and we reply as did our ancestors:

> Keep, ancient lands, your storied pomp.
> Give me your tired, your poor,
> Your huddled masses yearning to breathe free.
> The wretched refuse of your teeming shore,
> Send these, the homeless, tempest-tost to me,
> I lift my lamp beside the golden door.

THE EDITOR

Acknowledgments

The efforts of so many kind people go into making up a book of this kind that it is quite difficult to mention them in any detail. We are especially grateful to all of those who did pioneer work in the lives of many of the men contained in this book. All of us have drawn heavily from the results of their labors. Needless to say, the encouragement given our work by our Superiors and fellow Religious has been strong incentive for us.

The authors feel particularly indebted to the following: Rev. Francis Talbot, S.J., of New York; Doctor Bolton of the University of California; Rev. William Rice, S.J., and Rev. Zacheus Maher, S.J., of El Retiro Retreat House in California; Rev. Wm. Repetti, S.J., Archivist at Georgetown University, Washington, D. C.; Rev. Charles Chapman, S.J., of New Orleans; Rev. Edmond Lamalle, S.J., of the Jesuit Historical Institute, Rome; Rev. Val Roche, S.J., and Rev. James Macelwane, S.J., of St. Louis University; Rev. Eugene Zimmers, S.J., Rev. John Murphy, S.J., and Rev. Edward Warren, S.J., of Alma College, California; the Xavier University Library, Cincinnati, Ohio; and the Huntington Library, San Marino, California.

The map on the endsheet is the work of a Jesuit Scholastic, William Ryan of Sheridan, Oregon. The idea for this book and much of the historical research involved came from two of the authors, Rev. Wilfred Schoenberg, S.J., and Rev. R. I. Burns, S.J. Rev. Frank Costello, another author, was also of great help. Our Superior, Rev. Hilary Werts, S.J., in the theologate deserves our gratitude. And finally our thanks to the former Provincial of the Oregon Province, Rev. Harold Small, S.J.; without his quiet and effective encouragement, it would have been far more difficult to bring this book to successful issue.

Empire *was in the offing. One storied adventurer from Genoa had in his frail bark followed the sun west to this New World. Here in the hard, firm soil he planted the flag of Spain, claiming in imperative voice that these endless miles of mystery were now booty for a king.*

From glade and wooded cliff fierce-eyed redmen watched these intruders from over the waters. This was Indian land. Fear ran through their blood. Back across the continent drifted word that palefaces in large canoes were bartering and killing in this ancient home where before no marauder had ever been save the wild beasts and the storms, the Sioux, the Iroquois, and the Apache.

But on that jutting peninsula which is Spain there had been born suddenly such men of fortune and enterprise as the world had seldom seen—all bent upon exploit, on prying open the treasures of this fledgling world thrust suddenly upon their doorstep. There was Balboa scanning the Pacific with "wild surmise," Ponce de Leon stumbling on a lovely wilderness of Florida in his quest for the fountain of youth. Cortez had unsealed fabulous Mexico; Pizarro, a Peru. De Soto was rubbing wonder-struck eyes at the swells of the Mississippi.

Quick on the heels of her soldiers came the Padre with his Cross and his broad, flapping hat and beads. Laving waters poured upon the heads of Indian babes. Dominican priests had set up operations near Tampa in 1549. A year later the Franciscans could count eighty monasteries in America. Mexico University was chartered in '51 and five colleges in the New World were near their centennial before Harvard began.

Library and printing press, the sound of a church bell ring-

ing out clear in this virgin land: all stirred the pagan breast with envy and admiration. The white men spoke of great mystery, of Him Who made the sun drop red into the hills of the west at dusk. They squatted listening to this strange tale and old men shook their heads in wonder.

*   *   *

Born of Good Blood

Father Baptista Segura, S.J.

by Theodore Mackin, S.J.

Father Baptista Segura was a Jesuit provincial; he had been a rector three times over. So he was as used to worry in the mind as many men are to bad teeth in their mouths. Furthermore, like most educated worriers, he periodically lined his troubles up, ranked and filed them in order of importance, and then inspected them one by one, up and down, inside and out. And he perhaps altered their order, or cast some out, or tagged others with newer and more promising plans for riddance. That was what he was doing this particular midnight—and he knew he should not be.

He should be sleeping the same heavy-breathing, dead sleep as the other eight men—and the child Alonso—who lay huddled in their cloaks, spaced evenly around the faint-glowing camp-fire embers with feet toward it, like spokes toward a wheel hub. He was as exhausted as they. And with them he would again be staggering all the following day along the swamp-path and through the baking September humidity until he was numb under the weight of sacks and bundles and casks from the ship. This last afternoon's hauling had got barely half their supplies to the nearby Indian village.

· 2 ·

Instead of sleeping, he lay achingly weary, but wide awake. Against his will he listened to the flowing whisper of the Rappahannock over to the south a stone's throw, behind its hedge of willow and wild lilac and blackberry thorn, wending the rest of its 20 leagues down to the sea. And being bothered by the mosquitoes that sang and swarmed in from the stagnant pools along its banks. And getting his throat raw and beginning to feel chilled by the mist that rose silently off its surface and threaded through the tangle of brush and laced its way up into the tree shadows as midnight passed into early morning.

So he grew petulant with himself and more wide awake than ever. They would all have to be up with the first gray filtering of dawn through the trees east of the clearing. How far was it back to where the boat lay at anchor with the rest of the supplies? Five leagues? Six? It was next to impossible to judge the distance by the time it had taken them to make the one trip here to the Ajacan village. They had been forced to stop and rest so often under the weight of their packs. But if they were to get back to the ship, write the letter of instructions and put it under seal in the pilot's care, and then be ready to load sacks and bundles on their backs in time to make the return trip, they had best be there at least an hour before noon. And if, as Father de Quiros and the Brothers had suggested, the distance was six leagues, that would mean six hours' walking time there and almost eight back. Today it had been only one way and his legs had turned to stone. What would it be like tomorrow, after a night of tossing and turning and staring up into the darkness?

What about the Ajacan braves who had been so surprisingly alert and waiting for them as they climbed overboard and splashed through mud and weeds to the river-bank yesterday morning? Why could they not have helped with the carrying? They had found the biscuit cask soon enough, and at every stop had stuffed their mouths. Had the agreement not to hinder them for the present been a wise one? More than all else, the savages' friendship was wanted from the very outset. And the biscuit, though meant to be the staple diet for the nine missioners, may well have been the price of amicable beginnings. So at least Don Luis had assured them; and he was in a position to know.

But their refusal to so much as turn a hand toward carrying the smallest of the bundles—that was a piece of evidence that hardly fitted Don Luis' running description of his people during these last months before their leaving Havana. It was not that they had failed to understand the Jesuits' need for help. If he had obeyed, Don Luis had communicated the request to his tribesmen—as he was intended to communicate so many in the future. Even after nine years' absence he had apparently not forgotten their strange, guttural tongue. The conversation between homecoming chief and tribesmen had set a striking pace for the usually taciturn savage.

Another thing that failed to fit the pattern of Don Luis' narration was the physical state of his people. Instead of the tall, full-limbed braves he had described, there was the same gaunt, sallow look about them, the same body-sores that Segura had found so universally among the Florida tribes through the past three years. They told mutely of a diet of acorns and roots and of winter starvation.

And this group of native huts to which they had been brought at sundown yesterday—was it a representative Ajacan village, with five or six skin-covered hovels, their women no more clothed than the men in their breach-clouts? And what of the under-sized children, evidently suffering from rickets and probably (some of them at least) lung-sickness? If the Ajacans grouped in no greater numbers than these, then their hunting parties, if any, could not be large. And that, too, helped to explain their half-starved appearance.

Segura's mind wandered back to the morrow's task of hauling the remainder of the supplies. One way through the difficulty would be to ask Gonzales to order the Spanish sailors to their aid. It was a tempting expedient. But again, what of his long-standing resolution to allow these Ajacans no slightest contact with Spanish military personnel? The years in Florida had taught him lessons on that score. To say even the best about them, the sailors were incurably addicted to bartering. But was there any guarantee that they would limit themselves to bits of cloth and metal as enticement for the savages? Moreover, no matter how many might aid in the portage, the length of the journey would necessitate their staying overnight at the village. That, too, was something better avoided.

So he debated within himself, and decided after a long battle with thoughts that were scattered and intractable, that he, Father de Quiros, and the Brothers would do the carrying on the morrow as they had done it that day.

The largest worry was saved for last. To get attention centered on it involved something more tangible than trying to shove his tired mind into a pattern. For that Segura was grateful. He raised himself on one elbow and looked for a long moment at the figure of Don Luis stretched out a few feet to his left. Now he was no more than a shadow, motionless in the leaves and matted grass. But the coming of daylight would reveal the coarse-strung black hair, the aquiline nose and over-generous mouth, the high cheek-bones and broad face of an Algonquin Indian.

And when the group would have been aroused for the return journey to the supply ship, Don Luis would speak with the missioners in commendable Castilian, would enter familiarly and easily into the brief morning prayers, and would take without question a position of equality among them. And well Don Luis might take an air of ease and familiarity. Where in all the New World missions, reflected Segura, had so much honor been accorded the word of one Christianized savage?—and savage was what Don Luis had been when taken from this land nine years earlier. Indeed, Segura wished that the Indian were not quite so shrewdly aware that it was his power of persuasion that had got a Jesuit provincial (himself) to abandon his assigned area of operation and come 200 leagues northward into this wilderness of St. Mary's Bay, reshaping thereby the plans of a Spanish governor in the Caribbean and a Jesuit general in Rome. Had Don Luis actually ever gathered such accumulated realization into the front of his mind? If so, what had it done to him? Was his story of the malleability and of the readiness of these, his people, for Christianity sufficient warrant for all that had been upset in the missions to come to them? In the light of this question, their appearance a few hours earlier had been distressing. For just a second, as the Jesuits had staggered into the clearing and among the huts at sundown, all this vagrant fear had come together and coagulated in Segura's heart—or, as it seemed then, in the pit of his stomach.

Thus wondering and thus fearing, Segura sank back against his pillow of rolled-up soutane and tried to lace up the web of worry with a tired prayer. And like many almost neurotically active men, it was when he tried eventually to pray that he found sleep. A thought too poetic to have crossed his mind then was that this first sleep taken by men bringing Christ to these northern savages was where it should be: prone among the clods, leaves, and grass—with not really a place to lay their heads. Much less could he have suspected that that was also the way they would take their last sleep there. That kind of speculating is the plaything of the writer's fancy centuries later. Right then, as early morning hours wore toward the daylight of September 18, 1570, Baptista Segura's consciousness was closing out with the image of an Alqonquin Indian in doublet, breeches, and boots. And it was, after three short hours, to awake with it still there, like a sore that had festered during the night.

* * *

Father Segura had first heard Don Luis' story in April of that year, 1570, at Havana. The Spanish court at Madrid had heard it five years earlier. But the court was still in Madrid, whereas Father Segura was now hauling hammers, hoes, altar linens, hard tack, and a church bell on his back to the banks of the Rappahannock, making ready to build his dream-mission.

To lead a Jesuit provincial to such a task in such a literally outlandish place, it must have been a long-jointed story. Probably Don Luis had never limited himself to the following shorter version of it before his European audiences. But short though it be, it is just as complete. Briefly: his people on the 14-mile strip of land between what we know now as the Potomac and the Rappahannock rivers were not the lazy, thieving, syphilis-eaten, bigamous, and earth-bound aborigines on whom the Fathers had been wasting the last five years in Florida. On the contrary, nature and custom had inclined his Powhatan branch of the Algonquin nation to Christianity, to its theology and to its moral demands. So, if the Jesuits could see their way to sending some of the Fathers among them—with him, Don Luis, in the vanguard—they could expect in a consolingly short time to have one entire, new-world tribe within the Christian fold. And with said tribe as staging-area, point-of-departure, living example, interpreter, and co-worker, there was every hope of redeeming the barren years of Florida as much as thirty, sixty, and a hundred-fold among kindred Indians to the west and the north.

That was one story, and Don Luis was its author. How close to the facts it lay remains to be seen. (And how much initial sincerity lay behind it, God alone knows.) There is another that has to be told briefly if we are to understand how one New World savage ever got the ear (and captured the imagination) of a responsible Jesuit superior. This one is not by, but about Don Luis.

If it has a plot, and if the plot has a critical point, it is that Don Luis and his tale of bright hopes among the north-country Algonquins met the Jesuits at the very time when these latter were beginning to despair of their rack-and-ruin missions in Florida. So both parties have to be accounted for.

First, about Don Luis. He first met the Spaniards when, in 1561, a vessel from the Dominican mission of Santa Elena (about 9 miles below the present Charleston, South Carolina) lost its way and put into what the seamen then called Baia de la Madre di Dios (or alternately Baia de Santa Maria de Jacan), our present-day Chesapeake Bay. Some coastal Indians, among them a young *cacique* or sub-chief, came aboard out of friendly curiosity. When the ship set sail for the return southward, the young *cacique* went with it—though whether as passenger or as prisoner is not known.

He was escorted to Mexico City as a willing prize, and there instructed and baptized into the Catholic faith. His godfather was the viceroy of Mexico himself, Don Luis de Alvarez, who generously bestowed on the neophyte his own swash-buckling title.

At that time the great, heroic, and high-handed governor of the Floridas, Pedro Menendez de Aviles, was laying his first plans for a Dominican mission to the Chesapeake area. He saw immediately that the newly-Christian Don Luis would be a splendid front-runner for a Christianizing expedition back to his own people. And he secured him for just that role, but only over the protest of the prudent (or prophetic) Archbishop of Mexico, who put little apostolic trust in dripping-fresh Indian converts.

The expedition got under way. But Dominicans, soldiers, and Indian never reached the Chesapeake. They got to latitude 37°, returned to 36°, then back to 37°30′, without Don Luis' being able to recognize the coastal territory. Then a strong wind blew them out to sea. This the ship's captain used as an excuse to fulfill a longing of some months' duration: to return to Spain. And so he did.

There Don Luis was given the standing and financial maintenance of a noble by King Philip. Whatever the proportions of this grandeur, it was certainly larger than what he had grown up with back in the swamplands of Ajacan between the Potomac and the Rappahannock. This odyssey lasted for four and a half years and was mingled with intermittent doses of education at the Jesuit college of Seville, where he studied reading, writing, the Spanish language, and "other branches of knowledge," probably the rudiments of theology.

Don Luis' return to the New World was in February of 1570, with an expedition equipped and commanded by the same Menendez de Aviles. With them went three Jesuits, Father Louis de Quiros and two coadjutor Brothers, Sancho Zaballos and Pedro Linares. These were meant to reinforce the small corps of Jesuits who had three years earlier inherited the Florida mission from the Dominicans when these were moved west to push back the frontiers of Mexico. It is recorded significantly that on the voyage Father de Quiros won the special intimacy of Don Luis.

It was on the expedition's arrival at Havana two months later in mid-April that Don Luis and Father Segura first crossed paths. The latter had already been on the Florida mission for two years, was established as its superior (vice-provincial), and had just then returned from a month's discouraging sojourn at the Guale mission station up the Atlantic coast in present-day Georgia's Liberty County (between Ossobaw and St. Catherine Sounds).

And it was then that Segura first heard Don Luis' story—the one recounted earlier here, the one with which Don Luis had regaled first the Hapsburg court at Madrid, then Menendez de Aviles, and very probably his fellow-voyagers, Father de Quiros and Brothers Zaballos and Linares. And considering that Providence earnestly meant Father Segura to lead a Jesuit missionary band north to the Chesapeake—he being led in turn by Don Luis—it was the strategically perfect moment for the priest to hear that story. Why that is so is ascribable to the state of soul in which he heard it. And that, in turn, was due to the state of the Florida mission that he had just inspected.

If Segura drew up an itemized account of what his visitation had revealed (and according to rule that was what he was supposed to do), it probably read, in substance at least, as follows.

"Florida mission, west coast: three mission stations taken over in 1567, but occupied only successively by Father Rogel. The first, Tocobaga [today's Tampa] abandoned in January, 1568, when Indians massacred the Spanish garrison. The second, to the south at Charlotte Bay, also abandoned by Rogel, also because of massacre. The third, still further southward at San Antonio, abandoned by Rogel on Palm Sunday, 1568. Reason: no one else to exploit more favorable conditions at St. Augustine on the north-east Florida coast. A fourth station at Tegesta [now Miami] abandoned when Father Rogel took with him to St. Augustine, Brother Francisco Villareal. The latter had carried on alone as teacher and catechist after the natives, with ample reason, had burned the village and driven off the Spanish garrison. These four missions reoccupied in 1569, but now facing starvation and hostile Indians.

"Florida mission, east coast. Guale [actually in modern Georgia, as noted above]: food supply turned over to Indians by timorous garrison commander. Jesuits and settlers survived the winter just past (1570) on acorns. No planting done the year previous; settlers too weak on a ration of one-half pound of flour per day. Orista [15 miles inland from the Guale coastal mission]: abandoned by Father Rogel after initial success with monogamous, hard-working, and relatively sedentary Oristan families. Reasons: (1) Father Rogel confused an ancestral deity with the Biblical Satan; natives alienated. (2) Oristans antagonized by Spanish garrison captain's plundering of scarce food supplies. Massacre followed; mission destroyed." (Father Rogel, thanks be to God, escaped again.) [Actually the burning of the Orista mission was not until July of that year. But when news of it did get to Havana, it added to Segura's already long list of recorded disasters.]

To get back to the Provincial's report—"Relations with the Spanish military: unhappy. Areas of authority uncertain; Jesuit missioners sometimes held under military obedience and made to act as garrison chaplains. Spanish soldiers not infrequently pillage Indian supplies and domestic possessions, molest Indian women.

"External difficulties: French corsairs [who were financed by the Tudor Elizabeth of England and the Medici Catherine in France to pillage the rich Spanish Main] intercept supply ships and threaten coastal missions.

"Added factors: Spanish missioners especially susceptible to local fevers; Indians to imported European maladies. Father Antonio Sedeño and Brothers Francisco Villareal and Domingo Baez laid low by the tertian fever at Guale during the winter just past (1569–70). Brother Baez succumbed, and with his passing went the only man to have mastered the Timuquan and Yamassee tongues of the Guale natives.

"Long-range prospects: grim. Governor Menendez de Aviles meets increasing difficulty in wheedling funds from the royal *Contratacion*. And he has very nearly exhausted his own personal fortune on this colony of the Floridas. Jesuit superiors in Spain reluctant to assign sufficient men to the mission."

Such was the tangle of troubles that lay in Father Segura's soul when first he listened to Don Luis' story that April of 1570 in Havana. Could we say that he dallied with temptation when he listened to him, and when, with the added coaxing of Menendez, the incurable frontier-chaser, his thoughts, dreams, and ambitions began to stretch out toward the blessed freshness of the lands to the north by St. Mary's Bay? Not dallying, really, but only recognizing a better thing when he saw it—or rather (and here's the rub) when it was described to him.

However, even had the Florida missions not been falling into ruin one by one, there was an added task at Havana that might well keep him there duty-bound indefinitely. One of the projects assigned him as superior of the Florida mission was the founding of a college at Havana for the sons of Florida Indian chiefs. The idea was originally Menendez', although sold convincingly to the Jesuit General, Borgia. According to the governor's idealizing mind, the young chiefs were to become first educated, then Christians, and then finally the sons-in-law of wealthy Spanish colonists, thus accomplishing long evangelization in a short space.

What is more, those who habitually misinterpret missionary work as a sub-intellectual enterprise would advise that founding and administering a college was precisely what Segura's pitch and stress of character were measured for. A finely-strung Toletan who had earned his master's in philosophy by 19 and his doctor's in dogma and scripture by 26—so the critical appraisal might go—was, in any case, no one to command men in the desolations and dangers of a New World mission.

But by that April of 1570, when Don Luis and his story entered to siphon Segura's hopes and ambitions off in another direction, no solid and lasting steps had been taken toward establishing that first college in Havana. It would be wholly false, however, to say that Segura had failed in obedience to Borgia in not getting it started before considering a departure for the St. Mary's Bay country. In the first place, Borgia had left him a broad liberty of judgment in the matter of when and how to make the foundation—if, indeed, it was to be made at all.

Secondly, when he did ask the judgments of the experienced Fathers of the missions between April and July, the very months when he was weighing the pros and cons of taking off with Don Luis, the ship collecting the written answers was delayed over-long by storms. (As it turned out later, they advised almost to a man against the move.)

And Segura did post more than seven letters to Borgia during the same period, explaining the full fabric of his needs and purposes and posing the burning question, "Should he get the college started first and then leave for the north; or get the northern mission started and then come back and attend to the college?" But for reasons known only to himself, Borgia gave the letters a low priority on the list of matters to be attended to, and did not get around to answering Segura until late that autumn—to be exact on November 18. And that was at least three months later than the critical date for deciding finally to go or not to go.

But what Segura wanted least as spring passed into summer, and summer wore on through July, was delayed replies. If permission to set out were on its way (and it was, though Segura was never to know it), then it had best come in time for boat and supplies for a summer trip. Autumn would be too late; a northern mission would have to be relatively self-sustaining and insulated before the onset of winter. And a year's delay might find the Jesuits recalled to Spain, re-routed to Peru, or reduced to corpses by starvation and fever.

So there came to be a burning question number two: "Should he, Segura, wait for the replies, or take matters into his own hands and leave for the north without them?" Finally, knowing that whichever way he decided, decide he must, Segura elected to mount the expedition without hearing from either General or missionary colleagues. Accordingly he had, at Menendez's expense, a ship of especially shallow draft prepared at Havana. It must have been equipped as a kind of Noah's ark in miniature, because it was intended to carry not only supplies for the missionaries' immediate needs but also the beginnings of gardens, flocks, and herds for the St. Mary's mission. And the fact that, withal, the ship was small enough eventually to make its way up one of the Potomac tributaries promised the Fathers and Brothers more than a theoretical acquaintance with barnyard mores.

Sometime during the first week of August the party set sail from Havana. First in strategic value, if not in *de facto* primacy, was Don Luis—all eagerness and importance at leading God's missioners and king's men to the land of his own people. Then the Jesuits: Fathers Segura and de Quiros; the three coadjutor Brothers, Pedro Linares, Sancho Zaballos, and Gabriel Gomez; and the three catechists who had recently been received into the Order as postulants: Gabriel de Solis, Juan Mendez, and Cristobal Redondo.

Finally there was the nine-year-old lad, Alonso Olmos, taken along at his own begging as acolyte and house-boy. As the craft nosed its way through the Florida keys and up the east coast under a steaming August sky, it certainly never entered his young dreams that he alone of all the missionary band would survive to narrate the full flowering of Father Segura's decision to trust everything to the word of one Indian.

From historical silence on the matter it is presumed that the trip northward was uneventful—provided one overlooks a stop-in at the Santa Elena mission that found the settlers plague-ridden and their food-stores destroyed by fire. On September 11 the boat turned westward into St. Mary's Bay (the Chesapeake), where it stretches 14 miles from today's Cape Henry across to Cape Charles on the north. Past the flatlands where lies the modern Norfolk and its huge naval base, and past the mouth of the James River the craft glided ahead of coastal winds. North again past the mouth of the Rappahannock, and then, about September 13 or 14, westward into the broad mouth of the Potomac where it empties into the Chesapeake at Point Lookout.

From there they wound their way 60 miles up the Potomac to one of its tributaries, the Aguia. Then southward upstream on this latter, moving toward the Rappahannock until they reached the landing site just halfway between it and the Potomac they had left behind.

We have already seen that one of Father de Quiros' first moves was to pen a letter, put it under seal, and send it back with the ship's captain, who was to deliver it to Rogel at Guale. Father Segura, applying his weight as superior, added an urgent plea for further supplies. The Indians were already on meager rations because of poor hunting and a severely prolonged winter that year. So they were in no mood to sustain nine Spaniards out of their small hoardings.

To the letter were added verbal instructions to captain and crew. The Jesuits could hope to maintain themselves no longer than four months. Consequently the ship was to return with supplies before the end of January—and we can imagine the captain's reaction to suggested travel at that time of the year. At the outside they should be back by March of the following year (1571).

There were to be signs whereby the returning seamen would know that it was safe to land, or that it would be worthwhile landing at all. Indians would have reported their progress up the Potomac and its tributary. So some from their mission village would be sent to light fires at the mouth of the creek. But lest the Indians, having possibly disposed of the Jesuits in the meantime, should lead the crew into a trap (for the sake of their supplies), additional signs would await them at the original point of debarkation itself. Crosses and a roughhewn altar would be built there. Should they fail to find those, they would know that all were dead, and should not waste time and possibly lives in a fruitless search. Evidently the first few hours with the Ajacans had made Segura a coldly realistic man.

It should have taken no keen student of human nature to predict what Don Luis' status would be among the tribesmen from whom he had been nine years absent. Some of the glory and awe inhering in the blackrobes he accompanied undoubtedly, as the savages saw it, rubbed off on him. To them his ease and familiarity with the strangers was big medicine. It must be noted, too, that these Ajacan Indians were seeing their first Spaniards. Unlike the Florida and Carolina coastal tribes, they had not had long experience of corn and fish supplies raided, skins and weapons pilfered, their women seduced or raped by the Spanish soldiery—pastimes at which the Indians were primordial adepts themselves, and which, as a consequence, laid the Spaniards neatly in the same caste of common clay as themselves.

But here on the shores of the Rappahannock the Europeans arrived and moved in a mood of semi-deification. Don Luis had learned many things in the schools and courts of Spain (as we shall see), and one of them was the not-too-difficult art of turning a gratuitously favorable situation to his own glory. And in order to heighten the glory, he heightened the situation. By predetermined strategy of propaganda (justified in principle, but bungled in practice), he was set before his tribesmen as an equal of the Jesuits in every way—a token of collective Christian regard for the Indian and an implied symbol of what Christianity could do for the Indian.

So Don Luis played the proffered role for all that was in it. He strutted and preened among the home-town savages, and regaled them with many a magical tale of the white man's prowess—with the added suggestion that he had learned a trick or two himself. With that much of an exact statement historically available we can conclude for the rest that he commandeered the vehicle of primitive story-telling and ran it a bizarre and incredible course. Within three days or a week (which is as long as he stayed with the Fathers at their first settlement), the savages' collective mind-picture of the Havana of Don Luis' recent past, of the sea voyages and the remoter Saragossa, the college at Valladolid, of the court of Philip II at Madrid where he had been presented and feted by Hapsburg royalty—all these must have been a photomontage of Camelot, Babylon, and Land of Oz combined, with, of course, the figure of Don Luis upstage-center throughout.

The effect was the desired one. The villagers were induced to cooperate with the Fathers and Brothers to the extent of helping them knock together one crude building that was in function two: a chapel and, at the other end, living quarters for the eight of them. To the Indians probably fell the job of dragging timber selected and cut by the Brothers, with the carpentering done by the latter.

In the meantime (i.e., within the week or less since arriving) Don Luis had been begging for permission to visit his uncle and his village at a distance of four leagues (half a day's travel on foot) to the west. The request was certainly reasonable: not for nine years had he seen his kinfolk. But the Fathers' reasons for detaining him the five days, more or less, that they did, were equally solid. He was the sole medium of communication between them and the Ajacans. He had to be on hand to help direct the gathering of timber; and for as long as that need endured, he stayed. But of far more vital importance, he was to be the indispensable go-between in the work of religious instruction. The Fathers knew not a word of the Algonquin dialect. So if the savages were to hear of the three persons in one divine substance, of the mystery of the human nature united to the divine in Christ, of heaven, of hell, of the sacraments, of the necessity for baptism; if they were to learn the detailed rudiments of the Christian moral code so foreign to their ways— all this would have to funnel through the mind of Don Luis and what on-the-spot verbal imagery he could summon to sift theological sublimities for aboriginal minds. It would be that way or not at all. Plainly, Don Luis had his work cut out for him. And with still vivid recollections of what sun-up to sundown task-mastering Spanish pedagogues were capable of, he no doubt reasoned that he deserved a rest and a reward.

Father Segura agreed. Don Luis was to visit his uncle for a period of five days including travel time. The consequent delay in getting catechetical instructions under way could be used to advantage in enlarging and strengthening their domestic beachhead. So, with a promise to be back within the stipulated time, Don Luis departed.

What happened at the uncle's village would be easy to conjecture even were the few available facts not on hand. Don Luis, it must be remembered, was a chief in his own tribe. So his home-coming was a return to pre-eminence over and above that gathered from his association with the marvelous men in black from across the great waters.

Furthermore—and this is a pivotal point—one of the oldest and most honored of tribal customs was that of multiple wives, polygamy—a vice that had checkmated the missioners in Florida and which Don Luis had lyingly assured them was not to be found among his own people. Added to that was the prerogative of a chief's access to the village women of his choice. So Don Luis' homecoming shortly turned into a personal, but not necessarily private, bacchanal. In the flat-toned language of the sixteenth-century chronicler, "Acting more like a heathen than a Christian in his conduct, in his garb and in his whole manner of living, he . . . plunged himself into unbridled license and all kinds of sins, taking many women unto himself according to the pagan custom."

There could be a great deal of moralizing on how a man fresh out of five years' steeping in Christian education could desert his principles so easily. But the interpretation is not so central as the fact. What happened to Don Luis' morals is what happens to most morals under the overwhelming attrition of environment. It may likewise be too easily forgotten that such was the environment and practice in which he had been reared and lived a number of adult years, and from which he had been separated unwillingly by his Spanish abductors. So the continence forced on him under Jesuit surveillance, in the face of what he was surely shrewd enough to see in Spanish court life, must have rankled under the surface enchantment of being lionized from one end of the empire to the other.

At any rate, when Don Luis' rediscovered delight kept him tarrying with his uncle beyond the stipulated five days, Father Segura sent one of the Brothers to investigate and to bring the young *cacique* back to the mission. Obviously it was without the latter that the Brother returned; Don Luis' days of being led by the hand were decidedly at an end. But what the Brother did bring back were the ingredients of a lurid tale.

It was then that Father Segura's Castilian temper made its

entry in most lamentably ill-timed fashion. The chroniclers say that he forthwith dealt Don Luis a severe tongue-lashing, so it must be that he thought it worth the 24-mile round trip in order to do so. He had a sufficient head of steam up to carry him the distance.

But with that, what had probably been no more than Don Luis' human frailty began to turn into case-hardened and diabolic resentment. The motive of pleasurable indulgence was carried away before a torrent of spite. It was by no means the common thing for a tribal chief to be flayed before his people in the histrionic Castilian of those days. That they could understand not a word of Segura's impassioned utterance meant little if Spanish talent for gesticulation was then what it still is.

We are left to think that at first Don Luis took the public humiliation in sullen silence or, at worst, in negative, hamstringing non-cooperation. The Fathers and Brothers, on their part, remained at their newly erected mission, of no more Christian use to the Indians than eight deaf-mutes. But the one-man debauch suffered no interruption. He who had been set before savage eyes as the paragon of Christian living went wildly on, with his tribesmen beginning to agree, probably, that if there were anything to choose between their way of life and Don Luis', they had at least a slight edge in temperance.

For the missioners the fact of Don Luis' personal fall was chagrin enough. But such scandal on a broad and coarse scale is what brought turmoil to the souls of Father Segura, Father de Quiros, and the others. Long before he had even set sail for the bay of St. Mary, Segura understood that the success or failure of the mission (and in view of the Florida collapse, the entire Jesuit effort in North America) pivoted on the whim of one Indian. Every last man of his confreres knew it too, and those who could do so had warned him away from the long gamble. But Segura had taken the risk, and with it full personal responsibility. And now everything was going to ruin. He had been duped. There was that in the training as well as in the native character of the man that kept the focus of bitter remorse away from his own bad judgment. Indeed he had more than enough to distract him from the shame of imminent personal failure.

Within a few weeks they would be faced with the alternative of either starving or spending the major portion of their waking hours foraging for wild yams, chestnuts, blackberries, and even acorns. And with the coming of winter and immobility, there might well be not even that alternative. Game was not to be available. The ruling idea of the mission had been to leave behind firearms or any suggestion thereof. And Don Luis was seeing to it that they got nothing from native hunters. Of the four large barrels of biscuit or hard-tack that were to have been the staple of their diet, two had been consumed en route from Havana, while the Indians, it will be recalled, had pitched in generously to help the others disappear. How the missioners did eventually manage to keep body and soul together was by slipping quietly from hut to native hut, bartering a bit of brass here or a measure of cloth there for a few handfuls of corn.

There was likewise the prospect of the coming winter in their open-jointed, thatch-roofed hovels. How piteously dependent on the provender of Don Luis' erstwhile Shangri-La Segura had made the expedition is evident from the Fathers' eventually being reduced to begging furs and mats from the very tribesmen who were being taught to despise them.

So for the rest of September and on through October, November, and December, the eight of them went through the motions of living. Any meeting with the Ajacans began and ended in stony silence. The one person capable of bridging the language-gulf was gone—off on a career of alternate sulking and back-woods high life. Needless to say, there was no faintest suggestion of Christian catechizing. Mass and prayers were over with early. And then all took up the drudgery of foraging. So what was to have been the minimum concern became very nearly the absolute preoccupation. It was no longer a question of how many savages were to be instructed and baptized. All the urgency was now shifted to whether there would be Jesuits alive to greet the supply ship when it made its way north from Havana the following spring—or, by the wildest wishful thinking, before winter closed in. There was the comforting thought, too, that the marauding Jacques Sorie and corsairs might meanwhile have reduced the entire tottering Florida mission by slaughter and pillage. Were that to happen (and if it did, they would never know for sure), they would wait and wait for supplies doomed never to come.

All through autumn and well on into the winter Segura tried at intervals to patch up relations with Don Luis, but always on condition that he mend his ways and return to the mission. Time and again he sent the Brothers, Mendez, de Solis, Zaballos, Gomez, Linares, and Redondo, singly or in pairs, with messages to Don Luis urging his return. But just as often he greeted them with scorn or frivolous excuses, and they tramped back the increasingly familiar 12 miles of swamp and woodland into a winter dusk.

These episodes of pleading and refusal continued past Christmas into the new year of 1571, and on through January: the Jesuits stalemated and starving, Don Luis unrelenting and thoroughly reconditioned to tribal life. The last resort was to send Father Louis de Quiros in person. In times past, particularly on the voyage from Cadiz to Havana, he had won the Indian's attachment. If there was a man on earth, then, who could fashion a reconciliation, it was de Quiros. If he returned as futilely as the others, then there was nothing to do but hold on precariously until spring and the coming of the supply boat. Then they would either evacuate or strike out for a part of the St. Mary's area beyond the range of Don Luis' moral and physical sabotaging.

So on Friday, February 2, 1571, de Quiros, accompanied by Brothers Baptista Mendez and Gabriel de Solis, pushed out along the trail to Don Luis' village. Along with the task of placating the Indian, they had another and incidental one of securing some mats for the protection against the petrifying cold of the missionary hovel.

As was to be expected, they encountered sluggish resistance in getting even this second task done. Evidently it took two days of their best bartering and wheedling to get what mats they could. And there is evidence that they eventually got them, not at Don Luis' village, but elsewhere, because the Ajacan Indian witness who later recounted the sequence of events stated that it was when the three were "returning" that they stumbled on Don Luis and a group of savages, all carrying bows and arrows, and therefore probably on the hunt either for game or for Jesuits.

It was an unhappy coincidence of circumstances: Don Luis armed and surrounded by tribal underlings come suddenly on one of the Fathers and two of the Brothers who were currently the butt of his most livid threats and jests—and carrying Indian mats at that. Nevertheless, de Quiros is related to have tossed his bundle to the ground and come forward with signs and words of cordiality to Don Luis. The same savage witness (whoever he be) is supposed to have recorded that de Quiros began immediately to exhort Don Luis to a return to Christian ways. But how said savage, understanding no Spanish, could have ascertained the content of the short-lived dialogue is not explained by the early Jesuit chronicler.

Don Luis' only reply was to demand de Quiros' cassock. The priest complied, removing it, and handing it to the Indian. The motive for the request became evident immediately: it was wanted whole and entire, untorn by arrows and unstained by blood. Because Don Luis handed it aside, laid shaft to bowstring, sighted calmly at the chest of the man three paces in front of him, and drove it home with the sound of a spike splintering through a barrel-head. Pain and pleading surprise spread over de Quiros' face. His knees buckled. Don Luis caught him with another shaft as he fell, and then leaned over the weakly twitching body and finished the task with a war-hatchet.

Simultaneously Brothers Mendez and de Solis were cut down by the cohort that took its cue from Don Luis. In a matter of seconds they lay twisted and groaning a few feet from Father de Quiros, arrows protruding at grotesque angles from chest, neck, and stomach. It is rather amazing to know that Brother Mendez was not disposed of so immediately and easily. When the corpses were stripped naked and tossed onto a huge fire the next morning, his had to be searched for among the tangled blackberry thickets and frozen grass at the edge of the clearing. Apparently, and for reasons that will never be known, the victims were initially left where they had fallen. And with the coming of dusk Mendez had set out for the mission again, but in pathetic fashion—hauling himself along the ground by stones and clumps of grass, dragging himself and arrows inch by agonizing inch toward the return path, and leaving his life a dark red stain on the earth as he went. He had got a few yards from the scene of the slaughter when the cold and dizzy blackness rose up from within and swirled over him, and his head slumped against the earth—the same earth that was to be littered with the corpses of men in blue and in gray almost 300 years later at Fredericksburg and Spotsylvania Courthouse.

When the corpses had been burned and the ashes scattered to the four winds, the clothes were divided among the Indians.

With the murder of de Quiros, Mendez, and de Solis, Don Luis had committed himself to a chain of events that had to be carried through to the end. If Segura and the other three were left to survive, there was a possibility that they would get back to the governor, Menendez; and once they got to him, there was certainty that Menendez would be back for Don Luis. So for the others it was no more than a matter of time; and as he saw it, better sooner than later.

With the passing of Monday, February 5, then Tuesday, and on through Wednesday, and still no return of de Quiros and the Brothers, Segura likewise came to know that it was only a matter of time. He told the Brothers who were with him—Zaballos, Gomez, and Linares, and the boy Alonso—that de Quiros and his companions had almost certainly met with tragedy and that they had best ready themselves for the same. Surely, they might attempt escape down the creek to the Potomac, and then along the Potomac to the bay. But it would be on foot in the dead of winter. Native tribes would be hostile. There would be no point in going unless they hoped to continue on to the mission at Santa Elena. The distance, however, was prohibitive.

The over-ruling concern, anyhow, was to find out for certain what had really happened to de Quiros and the Brothers. This was the least he owed them as their religious superior. If dead, then their bodies deserved an attempt at Christian burial. And there was yet the faintest possibility that they were alive.

In the meantime there was nothing else to do but prolong the pretense, continuing the search among patches of snow and under piles of frozen leaves for nuts and acorns, and bartering with what Indians were willing for a bit of corn and fish.

The suspense ended about mid-afternoon of Thursday, February 8. One account has it that the Ajacans rushed into the clearing screaming like demons, with Don Luis at their head robed bizarrely in Father de Quiros' cassock. Father Segura is said to have stepped from the mission hut and begun to parley with Don Luis, who, in chorus with his tribesmen, set up a clamor for the missionaries' axes—and when they got them, immediately set about the work of murder.

But that narrative, in the light of Don Luis' need for reasserting his ascendancy over Segura by some stunt of clever devising —and doing it before his accompanying tribal audience—seems less likely than the following.

Don Luis did arrive in mid-afternoon of February 8, along with the mustered audience from his uncle's as well as other local villages. But Father de Quiros' cassock was nowhere in evidence. For the five days' absence of Father de Quiros and the two Brothers he had the bland but, on the face of it, credible explanation that they had spent their time foraging with the natives for chestnuts and acorns, had had some difficulty in securing the sought-for mats or furs, but would be along the following morning. He was aware of the Jesuits' pathetic shortage of food; one look at de Quiros and companions could have told him that, had not tribal communications otherwise kept him informed. So the explanation was bound to hold for as long as he needed to get done in the most adroit fashion what he planned to get done.

Whether Father Segura believed the lie and its added implication that Don Luis was returning with a change of heart is beside the point. Probably he did not. He was still in no position to force the issue. Even should de Quiros and the Brothers fail to appear the following morning, he would have to accept whatever added lies were used to cover the situation.

So when Don Luis demanded all the axes in the missioners' possession, explaining that he and his tribesmen intended to cut fuel with them the following morning, Segura's only recourse was to hand over the five that he had.

What follows is said by one narrator to have happened that same afternoon. Whether it did, or rather on the following morning, cannot be determined. Probably the latter is closer to the truth. The only witness who survived the ensuing brutality was the nine-year-old Alonso. And his story can, with the exclusion and substitution of a few details, fit either context.

Father Segura and two of the Brothers, Gomez and Linares, were at prayer in the cold and darkness of the following morning, or perhaps even at Mass, when Don Luis and three or four braves thrust their way abruptly but silently through the hide-covered doorway of the chapel. Gripped at menacing angles were the axes borrowed the afternoon before. It is recorded that Don Luis carried a Spanish machete. Considering the course of his recent years, the statement is credible. For a second they stood in the shadows outside the circle of flickering candle-light, breath frosting on the air. The thin monotone of prayer halted and the Jesuits turned surprised faces toward them. For another second each party eyed the other—priest and Brothers in momentary, mute expectation; Indians tensed and ready against a first move toward resistance.

Then at a gesture from Don Luis the Brothers had arms pinioned behind them and were thrust roughly but soundlessly out into the faintly graying dawn. In the dim interior Don Luis and Father Segura were left facing each other. The priest raised his hand in greeting, voice weakly attempting a cordiality, but eyes reading the evident intent in those of the other.

The Indian, still without a word, took one step forward, tensed, balanced the machete a second behind his right shoulder; and then with a grunt of effort and bringing it across in a short, vicious arc, he split the priest's face. The imploring voice broke off in a choke. Blood streamed, and Segura crumpled at the feet of the Indian—who then threw the machete aside and, seizing one of the axes, went to work on the body as methodically as on any cordwood, lunging and hacking as he went over legs, trunk, arms, and head. (The boy Alonso, who later helped bury the corpse, stated simply that "it was left covered with gaping wounds.")

While this incomprehensible and personal hatred was exhausting itself in the chapel, Brothers Gomez and Linares had been separated by the two groups of savages outside the hut. Their treatment was the same: borrowed axes swinging in the faint dawn with the strength of savage muscles behind them, and there were two figures in black lying twisted on the frost-hardened ground.

Brother Sancho Zaballos is said to have been out for firewood at the time of the savages' first assault. At any event he was away; and as he walked unsuspectingly back into the clearing an Indian cleft his head open with an axe.

Meanwhile nine-year-old Alonso was in the hut of one of the village *caciques*, either a brother of Don Luis or at least one of the conspirators. Aroused by the babble of voices that came from the crowd gathering around the corpses, the lad dashed out into the clearing. He glanced momentarily at the figures of the three Brothers and then entered the chapel hut to be greeted by a sight not quite meant for nine-year-old eyes.

In a second the child was seized in a paroxysm of grief. And the shock of what he had found in the cabin was not too great to dim out the realization that he, Alonso, was now alone, and terribly so, among savages in a strange and cold land, hundreds of leagues from the nearest Spaniard. His pleas for death were not ignored; they were refused. And the reason for the refusal, which could have come only in Don Luis' words since he alone knew Spanish, are the solid substantiation for later generations' calling Segura and his companions martyrs. In brief, according to Don Luis, Alonso was not a missionary, not one of the Jesuits. So he was not to be harmed. Possibly, too, Don Luis had pre-arranged with his brother that Alonso was to be kept unharmed as a hostage or slave. Such at any rate was the war custom of the tribe.

So the other *cacique* led or carried the child aside, but not so far away as to prevent his witnessing one of the strangest phases of the tragic sequence. Don Luis, sobered by now either at the sight of his grisly work or by the wails of Alonso, suddenly broke down himself in a spasm of tears and sobs. Before the astonished and brute gaze of his cohort, he stumbled about in most unchieftain-like fashion from corpse to corpse, face in hands, groaning under the deep bite of remorse—and choking out the one word: "martyrs." There will always be the suspicion that this part of the narrative is somewhat too likely, too ready grist for the uncritically pious reporting of the day. But until solid evidence to the contrary is adduced, Alonso's account must stand. He was the only witness and ostensibly told what he saw and heard. This much is certain about Don Luis' pathetic display: Satan had gone before and lain in wait for him among his own people; and having got him to do and do quickly what was to be done, he was now leaving him (according to age-old policy) to deal with the after-devils of remorse and despair on his own.

The display of weakness left Don Luis with still enough ascendancy over his tribesmen for him to order them to a quite untraditional task: the digging of a single large grave. In it were laid, side by side, the four mangled bodies—Father Segura's first, and then the Brothers'. It was probably then that either Alonso or Don Luis himself supplied the one Christian touch to the chain of events. Into the cold hands of priest and Brothers were clasped their missionary crucifixes. Lying thus the men were heaped over with Virginia earth, in a common grave that was deliberately left unmarked. Don Luis knew Spanish vengeance well enough to guess that it would come even as far north as his land of the Ajacans. No helping clues were to be left. But as for the Jesuits themselves, it is good to know that if their resting-place is ever found, the only possible and sole identifying remnants will be whatever is left of the crucifixes with which they were buried. While these were neither as good a defense in these lands as Captain John Smith's Pocahontas, nor as vivid an historical hallmark, still they do help to clarify a radical difference in attitude and intent.

* * *

Don Luis was right about the long reach of Spanish vengeance. However, the first of the returning boats was brought by a motive not quite that. It was solid, salutary fear on the part of the people in Havana that the St. Mary's missioners would be suffering beyond their limit in hunger and exposure. So by early spring, possibly March (a winter voyage having been impossible), hardtack, seed corn, oil, mattocks, and hoes were again on their way up the Potomac, and this time in charge of Brother Juan de Salcedo.

At the original point of debarkation none of the agreed-on signs were to be seen, neither crosses nor rude altar. Instead, as the Spaniards drifted cautiously in midstream awaiting some sign of welcome, the Ajacan tribesmen began gathering on the bank, shouting what seemed calls of welcome and urging them by signs to come ashore. Among them were a number of figures in the cassocks of the Jesuits. But the crude ruse was a failure and a final giveaway. Searching and questioning were unnecessary. Instead the captain ordered his crew sharply to the oars and the boat swung quickly about and headed back toward the Potomac and the bay.

The last attempt made at a search for the remains of the Ajacan martyrs and their slayers was on July 30 of the following year, 1572, when Menendez and Father Rogel set out with a fleet of three ships. At their arrival in the Ajacan district the two larger of the vessels were anchored in the bay at the mouth of the Potomac, while the smallest was sent up-stream with a captain and 30 heavily armed men. Their task was first of all to rescue the boy, Alonso, and then, if possible, capture Don Luis and the tribal chiefs. The matter of finding the remains of the murdered Jesuits and their mission would be taken care of once Indian resistance had been broken by the capture of the chiefs.

Alonso was nowhere to be found, but the Spaniards did succeed in luring some of the Indians aboard, chiefs included, with promises of gifts. Once aboard, they were seized and thrown into the hold, and the vessel was hurried back downstream, beating off the attacks of pursuing braves en route.

But just when it seemed that the Spaniards would have to fight their way to the rescue of Alonso, some *caciques* in a conciliatory frame of mind (and eager to be rid of the terrible Menendez) sent the boy under escort to the anchorage at the mouth of the Potomac.

The next move was Menendez'. Among the captives, apparently, was the chief of Don Luis' tribe himself. He was ordered to have Don Luis and two of his brothers brought for punishment within five days; if they failed to come, he and his Indian peers would be hanged as responsible for the murders committed in their territory. One of the captives was sent around the villages with this message.

But as expected, Don Luis failed to appear within the stipulated time. And Menendez was as good as his word: the chiefs were hanged at the yard-arm, after having been given the choice of Christian baptism.

This and the threat of further punishment spread terror among the Ajacan tribesmen. The most that is known of Don Luis is that he fled to the interior, probably westward to the fastness of the Blue Ridge Mountains; and there, one of the strangest figures in Spanish colonial history, he lived out his days with his all-too-well-educated conscience. The other Indians, now deprived of their chiefs, scattered southward to the peninsular land between the Rappahannock and the James rivers. It was there, still living in their semi-nomadic condition, that they were found 35 years later under the rule of Powhatan by Captain John Smith.

The most significant sequel to all this took place in the mind of Father Rogel. And one finds it hard not to be amazed at the spirit of the man and those of his type. The journey back down the Bay of St. Mary was a leisurely one; organized reprisal on the part of the Ajacans was no longer feared. So it is possible that some exploring of the coastal areas was done. And it was found that the natives there lived the most settled life of any yet encountered by the Jesuits.

Immediately Father Rogel's best missionary instincts were aroused. As soon as he had arrived in Havana, he penned the following sanguine lines to the General, Borgia: "If Spaniards were to settle there in such numbers as to impress the Indians with their power to avenge wrongs, we could preach the holy gospel more easily than elsewhere. We have this boy, Alonso, who would be a capital interpreter, for he speaks their language so well that he was losing hold of his native Spanish. And when asked whether he wished to return with his father, who had come with the expedition, or remain with us, he said he wanted to stay with the Jesuits.

"If your paternity decide that this project be undertaken, I should be delighted to be called to it. It may be that these pagans be found as hard of heart as were the others in our experience so far, and that much fruit will be reaped only after a lapse of time. Yet the attempt would encounter less discomfort and fewer obstacles here because the region is more thickly populated and the severity of the long winters holds them together and prevents prolonged absence from their huts."

But like so many of the communiques of that mission period, it was never read by the man to whom it was directed. Borgia had died on October 1, 1572, after issuing instructions for the abandonment of the Florida mission in that, its seventh year. Already earlier that year he had ordered Father Pedro Sanchez, who was shortly to leave for Mexico as founder and first provincial of that province, to recall his men from Florida to Mexico gradually unless there was good hope for a college in Havana.

There was not. The Spanish colonists there failed to provide sufficient foundation. And the Jesuits themselves were spreading their manpower to the ends of the earth. Already missioners were in Abyssinia and the Congo and South Africa. Xavier had opened fields in Japan; and Verbeest, Ricci, and Schall were to lecture shortly thereafter among the learned royalty of Peking. They were likewise in Brazil and Peru, and would soon be in

Chile and founding the paradisal reductions of Paraguay. By comparison the North American record was not good: 15 men sent; eight martyred. For the time being, at least, the entire continent was writen off as "not worth the risk."

It is probable that later generations have reversed that verdict. True, Fathers Segura and de Quiros and the six Brothers, for all their trouble, reaped nothing—except more trouble. Not to mention reaping, some would say they had not even sown. Axes swinging in the gray shadows of a February dawn had cut them down before even their first planting season.

But one article of the supernatural economy that drove them into the Chesapeake and up the Potomac has it that, better for one's mission than even sowing or reaping is to be oneself that seed that falls into the ground and dies. Despite some poor discernment of spirits here and some wishful thinking there, they must have fallen well and died well. Because at last count there were just slightly over 7000 men who are not only members of Segura's own Order 380 years later, but likewise citizens born of the soil he had irrigated with his good but (it seemed then) wasted blood.

And what is more, there were, by like count, some 31 million natives of the same land now professing the Faith they had tried not very successfully to bring. And strikingly enough, these same 31 million call their national capital a city within an hour's drive of the spot where Segura, de Quiros, and the Brothers lie buried.

Europe *lay in the toils of revolution. Bacon, Galileo, and Kepler, Pascal and Descartes were baring ideas that would rock the world. Richelieu's crimsoned figure bartered for the glory of France with human coin. In Ireland martyrdom walked the green sward and fell beneath Cromwell's boot. Proud Queen Bess went down into the grave with the blood of Scotland's queen and Tyburn's gallows upon her head.*

Across the waters in New Amsterdam, Dutch burghers plied their trade along the Hudson. They had settled near Albany, then bought Manhattan. With dogged, jolly determination the pantaloons and long stemmed pipes began to build as only sturdy Lowlanders could do.

Farther North, Cartier had long since followed the St. Lawrence. Champlain moved further into the interior, past Cape Cod, into Ottawa. Prospect of enormous fur trade stirred action on ancient shores. The first small fleets made their way across the Atlantic to America.

Liquor, meanwhile, set on fire the savage breast. Massacres would follow. The white men had come only to exploit and rob. These children of the forest conceived human relations in simple and primitive terms. Beads and blankets they saw could not repay them. They would be despoiled—their lands plundered—their wild nomadic wanderings held in check by steel rods that spat death and left widows to mourn around the campfires.

Across the waters robust sainthood flowered again on Europe's ancient soil. Her lagging spirit took new life from Vincent de Paul and John of God, Columbiere and Claver, Bobola and

Regis, Francis de Sales, Thomas More, and the martyred Bishop Fisher. Here was a galaxy of stars—to light men's darkened paths.

* * *

Memoir of a Martyr

Father Isaac Jogues, S.J. (Saint)

by Louis E. Haven, S.J.

Albany, New York
August 7, 1951

Dear Henry:

Tonight mother and I have just finished a visit to the Shrine of the North American Martyrs at Auriesville. It's beautiful and inspiring, with a constant stream of pilgrims visiting it. To think that I've lived most of my life so close to a place charged with great romance of missionary history and yet had never before known about it! You and Jean must stop by there when you come up-state next month. . . .

Yours as always,
Jack

The College of Rouen, France
June 14, 1632

Dear Father Provincial, Pax Christi:

For a long time I have been purposing to write you about two of the scholastics teaching here. You remember how Father

Brebeuf and Father Masse stopped at our houses to tell of their work among the Indians when they were forced home in 1629 after the English had captured Quebec. It is true that when they were here it didn't look as if the French would be able to continue their mission; but now that Richelieu has forced the English to give us back New France, two of the young scholastics are once more yearning to go on the missions as soon as they can be ordained priests. Knowing them as well as I do, I felt impelled to write you a word about their desires.

. . . . The second one is Monsieur Jogues. Even during the days of his novitiate he has wanted to be a missionary, and since then I have felt a premonition that he would ultimately go to New France, perhaps to die among the savages. He seems to me to have all the qualifications for the missions. He is one of the best athletes among the young Jesuits here; and he has a boldness of nature and a way with people which would fit him for enduring all the hardships connected with such a life. I know as well as you do how insistently the missionaries are calling for help, and so I thought that I must suggest his name to you. . . .

I know that since the Cardinal has decided that the Jesuits alone should be put in charge of his new mission, you have been looking around for fit men. I just thought that if I were to inform you of the qualifications of these scholastics before you make your visitation of our house, you would be prepared to question them more in detail about their aspirations and qualifications when you come to see us. . . .

I certainly hope that the Calvinist Hugenot interference will not ruin our work in New France as it completely succeeded in doing with the work of the Recollect Fathers ten years ago. . . .

Your devoted son in Our Lord,

LOUIS LALEMANT, S.J.

Dieppe, France
April 6, 1636

MOST HONORED AND DEAR MOTHER,

How could a good son fail to write a last farewell to his dear
mother when he was about to set out to sea. You most likely
judged from my last letter to you that we left here for the missions about Holy Week, but contrary winds have kept us from
sailing until now. The day after tomorrow we shall be on our
way.

I hope that God will give us a good and happy voyage, because many people very pleasing to God are praying for us.
Eight ships are sailing together, and that will make for added
safety.

You help us now, mother, to have a safe trip, by praying
often for us. You will help me most by a big hearted resignation
of your will to what God wills, by your wanting what Our
Father in Heaven wants for us.

Goodbye, dear mother. I thank you for all the love you have
always shown me, and especially on that day I saw you for the
last time. May God unite us in His Holy Paradise, if we do not
see each other again on earth!

Give my very best wishes to each one in the family. Heart
and soul I trust myself to their prayers as well as to yours.

Your most devoted and obedient son in Our Lord,

ISAAC

Orleans, France
May 1, 1636

DEAR FRANCOISE,

Your brother is on his way to New France at last. I imagine
you may have heard about his departure from Père Couture. I
have just received his farewell letter and must begin writing the
children about his holy words and desires. I have not wept since
the day I got his letter. God has given me a strength of mind I

· 34 ·

could not have dreamed I should have. Isaac will write me every year. I'll live from year to year in hope for his letters. You must pray very hard for him. He wanted me to write and ask you to do that.

I am very afraid for him, Françoise. We know so little about the savages of New France. They are more brutal than the Orientals were when the members of the Company of Jesus went to Japan. And what I dread most is that Isaac would like to be a martyr. He is very bold because his religious convictions are so real to him. Do you remember when Père Lalemant once said that he would die in New France? I think that the reason he said it was that he knew how Isaac desired to suffer and die for Christ. And that was many years ago now. Ever since he has belonged to the Company, Isaac has carried in his breast pocket a picture of that Pere Spinola whom the Japanese burned in 1622. He showed it to me on ordination day.

You have a holy brother, Françoise, but that is why I am so afraid. Have some Masses said for his safety, please. I have had many Masses said for him ever since the day three months ago when he broke the news to me that he was going away. It was the morning of his first Mass. His superior had told him that he was to be a missionary just the day before. That is one reason he was so overjoyed when he said his first Mass for us that morning. My, how I had pleaded with him as my dearest son to stay in France at least for my last years on earth. I know they will not be many. But I was very selfish. I was very selfish ever since he was a baby and I had prayed he would be a priest, but only a canon, so that he would never leave Orleans. I know that he was weeping for me that morning of his first Mass when he came down to the Communion rail to give me Our Lord to take his place. Perhaps it was the grace of that one Holy Communion that made me resign myself to God's wishes. Thank God, my Isaac did not have to leave me before I had become resigned never to see him again. Otherwise he should have had yet another cross to bear among his many hardships. . . .

Pray for me, Françoise, as I do every day for you.

YOUR MOTHER

I Lift My Lamp

DEAR MOTHER,

At last it has pleased Our Lord to allow me to land on the shores of New France, the goal of my longings. We arrived here eight weeks after our departure, on an island called Miscou, where two of our Fathers serve the French and attempt the conversion of the Indians. Two weeks later I set out for Tadoussac where I landed on the feast of the Visitation of Our Lady.

I do not know what it is to enter Heaven; but this I know, that it is difficult to experience in this world a more overflowing joy than I felt on my setting foot in New France and celebrating my first Mass here on the day of the Visitation. I assure you it was really a day of Our Lord's and Our Lady's visitation to me by Their goodness. I felt as if it were a Christmas day for me, and that I was to be born again to a new life, and a life in God.

My health has been so good that it has been a matter of wonder to all, since it is very unusual for any one to make such a voyage without suffering a little from nausea. It was a great consolation to me to be able to offer the Holy Sacrifice of Mass every day the weather was favorable, a happiness I should not have had, had you not provided me with the vestments. All eighty of the persons on board my ship confessed and received communion on Pentecost, Ascension, and Corpus Christi day.

It will be a special comfort for me to hear from you yearly as I have no hope of seeing you in our lifetime. May God in His goodness unite us both in Heaven to praise Him for all eternity! I know that this was the thought which urged me to beg so earnestly to be sent to these countries, where, there being so much to suffer, we can also give such sincere proof of our love for God.

I write this to you at a distance of more than a thousand leagues, and perhaps I shall be sent this year to a nation called the Hurons, who live at a distance of more than three hundred more leagues. They give some signs of sincere dispositions for embracing the Faith.

It matters not where we are, mother, provided we rest in the arms of Providence and His holy favor. This is the prayer offered every day at the altar for you and our family by him, who is your most obedient and humble son.

ISAAC

P. S.

I have just within this very hour received orders from Father Le Jeune to get ready to start for the mission among the Hurons in three or four days.

Ihonoteria among the Hurons
May 20, 1636

DEAR BROTHERS IN CHRIST,

With respect to your request from Quebec that I as superior out here among the Indians should send you some words of advice about the qualifications that a man should have if he should come to work among us, I submit the following points which, believe me, I know from experience are very important.

. . . . You must have sincere affection for the savages. To conciliate them, never make them wait in embarking; have a tinder box to light their pipes and fires for them; eat their sagamite, although it may be dirty, half-cooked, and very tasteless; eat all they offer, and when they offer it; do not carry water or sand into the canoe; do not be troublesome, do not ask too many questions, do not criticize; be and appear to be always cheerful; make presents to them of pocket knives, fish hooks, colored glass beads; do not stand on ceremony; wear a nightcap in the canoe rather than a broad-rimmed hat; help carry the baggage at the portages, if it be only a kettle.

Finally, understand that the savages will retain the same opinion of you in their own country that they will have formed on the way. One who has passed for an irritable and troublesome person will have considerable difficulty afterwards in removing this opinion. You have to deal not only with those of your own canoe, but also, if I may say it, with all the inhabitants of the country; you meet some today and others tomorrow and they do not fail to inquire from those who brought you what sort of man you are. It is almost incredible how they observe and remember, even to the slightest fault. When you meet savages on the way, as you cannot yet greet them with kind words, at least show them a cheerful face, and thus prove that you endure gayly the fatigues of the voyage. You will thus have put to good use the hardships of the way, and have already advanced considerably in gaining the affection of the savages.

This is a lesson which is easy enough to learn, but very difficult to put into practice. For, leaving a highly civilized community, you fall into the hands of a barbarous people who care nothing at all about your philosophy and your theology. All the fine qualities which might make you loved and respected in France are like pearls trampled under the feet of swine, or rather of mules; they utterly despise you when they see that you are not as good pack animals as they are. If you could go naked and carry the load of a horse upon your back, as they do, then you would be wise according to their doctrine, and would be recognized as a great man; otherwise, not. Jesus Christ is our true greatness; it is He alone and His Cross that should be sought in running after these people; for if you strive for anything else, you will gain naught but bodily and spiritual affliction. But having found Jesus Christ in His Cross, you have found the roses in the thorns, sweetness in bitterness, everything in nothing. . . .

Please remember us in your prayers.

Your brother in Christ,
JEAN DE BREBEUF, S.J.

Memoir of a Martyr

FOR REV. PAUL LE JEUNE, S.J., QUEBEC

DEAR FATHER SUPERIOR,

We were extremely glad to have Father Jogues sent to help us out with our labors, but we almost lost him to Heaven soon after he arrived. The very week that he came he caught the influenza; and before a couple of weeks were out, he almost died. The morning that we brought him what we thought was his viaticum, we in desperation decided to bleed him. Father Brebeuf did the bleeding, and a few moments later Father Jogues lapsed into a coma, which, thank God, seemed to mark his turn for the better; for when he came out of the coma, his fever was definitely abated.

It was a couple of weeks till he was recovered sufficiently to be up and around, though, and at one time Father Brebeuf and I were the only ones left well among the French, to do the nursing of the many missionaries and Indians who had come down with the malady. Soon the epidemic spread to all the other villages of this nation, and we were under a dark cloud of suspicion, since the Indians were persuaded by their medicine men that we were possessed of evil spirits and had brought the plague to them.

It is a wonder that someone didn't split our heads, but I think that their superstitious fancy that we held the secret of life and death made them fear killing us. As a matter of fact, during the time of the plague we were able to baptize a couple of hundred people. It is true that these were chiefly the baptisms of children, who later died; but this is, after all, thus far our great consolation in our work. The heavenly prayers of these innocent souls will finally work for the salvation of this whole people, I feel sure.

And some day, long after we are dead, this may finally be a greater Christian people than the nations of Europe. I cannot help but feel that there is something about the freedom of this land and the need of living with just the bare necessities of life that makes it the ideal land for Christianity.

Although there is an enormous amount of thievery and treachery and lying among these Hurons, yet there is a simplicity about them, at times, which is so different from the stuff of our European civilization that I feel once this nation is converted, they will live much closer to the radical concept of evangelical Christianity than we in Old France ever shall.

Since the time of the plague, which had claimed most of its victims by last January, we have given ourselves over to the most humdrum type of life. I won't say that it's completely uninteresting, but it is the kind of work that none of us could have the courage to persevere in without much faith and the grace of God.

We began on February the tenth to put our whole attention upon learning this barbaric tongue. You have scarcely any idea of how complex it is. There are no words for abstract notions. All Indian ideas are about material things. And this makes it a most difficult task, even when we have mastered the language, to figure out how we can put into their equivalents our tremendous ideas about God and His plans for men. Even such a simple generalization as the word *animal* is something beyond the intelligences of these natives.

We shall not be here at Ihonoteria much longer, I feel. The natives are restless. They have lived here now for about ten years, and normally that is the limit to the life of an Indian village. By that time, its huts are so rotting, and the whole district is so filled with filth and rubbish that they must move to establish a new town site. I think that we may accept the invitation of the tribe to the south of us at Ossossané to come and live with them when our own Indians break up and leave for a better site.

The fishing season is now beginning to get underway, since the cold has finally broken, and I take this opportunity to send a letter by the canoes which will be plying the waters of the river within the next few weeks.

I have written a complete account of the labors of our new

missionaries for the *Relations*, but I shall wait till summer to send them along to you, since the travel will be safer then.

Your devoted son in Our Lord,
FRANCOIS LE MERCIER, S.J.

Residence of La Conception, Ossossané
October 28, 1637

DEAR FATHER LE JEUNE:

I write this in great haste as it seems to all of us that we are perhaps at the moment of shedding our blood and sacrificing our lives to the service of our good Master, Jesus Christ. All of us unite in saying, "If He wills that at this hour we should die, Oh, fortunate hour for us! If He wills to reserve us for other labors, may He be blessed!" If you hear that God has crowned our insignificant labors, or rather our desires, bless Him; for it is for Him that we desire to live and to die, and it is He Who gives us grace for it. For the rest, if any survive, I have given orders as to all they are to do.

JEAN DE BREBEUF
FRANCOIS LE MERCIER
PIERRE CHASTELLAIN
CHARLES GARNIER
PAUL RAGUENEAU

P. S. I have left Fathers Pierre Pijart and Isaac Jogues in the residence of St. Joseph, with the same sentiments.

Ihonoteria among the Hurons
April 5, 1638

DEAR FATHER SUPERIOR:

I have almost nothing but bad news to report from the mission this year. If you received the message of last October from Father Brebeuf, sent in the name of all of us, then perhaps you will be happily surprised when the canoes bearing this note reach you. Because the Indians will be quick to inform you that we were none of us killed that fateful night when all the neighboring tribes had gathered to condemn us to death.

As they began their council that night, the Attigneenongnahacs grimly demanded our death, and there was not one Indian, even among the Christians, who would dare to defend us. But as the night wore on, the chiefs hesitated to pronounce the final sentence, though all were convinced that death was a just penalty for us and would alone save the nation from further ruin. They were afraid of the larger issue of thus nationally breaking their alliance and forfeiting their privileges with the French. If an individual committed the murder, they would not have objected in the least, for that would not carry with it the responsibility of the chiefs and ancients.

The whole trouble started last fall, after we had sent our last communication to you. We had thought at that time that the influenza epidemic had eased down, but by the beginning of July the sickness was as prevalent as it had been in the winter, and all the villages near Ossossané were stricken once more. There were reports, too, that the nations to the south and the east were being destroyed by the plague. Of course, there was a new hysteria as a result of all this. The sorcerers learned from friendly demons that we were the cause of it all. The pictures in our chapel blew out the disease. Our kitchen kettles exuded poisons. The cloth that one of us had hung on a tree near our cabin was a sign for the evil spirits as to which way they would send the disease. The box in the cabin which mysteriously beat tick, tick, all day and all night was a devil striking out death. When we walked about silently moving our lips as we held a little book, we were talking to the spirits. We had brought a baby's corpse from France and were hiding it in a little closet on the altar of our chapel.

Whenever we remonstrated against the awful accusations, the only answer we ever received was "everyone says it is true." We could not enter a single cabin, so that we had to remain at anchor, hoping the storm would blow over. On one afternoon in September a man had even gone so far as to aim his arrow and bend his bow to shoot at Father Pijart and me [Jogues], but a commotion arose at that moment at the far end of the cabin where he was lodged. Those who were surrounding Pijart rushed out of the cabin, and the man with the bow and arrow was left facing the two of us alone. I cannot understand what kept the man from letting his arrows fly at us. Certainly this incident jolted us out of whatever sense of security we had left in us, and we realized that it would take a long time before we could be reinstated to the position of favor which we had taken so many months to gain among these men, if we were left alive at all.

Already we knew that we had been condemned to death by a council of chiefs held in August, but the chiefs had decided that the matter must be postponed till there could be the general ratification of the plan by the war chiefs who were at that time on the trail. So it was toward the end of October that the final council was held. It was really almost miraculous that no one killed us after that business meeting. But strange to relate, we are all well, and we have not even been deprived of our few possessions.

However, since we are able to do almost no good among the savages here, till that perhaps distant date when we shall have recovered face, it seems a providential time for us to make some exploration of the country of the Petuns. Perhaps by the time you receive this communication one or more of us shall have set out on this new venture.

Please remember us to all of the Fathers at Quebec. Beg their earnest prayers for us amid all the difficulties of this far away land. Perhaps we shall never meet again this side of Heaven. But we shall always be united in prayer.

Devotedly in the Company of Jesus,
ISAAC JOGUES, S.J.

I Lift My Lamp

Ossossané among the Hurons
May 1, 1639

REVEREND AND DEAR FATHER IN CHRIST:

I thought that with the letters going to Quebec this spring I should let you know of the difference it had made to us on the mission to have had a change of superior this last year. Father Lalemant arrived here on August 26, and presented his papers to Father Brebeuf. Father Brebeuf was immensely relieved, as he has always felt that he was not qualified to be a good superior. However, it seems to me that he has been the best possible choice for getting the mission under way. He is so big that the Indians respect him very much. I can understand how he has been begging of you for years that you replace him, because I know what a fund of deep humility he has. He is a demi-god among the natives, equal to them in physical strength and their master in mind. I think that there is not another one among us who is so respected and so loved by them.

It seems to me that he was especially qualified to begin the mission because of his extreme tact. And it seems to me now that Father Lalemant is just the successor that was needed for him. If Father Brebeuf was noted for his tact, Father Lalemant is noted among us for his inflexibility, and that is what is needed these days to establish the mission on a firm foundation. He is a rigid disciplinarian, and tolerably irascible. If Father Brebeuf was an ideal clearer of the soil, Father Lalemant is the grand architect, the dreamer of tremendous projects. His first statement on the mission policy was to declare that we should travel all over the country which was first to receive us and make a census. Then we are to push farther on, and always on and on, until we have accomplished our task, which is only bounded by the setting sun.

It was not long till the new Father Superior had elaborated a regular order for the day. All rose with the ringing of the bell at four o'clock. From then, till eight, we meditated and said our Masses. Then the doors were unbarred. Formerly, the natives were allowed to enter the cabin freely, but Father has decided that since the importunity of these barbarians, lazy to the last degree, was unbearable, none were admitted except those who might be profited, or from whom profit might be gained. During the day, one Father is on duty in the cabin, and holds instructions for the children. The others of us visit the cabins and surrounding villages, each one having the care of specified families. Dinner is at two regularly. We say grace in Huron, for the benefit of any savages present, and read a chapter of the Bible. By four o'clock in the winter months the doors have been barred, but Christian Hurons might gain admittance. The evening is devoted to the study of the language, to conferences on the work of the day, to consultations on the general status and the future prospects of the Mission. Supper is at six-thirty, during which a spiritual book is read while we eat, around the fire seated on a log, without plates, on the ground. At eight, we have night prayers, examen of conscience, and points for the morning meditation. At nine we are at rest on our mats under the shelves.

I think that all of this order is very good for us, although I do know that none of us missed our spiritual exercises during the time that Father Brebeuf was superior. It is just that everything was much less formally organized. This way, though, we have much more peace and quiet for accomplishing our plans more efficiently.

We shall be sending our report for the *Relations*, Father, when we send our next caravan to Three Rivers. I am glad to report that the dissension is beginning to die down, and perhaps before a few months are up we shall be again doing as much as we did in the former year in the actual Christianizing of these poor pagans.

Please do not forget to remember us in your prayers, and especially at Mass. We shall continually pray for you.

Your devoted son in Christ,
ISAAC JOGUES, S.J.

The Archiepiscopal Palace
Paris
March 10, 1641

To Charles Hualt de Monmagny
Governor-General of New France

Respected Sir:

For a long time I have seriously understood the plight of your governorship of New France amidst the continual threats of the Iroquois. Believe me, it was with the greatest respect that I listened to the Jesuit, Father Charles Lalemant, whom you had asked to report to us on the conditions of your government a year ago. But I thought at that time that his plan was too ambitious a one for our limited finances.

However, this year I see the matter in a different light. I have already appropriated the sum of 10,000 ecus for the erection of fortifications against the Iroquois, for vessels to patrol the St. Lawrence, and for offensive expeditions into the savage lands. I shall also see to it that an additional amount of money is expended for the upbuilding of the fort Saint Marie among the Hurons. . . .

The servant of the King and of yourself, my Lord,

Richelieu
Prime Minister of France

Ossernenon, Nation of the Iroquois
June, 1641

Dear Father Vimont, the Peace of Christ!

What a surprise it has been for me to find an opportunity to write to you at Quebec from this village where I am the captive slave of the Iroquois. The Dutch came up the Hudson for some trading with the Indians this summer, and I found them extremely friendly. They made every effort possible to bribe our captors into releasing René, William, and me, and allowing us to go back to the safety of civilization with them. And although they did not succeed, I hoped then, but vainly, that the Indians set enough value on our persons not to kill us, knowing that it would incur the wrath of the Dutch as well as of the French. The Dutch kindness toward us will, I hope, go far toward banishing the traditional hostility between the French and them in this country.

I wonder if by this time you had been able to discover that I wasn't killed when our company was captured going up the river last July. It was a horrible experience, about which I can only tell you adequately when I am able to see you. And the rush of getting off this letter, in closest secrecy, allows me only a chance to tell you most briefly about our trials.

The Iroquois attack was a complete surprise. When the war whoops split the air and the first volley of arrows was let fly, Atieronhonk, the only non-Christian in our canoe, was pierced in the hand. I asked him if he wanted baptism; and when he answered yes, I baptized him immediately. It was a great consolation to me.

My canoe catapulted into the reeds, and I found a hiding place from which I could see the Iroquois downing, now René, now Chief Joseph, now everyone from the canoe of Eustace. I think that I could have outrun any of the savages and have escaped, but after arguing with myself, I determined I could never abandon even one of our Frenchmen, or any one of the Hurons who were already captured, especially those who were not baptized. I stood up boldly among the reeds and called out to the Iroquois. One guard advanced warily, then sprang on me and forced me down. Others leaped on me, stripped off my robe, and beat me.

A band of warriors burst into the open, wildly shouting, and leading Eustace, covered with blood and tied with strong leather straps. He had been recognized as the great war chief, the one above all others that they had sought to capture. When Eustace saw me, he shouted out with all the conviction in the world, "My Father, I swear to you that I shall remain faithful to you whether I live or whether I die."

Couture had shot and killed an Iroquois in the skirmish; and before he could move a step, a half dozen Iroquois were upon him and pinned him to the earth. Like maniacs they stripped him, kicked and stamped on him, beat him with their fists and the butts of their muskets. They knocked him senseless, then revived him by pulling out his finger nails with their teeth.

When their fury seemed somewhat abated from the orgy of torturing us, the Iroquois began hurrying to set out from the scene of the battle for their own country. We had a horrible torture trail of thirteen days. Much of the way we were forced to drag ourselves for miles at a time during the portages, almost naked, and aching from head to toe.

On the fourth day of the journey, René, who was assigned to the same master as I, offered his life to God by vowing with me for his witness, his perpetual poverty, chastity, and obedience in the Society of Jesus. I cannot tell you what a joy it was to me to have another brother of the Company by my side to strengthen me for what lay ahead.

The Mohawks seemed arrogantly proud that they had had to kill only two of the twenty-five of us whom they captured, and we were sure that they were saving our ultimate torture and burning for their triumphal entry into their villages.

On the eighth day after the battle we met a band of a couple of hundred Iroquois warriors and for their fiendish pleasure we were all stripped totally naked and forced to run the gauntlet, a double line of all the men armed with clubs and switches of thorny rods. They saved me for the last, as a special treat. I had scarcely stumbled along through the line a hundred feet till I fell and was kicked into unconsciousness. When I came to, I was lying on a hill where I saw my brothers on a platform being beaten. When it was discovered that I had revived, but was too weak to mount the platform, they dug my flesh with their nails.

One bit my thumb till it was so macerated that the bone was exposed.

Several days later we reached the actual country of the Iroquois. Each village we passed through had to give us this same wild treatment as the former, leaving us all of the day upon the blood-blackened platforms as public spectacles, to be tortured by any who might come along.

On August 21 we were finally led back to Andagaron, the first village we had arrived at, and were received peacefully till the chiefs of the nations should hold council about us. By nightfall we were told that we were not to die. The next day the council assigned René and me to be the slaves of the chief who had captured us. Only Eustace, Stephen, and Paul, the greatest of our warriors, were to be burned offerings to the demons of war.

I had the horror of seeing Paul burned the night that we were returned to Ossernenon. After they had butchered and burned him with fagots, they bound him to a pole and heaped up burning bushes around his legs. And as the flames enveloped him, he looked at me for the sign of absolution. With agony in my heart for his sufferings, I pronounced the sacred words; and within five minutes Paul was dead. An hour later I could see the sky glow red over Andagaron where Stephen was being burned, and I knew that further on in the next village that same evening our brave Eustace was enduring his last agonies.

I should write a whole chapter about the saintly death of René, Father, and I promise to do that for you when first I get the opportunity. I am convinced that he died a true martyr of Jesus Christ. Just because he had guided the tiny hands of a poor pagan child to his forehead, breast, and shoulders in the form of the cross, a savage split his head with a tomahawk. As he fell to the earth he called out, "Jesus, Jesus, Jesus," and I said the words of absolution over him, as he died. If I am allowed another opportunity of writing, I shall tell you more, Father. When I think of dear René, I know that I should write a whole book about his heroic existence here and of his death for Christ. We have had several martyrs for the Iroquois now, and surely

God will grant their ardent desires and convert these hostile people some day.

I fare quite well here now, being in the service of a chieftain. Fear of his anger provides a certain immunity for me now, and I am free to spend much time in prayer or in the study of the language, though I dare not yet teach about God unless I am asked questions about the beliefs of the French.

Do not worry about our future. It is in the hands of God. Whatever He decrees for us we are ready to accept. Please ask the Fathers with you and in the home province to pray continually for us in our trials.

Filially and in union with Christ,
ISAAC JOGUES, S.J.

At the Colony of Rensselaerswyck
in New Netherland,
August 5, 1643

REVEREND AND DEAR FATHER IN CHRIST:

A month ago I should not have dreamed that so soon I would be writing to my Provincial in France. The very great charity of Your Reverence, which in other days overlooked the multitude of my sins, will pardon me if there be some fault against the rules of decorum or language, in this my letter to you, for they will have been committed by a man who has lived for eight years after the manner and even in the appearance and dress of the savages. Still more, I fear that, rude in language, I may be more so in knowledge, "nor know the time of my visitation," nor remember that I sustain the character imposed on me by God, of a preacher of the Gospel, of a Jesuit, and of a priest.

This induced me to write to you; if, by chance this letter should sometime come into your hands, that I might be helped by your own Holy Sacrifices and the prayers of your whole Province, I who live in this dreadful region among the Iroquois and the Mohawks. I trust that this help will be given more

earnestly when you read this letter and see both how much I
owe to God, and how much I need the prayers of pious people,
in whose prayers, I know, a powerful protection is raised up
for me.

[Thereafter, through some thirty and more pages of fine script
he narrates in exact detail all that has happened during the past
fourteen months, from the time he left the Huron country till
that moment when the Dutch were striving to effect his libera-
tion. He concludes his letter as follows:]

The Indians have made this trip down to Fort Orange to bar-
ter with the Dutch and have brought me along to help with the
portage, and, as I think, to show off their prize in front of the
Dutch. The chief to whom I am assigned is quite proud to have
me for a slave, and quite kind to me. It has been surprising with
what freedom I am being allowed to wander about in the Fort.

The Dutch, too, have certainly been kind to me on this my
first visit to civilization, although they do not love the French,
though they detest Catholicism, and abominate, in particular, the
Jesuits. They deem it an outrage that any white man whatsoever
should be enslaved by the savages. Dominie Johannes Mega-
polensis, minister of the Reformed Dutch Church here, worked
especially hard to procure my release. He it was who bought my
breviary from the Iroquois and returned it to me.

But the days of my freedom have nearly ended, since the
Dutch have been altogether unsuccessful in trying to ransom
me. And although, in all probability I could escape, either
through the Europeans or through some savages living around
us, if I should wish it, I have decided to live on this cross on
which Our Lord has fixed me in company with Himself.

But now I am weary of writing so long and verbose a letter.
I therefore beg Your Reverence from my heart that you may
ever regard me, although unworthy, as one of your own. Even
though I may appear to be a savage in manner and dress, even
though I might seem to be without God in such a tumultuous
kind of life, nevertheless, I have always lived as a son of the
most Holy Roman Church and of the Society should live; and
as I have lived that way always, so also in that way I hope to

die. Obtain for me from God, Reverend Father, by your Holy Sacrifices, that though heretofore I have made poor use of the many helps God has given me to attain the highest sanctity, I may, at least, make good use of these last occasions which He gives to me.

Your charity assuredly owes this to your son who has recourse to you. For I live a truly wretched life, one in which all the virtues are endangered; faith, in the black darkness of paganism; hope, in trials that are so long and so harsh; charity, in the midst of so much corruption and in the lack of all the sacraments. Chastity, indeed, is not endangered here so much by delights; but it is endangered, nevertheless, by the promiscuous and intimate manner of living together of both sexes, in the free permission for anyone to dare or to do anything whatsoever, and most of all in the complete nudity. For here you cannot help but see, whether you wish it or not, what elsewhere is hidden not only from wandering eyes, but even from spying eyes.

Hence, daily, I groan to my God begging Him that He may not leave me without help amid the dead. Begging Him, I say, that amid so much foulness of the flesh, and such superstitious worship of the devil, to which He has exposed me, naked as it were and unarmed, "my heart may be undefiled in his justifications," so that, when that Good Shepherd may come, "who will gather together the dispersed of Israel," "He may gather us from among the nations to bless His Holy Name. Amen!"

Your Reverence's most humble servant and son in Christ,

ISAAC JOGUES, S.J.

Memoir of a Martyr

Amsterdam, Holland
May 1, 1643

To WILLEM KIEFT, THE DIRECTOR GENERAL OF THE DUTCH
COLONY AT NEW AMSTERDAM, FROM THE NOBLE, HIGH AND
MIGHTY LORDS OF THE STATES-GENERAL:

. . . . At the request of Anne, of Austria, Queen Regent of
France, we urge you to use all your good offices to aid and
save the French Jesuit named Isaac Jogues, who has been captured by the Iroquois savages.

COST VAN DER COLIJN

New Amsterdam
August 28, 1643

To GENERAL ARENDT VAN CORLAER,
DIRECTOR AND COMMANDANT AT FORT ORANGE:

The captain of the vessel which has just arrived here from
Rensselaerswyck has just informed me of the abortive attempt
which Isaac Jogues made to escape, at your insistence, and of
how you relented in your purpose and now hold him a prisoner,
disputing with yourself about whether or not he should be released to the Mohawks for fear of their reprisals upon you. I
command you in the name of the Lords of the States-General
to bring Isaac Jogues in safety to Fort Amsterdam at the earliest
possible moment.

WILLEM KIEFT
Director General

I Lift My Lamp

DEAR FATHER VIMONT, THE PEACE OF CHRIST:

Having sent a letter to you at Quebec together with that I addressed to Governor Montmagny only five months ago, I need not tell you once more about our dealings with the Iroquois. However, I have the strangest good news to relate. We had not left Rensselaerswyck on the way back to Mohawk country when a band of Iroquois appeared exulting in the recent summer capture of more Hurons and enraged once more at the French because you fired your cannons at them as they entered the French fort. The warriors came back to Ossernenon in a great rage. They blamed all their failure on me, thinking that I had advised the French to kill them. And now they demanded that I be brought back to the village and killed.

Van Corlaer sought me out in the camp and urged me to escape. Seeing the fresh fury of the Indians, he and his counselors felt that letting me be carried off from Rensselaerswyck this time would be cooperating in murder. My heart was perplexed at his words when he urged me to slip away from the camp and stow myself on a vessel which was lying at anchor. I began to doubt if it really were expedient for the greater glory of God that I subject myself to the certain prospect of death by fire when I might escape. I asked him to leave me free till the morning to make my decision.

That night I spent in prayer, earnestly beseeching Our Lord not to allow me to reach a conclusion by myself, but to give me light that I might know His most holy Will. Then, since I saw no way of helping the savages, and since I thought that my knowledge of the Iroquois language, their strength in war, their habits, their intentions, their country, and the routes leading to it would be valuable for the French and for the missioners, and that it would die with me unless I escaped, I thought that I had weighed before God, with all the impartiality in my power, the reasons for and against it, and that Our Lord would be better pleased if I should seize the opportunity to escape.

My actual escape was perilous in the extreme since I was sleeping between two Mohawk guards in some Dutchman's barn, and the farm was guarded by dogs, one of which had bitten me twice as I sneaked out of the barn in the early evening to survey the prospect of my route to the beach where van Corlaer's promised rowboat was awaiting me. However, I did make my way there with no one having discovered my escape, and after a horrible fifteen minutes struggling with the heavy boat, mired by a tide, at last I loosened it and made out to the ship. The captain came out once I had scrambled on deck and assured me that now I was safe for good. But he insisted that I should hide in the hold amid the cargo.

As soon as the surgeon had applied some ointment for the cure of scurf to my dog bites, I was lowered into the dark hold and the trapdoor was closed over me, with a heavy chest covering it to conceal it from chance prowlers. I was two days and two nights in the belly of that vessel, with such discomfort that I thought I would suffocate and die from the stench. Then it was that I remembered poor Jonas, and I prayed Our Lord to detain me in the country of the infidels if He did not approve of my escape.

Two days later I was brought on deck to face the Commandant of the fort who had decided that I must stay in the vicinity till the fury of the natives was somewhat abated, since they were blaming him for my escape and were threatening war on the Dutch. Consequently I lay concealed in the house of the Commandant for the next twelve days. The surgeon of the fort examined my leg once more and decided that he might have to amputate it since the medicine intended only for the scurf had gangrened the wound.

After these days I was moved once more to a garret of another burgher, uncomfortable in the extreme, where I had to remain again for a whole month, without being able to move thirty feet, and with scarcely enough food to sustain life.

Now, however, thanks to a command from Kieft of New

Amsterdam, I am safe here at last and have been royally treated here since I was brought down the river from Fort Orange in the north. Van Corlaer finally consoled the Mohawks with three hundred guilders. I have been honored by a state dinner here, with all the principal burghers present. No one can understand how I could have cast myself into such dangers as I had suffered, merely to spread the gospel of Christ.

I am surprised at the fact that so many peoples and of so many religions can live here in peace. There is officially no exercise of religion except the Calvinist, and the orders declare that none but Calvinists be admitted; nevertheless, that order is not observed. For besides the Calvinists, there are in this settlement Catholics, English Puritans, Lutherans, Anabaptists, etc. If the French and the Dutch can manage to live at peace with one another, this Island of Manhate may someday be a great meeting place of nations living all in harmony.

You would hardly believe what kindnesses have been heaped on me here, and what a joy it is to me to think that within a few weeks now I shall be once more in France with my brothers of the Society. Already the ship which we had hoped for is in the harbor and I shall be setting out upon it within the week.

Give my very best wishes to the Fathers in Quebec. By God's favor I earnestly hope to see all of you once more after a report to the provincial.

Your devoted son in Our Lord,
Isaac Jogues, S.J.

The College of Rennes, France
January 5, 1644

Dear Paul, P. C.

Isaac Jogues, the most famous and fabulous missionary of our day, is at this moment three doors down the hall, where he is trying to get some rest, after months of a most horrible life. Within a week all France will be amazed to know that he is home with us. And the Fathers and Brothers here are still almost stupefied at the realization that we have with us a man who has suffered such great things for Christ.

Here is the story of his arrival, as I know that your community will be as overjoyed and astonished as we are with the details. It was like having St. Francis Xavier drop in at our front door all unexpected this morning. I can think of no other comparison which could match the reality of the experience. At five-thirty this morning, just a minute after Brother had rung the bell for the community Mass, there was a pounding on the front door. I heard it myself as I was just passing down the hall.

When Brother answered it, he opened the door to a ragged man indeed, wearing an undersized overcoat and a peasant's cap which did not fit either. He told Brother that he had to see Father Rector, as he had some news from Canada and the Fathers there. Brother went to the sacristy where Father was vesting and told him about the strange visitor, and that he could not wait to see him. When Father Rector heard that he was poor and could not wait, he took off his amice and went to the parlor.

He greeted the poor man and asked him if he had really come from Canada. "Yes." Did he know of Father Vimont? "Yes, Father." And Father Brebeuf? "Extremely well." And Father Jogues, did he know him? "Yes, I knew him very well indeed." We have had word, said Father Rector, that he was captured by the Iroquois. Do you know, is he dead? Or is he still captive? Have the Indians not murdered him? "He is at liberty," he answered with a queer gulp. "Reverend Father, I am Isaac Jogues."

With this he fell on his knees at Father's feet, kissed his hand, and begged his blessing. Father Rector shivered and then burst out in a cry of joy. He lifted Father Jogues from his knees, threw his arms around him, and kissed him on both cheeks. In a loud voice which we heard in the chapel he called out that Father Jogues was here and we all came hurriedly and confusedly to the recreation room. Hardly anyone could say a word, but we embraced him and clasped his mangled hands and kissed him.

You can not imagine what a flood of emotion swept through

our little community. We got him a cassock and led him to the chapel at last, where Father Rector, thrilling with joy, said a Mass of thanksgiving and gave Father Jogues Communion. Our breakfast was more joyous than any first-class feast, I can assure you, though we spoke almost in whispers of awe. Father Jogues was seated at the Rector's place, with Father Rector next to him. What a meager sign of honor it seemed to us to be able to show such a man. But I know that he felt more honored at our brotherly joy in his presence than if he were being paraded through Paris.

God is good to give us such brothers as Isaac Jogues, is He not, Paul? I shall never as long as I live forget the joy of this day. I have a hundred details to tell you about the few hours that we have had him in our midst, but I want to get this off with a courier so that you may get word of what has happened by tomorrow if possible.

Let us pray for one another that we may live as worthy brothers of so great men as we have working for the souls of the heathen Indians of New France.

Your brother in the Company of Jesus,

JEAN

Paris

January 15, 1644

MY DEAREST MOTHER,

I trust you've received the surprising news from my letter of a couple of weeks ago. I have yet some better news for you. Father Provincial doesn't as yet know quite what he's going to do with the extra Jesuit he suddenly has on his hands, and he thinks that in the meantime I ought to pay you a visit and breathe a bit of fresh Orleans air. I shall see you within a week. I have much to tell you about God's goodness to me in all the trials He has permitted for me.

Your loving son,

ISAAC

Memoir of a Martyr

VERY REVEREND FATHER FILLEAU,

. . . . Men try to invent tragic stories, and use their imagination to concoct strange adventures to surprise one and to touch one's emotion. But here is a story of great adventures which have really happened; here is a recital of the most astounding deeds joined with the truest heroism. It is my royal wish that you send me Isaac Jogues, that I too may pay him my respects.

ANNE OF AUSTRIA
Queen Regent of France

Rome
February 10, 1644

DEAR FATHER FILLEAU, P. C.

The French Ambassador and I visited the pope the day after I received Father Jogues' letter. His Holiness insisted that I recount all I knew about his hardships; and when I had asked the permission that he be allowed once more to say Mass, with those hands now so deformed, the Holy Father answered, "With all my heart. It would not be fitting that a martyr of Christ should not drink the Blood of Christ. And with sincerest fatherly affection I bestow on him and his heroic brothers among the Indians the Apostolic Benediction."

. . . . I leave it up to Your Reverence's judgment whether or not to allow Father's desire to go back among his Indians this spring.

Your Reverence's servant in Christ,
MUTIUS VITELLESCHI, S.J.
General of the Society of Jesus

Quebec
May 23, 1644

DEAR FATHER PROVINCIAL,

. . . I cannot tell you what joy I have experienced in being back in Quebec soon to depart once more to Ville St. Marie (Montreal). . . .

Filially in Our Lord,
ISAAC JOGUES, S.J.

Ville St. Marie
May 2, 1646

MOST REVEREND AND DEAR FATHER LALEMANT:

The letter which it has pleased Your Reverence to send me from Quebec found me engaged in the exercises of my retreat, which I began after the departure of the canoe which carried my letter to you; it was a good time, for our Hurons here are now all away on the chase, and give us more silence. Would you believe me that, when I opened the letter of Your Reverence, my heart at first was seized as if with dread; for I feared that that which I desired and that which my spirit would prize as the greatest of all desires was actually to come to pass. My poor nature, which remembered all that had gone before, trembled.

But Our Lord, in His goodness, bestowed calm on it, and will calm it still more. Yes, Father, I desire all that Our Lord desires, and I desire it at the peril of a thousand lives. God's holy Will and His sweet command on us are well worth any difficulties. He who has preserved us by His holy grace without the aid of Mass and the Sacraments for eighteen or twenty months will not refuse the same favor to us who do not thrust ourselves into this position, but who undertake this work solely and only to please Him, and undertake it against all the instincts of nature.

The thing I would say about all these comings and goings of the Iroquois is that I see very few from the first two villages (Ossernenon and Andagaron); and yet it is with these that we must principally deal, and it was to these villages that those who were recently slain belonged.

There have been scarcely any Mohawks who have come here except from the third village (Tionontoguen), the one where Couture lives. It is not among these last that we shall have to live, but among those others whom we do not see visiting us.

If God wills that I go to the Iroquois, it is necessary that he who accompanies me must be virtuous, docile, courageous, one who would be willing to suffer anything for God, one who is able to make and handle canoes, so that independently of the savages we might be able to go and come.

May Your Reverence permit me to send my respects, if it so please you, to our Reverend Fathers.

I am your very humble and obedient servant.

Isaac Jogues, S.J.

Notre Dame de Recouvrance
Quebec
September 10, 1647

Reverend and dear Father Filleau, P. C.

At last after almost a year we have discovered the details of the death of Father Jogues. It was not until June that we heard the first report that he had been murdered months before.

Here is the story in brief, as I have heard it from the mouth of the very man who admits to the killing himself.

As Father and Jean la Lande trudged along the trail approaching the first Mohawk settlement, on October 16, two weeks after he had left us, all of a sudden a large band of Iroquois emerged from behind the trees on all sides and closed in on them with blood-curdling shouts. The two froze to the spot in terror and amazement. The Indians pounced on them, beat them mercilessly, and stripped them naked. Then they dragged their captives in triumph to their village. This time they would not escape. The Indians would slash them to ribbons, burn them at the stake, split open their heads, eat their flesh.

In the village a storm arose over the Frenchmen. Some struck them; others warded off the blows and pressed in to guard them. But the two were hurried by one of the chiefs into his cabin. Temporarily that made them safe, since no one would dare enter the cabin to harm them lest he should forever incur the wrath of the chief and all his relatives. But the storm continued. And that night the quarreling tribes gathered in a nearby village to decree whether or not the prisoners should die.

All the responsible men of the town were absent for the night. And at sundown, a brave came to visit Jogues' cabin. There were people in another cabin who wished to eat and talk with him. To refuse the invitation would be interpreted as an act of great discourtesy and would betray a suspicion that might breed greater ill-feeling. Jogues consulted with the members of his cabin. They feared treachery. Nevertheless, they agreed that he should go.

They sent the chief's grandson along to guard him. He and his charge followed their guide silently through the subdued paths of the village till they arrived before the long house where their guide turned to pause. The guide stepped back. Jogues looked at him quizzically and then, not to betray suspicion or fear, he pushed back the skin which hung down from the lintel and stepped inside. That was the last that he saw or knew anything. For a tomahawk crashed down from the upraised arm of a brave lurking behind the door. And Isaac Jogues was dead. The braves bent over the blackrobe, scalped him, cut off his head, and held it up streaming with blood. Then they began a wild procession to the gate of their stockade where they jammed the head of the martyr of Christ on the point of a pole where all could see it.

The next morning the returning chiefs brought the news that the Frenchmen should be released and sent back to their country. But it was too late. The evil work had been accomplished, and war had by that fact once more been declared upon the French and the Hurons. The date was October 18, 1646.

It has taken a long time for the news finally to reach us about the details of the murder. But we had suspected the worst for several months. For we had not seen a trace of the Iroquois during this mild winter when we should have expected to meet them occasionally on their hunting expeditions to the north.

Strange to say, we have captured just lately a man who finally confessed that he was the murderer. But now he is so repentant and so desirous of baptism that he will be received into the Church here at Quebec and will be given the name he most desires, Isaac Jogues.

God's ways are unpredictable and strange. But we have already seen the first fruits of the martyrdom of René Goupil and Isaac Jogues. Some day the warring will cease, and the heavenly prayers of these men will gain these fierce and treacherous savages to the meekness of Jesus Christ.

Fraternally in Christ,
JEROME LALEMANT, S.J.

St. Louis College
St. Louis, Mo., U. S. A.
November 3, 1840

DEAR FATHER GENERAL ROOTHAN:

I am again writing about the Indians off to the west in the Rocky Mountains. This last fall they made a thousand mile trip down the Missouri from Fort Benton, Montana, to ask for a blackrobe. It seems to me that their whole nation is ready for the harvest if only we could send a couple of workers among them.

Some Iroquois visitors to the west coast have told the Indians there stories about the wonderful virtues of the blackrobes and of their God. This is indeed another Macedonian cry to come over and help. . . .

I shall await your answer to my earnest request with eager longing, praying God at Holy Mass each morning that I may be worthy of so great an honor as to work among the Indians.

Your humble and devoted son in Our Lord,

PETER DeSMET, S.J.

[Author's Note: The letter form of this sketch has been adopted chiefly as a literary device. However, the substance of what the letters tell was actually the subject of correspondence of the time. Many important details had to be omitted because of the brevity allowed for this account. Those who may wish to know the exact and complete story should consult *Saint among Savages*, the definitive biography of Isaac Jogues, by Francis X. Talbot, S.J. It has been the basic source book for what we have written.]

ENGLAND *meanwhile had become a mighty power. Her sea dogs ventured to the farthest lands. No travelers could be sure that dawn would not bring her pirates in search of booty. Then drawn swords made the waters blush. Drake, Cabot, Walter Raleigh had won their spot in England's statuary. Conquest and discovery were abroad.*

The seventeenth century was only a few years old when John Smith fell in love with Pocahontas. Jamestown represented a firm toe-hold in Virginia. In a little while Negro slaves and white women and tobacco planting had become institutions on the new soil.

Up the rocky coast past the Dutch more English landed. They were Pilgrims in search of religious freedom, stern men who brought Calvin's spirit to American shores. Plymouth helped to cradle American history. Miles Standish, John Alden, and Priscilla walked into the history books and tintypes and folklore of colonial love.

Men began building Boston on a harbor. New Haven and Hartford, Salem and Providence followed in the colonial theme. Small rivalries, the dogged individualism that characterizes pioneers, calculating religious devotion that bordered on frenzy typified the early New Englanders and plagued these refugees seeking asylum in a far country.

Suspicion stalked even the innocent. Aged women tottered to execution, condemned as witches. Inclemency and roughhewn bigotry wrapped its poisonous shell around the buoyant soul that was inchoate America. A far cry from the toleration they had supposedly come to seek!

* * *

Patriot on the Potomac

Father Andrew White, S.J.

by W. P. Schoenberg, S.J.

Roman weather that November was "unusual" and there were some who said it was due to Richelieu's wars in the North. The summer had been most excessive in its extremes; now the chilly, piercing dampness was excessive too. It would never do for Father Mutius Vitelleschi to grumble at these deplorable vagaries of the elements, because he was General of the Jesuits and might be expected, if anyone were, to set an example of indifference. Yet he couldn't help but react as others did. He was cold, clammy cold all that morning; and though grumbling wouldn't have changed the temperature, it would certainly have appeased his sense of justice.

He reflected ruefully on New France where his Jesuits were being scalded and roasted by barbarian redskins, and about reports, lately received, of the last Canadian winter. Blizzards, icy trails, smoke-filled bark shambles where one could freeze as conveniently under-roof as without.

In India, Tonkin, Paraguay, Abyssinia, the complaint was heat. In China it was Confucius and in England the Bishop, who was trying to discredit all the Religious Orders. Everywhere something—just to keep that nice balance between seeking and receiving.

Now what had the English Provincial to say this morning? Father General scanned his letter and shivered decently. Father Andrew White would leave with Lord Baltimore's colonists—a touchy business. These Englishmen were inveterate travelers, pirates if not gentlemen. Hm-m-m. He would go as an "adventurer," no status as an official, clerical or otherwise. A new experiment, they called it. No state patronage of religion. . . .

Father General didn't exactly disapprove of the innovation. The Jesuits Suarez and Bellarmine had recently been saying a good deal on the subject—by the way, for the benefit of those Englishmen. This nobleman Baltimore, where had he got his ideas? Perhaps Father White . . . . he had been a friend of Baltimore.

Well, they would go—it would be a noble experiment.

Father General remembered the last Canadian winter. Br-r-r-r, Rome was cold too.

Standing boyishly on the deck of the *Ark*, relishing its race with a merchant-ship, Father Andrew White was not conscious of his unique position in history. At the moment other matters were more compelling, like the race—which the *Ark* lost—or adventures distant, or the care of his two Jesuit companions. One of the latter was at his side, fragile as a reed and much less resilient. Would Father Altham survive the trip? He wondered that God had sent such a frail specimen into the wilderness. The ways of Providence, like sea-depths, were unfathomable.

Of Brother Gervase the superior felt more confident. The Brother was strong and healthy, in the prime of life and full of enthusiasm. Surely he was well qualified for his assignment. A jack-of-all-trades, typical of the English seaman of his day, capable of performing the duties of anything from buccaneer to butler: Father White complimented himself on finding so suitable an assistant.

He could hardly know that Brother Gervase was sailing to his death. Nor could he even suspect the killer, an insignificant little mosquito—after the jails and treacheries of all London, a colossal irony. Happily this irony was hidden among the ripples of Brother's laughter. The superior could lean on him with quiet composure.

Not that Father White had to lean on anybody. He was no ordinary Englishman, though in his veins he carried perilously the honest English blood of many centuries. He was an English outlaw, a gentleman-outlaw, too, with learning and wits about him. For he had passed many years as a professor in Jesuit theologates on the continent. Had he been willing to sever his ties with Rome, his status could easily have been reversed. Native England with, perhaps, Anglican purples, episcopal and plush, instead of disguise and the deck of the *Ark* bearing him into exile.

While Father White still pondered Providence and took his pleasure in the sturdiness of Brother Gervase, bad news for Protestants aboard ship finally broke out, and they came forth to stare. Three Jesuits were on the *Ark!* The expedition had been cursed from the beginning. Now this! Ah, they had been told to avoid that Papist Calvert and all his schemes.

Some of the Protestants were sailors, though most were not. Most were colonists who had accepted Lord Baltimore's terms for opportunity in the New World, hard terms because the second Lord Baltimore kept his purse strings tight. It was quite enough for any of them to drive a bad bargain, but to get Jesuits too, that was the limit. It was beyond endurance. So they stared furtively at the three miscreants (did they really have cloven-hoofs?) and let their resentment swell within them.

Father White was not much disturbed by these dark and furtive looks. He paced up and down before them and "good-day'd" them with the poise and aplomb of a Roman and self-assured archbishop, chuckling to himself at their gruff reactions. Did all Jesuits secretly enjoy the suspicion and awe others manifested toward them? Father White thought they did. Too funny to be taken seriously. It was ignorance, anyhow, not malice.

The Protestants found no cause for chuckles on deck that morning. Everything was wrong—like the Jesuits they had got. First they had taken the oath at Gravesend (God bless King Charles), then the ship had proceeded to Cowes, Isle of Wight, where the Papist boarded her. No sign of Jesuits there. Evidently these latter recusants had climbed aboard during the night. Ho now! Let that fellow White pace and smile—he would change his tune soon enough. The journey was just beginning. . . .

The following day was Sunday and there was no Mass. Winds were howling and creaking through the rigging above deck, and below, the Colonial governor, Leonard Calvert, with twelve gentry and a few-score Catholic poor folk were attending Father White's "services." A long prayer (it seemed long), a brief homily on confidence in Mary, Star of the Sea, and after that a solemn promise.

During the night the *Ark's* little-sister ship, the *Dove*, hoisted a distress signal, two lanterns high on the mast, and then had been carried off into the teeth of the storm. For a while the *Ark* followed, till the *Dove* had disappeared. Father White and his companions were mourning her now. They said she was lost, and they too would be lost if the storm didn't abate.

Their grief was tainted with fear. With their ship's rudder out of control, they were drifting helplessly, tossing like a tub in mountains of water.

"I suggest," said Father White, scanning his congregation's frightened pinched faces, "that we place our ship under the protection of God, of His most Holy Mother, of St. Ignatius, and all the Angels of Maryland."

He hesitated and the oak beams above them groaned ominously. "I have a suggestion," he said; "let us dedicate the new country beyond the seas to the Immaculate Virgin Mother. It will be her dowry, a new one to take the place of England."

With heads bowed the colonists dedicated Maryland. In their hearts they knew all along it was Mary's land, despite the king's insistence that it honor his queen.

A new dowry, Maryland. It sounded like a poem. . . .

After three days the storm blew itself out and the *Ark* was left to coast serenely along the shores of Spain. Father White saw in the fleeting shoreline the land of his student days, of his professorship at St. Alban's, Valladolid. Then Spain went down into the sea, and the tip of Africa came up. The *Ark* turned west, past the Canary Islands, farther, farther, farther. On January the third they reached Barbados in the southern Antilles. The crossing had been the most tranquil the ship's captain and crew had ever seen, a circumstance not lightly regarded by

Father White. It was due, he said piously, and we ought to believe him, to the intervention of the Virgin Mary whose dowry they would restore.

Barbados was propitious. It gave them what was lost to them, their tiny pinnace. The *Dove*, as though brought to life again, came sailing in from the high seas, just like themselves. There was a gala reunion, solemnly sanctioned with singing and rum, more rum than singing, and the two boat-loads made a noisy assault on the island.

There were few Catholics in Barbados, mostly English and Irish who had been fetched there as indentured slaves. The rulers were crafty and sometimes harsh, demanding exorbitant prices for their produce.

"Nothing could be had," wrote Father White, "but it cost us our eyes. A pig six weeks old was five pounds sterling, a turkey fifty shillings, and a chicken six shillings." The only liberality shown was in the matter of potatoes, which root was so plentiful that one could have cart-loads for the taking.

It was the pineapple which caught the voyagers' fancy. Was there anything like it in Europe? Nothing. Father White tried to describe it, but found concepts inadequate. "I did wish I could send with this letter just one pineapple—for nothing but the fruit itself is adequate to the task of showing worthily what it is."

During the night of January twenty-fourth, the two vessels weighed anchor and made for the Carib Islands. Here they scarcely stopped, then hurried on through the West Indian chain where place names sounded like a litany. In Montserrat they found many Irishmen who had been expelled from Virginia for their Catholic faith. At St. Kitts they were entertained by the English and French governors. A sea-battle was raging nearby, they were told, English and Dutch on one side, and the Spanish on the other. They kept a safe distance, though they boasted that their ship was "well gunn'd and man'd."

From St. Kitts they touched land no more till they arrived at Point Comfort in Virginia on the twenty-seventh of February,

1634. They had come to the land of dedication at last, Mary's dowry.

The new arrivals, though ordered to silence, were all agog that February morning. Hold their news? Impossible. They trooped ashore and gabbled away like a flock of fish-wives.

They were going to found a colony! Why yes! King Charles (God bless him) had granted almost unlimited rights. A proprietor, no royal governor! Religious equality for all!

The news resounded like a thunderbolt over Port Comfort. Did these Papists actually think they could claim part of Virginia to the North? Did they expect to make that stick? It was unthinkable that the head of the Church of England would grant more liberal terms to Papists than to Anglicans. Were there documents to confirm this preposterous assertion?

Point Comfort's citizens pored over the letters and tracts that were spread before them. It was true, they said. King Charles had betrayed Virginia. King Charles was a fool.

While these disturbances were alarming the populace, Leonard Calvert sought out and found Virginia's governor to prosper his business. Rendering him benevolent, Calvert produced two casks of fine white wine; Governor Harvey was no Puritan. Calvert sipped some of it daintily while he displayed the royal documents.

Virginia's governor was delighted. Let the commoners roar, he said; he was running things and Maryland would have what it needed.

They shook hands on it.

A last point, said Calvert. Was there a Captain Claiborne in Jamestown, who, he was given to understand, occupied a certain Kent Island in Maryland territory? He had a message for the Captain, a message from Lord Baltimore himself.

Governor Harvey said yes, the Captain was in that very building, for he was secretary of the colony.

Captain Claiborne blustered in. As one of Virginia's wealthiest planters, he wielded great influence. When he talked with Leonard Calvert, all Virginia, except its governor, talked.

Did the honorable Captain Claiborne occupy an island on the Chesapeake, known as Kent Island, Governor Calvert wanted to know.

He did. He had it by license under the seal of Scotland and the governor of Virginia.

Would the honorable Captain Claiborne be willing to occupy Kent Island as a tenant under Lord Baltimore, acknowledging this illustrious lord as the rightful sovereign of Kent Island?

Ridiculous! The Captain couldn't think of it! Kent Island was his—he could acknowledge no lord and sovereign.

Very well, Governor Calvert had his orders. He was to allow the honorable Captain peaceful possession for one year. After that—! The Captain would know.

Captain Claiborne retired to consult the colony's notables. Was it true that the king had granted Baltimore this territory north?

It was. With their own eyes they had seen royal letters.

But the king had already given that land to Virginia!

The king was a fool. He gave the same land away twice—more than twice. He gave what belonged to another.

Should the Captain withdraw from Kent Island?

A thousand times no! Possession was nine points of the law; in America, ninety-nine. Kent Island was a wedge. . . . There would be a day of reckoning, wait!

Was it true that Jesuits had come?

It was, three of them.

America wasn't big enough for Popery and Jesuits. No, by heaven, not big enough! Captain Claiborne thumped his fist determinedly and frowned his dark, mysterious frown that he reserved for extremely grave climaxes. Then twirling his cavalier moustache, just like one of those villains in a sorry melodrama, he stomped rudely out without saying another word.

In mid-March the *Ark* and the *Dove* and a second pinnace purchased from reluctant Virginians entered Chesapeake Bay and cruised cautiously westward. Armed and dusky warriors lined the shoreways. Fantastic reports had been circulated among them; a canoe "like an island" had entered the red-man's world. Men more numerous than forest trees. They were "Spaniards" come to conquer and destroy. By day, cold expressionless eyes watched the advance from behind trees, and at night fires blazed throughout the whole country.

But the tiny fleet persisted. Up the bay, into the Potomac it coasted, alert to a possible attack, till at length it reached a wooded island.

"This is it," they told one another.

Father White found a name for them and the island was christened St. Clement's, the priest said, because on St. Clement's day they had begun their voyage. Even the Protestants approved —they had long since come to respect "Mr. White."

As the beach at St. Clement's was sloping, they had to wade ashore. This occasioned some minor crises, like women falling into the water and linen being swept away by the current, but no lives were lost, nor were there Indians waiting with arrows to murder them. They took possession peacefully, almost in a trance. They gazed around them, at the beach, the coves, the forests stretching in some places to the water's edge. All for the taking. Theirs. Young men ran to examine the nearest trees and they laughed as they snapped twigs of cedar and sassafras. This land, these trees, grass, flowers—all theirs.

And then they made camp for the night. Guards were assigned and wood-cutters and water-carriers and cooks. A cross was hewed from a mulberry tree. It would serve on the morrow. A site was selected for it and the ground prepared. Stars came out and all was well.

For Father White, all was especially well. Come morning, the feast of the Annunciation of the Blessed Virgin Mary, he would say Mass for his first time in this remote part of the world.

When Governor Calvert and Father Altham returned from their council with Indian chiefs, they found Indians swarming all over St. Clement's Island. Among them, judiciously jocular, was Father White. He was gesticulating madly to convey white-man's concepts to primitive minds, while *his* Indians were admiring everything the pale-faces had brought. The center of interest, surprisingly, was not the cannon which boomed now and then to impress anyone who needed it. The center of interest was the ship bobbing off shore—where in the world had the pale-faces got so large a tree? And how had they managed to dig it out to make so vast a canoe? Not even with an interpreter could Father White enlighten them on these points, so he left them awe-struck and displayed other wonders that might impart a wholesome fear.

The governor brought good news. Captain Henry Fleet, once of Virginia, had come to their aid, the governor said. He had shown them the best site for their colony and had negotiated for them with the Indians. They had paid for thirty miles of land with axes, hatchets, hoes, and cloth, and the natives were well-pleased with their bargain. Indeed, if Captain Fleet could be believed, the Indians really were eager for white-men, because fierce tribes to the West had been ravaging their homes. As soon as they could get started, the governor said, they would leave St. Clement's for their permanent home.

In a couple of days the tiny fleet set sail again. It moved down the Potomac some twenty-five miles, then into a bay on the left. And there was land, lots of it, fallow, rich, and abounding in game.

With mixed feelings of awe and gratitude they stepped ashore at St. Mary's. They knelt, Catholics and Protestants all, while Father White thanked God for His bountiful goodness, and barbarian red-skins watched with increasing wonder.

In the weeks that followed the colonists planned and settled their village. Spring planting was begun. Seed-corn purchased in Barbados was put into the soil already prepared by the Indians. Seeds, cuttings, and roots of all kinds brought all the way from England were set out; and before the summer was over, St. Mary's had achieved a cultivated luxuriance hitherto unknown in the New World.

More flourishing yet was their friendship with the Indians. In other colonies, with the exception of Pennsylvania (which came much later), Englishmen plowed their fields with their muskets on their backs. Not so in Maryland. Indians helped plant and harvest the corn. Squaws showed their white sisters how to bake it into bread. Indian braves instructed the white men how to hunt and fish, and accompanied them in the chase. Strict laws protected Indians from trade-sharks and liquor, and treaties were drawn up for every eventuality and signed with a feast and an exchange of gifts. No treaty was ever broken. No Marylander had to barricade his door, keep a musket loaded, fear for his family when he was away.

St. Mary's had become more civilized than London.

On St. Mary's Bluff, near the point of land which pierced the belly of the bay, stood an ancient and solitary mulberry tree, rooted like a symbol of Maryland's vigor. Beneath its spreading branches the colonists had often gathered for official proclamations and treaties with Indian chiefs. Here Father White had said his first Mass at St. Mary's. Here he had often read his breviary, beside his shining bay, beside lovely St. Mary's.

One misty morning, Governor Calvert's secretary approached the tree and tacked thereon a bulletin so that all might know what state of affairs existed between the colony and that scalawag Claiborne. Be it known, the bulletin said in effect, that Maryland was at war with Captain Claiborne and his Kent Island associates. Be it known, the bulletin continued, that a "sea battle" had been fought between Claiborne's ship, the *Cockatrice*, and two of Maryland's pinnaces, during which engagement six men were killed. The *Cockatrice*, the bulletin said, had been captured. God save the King!

And at the bottom of the secretary's bulletin was the date: April 24, 1635.

During ensuing months the secretary had many trips to make to the old mulberry tree. Some were great triumphs, enjoyed by the secretary as though he alone had been responsible. Others were less gratifying, but on the whole favorable to Maryland. In any case, the secretary was wont to say (louder when the news was bad), "War is war, a bloody business. Sad report with the good and so to victory."

The secretary was a cheerful man.

News of Maryland's war on the Chesapeake drifted down the coast to Jamestown and excited some twelve thousand Virginians, who were anxiously waiting for excitement. A crisis could rid them, perhaps, of their governor. If so, a crisis was welcome.

Governor Harvey was not a prudent man. It was commonly said that he was too fond of money and not particular how he got it. His manners were rude. He strutted about Jamestown like an ill-mannered rooster; and when councilors got in his way, he assaulted them like a champion of the same breed, using his fists for spurs.

But the crowning grievance was infinitely worse. Governor Harvey was a friend of the Marylanders. "A pox on Maryland!" the Virginians said.

The governor had sold them cattle? The governor was a traitor. Better knock cattle on the head than sell them to Maryland!

Now the Kent Island affair. It annoyed Harvey as much as it did Claiborne. Claiborne was a nuisance and a knave to boot. Claiborne, his own secretary! Well, the governor would settle that. He removed Claiborne from office and the storm broke loose.

It began with a parson calling the new secretary a "jackanapes," which must have been a terrible word in 1635 because the poor parson paid later for it by banishment.

The new secretary was a jackanapes, most Virginians decided. The "jackanapes" was seized and with him Governor Harvey. Angry councilors decreed a new administration, sent Harvey off in chains to London.

Peace settled again on the James River, a peace breathed upon and warmed by the most excellent Captain Claiborne.

But Claiborne should have saved his breath. He had failed to reckon on his London partners, and now there would be a warming of another kind. Letters came for Captain Claiborne. Could Captain Claiborne put in an appearance at London? the partners wanted to know. If not, he had better find a way. There was going to be a lawsuit, the London partners said. War on the Chesapeake had ruined Kent Island's fur business.

Captain Claiborne was forced to yield to their good pleasure. In an evil mood, less disposed toward Maryland than ever before, he boarded a ship and sailed into a rising sun for London.

The affair went badly. Claiborne returned a year later, legally stripped of his island, but determined that, when fortune's wheel had turned again, he would have it back. He soon did.

In August, 1637, Brother Gervase sickened with yellow fever and, seemingly impatient to leave, died in a hurry. His funeral was celebrated in the handsome brick church he himself had just finished; Father White read the funeral Mass. The church, though a vast one, all of thirty-two feet long, was jammed like a duke's obsequies, because the Brother was a favorite. And besides, most of the Protestants had recently become Catholics—they nearly doubled the Catholic congregation, but not the size of the church.

Many Indians came to town for the funeral, mostly friends with whom Brother had gone turkey hunting. They were tawny of skin, dressed scantily in deer-hide and reeking with the odors of the forest, especially an oil repelling mosquitoes. But no one minded these crudities. Brother Gervase was dead, their pastor's "two hands," and that was so memorable nothing else could be noticed.

In the nearly four years since his coming, Father White had aged like one who grieves. He wasn't the grieving kind, but these had been particularly strenuous years—he had, as it were, represented the whole Church in this noble experiment of seeking new adjustments between Church and state. He couldn't say yet whether he had bent to or fro; perhaps he had stood so straight that he had fallen backwards. He didn't really know. What bothered him most was that he could foresee a storm on the horizon; misunderstandings between Lord Baltimore and the Jesuits were brewing. God willing, Father White would be spared the trouble when it came.

So far the experiment had been a grand success. Catholics and Protestants had got along fine together, like lambs among lambs, and this was evidently a great phenomenon in those fervid days. There was no state support for any religion (quite a departure from the European tradition), and officials, all Catholic, had carefully preserved the religious and civil rights of everyone, whatever his sect. Maryland was unique in all the world, but since it was, Father White had had to tread cautiously; on him more than on civil authority rested the chances for success.

When he had first come, he had done double duty, domestic along with his priestly work. Like St. Paul he had been a tent-maker of a sort to support himself. So had Father Altham. Now their homes were built, the church finished, and the farm supervised by a layman, and physical labor was no longer necessary. They could devote themselves to their congregation and, somehow, to Indian languages.

Father White struggled continuously to get the latter into his fifty-year-old head, and he came up in due time with a catechism, a grammar, and a dictionary. His manuscripts, produced with so much weariness and patience, symbolized the man.

For the most part, mission work had been denied him these several years. The governor, fearing that hostile Indians to the West would carry him off as a hostage, forbade prolonged or distant trips among the tribes. This restraint on his zeal but added to an already heavy burden; however, wait he did, and with the death of Brother Gervase a new era began.

First some new Jesuits arrived, among them Father Copley, who took White's place as superior. White was free now to live among the Indians if—would Governor Calvert allow it?

Yes, the governor decided, he would, and Father White went gaily off with everyone's blessing to live among the Piscataways who resided somewhere near the ends of the earth, one hundred and twenty miles from St. Mary's. The journey to this remote heathen-land was a happy mixture of exploring, vacation, and penance. There were three, Father White and two hired guides. They traveled in a row-boat, two at the oars in turns and the third at a crudely devised rudder. In a basket they carried provisions, bread, cheese, and dried roasting ears of corn. In one chest they had the articles necessary for Mass, and in another presents for the Indians Father White hoped to convert. When nightfall overtook them, they pulled their boat on to some sheltered beach; and while the priest gathered fire-wood and put up a tent, his companions beat up the adjoining woods in quest of game. It was all quite a lark, even if Father White wasn't as young as he used to be.

The Piscataways called their village "Kittamaquund" and their head chief "Tayac," meaning Emperor. At least theoretically he was "king" over the many Indian chiefs who roamed the hills of Maryland and Virginia.

Tayac was a wily one. He had killed his brother for the "throne" and collected what he considered to be a royally respectable flock of wives, and then began his rule with all the native pomposity he could muster. His people liked him: at least he knew what he wanted and he knew how to get it.

When Father White appeared in his village, Tayac was not slow to learn of it. His braves herded the Black Robe's party into the presence of the terrible Tayac.

For a moment Tayac stared at the priest, startled by his garments. "The Black Robe!" he exclaimed; and he rushed to embrace Father White, Indian fashion.

Tayac's companions, perplexed as the priest over this sudden gesture, looked at one another soberly and wondered whether an evil spirit possessed Tayac.

"Black Robe, you are welcome," said Tayac; "come remain at my palace." He waved his arm grandly over a bark shack in the last stages of disrepair. "My brother Uwannus had a dream," he said. "He saw two Black Robes and he told me that Black Robes truly loved redskins. Black Robes would bring redskins happiness."

Father White was elated with his prospects—he would live at the "palace!"

"Stay seven years," said Tayac. "You will instruct my sons."

That was the beginning of Tayac's conversion. He soon cleared out his flock of wives, keeping only the best one, and he studied Christian doctrine with the fervor of any good Irishman. He asked for baptism, too, but Father White said no, not yet.

Then Tayac got sick, very very sick. All the medicine-men of the countryside, all forty of them, poured into the "palace" to practice their black art and so get credit for curing royalty, the best recommendation possible. They all failed, and Tayac got worse instead of better.

At this point Father White intervened. He scolded Tayac for receiving medicine-men, and told him that was no way at all to get baptism. No more superstitions, he said, or the Great Spirit would be angry.

Tayac agreed.

Then Father White prepared some medicines of his own invention, giving them in little doses to the royal patient. Tayac recovered, and all Kittamaquund made merry.

Could he have baptism now, Tayac wanted to know.

Not yet, but when the Black Robe returned from St. Mary's. The Black Robe had to go, but he would surely be back.

Tayac also went to St. Mary's. He continued his studies through the late spring of 1640, then hastened back to Kittamaquund to build a "chapel" for his baptism.

On July 5, Tayac's great day dawned. The governor was there, other Colonial officials. And *two* Black Robes, White and Altham. Father White was making it as solemn as possible—the fame of Pocahontas' Anglican baptism had reached even the Potomac, and it would never do to be less solemn for a Catholic emperor. There were prayers and hymns and candles and lots of flowers brought all the miles from St. Mary's. There were uniforms, too, and ribbons for the ladies. A most solemn occasion, to be sure.

First Father White performed the rite over Tayac, baptizing him Charles—in the name of the Father and the Son and the Holy Ghost. Then Tayac's chosen wife (she who survived his housecleaning), who took the name of Mary. Then a couple of lesser celebrities in the tribe, whose Christian names history has not thought fit to record. While the two priests chanted the Litany of Mary, Tayac and the governor carried a huge cross in procession, setting it up in the center of the village and kneeling beneath it till the chanting was done.

After that there was a big feast of roast turkey and cornbread, and all Kittamaquund was happy. Their Tayac had finally got what he wanted.

The exertions of the big day proved to be too much for the Black Robes. Both came down with a "malicious fever," which could have meant anything in the seventeenth century.

Four months later Father Altham was dead.

In the year before the Marston Moor (Cromwell's victory which changed the course of English history), Virginia got a new governor. He was Berkeley, Sir William Berkeley, if you please, and a more implacable royalist no one ever did see. This Berkeley had a grievance against Puritans, so he began his rule by passing laws forbidding the godly sect. The governor of Massachusetts had sent three Puritan preachers with his compliments? Fie on the governor of Massachusetts! Get them out of Virginia! Sir William ordered and swore and threatened till he was out of breath.

Then business called him off to England and he sailed away with the regrets of a job half-done. Only half the Puritans had been gotten rid of—the other half, the governor said, were a pestilence like the frogs of Egypt.

In Massachusetts, too, there was an epidemic of squabbles. Puritans versus Puritans, and about all any of them could agree on was that it was a rotten shame Mass was being said in the New World. There were some in Massachusetts who longed for the more congenial climate of the South, of Maryland, for instance, but they'd just as soon have pitched their tents on the edge of perdition as settle under Papists.

Maryland, caught between these two trouble-spots, saw her position grow more difficult by weeks. No longer was the friendly Harvey in the Virginia capital. Massachusetts Puritans considered it sinful to exchange fish for Maryland corn, though they were quite willing to trade with heathen Indians. When the *Dove* entered Boston harbor for purposes of trade, an attempt was made to arrest all the "culprits" aboard, meaning Catholics. If a priest entered Massachusetts, he was told to get out. If he returned, he was hanged.

Despite this Protestant intolerance on either side, Maryland offered asylum to all who were not wanted elsewhere. From Virginia came ship-loads. From Massachusetts came a scornful rejection. Settle under Papists? Never!

At the moment Maryland had a more urgent problem centering about one Master Richard Ingle, who was a Puritan swashbuckler with two itchy hands, one big mouth, and at least one ship for tobacco trading. It was rumored abroad that he ran a pirate's business when his friends weren't looking. If he really wasn't a pirate, he was at least a Parliamentarian, and in Maryland waters that was something almost as bad. Indeed the king (God bless King Charles) had given explicit orders that the ships of all Parliamentarians were to be seized and held for a manifestation of the royal displeasure.

Accordingly, when Master Ingle's ship anchored off St. Mary's, the acting governor, Brent (Calvert was in England at that time), was alerted, and the populace trooped over to the bluff to see what would happen.

"I am a captain for the Parliament against the king," said Ingle when he swaggered ashore. "In fact, your King Charles is no king at all; and if I had Prince Rupert on board my ship, I would flog him at the capstan!" He brandished his cutlass and made sly threats about cutting off heads—his companions said this ferocity was a "habit of his."

Now this was traitorous talk. Brent ordered him arrested and turned him over to the sheriff.

Had it all ended there, in St. Mary's jail, my story would be quite otherwise, because, in all likelihood, Father Andrew White would have breathed his last in a Maryland bedstead. But Master Ingle was a resourceful prisoner. He soon talked his way out, with the aid of Maryland's leading officials, who escorted him to his ship, and he sailed away to plan a hasty return.

And here a most familiar villain enters the scene again. The honorable Captain Claiborne had been waiting a long time to play his part, and he had rehearsed it so often he was certain to do well.

That Ingle was a Parliamentarian and a Puritan never seemed to bother Claiborne one single moment. Not even in the year before the Marston Moor. That Ingle claimed to be commissioned by Parliament and Claiborne's pretended charter came from the king made no difference either. Whatever their political or religious disaffections, the two had a common enemy, Papist Maryland, and that was enough to unite them in a flawless alliance. Even in the year before the Marston Moor.

Together they plotted their course, "their road back." Claiborne, it was decided, would seize Kent Island—nothing would suit him better—while Ingle would spew his wrath on lovely St. Mary's.

In the fall of 1644 they started out. All went well for them, exceedingly well. Because Calvert had not yet returned, Marylanders lacked a leader—they were still quarreling among themselves over how and why Ingle had escaped. So Ingle's rowdies thrashed them soundly and took possession of the finest homes in St. Mary's.

During these supreme triumphs Claiborne tried to talk his way into possession of Kent Island; failing in this, he returned to St. Mary's to get help. Back to the island he hurried, this time in force. There was a ringing battle. Claiborne, as usual, did no fighting; but when it was over, he held the field. How sweet the soil of Kent Island!

There was but one more score to settle—that Jesuit White!

It was a hard thing for Father White to leave Maryland in chains. It would have been hard in any circumstances, but in chains—heartbreaking. Perhaps more than anyone else he had been responsible for Maryland's prosperity. He had aided the first Lord Baltimore in formulating its plan of government. He had composed a tract, "An Account of the Colony of Lord Baltimore in Maryland near Virginia," which Baltimore used to attract his first colonists. He had won the confidence of all and brought them into a spirit of harmony and cooperation. He had guided the Church in its new venture. He had pacified the Indians. Most of all, he had brought God's blessing on the colony, a force that is most evident when it is absent.

Father White, the Marylanders often told one another, was more than an administrator, pastor, missionary. He was a "saint"; and because he was, Maryland had become what it was.

Unfortunately there were others besides himself who disagreed with Marylanders. They called him "traitor" instead of "saint"; and to show that they meant it, they put him in chains, heavy chains, for he was "hardened" too. Under double guard they dispatched this "hardened criminal" to London for trial.

For several months Father White rotted in London's prison. The charge of treason lay heavily on him, and he got little or no sympathy from anyone. They wouldn't even listen.

But his trial finally did come up. By this time it suited His Majesty's government to drop the charge of treason and to accuse the old priest of returning despite the law forbidding it.

"But I was forced to," White told the court. "They brought me here in chains."

The shot had misfired; and White was acquitted, but "banished forever" as an incurable Papist.

He went to Belgium where he begged superiors to send him back to Maryland. There were still some Indians to be baptized, he said, and nothing would suit him better than to sail the seas again with redskins in his dreams.

Superiors said no, White was too old, etc., etc.

"If not Maryland," said the incurable Papist, "then at least England." Couldn't an old man, too feeble for baptizing, be expendable on the gallows?

He went back.

For seven years he worked under the sensitive nose of Sir John Bull, and then his crime was discovered again. Murder, after all, always comes out.

Back to jail they took him, a chronic offender at best, perhaps even "desperate." Here he fasted every day and counted the hours patiently, waiting for martyrdom. But those particular Englishmen were too compassionate. When they saw that he was nearly dead, they kicked him out and told him to die elsewhere.

The poor old man, white-haired and helpless, wasn't even granted his dying wish, martyrdom. He had to die in bed, a soft bed under a friendly roof, while the Catholics in Maryland wept for him. They missed him more than ever, now that the Puritans had ousted them and were ruling Maryland with a stiff and righteous arm.

BRAVE men and the mercenary labored together. It was a strange gathering, this, the good souls and the greedy come to these alien shores, God-fearing men and ruthless, martyr and knave. The French, the English, the Spanish, the Dutch—there was little to distinguish one from the other save a shade of color in the skin, the emblem on a flag unfurled above a colony, and that deeper allegiance they swore to their Christ seen through the eyes of stanch heretic or valiant defender of the ancient Faith.

By middle seventeenth century the Hollanders began to lose ground in Manhattan and their holdings on the Delaware which they had taken from the Swedes. The Netherlands, after all, was only a stripling among the older powers. Up the eastern seaboard, English Elders gave humble beginnings to their Harvard. Quebec was not large enough for France, and so she laid the cornerstones of beautiful Montreal.

Far across land and water in the fabled Orient, Japan was martyring or expelling the last priest. For two centuries her Christians would carry on alone. Ricci's Chinese rites were frowned on by Rome, and the Jesuits went begging for new avenues into the heart of the mysterious Mongols.

But there was mystery in America too. A vast interior lay almost untouched. Buffalo roamed the wide plains. Endless miles without habitation, mountains never scaled, great rivers that had flowed on silently for centuries into the sea, her flatlands and hills and valleys dried and moistened with the eternal seasons. How lavishly Providence had blessed this New World.

* * *

A Stranger in the Hall of Fame

Father James Marquette, S.J.

by CHARLES A. WOLLESEN, S.J.

"A Jesuit in the Capitol!"

"Be it resolved by the Congress of the United States of America that the placing of this statue in the Capitol is not only without authority, but in direct violation of the law."

"Be it resolved that this statue be removed from the Capitol."

The congressman from Michigan was spearheading the attack against James Marquette, discoverer of the Mississippi. Congress had expressly requested statues of America's famed historical characters. Congress had officially accepted the beautiful Marquette memorial in white marble. Yet a division split the excited House of Representatives.

The delegate's voice was charged with irony. "A glorious triumph for America! I tell you, our country's ideals are being forgotten, and that because of a sinister Jesuit! Look at the statue; see it there in the Hall of Fame. A clergyman, and nothing but a clergyman, pious with his rosary and other such absurdities. His cassocked figure dwarfs even the great Lincoln at his side."

A wiry little man bobbed up nearby. From between trim grey sideburns, his weak voice crackled in scorn.

"Sirs," he spat, "take the Goddess of Liberty down from the dome, put St. Peter there, and the Hall will be a perfect cathedral. Monks and saints, it seems, already own the interior."

Having graciously imparted his acute observation to the House, he eyed the assembly over his glasses, looking for unanimous assent, then sat down a very satisfied little gentleman.

A Stranger in the Hall of Fame

The first Congressman again took up the whip. "I have seen an elderly lady pause before the priest's image and teach her smudgy-faced nephew to make the sign of the cross. Then the two of them stood and prayed. Right there in the main corridor of the Hall of Fame!"

A reaction of muffled laughter killed the intended seriousness of said observation. But he brought out another line in his argument.

"The blackrobe," he urged, "was not even a citizen of this country. Of American liberty, what did he know? You have proclaimed him a hero of Wisconsin. Yet he never heard of that great State. Is it not outrageous that a foreigner and a priest should be honored in our national Capitol? It is the place set apart for heroes of our nation, for our pioneers, distinguished in civic and military achievements. In the Hall of Fame we have no room for weak, commonplace churchmen.

"In the name of the State I represent, in the name of all sane Americans, I insist that this statue of the priest, Marquette, be removed from the Capitol." Exasperated, he emphasized his insistence by pitching himself into his chair. There was a stony silence, an embarrassed shuffling of feet, amens of agreement here and there. The business of the day went on.

But speakers and columnists throughout the country took up the cry. In other cities, too, clubs and secret associations began forming plans to oust the Jesuit from his place of honor. Open threats of violence appeared. "Rid the country of Marquette—or with our own hands we'll topple this proud Jesuit from his pedestal!"

It is a fact of history that the cloudburst of fanatical protestations thundered so forcefully that it silenced all laudatory speeches when the Jesuit's statue, at the express desire of Congress, was received into the Capitol and there unveiled. The low-hanging storm of hostility caused guards to be stationed before the Hall night and day.

The Senate, nevertheless, on April 29, 1896, wrote in the Congressional Record its official thanks "for the statue of James

Marquette, the renowned missionary, explorer, and discoverer of the Mississippi River."

The Jesuit, meanwhile, remained standing among America's foremost heroes. There was Abraham Lincoln on his left, Major General Phil Kearny on his right, and round about, many another eminent pioneer. In size, if not in majesty, the newcomer topped them all. Eight feet he stood in white marble, map in hand, eternalized in action. As one looks up at the man, he sees an earnest face, calm amid the tempests of controversy. The sculptor had realized in stone that indefinable something more than banal conquest of earth and water.

The figure was that of a priest. Soutane, rosary, crucifix symbolized the further quest.

The form was that of an adventurer, too, among the first pioneers breaking open a wilderness of inland wealth and beauty.

Priest and adventurer joined to make the missioner. And the missioner found the greatest water route through the heart of America.

As discoverer of the Mississippi, Congress thought, Marquette ranked with the outstanding builders of the nation. What he had done merited the Hall of Fame. When controversies should arise, merit investigated would become merit acknowledged. The taunt that Marquette had not been a citizen of the United States was really not too hard to answer. Who, in 1673, was a citizen? The nation had not yet been born. Men did not find the spirit of America here; they came here and forged it out of their own dreams.

It was across the ocean in the land of Lafayette that the ancestral home of the Marquette family had stood. There on the slope of Caesar's Mount Bribrax, some seventy miles from Paris, young James Marquette had grown up, playing and working in the sunny vineyards till his seventeenth birthday. Then, in 1654, he had left his birthplace at Laon to wear the cassock of the Jesuits. He was in the same Order, wearing the same garb, that Francis Xavier had glorified a century earlier. Like Xavier, Marquette found his heart quite afire with hopes that spread farther than the Pyrenees or the Isles, farther even than the great ocean itself. But he was not merely a dreamer. The counterbalance of a mind persistently directing all to a single objective offset long years of intense preparation. The sacred studies slipped by swiftly, interrupted once by a few semesters of teaching. Very soon after his ordination to the priesthood in the Society of Jesus, Marquette was on a lone ship, heading across the Atlantic and into his life's work.

Young yet—only thirty years old—he saw a world fading behind him forever. He thoughtfully watched, of an evening, the setting sun build a shifting bridge of crimson over the waves. He could hardly fail to see in it a bridge of blood running westward, across which he must travel to reach the heart of the new world. He knew that his brother Jesuits, Isaac Jogues and Gabriel Lalemant, had begun to cut through the vast darkness beyond with the hard red wedge of martyrdom. At the end of this same bridge, he knew, he would find himself among death-dealing savages whose souls were darkened and whose bodies scarred by their own barbarism. Then the ocean's bridge of living flame collapsed with the buried sun. As the black waves powerfully rose and fell beneath the ship, Marquette could well have taken the American martyrs for his patrons, and made his prayer a prayer for strength.

"Wilderness, want, loneliness," his heart may have said, "these will make my vowed life not unlike the best of missionaries. Like them, O Christ, let me burn my life out alone, apart from all save You, my God. Give me Thy love and Thy grace. I ask for nothing more." Nor were these idle words, piety of a sort—he meant what he prayed.

Then, after some six weeks in the creaking wooden ship, Père Marquette sighted the outline of land. It was the mouth of the St. Lawrence, with its tall stone capes wrapped in fog. Soon he felt stern fir-clad shores lock the ship in their crude embrace. North America must have inked a forbidding first impression on his expectant memory.

But as he leapt ashore at Quebec, many a cordial *Bon Jour* rang in his ears. The warm exchange of greetings with his brother priests moved him so that never did he doubt that this was the land for him. In all the arduous years to come, not once did he look back longingly to France. The New World was his, and to it he belonged heart and soul.

Impelled by a really great zeal and impatient to begin an active missionary apostolate among the savages, he at once nailed himself down to learn the uncouth sounds and peculiar idioms of the red men. Always before, languages had come hard; now with surprising rapidity he gathered a working knowledge of six distinct Indian tongues. It was not long before superiors as far away as Rome were beginning to hear of Marquette not only as a Jesuit with robust body and excellent character but also as one well versed in the languages and highly acceptable to the Indians by reason of his gentle understanding ways. They considered him ready to begin.

Orders came: go to Sault Ste. Marie, in the land of the Hurons. South and southwest he traveled, down through Lakes Ontario and Erie; then, turning northward, up through Lake Huron. Narrow rapids raced ahead. More than once the missionary, after paddling all day, sloshed through icy water, tugging his canoe between boulders. Portage after portage was frequently necessary, and he willingly shouldered boat and baggage and threaded rocky trails till his feet were bleeding. It was his initiation. Often during the day the accompanying savages scoffed at his clumsiness with insults and taunts. Night meant rolling himself in a blanket and growing accustomed to a bed of cold earth or rock. Stiff the next morning, he took to the canoe, and paddled on for what he knew to be the greater glory of God . . . . a beautiful ideal turned suddenly hard and harrowing.

Still, after ascending the dangerous rapids at Sault Ste. Marie, the travel-weary blackrobe was rewarded. For the Indians gathered about him and showed their eagerness for instruction by leading him to a small log hut. Here, ready built, not very fancy, but substantial, was Père Marquette's new mission station, his chapel, his home. Now to begin the labors he had dreamed of.

Among the chain of explorers and traders that passed through the station in 1668 came that young restless spirit, Louis Jolliet.

Marquette's gentle hospitality quickly won a new friend who in a few years would share with the Jesuit the pains and glories of discovery. It was no wonder they struck it off well together. For both of them had vision, and courage ran in their veins.

Off to the west some five hundred miles was another mission run by the priests for the Ottawa Indians. "This mission is one of our roughest," Marquette wrote to a friend. "There are some fifty-six portages to make before you reach it. For three or four months out of the year you have nothing to eat but bits of bark." Leathery old frontiersmen reckoned it the most difficult and hazardous of all the missions in New France. Time and again the unresponsive natives had nearly caused it to fold. Then, unexpectedly, one whole tribe of Kiskakons resolved to embrace Christianity. The frontier settlement was now to be maintained. Marquette volunteered for the task.

It was there at Holy Spirit Point, near the westernmost tip of the Great Lakes, that Illinois warriors kept straggling in with more detailed information concerning a great river in their land. With keen attention the blackrobe listened. In the long cold evenings of 1669–70, he set himself to learn a new tongue with a young Illinois slave as tutor. "Some day," he promised himself, "some day I'm going to explore the mysterious reaches of that distant waterway and bring the cross of Christ to its peoples."

In 1671 the ravaging Sioux forced the Hurons eastward. Père Marquette's mission fell. But a new mission overlooking Mackinac Straits was soon set up. St. Ignace it was called, in honor of the Jesuit founder whose sons were being martyred for the North American Indians.

It was here that Jolliet again surprised the lone missioner. This time he burst into the hut jubilant with the news he bore.

"Père Marquette," the young Canadian shouted as he crossed the tiny room in two strides, "take a look at this letter. It's from Count de Frontenac, governor of New France."

Above the Count's ambitious signature was expressed in a few historic lines a commission to explore the West, to find the rumored river in the expanse of Indian country.

With a boyish smile playing on his lips, the twenty-seven-year-old Jolliet swung a leather bag off his shoulder. His fingers were toying with another letter. He tossed a rolled parchment to the priest. "Read this, *Mon Père;* you've seen only half the story."

"By colonial command," he read, "Père Jacques Marquette of the Society of Jesus is hereby commissioned to serve as member of the expeditionary force. He is to be Louis Jolliet's associate, and chaplain on the perilous journey to find the Mississippi."

The two partners vigorously traded congratulations.

Jolliet was envisioning a fertile valley deep in the heart of the continent, cocksure he would find it. He knew that Louis XIV, his king, would recompense his discovery of this "corridor to the Orient," which should be turned into a channel of commerce, a path for civilization. Hopes for fame and fortune danced in his feverish young blood.

But thoughts of quite a different kind beat in the priest's mind. Far down that storied river would be barbaric nations, pagans needing the light of the Gospel, souls to win to his Lord's allegiance. Many times he had hoped, often prayed, that someday as a priest he might work among them. Now on the feast of the Immaculate Conception so dear to his heart, Jolliet had brought heaven's response. "What tremendous joy this good news has brought me," he wrote. "Now my plans are to be realized. A strangely providential order of obedience seconds the longing I have to expose my life for the salvation of all those western peoples."

Till spring the pair eagerly gathered available data, drew up tentative routes, fashioned their equipment. Then on May 17, 1673, they set out from St. Ignace "fully resolved to do and suffer everything for so glorious an undertaking." In their two bark canoes no pabulum was packed other than hard Indian corn and tough smoked meats. With the Jesuit and Jolliet were a few French *voyageurs,* five in number. Rarely in all history had so small a party risked an enterprise of such great moment.

Every heart in the little band thrilled as the prows pushed the first ripples before them. The toil and drudgery would fall upon them soon enough. But it was in high spirits that the expedition paddled through the quiet head waters of Lake Michigan and on up into Green Bay to the west. As the singing *voyageurs*' powerful strokes made the boats glide along, the two leaders settled down to record invaluable data. Every detail was of interest: the water depth, the ebb and flow of wind tides, the changing geography, the species of game and innumerable types of vegetation, Indian tribes, their strange habitats and customs.

Stopping over at the Mission of St. Francis Xavier at De Pere, a shadow of Indian prophecy fell across their joy. Marquette had returned to the shore after conversing with the natives. Beckoning for the two canoes to pull close together, he repeated what the excited savages had divulged. He was studying the faces of his men as he spoke.

"The savages here have wild stories, stories that may not be without foundation. When they heard our plans, I could see terror in their eyes. 'The nations the blackrobe wishes to visit,' they said, 'kill like bears. They torture intruders without mercy. They bury tomahawks in whiteman's skull.' 'Blackrobe,' one old chief muttered, trembling as he described what haunted his mind, 'Blackrobe, every river is a scourge. In the white rapids, horrible monsters and demons howl, and bar the way, hungering till they devour whitemen, canoes, all.' "

Marquette had calculated the reactions of his men to such exaggeration. Yet it strengthened him, no doubt, to be reassured that they were wholly of one mind with him.

Returning to the Indians, the missioner's lips spoke thanks for the warning; but his heart was saying, "I dare not follow your advice to turn back. The salvation of thousands of souls is at stake. I, and my men with me, are gamblers enough to delight in risking our lives for this cause."

Père Marquette led the people in prayer, and by instruction sifted perhaps a few seeds of grace into their fearful pagan hearts. Then blessing them, he rejoined his waiting companions.

The party continued moving up through the cold waters of the Fox River and the passage began narrowing. Swift currents cut the only avenue of advance through huge jutting rocks. Nervously the paddlers fought the rapids. Sometimes they conceded victory to the river and patiently towed their boats, wading barefoot over sharp stones as the currents tore at their legs.

With this painful lap of the journey behind them, they had reached the remotest border of the whiteman's advance. They were near the center of what is now the state of Wisconsin, but then it was Machkouten territory, the land of the "Fire Nation." There on a central eminence surrounded by fields of Indian corn, they found three tribes banded together in one village. With rude Maskoutans were the pastoral Kikabous; both were dominated by the excellent Miami warriors.

Jolliet had to stand before a council of somber Indian elders. Stating briefly that he himself was seeking new lands for the King of France, he went on to speak in behalf of his chaplain friend.

"The blackrobe has come looking for nothing but yourselves. His commission is from the King of Heaven, and he brings to you the fire of a new life."

As the ring of copper faces tightened with interest, the young ex-seminarian pressed on. "There is one great God, Chieftain over all your lives. He intends that your nations may know Him. His priest has come through great dangers to teach you. Because he is sent to you by the undying Manitou, the blackrobe is ready to suffer scalping and death, but he will not turn back."

By this time the eyes of all the assembly were studying Christianity as it stood incarnate, clothed in the Jesuit cassock. Admiration heightened by astonishment would have caught Marquette's glance. But his head was bowed . . . . and he was praying.

Next day two Miami guides skillfully conducted the adventurers along a winding channel completely covered over with wild oats. Some distance further, they leapt ashore on the soft mud bank and helped Père Marquette's party carry canoes and supplies over a mile-long portage. At the edge of a waterway they set them down again, but this river was not flowing toward Quebec. This river—the Wisconsin—was streaming off to the West toward totally strange and unexplored lands.

When the savages had slipped silently back toward their village, Marquette turned to the West, and with a resolute heart studied the horizon beyond which lay the land of a missioner's dreams. He gathered Jolliet and the *voyageurs*. On the shore of this westward moving river they knelt to dedicate anew their voyage, their lives, their all, to the Blessed Virgin Immaculate. Children, when they are afraid, turn to their mother.

Down the sandy-bottomed Wisconsin they drifted, past banks pregnant with iron ore and colored by oak or walnut trees, frightening many a timid deer, down through unknown lands for over a hundred miles. Then, on June 17, just one month from the day they had left St. Ignace, the two canoes shot out from the mouth of the Wisconsin into the great southward rolling waters of the Mississippi.

The impetuous Jolliet all but upset his canoe, shouting in wild enthusiasm. Wrestling him back to his seat, the *voyageurs*, silent giants through many a fate, showed by their lighted faces that never had they known a thrill to equal this. Here was the renowned river, and, as they thought, Christianity's waterway, America's corridor to a distant sea. Here was the fulfillment of their quest. The two boats swerved into line with the deep broad swells of the Mississippi there where Prairie du Chien still watches its incessant moving.

Checking their latitude, measuring the water's depth, estimating the river's expanse from time to time, the voyagers, glowing with satisfaction, began now jotting down what was to become unheard of news for all the outer world.

Huge catfish leapt at the side of Marquette's boat. A sharp-nosed wildcat swam out from shore, curious to see the unprecedented visitors. As the expedition dropped farther southward, the mountains fell behind, and on limitless plains roamed *pisikious*, wild buffalo. As yet, no trace of human life was apparent.

Knowing, though, that they were in savage country, the adventurers took no chances. A small well-concealed fire in the evening for boiling wild game was all they allowed themselves. Afterward they deserted the coals in case an Indian's keen eye had perhaps caught the betraying column of smoke. In the dark, they anchored some distance out from shore. Waiting for a surprise attack, each took his turn as sentinel there in the unbroken blackness.

Finally on June 25, Père Marquette spied the tracks of men on the water's edge. A narrow, somewhat beaten path was seen leading up to a broad prairie. Charging the other members of the group to stand on guard, Jolliet and the priest noiselessly, nervously, paced off all of what turned out to be six full miles.

A village sprawled out before them. Not far distant two more camps were baking in the prairie heat. Realizing they were walking into a murderous tribe, half-expecting to hear the fatal whiz of arrows at any moment, the two men earnestly commended themselves to God and kept going. So near did they creep unseen that savage voices could be heard.

There was now no alternative. They must reveal themselves and hope for the best. Stepping out into the open, the men shouted with all their energy. Swarms of Indians quickly issued from their cabins. Four chieftains, seeing that one of the intruders was a blackrobe intending no harm, advanced slowly. The chiefs, as they came, lifted ornate calumets to the sun—a sure sign of peace—but not a word broke their silence. They stopped quite close to the blackrobe and his companion, scrutinizing them mutely. Their red flesh glowed in the sun's hot rays.

With a dry mouth, Marquette ventured: "To what nation does your camp belong?"

"Illinois," came the reply.

In a moment Marquette was gratefully lifting the magic pipe of peace to his lips. God had brought him safely to the very people he had come so far to find and to save. For the Illinois knew the blackrobe. Warriors returning from St. Ignace had announced his coming. Illinois tribes had waited long for Father Marquette, eager to hear from him more of the great Manitou he worshiped. Their leader intoned a welcome.

"How beautiful is the sun, O Frenchman, when you come to

visit us! Our whole village awaits you. You shall enter all our cabins in peace."

As Marquette and Jolliet were escorted through the village, hundreds of those children of the plains, crouching in the grass, devoured them with eager eyes. Never before had they seen whitemen. Now they glutted their curiosity. All was profound silence, save for the repeated utterance: "How good it is, my brothers, that you should visit us."

That night a great council convened, presided over by the supreme captain of all the Illinois. Glowing welcomes and oratory were concluded. An elaborate war dance, unsurpassed, the visitors thought, by any polished French ballet, was performed in honor of the whitemen. Then Marquette rose to speak.

"We have come to you on a mission of peace. The God who created you has sent us to your great nations here in the West. He wishes that all, whitemen and Indians alike, should know Him. For many suns, your tribes have wandered without the true Light of the World. Now you must serve Him who is sovereign Chieftain over all your lives."

The reverent leader of the savages bowed to the missioner and to Jolliet. "I give you our thanks, Blackgown, and you, O Frenchman, for having taken so much trouble to come and visit us. It is you who know the great Spirit who has made us all. It is you who hold converse with him, and hear his word. Beg of him to give us life and health, to come and dwell with us that we may know him."

As a pledge of his sincerity, the chief, resting his hand upon the head of a little slave, continued. "Here is my son. Take him with you as a seal of our friendship." Then folding the priest's fingers round a weirdly beautiful calumet, the old Indian shared his wisdom of the West. "In all your journeys," he said, evaluating the pipe much higher than the lad, "in all your journeys, you must carry this with you. It is more powerful than many bows. It is the Indian symbol of peace. The calumet will save your life."

The savage had been pleading that his blackrobe visitor go no farther on his southward route. How great were the dangers that lay ahead he knew by years of experience. But it was to no avail.

"I do not fear death." Marquette answered altogether without pretense, like a man attentive to some greater concern. Love of Christ and souls was his pre-occupation, and he added, "To me no happiness can be greater than to lose my live for the glory of Him who has made us all."

With admiration and numerous tokens of respect, the chief and several hundred Illinois stood by to see the missioner depart. The priest's promise remained in their hearts that he should return the following year to live with them and instruct them. But for the present he must continue his journey.

Southward the two canoes floated. Painted on huge impending rocks along the shore, hideous monsters glared at the trespassers. Were these the demons that so inspired fear in native hearts? When the whitemen first looked up, even they were terrified. Marquette, after swallowing hard, studied the weird representation. Out came his quill, and he sketched each grotesque detail.

"The monsters have faces strangely resembling those of men. But a beard like a tiger's, and red eyes burning in their sockets, make them repulsive to look upon. Antlers curve fantastically upward from the head. Around the creature's black scabbed body a satanic tail winds in coils of green. A savage masterpiece."

As the men were discussing these mysterious terrors, a crashing as of giants in conflict alarmed them. Their tiny boats were trapped in a swirl of accumulated debris, uprooted trees, jagged branches, and floating islands of soggy soil. The water was thick with mud. It was the opaque Missouri River rushing down to meet them and merge in conflicting currents with the Father of Waters.

Is this river, the blackrobe wondered, really a path to the Pacific as some men say? Should he investigate? No, not on this trip, he decided; he had more than enough to do already. The boats continued southbound. The unbuilt city of St. Louis passed unseen.

A Stranger in the Hall of Fame

The waters, before long, began to assume a bloody tinge as they washed the banks of red clay. Fine setting for the trap into which the expedition was heading. For another of superstition's demons roared in their ears. Rock banks like huge stony arms clutched the broad Mississippi, throttling it down to a narrow neck of water. Angry currents blasted at the high portal boulders only to be tossed back in confusion and deafening reverberations. A needle-eyed channel was all their violent struggling could split open.

Gripping the frail walls of his canoe while paddlers poised for quick emergency strokes, Marquette bolted through these Indian hellgates. Jolliet's tiny craft shot after him. "All in a day's work," one nodded to the other. But every man of them was wet with river spray, sweat, and fear.

From here on, tall swaying reeds flanked the river. Through them buffalo forced their way to the running water. Mosquitoes began to swarm about the blistering travelers.

It was now that the chieftain's mysterious calumet proved to be worth its weight in gold. For down ahead savages were lining the banks, armed with guns, waiting for the two canoes. The blackrobe, raising himself to full stature, waved the red-plumed pipe of peace, master-key to Indian friendship. It worked. Within the hour he was feasting on dried buffalo meat and wild white plums, while friendly savages told of whitemen's settlements only several days distant.

Leaving this camp, they approached Mitchigamea, an Indian village not far from the present Memphis, Tennessee. The war cry again rang in their ears. Savages, with terrifying yells, were running to the shore commencing an attack. The voyagers prayed as they had never prayed before when they saw the moving mass of bows and arrows, hatchets, clubs, and shields driving toward them for the slaughter. Long wooden canoes, filled with swiftly paddling Indians, shot out into the water. One group headed upstream along the shore line; others waited below to intercept the surrounded whitemen. Young braves swam out into the strong current to seize the canoes. As Marquette stood frantically waving the calumet, a tomahawk slashed the air close above his head.

The Indians in their sudden attack had not seen the raised pipe of peace. Perhaps the glaring sunlight made it imperceptible. But at the last moment, an old chieftain on shore detected it, and immediately commanded the attack to cease. In but an instant, war cries died across the water; bows were relaxed. As the frightened Marquette pulled up to the shore, two of the leaders apologetically cast their bows and quivers into the boat at the blackrobe's feet.

It was not without some anxiety that the little crew passed the night within the borders of that encampment. Next morning, however, the tribe proved their loyalty by escorting them to Akamsea, some miles above today's Arkansas City. As the flotilla drew near, singing redskins paddled up to receive the visitors in honor. The Jesuit, after being conducted into the center of a distinguished ring of elders and warriors, again seized the opportunity to speak to them of the Savior of all mankind. Listening in admiration, they earnestly desired the blackrobe to stay with them and give further instructions.

Then a banquet was in order. Very obligingly savages served on broad wooden platters the smooth flesh of a boiled dog. Seeing his hosts loath to delay, the missioner, trying to chat as pleasantly as he could about distances to the sea or about intermediate tribes, took up a piece and began to eat.

But his greatest dangers were not from food. A handful of younger zealots convened secretly that night to plan the scalping of these white intruders. One of the elder chiefs luckily stumbled upon the plot in time to check it. The Jesuit got profuse apologies for the tribe's misbehavior, and since it seemed to be the thing most needed, another splendid calumet.

Next day, however, Monsieur Jolliet and Père Marquette thought it was time they should call a council of their own. Ought they push on farther? There remained but a short two or three days' journey to the Gulf of Mexico. They had ascertained for certain that the Mississippi did not flow east into the Atlantic, nor westward into the Pacific, but ever toward the south.

A Stranger in the Hall of Fame

All desirable information they had carefully gathered. To proceed now would be to risk losing everything; for hostile Indians, equipped with whitemen's guns, waged incessant warfare along the southward route. Spaniards, too, even in the New World, were fighting the French, and held the coastal settlements. To fall into their hands meant imprisonment or death.

The expedition's purpose, the pair decided, had been attained, and with remarkable success. It was best to call a halt here at the Arkansas River camp. Here they would rest a day or two with the Indians, and then begin the interminable trip homeward.

It was just one month from that memorable day their canoes had first plunged into the Mississippi that the prows pointed again northward. That meant mid-July, a sweltering time of year. To fight the south-bound waters all the way from that remote village of the Akensea to the distant Canadian border was no easy pull.

Acting on a sage old Indian's advice, the tired crew swung eastward at the Illinois River fork, cutting short the distance to Lake Michigan. One historic portage where Chicago now stands, and they were on the Great Lakes. From there back to the Jesuit mission of St. Francis Xavier at De Pere was a relatively easy finish to the innumerable hardships of their 2,800-mile voyage.

Tired but exultant with success, the zealous missioner hardly realized that so gruelling a test of endurance had broken his health. Rough Indian food, the inclemencies of several winters, and now the strain of four months' continuous traveling proved too much. The Jesuit had to brush aside the shadow of impending death as he forced a smile and beamed a gladsome *Bon Voyage* to Louis Jolliet paddling away from the mission to make his report at Montreal. Wearily the veteran blackrobe turned back to the chapel. All that winter and all the following summer a painful disease pinned him to the mission's narrow boundaries.

In the cold dark evenings of that year, as he relived his voyage, his quill captured the wondrous story. It was his

Journal that broke the discovery of the great river to the astonished outer world. An account it was of epic color, but simply-written truth. For centuries it has fascinated lovers of adventure, and has become a foundation stone in America's history-house. Engraved on its rugged face, for all ages to read, are the names of Louis Jolliet and the Jesuit James Marquette.

Fortunately Marquette did not fail to carve and to lay that stone. Had he not done so, the rich quarry opened by their expedition would, in all probability, have been earthed over by obscurity. For young Jolliet, with history on his tongue and glory at his fingertips, hit disaster. His canoe, loaded heavily with invaluable maps and scientific recordings of the entire Mississippi trip, with samples and souvenirs and Indian gifts, with himself and his loyal associates, had been caught in the treacherous Lachine right within sight of Montreal. Jolliet had clung despairingly to the upturned canoe for four whole hours as it plunged and swung madly in the raging current. He was the sole survivor. But as he faced the governor of Quebec and told his fantastic story—an undocumented, unproven, un-believed story—he would rather have perished. Without Marquette the story of Louis Jolliet would be but a stillborn myth.

But Père Marquette's quill, there in the candlelit evenings at De Pere, traced on the pages of American history a monument of triumph for the tragic hero. As for himself, the worn mis-sioner cared little for any such glory. He had promised the Indians they should see him before the sun rounded another year. His only desire was to return to those children of his heart.

He did return, in fact, in that fall of 1674, but sickness and winter exacted a heavy toll. Their price was his death. He had painfully struggled to the Chicago portage. In Holy Week, within the Indian camp, he had preached in eloquent simplicity on the wonderful love of Christ, suffering to ransom souls. He and his people had offered up the Victim of Calvary in one of the first Masses celebrated in that territory. An embryonic mission had been established and named for the immaculately conceived Mother of God. Then the dying Jesuit turned again home.

People have a way of wanting to go back to their origins, finding out about how things got started in their little acre. And somehow when the people of the heartland of America began taking a look at who first edged into the country around them, Marquette's name kept cropping up . . . all through the Great Lakes area and down the Mississippi.

His story and his name became so great that they seemed more legendary than real. Secular historians might take a long time in coming around to see the point, but this French priest belonged right by the side of America's Greats . . . in a sense he ran before them, enkindled the spirit that would survive long after he had ended his young years. He was the old world crossing over to the new, bringing with him the hope and vision that was western man's heritage, and which stood in such danger of being snuffed out in the battle and bitterness sweeping through Europe with increasing frequency. Like all men of his stature, Marquette's valedictory could never be uttered, because he would really never leave. His presence would abide always.

THE LOOSELY *federated duchies and kingdoms of central Europe had gathered now to promising greatness. Prussia was born. Wars plagued the continent, the struggle of the "30 years," Sobieski's rout of the Turks, Queen Anne's War, and the Spanish Succession. There was King William's War and also fateful Augsburg.*

In the new world, Bacon's Rebellion threatened to undo Virginia; raids were perpetrated by the Carolinas on Florida missions. Quiet William Penn had been granted his charter and plot of land for the Quakers of Brotherly Love. In the offing was Georgia. Relations with the Indians stayed stormy: at times unprovoked assault, then the peace pipe. Old chiefs could not handle young braves. Hard bitten traders meanwhile scrupled at no trick to get their skins.

Yet bit by bit the white man was inching his way into the land of Hiawatha. Thrifty English colonists strapped the crude plow to oxen and turned American soil. Everywhere fertility, abundant harvest in the gold brisk autumn. Then, before the snow fell, came thanksgiving when the Pilgrim blessed a just God Who had dealt kindly with His children.

Great gabled mansions to house English soldiery and Southern planters began to dot the countryside. Little villages and heaped up barns broke the undulating sky. The sound of hammer on anvil pierced the thin air.

Far in the West new movements were afoot. Keen Spanish eyes surveyed the western slopes of the continent from the white frozen lands down to the gentle plateau lands of Mexico. And the Franciscans meanwhile marveled at what extravagant beauty God had flung from His fingertips, purple grandeur lost here for these long ages.

* * *

Padre on Horseback

Father Eusebio Kino, S.J.

by WEBSTER T. PATTERSON, S.J.

Darkness had descended over the rugged mountains of Sonora in Northern Mexico. In the little adobe house near the mission Padre Kino sat alone this Christmas Eve reading his breviary.

A fireplace blazed brightly, casting flickering shadows on the thick adobe walls and dark beams of the ceiling. Now and then he paused, reflecting with devotion on the words of a psalm and lifting up his heart in frevent prayer.

As he turned again to his reading by the fireside, a loud clear knock suddenly sounded on the door without. Instinctively his eyes looked up, riveted on the rough pine-wood door at the end of the room. A turn of the latch, then slowly, gradually, the door opened. Against the blackness of the night, in the half-lighted archway, towered a square-jawed, hawk-nosed giant in flowing black.

"Buona sera, Reverendo Padre!" said the stranger.

Kino rose in startled wonder at the sound of his native Italian.

"I am Padre Juan Salvatierra," smiled the visitor graciously, "your new superior."

It was a joyful meeting between these two countrymen and brother Jesuits. Cultured, scholarly, men of noble birth, either would have done credit to any university in Europe. But in the midst of a North American wilderness they now sat discussing things far more important to both of them than personal ambition.

Over a cup of chocolate they fell to talking of the conversion of the Indians in a great land to the West. Little did he know, but in Juan Salvatierra, Kino was to find the answer to his life-long ambition.

California! Kino's eyes sparkled when he mentioned the name. Only a few leagues to the West it lay—a long crooked finger jutting down into the Pacific parallel to Mexico. Drake had called it an island and as such it was represented on the maps of the day. It must be so.

A scorched, barren country—this Baja California, a land ribbed through with massive granite mountains and burning deserts: in parts, little life at all, only the painted lizards that dart in and out of the prickly cactus and lie panting in the white-hot sun.

Cortez and two Spanish kings failed to settle this lonely wasteland. But there were Indians to be converted; and this was Kino's ambition, the one he now laid before the listening superior.

Two years before, he had first visited California, landed there with Admiral Isidro de Atondo in 1683. Together they took possession of this new province, Santissima Trinidad de la California, the Most Holy Trinity of the Californias. A palm-fringed shore, knights in armor, a scarlet banner that soared aloft as drums rolled and muskets cracked, the hills that echoed three times to the cry: "Viva Carlo Segundo!"—he remembered the scene well.

To the service of two Majesties they had hoped to win this stubborn new country: Atondo as military leader, Kino as missionary and royal cosmographer. Spain wanted the land as a stopping off base for the Manila galleon, constantly harassed along these coasts by Drake and the English pirates. The Church wanted the land also, for the souls of its brown skinned natives.

For nearly two years Church and State had struggled. Some progress had been made, more by Church than by State. To his tireless giving, the Indians had responded with their love and devotion. For his part Kino had acquired an undying affection for these abandoned savages of the desert.

But from the beginning difficulties abounded. Discontent

among the soldiers, scurvy and drought, shortage of food—
then as a climax to it all, the Spanish viceroy announced the
California experiment was too great a drain on the royal
treasury. The government was no longer interested in pouring
its pesos down a rat hole. Thus the venture had to be
abandoned.

In the meantime, from Padre Gonzales on the far-off mission
of Northern Sonora came heart-rending pleas for more missionaries. Once more the Apaches were ravaging the Spanish
frontier. Further assistance was imperative. The Jesuit provincial did what anyone in his circumstances would have done.
The California mission was closed. Kino was sent to Sonora in
Northern Mexico.

So it was that he found himself headed out of Mexico City
that November of 1686. His heart was still with his savages in
California. But obedience was the thing: God's will shining
through the orders of his superiors. This was the supreme rule
of life for a Jesuit, an ideal above all personal schemes and
ambitions. He would not forget California. Someday, somehow,
he would return. But in the meantime California could wait.
Sonora could not.

After five months of travel by horseback through the rugged
mountains of Northern Mexico, he arrived at his destination,
the dusty little Spanish pueblo of Curcurpe, last outpost of
civilization on the Sonora frontier.

On the great high bluff of Curcurpe he dismounted and
looked out over the new territory that had been assigned to
him. Far to the north and west it rolled, thousands of miles
of rugged mountain ranges and pathless deserts, totally unexplored, even uninhabited save for the wild Seris, half-tamed
Pimas, and fierce maurading Apaches.

It was fifteen miles north up the San Miguel River from Curcurpe that he chose the site for his own mission which he called
Nuestra Señora de los Dolores (Our Lady of Sorrows). This
he had chosen for his headquarters. From here he would radiate
out to all points of the compass, founding other missions,
establishing stock ranches to support these missions, setting

forth on trips of exploration a thousand miles north through unexplored territory to the banks of the Gila and Colorado rivers.

Of his mission site he was especially proud. Built on a lofty mesa approachable only from the west, Mission Dolores commanded a beautiful view of the San Miguel Valley. Hundreds of feet below, the river roared and churned through the canyon; and far in the distance in every direction rose the tall Sierras, their granite peaks shouldering the cloudless Mexican sky.

Atop this jutting promontory only a few months ago he had begun the building of his mission. Under a broiling sun he and his Pima helpers toiled, clearing ground, making adobe bricks, cutting and hauling wooden beams from the nearby mountains. Hills echoed to the ring of hammer and saw. Indian mothers looked on while fat brown babies squawled and played in the sun. Slowly the walls of Mission Dolores began to rise.

At night by firelight, he scratched out a record of the mission's progress, told how the natives worked with "very great pleasure and with all willingness . . . making adobes, doors, windows, etc., for a very good house and church to replace the temporary quarters."

The Indians had never seen bells before, and he recorded how "the natives are very fond of listening to their peals, never before heard in these lands." With the greatest awe and pleasure they viewed the ornaments and pictures in the church, and some would even talk to the pictures and statues as though real people were present. At Easter time he had noted with pride his forty newly baptized Indian children "whom the Spanish ladies of the mining town of Opodepe dressed richly and adorned with their best jewels, like new Christians, for the procession of the Blessed Sacrament, to the delight of all."

The Pimas of Sonora had won his heart, but now at Christmas time his thoughts were once again turned to California and he was more conscious than ever of the savages he was so tragically forced to abandon. He yearned to return to them, to reopen the mission on those western shores.

I Lift My Lamp

* * *

Kino finished his story. He had traced his whole history the past two years, how he first had gone to California, and then come here to Sonora. Salvatierra was silent for a time. He studied thoughtfully the Padre who now stood silhouetted against the leaping flames of the fireplace. Strong and wiry, bronzed by constant exposure to the desert sun, he little resembled the brilliant mathematics professor of just a few years before. Ingolstadt University would scarcely recognize him now! How much can circumstances change a man! Kino had come to resemble his Indians even physically, he mused.

But it was the Padre's ambition that interested the superior now. Padre Juan had been deeply impressed. Eagerly he sketched a plan for the re-establishment of a mission in California, even without the aid of the Spanish government. He proposed the building of a small ship on the Sonora side of the Gulf. From the fertile missions of Sonora they might transport supplies across the Gulf to support settlements in the sterile wastelands of California. And together they might undertake the founding of a new mission higher up the coast.

Far into the night they talked, planning together the things that might be done to reopen the mission. When at last they retired to sleep, it was the superior who had caught the fire of inspiration from his subject, a spark that would later flame forth in his own great deeds in Baja California.

Kino lay awake long that night, listening to the sounds that are only heard at night in the wilderness of Northern Sonora. After sundown the dry parched land seems once more to come to life. Small animals emerge from their hiding places and whisk to and fro over the moon-bathed sands, filling the night air with their soft mysterious noises.

As he lay listening to these haunting sounds of the night, Kino pondered over his long talk with Salvatierra. Before his mind flashed the faces of those Indians whom he had left behind on that far-off shore and who without a priest would be without the means of salvation. Especially for the children was he concerned; little Francisco who had cried so bitterly when his parents tried to remove him from the mission. And Manuel, the three-year-old, whose chief delight it had been to ride in the saddle behind the Padre. And the little Indian girl who knelt before a picture of the Virgin Mary and begged permission to hold the Christ Child.

Such as these he could not abandon to darkness just as they were beginning to receive the light of salvation. Somehow, he would return. He fell asleep praying to the Mother of God that she would not abandon his brown-skinned children.

In the meantime there was the work to be done in Sonora. Almost single-handed Kino had been set over an expanse of wilderness larger than any state east of the Mississippi, a land comprising tens of thousands of unruly natives. To him fell the task of converting, controlling, and civilizing these wild and bloody tribes which were constantly warring among themselves. Besides teaching, catechizing, and administering the sacraments, he was obliged to attend to countless details of a merely administrative and practical nature: stock-raising, planting and harvesting, building, exploring and mapping new country, defending the frontier against Apache raids, corresponding continually with authorities in both Church and State.

He was both missionary and frontier diplomat. Through him the Spanish military dealt, when they wished to levy Indian troops in their constant wars against the Apaches on the northern frontier. Upon his shoulders fell the responsibility of training these ignorant and primitive savages in the ways of Christian living, completely unaccustomed as they were to civilized ways. Without outside assistance, he must teach them the skills that were necessary for building, carpentry, cooking, bricklaying, farming. From the Padre they must learn to be farmers, cowboys, mechanics, all the various professions which accompany civilized living.

Kino's practical genius soon showed itself equal to the task. Pack trains of sixty and more mules wound through the mountain ranges to Dolores and the other missions that he gradually set up (there would be twenty-five in all), carrying tools, beads, blankets, metals of various kinds, and other goods necessary for mission building. On horseback each week he made a round trip to the missions at Remedios, Cocospora, and back to Dolores, a journey of a good one hundred miles.

At nineteen of his missions, he gradually established stock ranches that would be permanent supplies of livelihood for the Indians. Other ranches, independent of the missions, he founded to supply meat and horses for the soldiers who constantly patrolled the frontier. Managed and run entirely by the Indians, these ranches were the beginning of the cattle industry of Northern Mexico and Southern Arizona.

To tend to his many widely scattered missions, Kino now spent much of his time in the saddle. Hard riding became his daily program. Day after day, over mountain ranges and through pathless deserts, he sped tirelessly, stopping only to instruct and baptize or to obtain fresh mounts to continue his journey.

A typical three days was the trip he made with Padre Leal in November, 1699. Supervising the beginnings of stock ranches, preaching to the Indians and establishing mission stations as he went, Kino rode north into the Santa Cruz Valley and Southern Arizona. They had traveled twelve days when he left Padre Leal and with Don Matheo Manje rode to the northwest where he heard some sick Indians awaited baptism. This was the eighth of November. On the ninth he rode to a village where he took a census of 400 Indians, preached to them, then rode on to another village, making some sixty miles that day.

It was here that he assembled 300 natives, distributed presents, baptized three sick natives, then immediately mounted his horse to gallop seventy-five miles through the rugged mountain passes to arrive at Sonoita by nightfall. On the way he had stopped at two native villages to baptize and give instructions. That night he preached to the Indians, took four hours' sleep, was up before daybreak to ride the next day and night 125 miles to Busanic where he rejoined Padre Leal.

During the past three days, Kino had traveled close to 300 miles, catechizing and baptizing in five native villages en route.

On the fourth day, he was up again at sunrise to celebrate Mass, preach to the Indians, and supervise the butchering of cattle on the mission ranch. This was a strenuous life for a man of fifty-five. Nor would he slacken the pace for several more years to come.

To the East, to the North, and to the West he rode, extending his territory in ever increasing circles. Mission churches and great ranches grew and flourished under his supervision and ceaseless activity.

But it was Dolores that was the apple of his eye. Within two years after its founding he was able to write: "This mission has its church adequately furnished with ornaments, chalices . . . bells, choir, chapel, etc.; . . . likewise a great many large and small cattle, oxen, fields, a garden with various kinds of garden crops, Castilian fruit trees, grapes, peaches, quinces, figs, pomegranates, pears, and apricots. It has a forge for blacksmiths, a carpenter shop, a pack train, water mill, many kinds of grain, and provisions from rich and abundant harvests of wheat and maize, besides other things, including horse and mule herds, all of which serve and are greatly needed for the house, as well as for the expeditions and new conquests and conversions, and to purchase a few gifts and attractions, with which, together with the Word of God, it is customary to contrive to win the minds and souls of the natives."

In over two dozen different locations throughout Northern Sonora little centers of civilization had begun to rise because of the industry of the Padre of Dolores. Like the great monasteries of Europe in the early centuries, these missions of Kino became nuclei from whence religious, educational, and civil influence would radiate out in all directions to transform the country. Buildings rose, crops were planted, orchards set out; from the wilderness came forth thriving communities.

To manage and run all these activities, he set up a complete system of native government on the civil, religious, educational, and industrial levels. "In Dolores," he wrote in his diary, "besides the justices, captain governor, alcaldes, fiscal mayor, alguacil, topil . . . masters of chapel and school, and mayor domes of the house, there are . . . cowboys, ox-drivers, bakers . . . gardeners, and painters."

While carrying on all these activities he found time to ride out on numerous trips of exploration. In Arizona he discovered the Casa Grande, remains of an ancient castle left long ago by prehistoric Indians who once inhabited this territory. In 1697, he rode north 800 miles to the Gila River, a journey he made in thirty days through country unexplored by white men. The following year he made the same trip in twenty-six days; in 1700, a journey of one thousand miles through the same wild territory, then another of eleven hundred miles in thirty-five days, averaging often thirty miles a day over the roughest mountain trails and deserts.

Spaniards soon began to talk of the Padre on the San Miguel and to recount his deeds. Much of the night he devoted to prayer; the days were spent in ceaseless toil and hard riding. Once he had been discovered scourging himself as a penance. Everything he received he gave away to the Indians; and while on the trail he slept on his horse blanket for a mattress and used his saddle for a pillow.

* * *

Of such things two members of the Sonora military were talking one day as they jogged over the desolate waste on their way to the garrison at San Juan. The heat was stifling. At twenty-five a young caballero relishes heat and hardship. He has yet to win his spurs and prove his mettle in the face of difficulties. But at forty-five, a soldier has lost his appetite for the rigors of a desert journey. He sits heavier in the saddle and cannot endure the heat as well.

Reflecting on this, General Don Domingo Jironza mopped the sweat from his fat face and turned again to take up the conversation which he had begun with his young nephew, Lt. Don Matheo Manje.

"How can a college professor," young Manje had asked, "be of any use on the Sonora frontier?"

Padre on Horseback

"I tell you, Don Matheo," Jironza replied, "this Padre is of more military value to me than a well-armed garrison of soldiers. You will see what I mean."

As Spanish frontiersmen were soon to find, the General's esteem of Kino as an Indian agent was not misplaced. The Padre had come to exercise an influence over the natives which made him virtually the sole ruler over all the tribes of Northern Mexico.

Somehow, Kino seemed to hold a special charm for these wild sons of the desert. Decked out in gaudy blankets, bright-colored bracelets, and feathered headdresses, they came in increasing numbers to Dolores from all parts of Sonora. On the lofty mesa above the San Miguel was the Great White Father whom they had come to love and revere. Like a magnet the Padre drew them. They brought him presents; they loved to talk with him; they waited upon his every wish. They could never seem to do enough for him.

* * *

One day a great chief came to see Kino from a village far to the Northwest. A powerful man, tall and stately, El Coro was famed throughout Pima Land as a mighty warrior. Many times he had met the Apaches on the field of battle, and each time had left the field victorious.

When El Coro spoke, his great voice boomed and rumbled, "like a chorus of men talking," the Indians had observed. For this reason had they named him El Coro—the chorus. And they had come to respect him greatly for his strong character and brave deeds.

Kino had met El Coro at his village of Quiburi on his trips of exploration and had always been received by him with the greatest kindliness and consideration. El Coro had even presented his son to Kino for baptism.

To the Padre Grande this time El Coro had come to ask for a missionary and to offer his aid to the Spaniards against the wild Apaches. His people had always fought the Apaches, he said. They had always been friendly to the Spaniards. They wished to fight for the Padre against their traditional enemies.

Kino's heart ached; the harvest was so great and the laborers so few. How he yearned to send north a missionary for the land of this friendly chief. But he would not forget El Coro, nor the chief's offer. Little he realized then how soon he would be needing it.

Between these two men, the chief and the Padre, so different in race, background, and culture, there grew up as time went on an intimate bond of friendship. When gossips spread rumors and doubts and suspicion on all sides, these two never wavered in their fidelity to each other. Stanchly Kino defended the loyalty of El Coro against the Spaniards; and the chief never betrayed the confidence the Padre had placed in him.

Around a blazing camp fire one night, Padre Eusebio talked to the Indians in the Santa Cruz Valley far to the North. Here he had come on a long tour of inspection with Padre Juan Salvatierra. Never before had these Indians seen white men. Wide-eyed and wondering they listened spellbound far into the night to this black-robed charmer.

"I spoke to them of the Word of God," wrote Kino in his diary, "and on the map of the world I showed them the lands, the rivers, the seas over which we Fathers had come from afar to bring them the saving knowledge of our Holy Faith. To these and other talks concerning God, heaven, and hell they listened with pleasure and told me that they wished to be Christians and gave me some infants to baptize."

On all sides as they traveled through this unexplored country they found the natives friendly and eager to receive them. New horizons of mission expansion opened up. Indians constantly came to them, many from distances of two hundred miles, begging for missionaries. Salvatierra was indeed impressed.

"Father Rector," he said turning to Kino, "not only shall it not be a matter of taking away from this Pimeria any of the four Fathers granted us, but an additional four shall come, and I with the help of divine grace shall endeavor to be one of them."

Padre on Horseback

This land through which they rode would be at a long-future date the present state of Arizona. Near the present ruins of Tumacacori mission, Kino celebrated Mass, the first Christian service on Arizona soil. Again he would return many times up this valley of the Santa Cruz, here to found the great mission of San Xavier del Bac, now a national monument in Arizona.

Back they rode to Mission Dolores, teaching, catechizing new villages as they traveled. Already the fruits of Kino's labors were bringing untold consolation. Success abounded on every side.

Would that it could have continued! But soon the Padre of Dolores would be torn with sorrow and grief. Already the trouble had been brewing.

* * *

Down the dusty main street of San Juan one day Lieutenant Matheo Manje galloped at full tilt and reined up in a cloud of dust before the military garrison. In a single bound he was off his horse and at the door of General Jironza.

"The Pimas have revolted, Domingo!"

Jironza half-rose in wide-eyed amazement.

Between gasps of breath, Don Matheo poured out the gruesome story. Slowly Jironza was able to gather the facts and piece them together.

Sent by Kino from Dolores, Don Matheo had ridden at breakneck speed most of the day. The trouble had started at Tubutama. Antonio, a brutal Opata herdsman, had knocked down the Pima overseer and was mauling him with his spurs. Responding to the overseer's cries for help, Pimas pursued Antonio and filled him with arrows. With passions fully aroused, the Pimas went on to kill others and finally to attack the mission of Padre Saeta at Caborca.

Padre Saeta was inside at the time. Hearing a commotion, he came to the door. There, before his very eyes, he saw his faithful Indian servants being slaughtered in cold blood. Saeta called for help. The military captain failed to respond. Saeta saw that his time had come.

With arms extended he knelt down in the doorway and there received the arrows into his breast. Streaming with blood he rose and went inside. By the side of his bed he grasped a beautiful crucifix he had brought from Italy. Kneeling, he died.

Excitement now shook the frontier. Jironza had once remarked that Kino was of more military value to him than a well-armed garrison of soldiers. It was true. For that reason Kino had never been allowed to return to California. And had this delicate situation now been left in the hands of Kino, a speedy peace and punishment of the guilty might easily have been accomplished.

But such was not the case. Captain Solis, a hot-headed young officer, took things into his own hands. He arranged a peace talk with fifty of the Pimas who had not taken part in the out-rage. Not more than eight had even been involved in the massacre. Trusting the assurance of Solis, the Pimas came to the conference, unarmed, humbly, and with crosses in their hands.

In the midst of the conference, one Indian grabbed another by the hair of the head and cried: "Here is one of the murderers!" Immediately Captain Solis seized a cutlass and struck off the accused Indian's head. Panic-stricken, the remaining Indians bolted for freedom. Solis's soldiers opened fire. What had begun as a peace talk now became a slaughter. Out of the fifty Indians present, forty-eight were killed, the majority of whom were innocent.

When Kino received the news at Dolores, he was prostrate with grief. Even the soldiers regretted the incident. Jironza mistakenly thought the Pimas were now cowed, and would give no more trouble. But little had he calculated the temperament of the red man, as following events would show.

One day at noon time, Kino and Manje had just settled down for their noon meal on the cliff top at Dolores. Suddenly the door burst open and an Indian messenger fell prostrate at their feet. Between sobs, he told of a new insurrection, how the

Pimas had burned San Ignacio to the ground. The missionary, Padre Campos, had made good his escape over the mountain passes, "the Padre in the middle and two soldiers on each side restraining the fury and fighting the whole two leagues which the enemy pursued." Even now the Indians, three hundred strong, were descending on other missions and would come to Dolores.

"Instantly," wrote Manje later, "I mounted a good horse and rode *a rompe-cinchas*—at breakneck speed—the sixteen leagues to the pueblo of Opodepe, where I arrived at three o'clock in the afternoon, finding the Reverend Father. . . . Kappus and General Jironza drinking chocolate."

The three of them mounted fresh horses and galloped through the mountain canyons to Curcurpe, arriving there at nightfall. Don Matheo had ridden seventy-five miles that day. Next morning, Manje with two soldiers set out for Dolores, fearing the Indians would set upon it next. There he found Kino alone, everyone else having deserted.

"We stole forth in the silence of the night," wrote Don Matheo, "to hide in a cave a league away the boxes of ornaments, vessels, books, missals, and other treasures of the church and of the Padre. But although I protested to him that we ought not to return to the pueblo, he assured me that nothing would happen, and setting out, we arrived at daybreak."

Manje was convinced the end had come. "I confessed myself as for death on account of what might happen, in order not to desert the minister of the pueblo." Through the long dreaded night they waited anxiously; but their enemies never came, although every other mission was burned and ravaged. Only the mission of Dolores was exempt.

"I attribute this," says Manje, "to the virtue and the continuous and fervent prayers of Father Eusebio Kino, first missionary of that revolted nation, for, since he had been their spiritual Father and had wiped their tears in their times of need, affliction, and trouble, defending them always, gratitude perhaps kept them from burning and destroying his mission and his spacious painted and adorned church."

Little by little, Kino restored relations once more between Spaniard and Indian and began to rebuild his missions in Sonora. His heart was filled with sorrow. Against the Spaniards he had always defended the loyalty of his beloved Pima Indians. What could he say now after the rebellion? His only consolation was that the really guilty were few, that the bulk of his Pimas had never intended to revolt and never would revolt against the Spaniards. He still believed in them, trusted in them, whatsoever the Spaniards might say against them. But he needed proof of their loyalty. An occasion would be offered sometime later.

* * *

In the meantime Kino was busily occupied in sending supplies to his friend Salvatierra, who had since reopened a mission at Loretta on California soil. Cattle, food, clothing he sent across the Gulf by ship. But the waters of the Gulf were dangerous, and the process extremely difficult and costly. If only a land route were possible!

That California was an island was a fact accepted by all the leading geographers of Kino's day. But as Kino reflected on the results of his own explorations to the North, he began to wonder. Was it not possible that California was a peninsula? It was a glorious thought! What it would mean to the missions!

Once on a trip north to the Gila River, Kino had been presented with some blue abalone shells. It was not until he started back to Dolores that the thought occurred to him: were not these the same kind of shells he had once seen on the shores of California? And if that were so, then the Indians must have brought them overland, for they did not navigate the dangerous waters of the Gulf!

The more Kino pondered the meaning of the blue shells, the more the idea of a land route to California possessed him. Perhaps the map makers were wrong. Perhaps Drake was wrong. The thought grew in his mind. *California no es Isla, sinó Penisla!* California is not an island, but a peninsula!

All his hopes and dreams suddenly became related to these blue shells. The plans and the schemes of years flashed before the mind of Kino:—the missions that would be built in California; the herds of cattle that could be driven from Sonora; the thousands of poor savages that would know Christ—these were the things that he saw in these glistening bright blue shells.

But he must be certain. Indian messengers were sent out to inquire about the origin of the blue shells. At Dolores, Kino anxiously waited.

Another message came to Kino, however, before he learned the meaning of the mysterious blue shells, an S.O.S. from General Domingo Jironza. Not the Pimas this time, but the Apaches and Jocomes threatened peace and security in Northern Sonora. Six hundred strong they had descended upon Cocospora. Having sacked and burned this mission, they were on their way to Quiburi to do the same. Jironza was helpless. Most of the garrison was away on another campaign. Even the few soldiers present could not reach Quiburi in time to save the village. Would the Padre help, perhaps appeal to his Pimas whom he had always defended so loyally?

Now was the test! It was the opportunity to vindicate his Pimas! El Coro's offer would not go unheeded!

Upon receiving Kino's call for help, El Coro instantly summoned his warriors and with a war cry set out to the rescue. A scene of carnage and slaughter greeted the chief when he arrived at Quiburi. Apaches, covered with buckskin armor for protection, had come close to the fortification, climbed upon the roof, and were now shooting at those inside. Others were enjoying a feast as though already victorious.

When Capotcari, chief of the Apaches, saw El Coro with his Pima warriors, he taunted the Pima chief, calling the Pimas women, and the Spaniards for whom they fought, cowards.

Capotcari, great chief of the Apaches, was the bravest of all warriors! He caught flying arrows with his bare hands! He, the great Capotcari, challenged the Pimas to a duel! They would fight in two groups of ten; five Apaches against five Pimas; five Jocomes against five Pimas. To the winner of the contest would go the victory!

El Coro accepted the challenge. The contest was on!

"They began firing arrows," wrote Kino much later, "and as the Pimas were very dexterous in shooting and also in parrying the arrows of their adversaries, and as the Apaches, although expert in shooting arrows and with the lance, are not dexterous in parrying the arrows, five Pimas soon wounded five Apaches, who were their antagonists, as did four other Pimas their adversaries, the Jocomes and Xanos."

Now the battle was narrowed down to two, Chief Capotcari and his personal antagonist, who locked in deadly combat.

"Capotcari was very skillful in catching the arrows, but his opponent, a valiant Pima, grappled with him . . . threw him to the ground and beat his head with stones."

When the Apaches saw their chief lying lifeless on the ground, his head pounded to a bloody pulp, they became frightened, turned on their heels, and fled with the Pimas in hot pursuit. As they followed, the Pimas shot at them with poisoned arrows until the ground for many miles was littered with Apache dead. More than three hundred bodies were counted.

El Coro immediately sent news of the great victory to Kino on a notched stick, the notches indicating the number of enemy dead. Another messenger was dispatched to Jironza. Spaniards in every mining town and frontier settlement were jubilant. El Coro's great victory was the talk of the hour. Bells pealed in churches; special Masses were celebrated in thanksgiving.

But none was more jubilant than the Padre of Mission Dolores. At last his Pimas were vindicated in the eyes of all. And in El Coro the Apaches had met their match. The Pima chief was the hero of the hour; and Kino received many letters of congratulation.

* * *

All this time the Padre had not forgotten the blue shells. At every opportunity, he made deeper inquiries into their origin. The final clue came when a chief one day came from near the Gila River with a present of a cross and a string of twenty blue shells. Kino was convinced. He must again go north to inquire about the blue shells, and again seek a land route to California. As Kino prepared to set out, his new report of the blue shells aroused enthusiasm among his fellow Jesuits. Wrote Father Kappus:

"I thank Your Reverence for your most delightful letter and also for sending the blue shells. . . . If Your Reverence accomplishes the entry by land into California, we shall celebrate with great applause so happy a journey, whereby the world will be enlightened as to whether it is an island or a peninsula, which to this day is unknown. May it redound . . . to the glory of God, thrice holy and mighty."

"If you accomplish this," wrote Father Gonzalez, "we must erect to you a costly and famous statue. And if the way is short, there will be two statues."

Hopes ran high as tireless Kino jogged north up the Santa Cruz Valley where he had first gone with Salvatierra years before. Teaching, catechizing, baptizing all the way, Kino arrived at Bac a few miles south of modern Tucson. Here, while awaiting the arrival of the Indians, he set about organizing and founding the mission of San Xavier del Bac.

Over three thousand tribesmen assembled from far distances. Into the night he talked to them of God and "at the same time I made further and further inquiries as to whence came the blue shells, and all asserted that there were none in this nearest sea of California, but that they came from other lands more remote."

Thoroughly convinced at last, Kino returned to Dolores to prepare for a trip down the Gila and into the land of the giant Yuma Indians whence had come the blue shells.

With ten natives and sixty pack animals, the Padre set out in September, 1700, on the trail of the blue shells. The year before, Indians on the Gila had run terrified at the sight of his horses which they had never seen. But this time they were not frightened, and the "Indian boys were much pleased to find that the horses ate grass and not little boys as they thought before."

Down the south bank of the Gila he went till he came to the land of the brawny Yumas, tall awe-inspiring men who had never seen a white man. Not since Coronado passed through in 1540 had a European set foot in this territory.

The Yumas were friendly, "even giving the dog which was with us water and pinole in a little basket, with all kindness, as if he were a person, wondering that he was so tame and faithful, a thing never before seen by them."

But Kino's Indian guides were uneasy in this land of brown-skinned giants, and the Padre was obliged to yield to their entreaties to go back. But first he must have a last look from the nearby mountain peak.

It was evening when Kino unslung his telescope and stood on the windy dome against the full glory of a desert sunset. Far below he saw the junction of the Gila with a mighty river from the North, the Colorado! He was sure now that this was the same great river the old geographers called the Rio del Norte. Southward his eye followed it, a great gleaming ribbon threading its way through the windswept desert until it emptied into the Gulf of California.

To the North and West and South, over a hundred miles of desert country, he saw only continuous land, an unbroken range of jagged mountain peaks running southward to be lost in a golden haze in California. He was above the head of the Gulf! The proof was complete! *California no es Isla!*

Kino looked long that evening, watched the desert shadows lengthen, and conjured up a vision of the unknown lands that lay out and beyond in the outermost confines of this raw wilderness that stretched away unendingly in every direction. It was a vision of a new Christendom he imagined, a New Navarre wherein seven new kingdoms might replace the seven Cities of Cibola which led Coronado on with his adventurous thousand in search of fabulous riches.

Seven new kingdoms! Only the riches in these kingdoms

were not the gold of Coronado's dream, but the countless souls that might be saved. On the banks of this mighty Colorado a great Spanish city could be founded, and from here new advances made to the West, into California Alta and the South Sea (Pacific) and its famous port of Monte Rey and to Cape Mendozino; and from here, still farther northwest a shorter route to China and Japan!

And up the Colorado to the North and East, the great nation of the Apaches might be converted and through them, the faith might reach New Mexico and its nearest provinces of Moqui and Zuni, and from here, with new conquests and conversions, communication might follow with the Jesuits of New France—a new road to Canada, even to the lands and the great Sea of the North which Hudson discovered!

It was a glorious dream, the vision Kino caught that evening above the mighty Colorado, but a vision he was not destined to realize. Limitless conquests for souls still opened up before him, but the Padre was growing old and his days in the saddle were numbered. A few years yet remained, years in which he would three times again go the thousand miles north, each time to gather more evidence for those who still doubted the land passage to California.

But his main work was done. The trail of the blue shells had proved his point; he had clearly demonstrated the possibility of a land route to California and joyous congratulations awaited him from every side.

"I esteem the blue shells above my eyes," wrote the Jesuit Rector Kappus from Matape. "May Your Reverence live a thousand years!"

And with deep emotion, Kino's old friend, General Jironza, embraced the aging Padre exclaiming: "In the name of the King, Padre Eusebio, I thank you!"

Kino was sixty-six now. His graying head and weatherbeaten features were a familiar sight as he still made the rounds on horse-back to his missions in the San Miguel Valley. With awe and veneration Spaniards and Indians regarded the veteran missionary as he jogged over the rough mountain trails to and from Dolores.

A life-time of incredible activity lay behind him, a life in which he was forced to accomplish the work of many men, to play the role of explorer, surveyor, diplomat, builder, and cattle king, as well as that of missionary. He had been first to introduce civilization into Arizona, the first to discover a land route to California. Future generations would marvel at his feats in the saddle, his amazing journeys made alone and unprotected through the Southwest's deserts. The trails which he sought out and was first to use would one day become the future highways of Northern Mexico and Arizona. His water holes were to be those of future generations. Geographers would praise his maps; historians would treasure his diaries as the earliest recorded history of the great Southwest.

But above all, it was the man himself and not his deeds that would remain longest in the hearts of those who had known and loved him. A man of keen intellect and resolute will, his life had ever been dominated by one overwhelming purpose—the conversion, the care, and the well-being of the thousands of Indians who had come under his charge. For him these ignorant savages were children of God, destined to eternal happiness with their Maker in heaven. The responsibility for their salvation ever weighed upon his shoulders. With a true and fatherly affection he loved them, worked and prayed for them up to the end. This was the single purpose which ruled and guided his life. It was the only motive which could have driven him on for so many years, the vision that would have led him over the whole of North America in his search for souls.

* * *

It was at the mission of Magdalena that the Padre dismounted for the last time. In the midst of a dedication ceremony in honor of his patron saint he suddenly became sick and soon afterward died.

"He died as he had lived, with extreme poverty and humility.

In token of this he did not undress during his last illness. His death bed, as his bed always, consisted of two calf-skins for a mattress, two blankets such as Indians use for covers, and a pack saddle for a pillow."

Thus wrote his successor at Dolores, Father Louis Velarde. Unrealized were the dreams that Kino held for the conversion and settlement of California. Two generations later, Spaniards opened the ports of San Diego and Monterey. A few years later, and San Francisco was founded. The Padre was in advance of his times, for these were the realities of which he had dreamed and would have accomplished had not death intervened. But he had laid the foundation. Upon this foundation the great Junipero Serra erected his famous chain of California missions almost a hundred years later. San Juan Capistrano, San Carlos, San Luis Rey—twenty-one they are in all. And they all look back for their earliest beginnings to the trail of the blue shells and the Padre on horseback.

IT WAS *an age of historic upheaval. Giants strode the stage for their brief hour, Frederick the Great, Maria Teresa and Emperor Joseph of Austria, Catherine of Russia, Robespierre and Bonaparte. There was Madame de Farge knitting in the slums of Paris where she saw nothing. The Poles and the Irish went on being nailed to the cross.*

America, too, lay in the throes of revolution. English tyranny had worn thin colonial forbearance. Talk of rebellion ran like fire into the backwoods of New England and the South. Too long had these pioneers chafed beneath the yoke of subjection. The Boston Tea Party let the British know the Yankee temper.

Patrick Henry, Tom Paine, John Carroll, Paul Revere, Ben Franklin—all heroes—would rather die, they cried, than listen further to the clanking of chains in Boston Common. So the spirit of great men sparked resolve to strike a blow for freedom.

The shot was fired that was heard around the world; brave, rough-clad minute-men stood their ground at Lexington Square, at Concord by the rude bridge that arched the flood, at Ticonderoga, at Trenton and Bunker Hill. General Washington with breaking heart saw in the snow the bleeding footsteps of his men at Valley Forge.

But freedom triumphed. Like heady wine its spirit ran through the thirteen colonies, put Cornwallis and his redcoats to naught. In Philadelphia, Liberty Bell rang out over cobblestone streets. America was sovereign at last. Now could the oppressed of all ages, the poor, the maimed, the persecuted, the martyred sit in the councils of her wise men and tell them what to write in their laws, how to ground the structure of this state in truth and justice for all.

* * *

Thoroughfare for Freedom

Father Anthony Kohlmann, S.J.

by Frank B. Costello, S.J.

I

He stepped from the brilliant April sunshine and melted into the gloom of the Gesu. No one looked twice at his black cassock, black cloak, and the round crowned hat held in his hand. His tall angular figure and frightened round eyes hardly distinguished him in that crowd. Had he spoken, a Yankee twang might have been noticed in his hesitant Italian. But in the great church of the Jesuits that morning in 1836, Father John Mc-Closkey, priest of the diocese of New York, was just another cleric, and clerics in Rome were as common as swallows.

He had come to the Gesu for the funeral of a fellow priest, Father Anthony Kohlmann of the Society of Jesus. Low voices mumbled from the depths of the church. Moving down the side aisle he saw the candle-flanked casket in front of the altar of St. Francis Xavier. Surrounding it were Jesuits from the General's residence next door. Theirs were the voices, reciting the Office of the Dead, he had heard when he entered the church. He hesitated to intrude on this family gathering of Jesuits. It would be better to wait until they had gone. The Mass of Requiem was just beginning anyway. Then he noticed the Father General in the group.

John Roothan, General of the Society of Jesus, knelt inconspicuously among his fellow religious. As Superior of his Order, he felt keenly the loss of a talented man like Anthony Kohlmann. The Holy Father told him that Father Kohlmann's death was also a great loss to the Church. Men like him were needed around Rome, and the vacancy he left would be hard to fill.

It had all happened suddenly. He had worked too hard, as usual, during Lent. By Easter Sunday, though, he had seemed recovered and continued his confessional work. The following Friday he collapsed at his job and was taken to the infirmary next door. Sunday he was dead. One of his penitents was told Friday to pray for him during the next two days. Perhaps he had a premonition of death. Now it seemed that nearly every-one in Rome, cardinals, bishops, priests, and people, all had rea-son to regret his death. They kept coming to the Gesù to see him once more. But John Roothan, more than the others, would miss him.

Their paths had a strange way of crossing. Thirty-one years ago he first met Anthony Kohlmann at Dunabourg in White Russia. Roothan himself was just a teen-ager in his second-year novitiate, trying to become a Jesuit. That was never an easy job. At Dunabourg it was harder than usual. But when Father Kohl-mann arrived, famous already for his work in all parts of Europe, he fitted in as one of them. If the novitiate was hard for the younger novices, it should have been much harder for an ordained priest. He never let on if it was.

At thirty-four he was still young for a priest with nine years of the ministry behind him. But lines in his face made him look much older. Christ at his age had finished His work; he had hardly begun. It had been a long weary wandering, but he was a Jesuit at last, and that's all that mattered. Once in a while the novices could persuade him to talk about what had happened.

Kaysersberg, a little Alsatian town, saw the beginnings on June 28, 1771, the day he was born. At first nothing unusual happened. Nothing unusual ever happened in Kaysersberg. But when he was nine, his simple life was saddened by his father's sudden death. Mrs. Kohlmann was left with five children, all under eighteen. She was one of those valiant women who Scrip-ture admits are rare. When the terror of the French Revolution broke into the quiet life of Alsace, she proved her bravery. The local pastor, Father John Adam, had refused to take the schismatic oath of the clergy. He was deported from France, but managed to slip back in. Found hiding at a farm, he was dragged back to Kaysersberg for trial. Mrs. Kohlmann was the first to see the posse with its prey. She raced through the town alerting her friends. All at once a mobile brigade of wild women descended on the posse. The police squad, probably composed of married men, knew better than to resist. They broke up and vanished, leaving their prisoner behind. Mrs. Kohlmann led the triumphant procession to the rectory.

Such was the mother whose devotion to the priesthood was rewarded with two priest sons of her own. Anthony had followed his older brother to Switzerland in 1792 in order to study theology. His four-year course at the College of St. Michael, Fribourg, was capped with the degree *cum laude prorsus insigni*. On March 26, 1796, he was ordained a priest at the tomb of Peter Canisius in the college chapel. Within a month, a chance meeting, like an accidental jar to a plane's automatic pilot, changed the whole course of his life Jesuitward.

In 1773, two years after his birth, the Society of Jesus was destroyed by the "Bourbonic plague" that swept over Europe. Determined Bourbon courts kept threatening the Pope until he reluctantly signed the decree of death. Jesuits by the thousands were wiped out. Only in Prussia and Russia were they comparatively immune from the contagion. Frederick the Great and Catherine II refused to take orders from either the Bourbons or the Pope. Under their perverse benevolence, then, Jesuits continued to live in Europe's northeast corner. Since no new recruits were added and the old men were dying off, what remained of Jesuit life was running out fast.

With the death of the Jesuits, a great gap had been left in religious life. Before too long a group of young priests, catching the inspiration of St. Ignatius' ideal and wanting to practice his rule of life as nearly as possible, organized to try to bring this about. Their congregation would substitute until, they hoped, the Society itself was restored. The first founders were two Frenchmen, Fathers Tournely and Broglie, students of St. Sulpice in Paris. Driven out by the Revolution, they set up shop in Louvain in an old house of the Jesuits and became the Society of the Sacred Heart. The Revolution at last reached Belgium and forced them to transfer headquarters to Germany.

At the beginning of 1796, Father Tournely, superior of the group, headed for Rome to put his new congregation at the disposal of the Pope. His route lay through Switzerland. In the early days of April he arrived in Fribourg and met the newly ordained Anthony Kohlmann. Kohlmann was captivated with the ideal of the new group and decided to join them. Since war in Italy prevented the continuance of the journey to Rome, the new recruit returned with Father Tournely to Germany. He was a valuable acquisition to the little group. Besides his great theological learning, he happened to be bi-lingual, speaking both French and German with ease. He was put to work teaching the Fathers German at Goggingen.

If he expected this quiet monastic life to continue, he was doomed to disappointment. For the next nine years he would wander over Europe on an Odyssey which would finally lead him to the Jesuits. The Napoleonic wars moved into Austria, and the Fathers moved out to Hagenbrunn. Here Kohlmann pronounced his vows in November, 1797. The Lent of 1799 found most of Hagenbrunn prostrate in a terrible epidemic. Even though sick himself, he was given the job of nursing the sick, and this he did day and night without rest. When the scourge finally passed, his name was on every survivor's lips.

Interestingly enough, just about this time, while the Fathers of the Sacred Heart were keeping the lamps burning for the Jesuits, another group with the same idea in mind had started up in Italy as the Fathers of the Faith. Their founder, Nicolas Paccanari, was an unusual character. Though not a priest, he persuaded priests to join him and then made his way from bishops to cardinals and cardinals to the Pope until he won approval for his organization. Besides, he had persuaded the Pope that the two similar groups should be amalgamated. The Fathers at Hagenbrunn had not even heard of the other organization when a letter from Paccanari arrived announcing that he was their superior. Finally putting in an appearance in Austria, he had himself elected General, and suppressed the Fathers of the Sacred Heart. There was growing suspicion that Paccanari was not waiting for the Jesuits to be restored, but intended to carry on independently. He broke up the group who were loyal to their first ideal. In the shuffle Father Kohlmann was sent to Italy to work among sick and wounded soldiers.

It is difficult to form even a faint idea of the hardships Father Kohlmann underwent in the hospitals of Padua and Pavia. At Padua they found several military hospitals filled with men of every nationality, far from their homes, wounded, fevered from typhus, piled upon and infecting one another, without any of the sanitation of our times. From the heat and stench of one hospital the Fathers hurried out into the cold toward another, begging food on the way. Sometimes they would arrive there with only a crust of bread. Then would follow hours of hearing confessions in the midst of such filth and vermin that they weren't able to sleep at night. Father Kohlmann had the consolation, though, of bringing the sacraments to nearly all the Catholics and converting several hundred Protestants.

He was at last recalled from Italy to take charge of a newly opened seminary back in Austria at Dillingen. This was old Canisius country and as professor of theology and master of novices he was imitating the great apostle of Germany. It had been at Dillingen that Canisius received young Stanislaus Kostka for the Society.

The relative peace of Dillingen lasted two years. A new college had been started in Berlin: Kohlmann was sent there. Later it was abandoned and he was moved to Holland. Reaching Amsterdam in April, 1803, he remained only a few months. That same year he crossed the Channel to Kensington College, England.

It was while he was in Amsterdam that he came under the influence of Father Adam Beckers, who had been instrumental in directing John Roothan, a local boy, to the newly opened novitiate of the Society of Jesus in White Russia. News that the Jesuits were accepting candidates again electrified the Fathers. A crisis arose when some petitioned the Jesuit General to be admitted as a group. The General wisely refused, insisting that they apply individually and be tested by the usual experiments. Father Kohlmann applied for admission.

Meanwhile he was sent to England and placed in charge of Kensington College. The letter admitting him to the Jesuits reached him there, but he was told to wait further word before proceeding to Russia. By March, 1805, that approval came, and he left London in June for Dunabourg. Arriving there on July 3, he began his novitiate. His joy was complete as he wrote a London friend. "You're right, dear Father, to congratulate me on my happiness and I am grateful for your best wishes . . . Here truly is the gate of heaven and the house of God; above the Society of Jesus all that is left is heaven's happiness. You have no idea until you have experienced this. I have read and heard many good things about the Society . . . but I happily acknowledge that the reality infinitely surpasses all that I have conceived. I can understand very well how St. Aloysius Gonzaga was able to say without exaggeration that if he had to pass through the flames of hell to find the Society of Jesus, he wouldn't hesitate a minute to do it. My great wish is to see all my friends sharing my happiness. As for myself, I have nothing left to desire on earth, but to love God more Who has loved me so tenderly."

It was evident that a novice with such sentiments did not need the complete two years of formation. It surprised no one when the General assigned Anthony Kohlmann to the American Mission only a year after he had come to Dunabourg. John Roothan was one of those who reluctantly saw him leave for Hamburg to sail to Baltimore.

The General of the Jesuits caught himself in these reminiscences when those around him began to leave the Gesu. The funeral Mass was over. He walked slowly to the opened casket and looked down for the last time on the peaceful features of Anthony Kohlmann's lined face. When he had said good-bye at Dunabourg, he had never expected to see him again. But Anthony Kohlmann had only begun his work. After long years he and John Roothan had met again in Rome.

II

They had all gone. The coffin stood for the moment alone in front of the altar. Father McCloskey stepped quietly to its side. The candles limned his features, casting shadows around his deep-set owl eyes. The same light softened the face of the dead priest. That face, which had told John Roothan a story of struggle, held another history for John McCloskey. It was his last link with home. He was losing the only real friend he had in Rome, someone who knew all his family, someone who remembered Brooklyn, the Bowery, Bowling Green, old St. Peter's on Barclay Street, and the new St. Patrick's on Canal. His mother would be happy that there was a representative from New York at Father Kohlmann's funeral. She would probably cry when she heard that he was dead. She always said that Bishop Carroll was very good when he sent Father Kohlmann to them.

The Church in the United States had been growing too fast for Bishop Carroll. When Father Kohlmann and Father Epinette stepped from their boat in Baltimore on November 4, 1806, four months out of Hamburg, they were received with open arms by Carroll who, as Bishop of Baltimore, had the whole United States to administer and almost no priests to help him. The Jesuits first had to report to headquarters in Georgetown, a flourishing little place watching the new city of Washington grow up from the swamps beside it. A college was there and a novitiate, too, where ten novices gave hope for the future of the newly restored American Jesuits. Father Kohlmann, though only a novice himself, was made assistant to the Master of Novices; it was his job to form the young men in the spirit and customs of the old Society as he had learned them in Russia. He could also help teach some philosophy in the college.

But the Bishop wasn't going to allow Kohlmann's talents to be buried at Georgetown. He was sent on excursions into Virginia, Maryland, and Pennsylvania, visiting the scattered Catholics. The English he had learned in London was invaluable. In Philadelphia he had to help out poor old Father Adam Britt, who was so helpless before the subtleties of English that after being in the country thirteen years he couldn't speak even one word of the language. He could only hear a few German confessions. Father Kohlmann's facile bridge of both languages eased the old Jesuit's embarrassment.

In April, 1807, he was assigned to give a mission at the German parish in Philadelphia and followed this with a swing through the state, visiting the German settlements. The trip ended with a triduum at the Baltimore parish. Bishop Carroll had been watching his new helper and was planning even bigger things for him. In response to the Bishop's frequent pleadings, the Holy See had decided to carve up his vast diocese and relieve him of some of the burdens and responsibility. Early in 1808, Carroll became an Archbishop, with suffragan sees in New York, Boston, Philadelphia, and Bardstown, Kentucky. An Irish Dominican, Luke Concanen, was named bishop of New York and consecrated in Rome. Since the French embargo on American ships prevented his leaving Italy, he wrote Archbishop Carroll requesting him to appoint a vicar general in the new diocese with full powers of administration. Kohlmann was the logical choice for this important post. Accompanied by his fellow Jesuits, Father Benedict Fenwick and four scholastics, the Vicar-General of New York arrived in the city in October, 1808. His jurisdiction covered all of New York State, including Long Island and part of New Jersey. But most of his flock was crowded into the lower tip of Manhattan Island. There he assumed responsibility for a debt-ridden parish and cemetery, and some 14,000 destitute Irish Catholics.

New York was in the depths of a depression resulting from President Jefferson's embargo. During the first three months of this boomeranging attempt at reprisal, 500 ships rotted at the wharves, and there were 120 business failures amounting to five million dollars. Thousands of his parishioners were out of work.

What was worse, they were in a spiritual depression too. "The parish was so neglected," Father Kohlmann confessed, "that it goes beyond all comparison." He saw at once that one church couldn't possibly take care of them all. The bishop waiting in Italy would have a new cathedral worthy of his dignity. Canal

Street between Broadway and the Bowery Road was selected for the site. Father Kohlmann, knowing that the Irish would have to bear the expense of the new church, wheedled them by calling it St. Patrick's. Meanwhile he and Father Fenwick worked on the spiritual life of those who could crowd into old St. Peter's.

"The whole day, from early in the morning until the evening, is occupied either in hearing confessions or calls for the sick, superintendence over the common schools, instructions, collecting money for the sick or for the embellishing of the church." Shortly afterwards he was able to report the results: "The communion rail is daily filled, though deserted before; general confessions every day . . . three sermons, in English, French, and German, every Sunday, instead of the single one in English; three catechism classes every Sunday, instead of one; Protestants every day instructed and received into the Church; sick persons attended with cheerfulness at the first call, and ordinarily such as stand in need of general confession and instruction; application made at all houses to raise a subscription for the poor, by which means $3,000 have been collected, to be paid constantly every year."

No wonder the McCloskeys were grateful that Archbishop Carroll had sent Father Kohlmann to them. They had arrived from Ireland and settled in the straggling village of Brooklyn about the same time he had come to New York. Their first baby, John, had been born in March, 1810, and by May it was warm enough to venture with him across the East River in a row boat for the baptism at St. Peter's. Father Fenwick administered the sacrament to twelve others that day, the early spring crop of babies in a place where the harvests were plentiful.

The Jesuits were in New York only a few months when they were called to the deathbed of America's great agitator, Tom Paine. The famous author of *Common Sense*, who had done as much as any single man to set the Revolutionary War in motion, was dying deserted in a New York shack. The idol of America at one time, he had gone to France where he got tangled in the meshes of the very French Revolution he was

trying to promote and only escaped the guillotine by an accident. His later work, *The Age of Reason,* a bitter attack on
Christianity, had lost him his American following. A long letter
to Washington, published in 1796, which attacked his military
reputation and presidential policies, didn't recover popularity
for him. Disillusioned and discredited, he returned to the United
States to die. Two weeks before his death, abandoned even by
his doctors, Paine became desperate.

He was heard crying alone at night: "Lord, help me. My God,
what have I done to suffer so. But there is no God. If there is
no God, what will become of me?"

Afraid to be left alone, he begged to have at least a child
alongside his bed where he wallowed in filth. A Quakeress
whom Father Fenwick had just baptized told Paine that no one
but a Catholic priest could cure him. When Father Fenwick
arrived with Father Kohlmann, and they began to speak of his
soul, instead of prescribing a remedy for his bodily pains, he
ordered them out of the room. "Paine was roused to a fury,"
wrote Father Fenwick; "he gritted his teeth, twisted and turned
himself several times in his bed, uttering all the while the bitter-
est imprecations. I firmly believe, such was the rage in which he
was at this time, that if he had had a pistol, he would have shot
one of us; for he conducted himself more like a madman than a
rational creature.

" 'I was in peace until you came,' he said. . . . 'all that you
have uttered are lies—filthy lies; and if I had a little more time I
would prove it, as I did about your impostor, Jesus Christ.' "

"Let's go," Father Fenwick said to Father Kohlmann; "we
have nothing more to do here. He seems to be entirely abandoned by God." Paine died a short while later.

Jesuits hardly ever have their sleeves rolled up in a new field
of work before they start a school. Somebody had said that if
two of them arrive in town in the morning, one of them has
founded a college by noon and the other has a high school going
before dark. And then they both teach in the night school after
supper. Archbishop Carroll had a school in mind when he sent
the scholastics with Kohlmann. Without the inevitable scholas-

tics, Jesuit schools would lack much of their enthusiasm. The New York venture had its beginning in a rented house on Mulberry Street near the new cathedral site. The next year it moved around to Broadway. Prospects were so promising that Father Kohlmann decided to plunge into real estate. He found a new site "far out in the country . . . the most healthy spot of the whole island. . . ." It was part of the little village of Elgin, and they laughed at him for paying $11,000 for property half way to the Canadian border. It is now worth a fabulous price as the present site of the St. Patrick's Cathedral, Fifth Avenue and Fiftieth Street.

Though burdened with the name *New York Literary Institution*, the school in the country prospered. Kohlmann next year was enthusiastic. "Everyone thinks that if the reputation of the house is kept up, it will in a short time rival any college in the country. . . ." Friendly relations were established with Columbia College; this resulted in an invitation to attend their commencement exercises. The Jesuits were also attracting some of the sons of important families. One was the son of former Governor Livingston and the other the son of Governor Thompkins, later vice-president of the United States. By 1813 the school had seventy-four boarders.

Then he got into trouble. Not too many Jesuits have ever been hauled up before a grand jury. But that is just what happened to Anthony Kohlmann early in 1813. It had all been innocent in the beginning.

One day in the confessional he handled a routine case of restitution of stolen property. As confessor, he was asked to be the agent for the return. In this particular case, it was one of his parishioners, James Keating, who had been robbed. He naturally enough had reported the theft to the police. Shortly after this, he received his property back through the instrumentality of Father Kohlmann. When he attempted to have the whole matter dropped, the police became suspicious and threatened to prosecute him unless he revealed the name of the man who had made the restoration. It was pointed out to him that it was his duty to tell the whole truth and the duty of the police to inquire into it and enforce the penalties. Reluctantly he admitted that he had received the property from the hands of his pastor, Father Kohlmann. When the latter was summoned, he refused to testify, denying the right of the court to question a priest on facts unknown to him except through the confessional. The case was sent to the grand jury and the pastor was subpoenaed to appear before it. He showed up, but again refused to answer questions. The case was causing a stir in legal circles and all New York was talking about "the Catholic question."

When the case finally got under way, the court was presided over by the Honorable De Witt Clinton, Mayor of New York and President of the Court of General Sessions. Only a few months before, Clinton had been narrowly defeated by James Madison in the electoral college ballot for the presidency of the United States. No sooner was the court in session than Father Kohlmann was called and sworn in. Mr. Gardinier, the district attorney, questioned him. He begged leave of the court to state his reasons for declining to answer:

Were I summoned to give evidence as a private individual (in which capacity I declare most solemnly that I know nothing relative to the case before the court) and to testify from those ordinary sources of information from which witnesses present derived theirs, I should not for a moment hesitate, and should even deem it a duty of conscience to declare whatever knowledge I might have; as, it cannot but be in the recollection of this same honorable Court, I did, not long since, on a different occasion, because my holy religion teaches and commands me to be subject to the higher powers in civil matters and to respect and obey them. But if called upon to testify in quality of a minister of a sacrament in which my God Himself has enjoined on me a perpetual and inviolable secrecy, I must declare to the honorable Court that I cannot, I must not answer any question that has a bearing upon the restitution in question, and that it would be my duty to prefer death or any temporal misfortune, rather than disclose the name of the penitent in question. For were I to act otherwise, I should become a traitor to my Church, to my sacred ministry, and to my God. In fine, I should render myself guilty of eternal damnation.

Lest the open and free declaration of my religious principles should be construed into the slightest disrespect to this honorable Court, I must beg leave again to be indulged in stating as briefly as possible the principles on which this line of conduct is founded. I shall do this with greater confidence, as I am speaking before wise and enlightened judges, who, I am satisfied, are not less acquainted with the leading doctrines of the Catholic Church than with the spirit of our mild and liberal Constitution.

The question now before the Court is this: Whether a Roman Catholic priest can in any case be justifiable in revealing the secrets of sacramental confession? I say, he cannot: the reason whereof must be obvious to everyone acquainted with the tenets of the Catholic Church respecting the sacraments.

The stilled courtroom listened attentively as Father Kohlmann briefly outlined the nature of the sacrament of penance and the obligation of perpetual secrecy implied in the notion of confession itself. There was the eloquence of centuries of the priesthood in his final plea:

If, therefore, I, or any other Roman Catholic priest (which God forbid, and of which Church History during the long lapse of eighteen centuries scarcely ever furnished an example), if, I say, I should so far forget my ministry, and become so abandoned as to reveal, either directly or indirectly, any part of what has been entrusted to me in the sacred tribunal of penance, the penalties to which I should thereby subject myself would be these:

First. I should forever degrade myself in the eye of the Catholic Church, and I hesitate not to say, in the eye of every man of sound principle: the world would justly esteem me as a base and unworthy wretch, guilty of the most heinous prevarication a priest can possibly perpetrate, in breaking the most sacred laws of God, of nature, and of His Church.

Secondly. According to the canons of the Catholic Church, I

should be divested of my sacerdotal character, replaced in the condition of a layman, and forever disabled from exercising any of the ecclesiastical functions.

Thirdly. Conformably to the same canons, I should deserve to be lodged in close confinement, shut up between four walls to do penance during the remainder of my life.

Fourthly. Agreeably to the dictates of my conscience, I should render myself guilty, by such a disclosure, of everlasting punishment in the life to come.

On the somber note of eternity Kohlmann finished his plea and the silent courtroom watched the immigrant priest of only six years' residence in the country return to his defendant's seat.

It was the District Attorney's turn and he fired questions at him, one of which was whether he had ever had the stolen goods in his possession. The Mayor and Court Recorder immediately objected to the question, saying that either the law allowed the exemption claimed or it did not, and that was the question which must be determined first. Kohlmann's attorneys, Sampson and Riker, agreed to argue the point, and the jury was adjourned until June 14 to give the court time to hear the argument and give its decision.

Richard Riker, as Kohlmann's counsel, based his claim for the exemption on two propositions: the 38th Article of the Constitution of the State of New York and the known principles of English common law. With clever use of evidence, he cited precedent after precedent in British courts and included as a clinching one a quotation in his favor from that authority among all commentators, Sir William Blackstone. It was like proving a point in a theological debate by firing at the opposition a canon from an ecumenical council.

The district attorney answered for the prosecution that it was one of the principles of common law that a primary duty of a citizen was to disclose all his knowledge concerning matters connected with the common good. There might be a danger to the state if the priest could not under certain circumstances reveal the confidence of a confessional, especially in view of some of the tenents of the Church on the power of the papacy.

Mr. Sampson, Riker's colleague, took him up on the insinuation that the Catholics might be dangerous citizens. The War of 1812 was in the headlines, and things were going very well for the British. There was talk that they might invade New York. The counsel must certainly have consulted Father Kohlmann before he declared:

I shall, therefore, knowing as we all do, who they are that compose the bulk of the Roman Catholics in this city, content myself by supposing that they will not give the city to the English. No, not even if the troops of His Holiness himself should join in alliance with the British to invade it. And I maintain in the presence of my clients, and in their name, that doctrine boldly and firmly. That though Catholics must acknowledge the pope as supreme head of the Church, yet they know their duty as citizens would oblige them to resist him as a temporal prince, if in that character he should make war upon that country, which is theirs, and theirs by choice, the strongest of all ties. Yes, and if the government was too slow in providing them with arms, they would with their pick-axe, or their spade, or their cart-rung, or peradventure, some old sanctified shillelah, the trophy of days that are past, drive the enemy from his cannon, as it has happened before. And I suppose furthermore that there is only one way to make such persons dangerous; that is to put their clergyman in prison for not betraying the most holy of all engagements towards God or man.

Thus the two Protestants who were Kohlmann's counsel closed their case for the defense. On June 14, 1813, De Witt Clinton, another Protestant, delivered the decision of the court, which was unanimous, acquitting Kohlmann. With remarkable insight and tolerance the Mayor outlined the facts of the case, explained the Catholic doctrine on the sacrament of penance and the obligation of secrecy on the part of the priest, even quoting the authority of the Council of Trent. Then in measured tones he continued:

It cannot therefore for a moment be believed that the mild and just principles of the common law should place the witness in such a dreadful predicament; in such a horrible dilemma, between perjury and false swearing: If he tells the truth, he violates his ecclesiastical oath—If he prevaricates, he violates his judicial oath—Whether he lies or whether he testifies the truth, he is wicked, and it is impossible for him to act without acting against the laws of rectitude and the light of conscience.

The only course is for the court to declare that he shall not testify at all.

We speak of this question not in a theological sense, but in its legal and constitutional bearings. Although we differ from the witness and his brethren in their religious creed, yet we have no reason to question the purity of their motives, or to impeach their good conduct as citizens. They are protected by the laws and constitution of this country, in the full and free exercise of their religion, and this court can never countenance or authorize the application of insult to their faith, or of torture to their consciences.

Father Kohlmann walked from the courtroom that day a tired man. It was the last thing in his mind that through all this notoriety and humiliation he had built a bridge along that thoroughfare for freedom which is the arterial highway of American life. Fifteen years later, while De Witt Clinton was Governor of New York, the substance of the Kohlmann decision was incorporated into the Revised Statutes of the state.* Since his day, twenty-nine of the forty-eight states and in addition the five United States territories and the Philippine Republic have adopted specific statutory enactments exempting as a witness any priest whose knowledge in a case was received in the confessional. But Father Kohlmann wasn't thinking of these things when he returned to St. Peter's that day. He was worried about the future of his Jesuit school in New York. And he was also in trouble with the Father General.

About his school. Though in 1813 they had seventy-four

* "No minister of the Gospel or priest of any denomination whatsoever shall be allowed to disclose any confession made to him in his professional character in the course of discipline enjoined by the rules and practices of such denomination."

boarders with prospects of many more, Jesuit Superiors at Georgetown thought it should be closed down. Father Grassi in a letter to Kohlmann wrote:

The Rev. Mr. Maréchal, a Sulpitian [*sic*], paid a short visit to this college (Georgetown). It is confidently asserted that he is to be Bishop of New York, and the great concern he showed for the Literary Institution confirms me in this idea. I exposed to him our situation, the want of members, and he was sensible that such an institution was an *onus insupportabile* for us, in our present circumstances, and for several years to come. I consulted again, quite lately, the Most Rev. Archbishop Carroll on this very subject; and he answered, that as the want of persons to carry it on is evident, this ought to be represented to those who are concerned in it.

Father Kohlmann was stunned by the decision. With a keen feeling for the future, he had predicted that New York would "always be the first city in America." Later he wrote:

The State of New York is of greater importance to the Society than all the States together. A mere Mission in New York is not enough; a solid footing should be obtained with a house of education. Georgetown College should be transferred bodily to New York; and its place occupied by the Novitiate. When there was question of sacrificing one college or another, that [Georgetown] ought to have been sacrificed in preference to the other [New York Literary Institution].

It would be a great mistake, he warned, to doom the Society to the woods of Maryland. But Father Grassi's view prevailed, and Father Kohlmann turned over their New York school to the Trappist monks who had just arrived in the city.

Ordinarily, a Jesuit can present his case to higher superiors. But over in Russia Father General Brzozowski was already displeased with him for taking the job as Vicar General of New York. Because of the Jesuit vow against accepting dignities, the General argued, Kohlmann could only have taken the position at the command of the Sovereign Pontiff. Bishop Concanen had died in Italy before he had a chance to claim his new diocese. That left Father Kohlmann holding his authority. The situation was unique, and he felt himself squeezed in a vise. He hadn't asked for the post. There was no competent authority in America to relieve him of it. Neither could he subdelegate his own authority. He would have to stay on the job as vicar general until a new bishop came. Fortunately, the Holy Father soon named another Irish Dominican, John Connolly, as Bishop of New York. That ended the crisis and he was recalled to Maryland as soon as possible.

They made him Master of Novices at White Marsh as soon as he got down there. Father Kohlmann was eminently a trouble-shooter for the Jesuits. When Father Grassi, superior of all the American Jesuits, left for Rome in 1817, Father Kohlmann was given his job. He moved to Georgetown, becoming rector there at the same time. That year, the Lutheran tri-centennial, he turned out two important theological works, answering the Protestant problems all over again. Later in a tilt with the Unitarians he gave further evidence of his brilliant theological ability. His books were best sellers in their day, going into a third edition within a year. His writings were probably responsible for his summons to Rome. Leo XII had restored the Roman College to the Jesuits and their most capable theologians were called in from all parts of the world. Early in 1824, Father Kohlmann left America for good.

John McCloskey had been down in Maryland himself those days, studying for the priesthood at Mount St. Mary's, Emmitsburg. Now twelve years later he caught up with Father Kohlmann again in Rome. The Gesu was very still as he said his final good-bye. Turning quickly, he moved back up the aisle to the door and stepped blinking into the sunshine of Rome. The squint in his eyes was partly from the sun and partly from watching the hills of home.

III

Spring hung heavy over the valley of the Maine; the City of Angers dozed in the sun like a little old French lady. Only up at the *Généralat* of the Good Shepherds were there signs of activity. Construction work on the new additions was in full swing. Under Mother Euphrasia's direction things always grew. She was busy this morning dreaming. The Sisters would have a house in Rome. At the very center of Christendom they would carry on their work for penitents. She had influential friends in Rome to help her with her pet project. Cardinal Odeschalchi especially could contact the right people to get permission.

A timid knock at the door brought her back to France. She turned from the window to see one of her assistants standing in the door. Something was wrong. Sister's face betrayed bad news.

"Mother, Father Kohlmann is dead."

Mother Euphrasia's dreams crashed around her feet. Father Kohlmann was one of the friends in Rome she was counting on for help in founding her new house there. Though she had never met him, they were old friends. His death was like having your guardian angel drop out of existence. Yes, Father Kohlmann was just like a guardian angel to her in Rome. She was vain enough to think that God placed him there just to help her out. God did things like that. She knew that he had been brought from America to teach at the Roman College which the Pope gave back to the Jesuits in 1824. The Jesuits had scoured the provinces to get their best theologians. Five years of teaching, and he was ready for a rest. But the move to the professed House found him spending most of his day with a long line of penitents in the church of the Gesu. He was a favorite confessor for the colonies of English, Americans, and Germans in Rome.

The Pope made him consultor to the Congregation for Extraordinary Ecclesiastical Affairs, with special reference to German problems. Later he held the same job with the Congregation for Bishops and Regulars. Some said he was a cardinal *in petto*; but he didn't need to be a cardinal to be very useful to the Holy Father and to be of great help to Mother Euphrasia.

The primary work of the Good Shepherds is reclaiming wayward girls and giving them a home where they can live again in self-respect. The Sisters couldn't begin to fill all the requests

for houses in France. One reason was that each house was independent, and there was no central organization. Mother Euphrasia at Angers wanted to set up a mother house there with
branches that could be staffed from it. This plan aroused opposition. The only thing to do was to write to Rome and get papal
approval. It came as an impulse during Vespers on the Feast of
the Assumption, and she left the church to compose the letter.
"Behold the handmaid of the Lord" was her first line and after
stating her request she closed with: "Eminence, I prostrate myself in the dust before you; I am at your feet. I desire but the
glory of God."

When the letter came up before the assembled Cardinals,
Father Kohlmann read it aloud, then laid it on the table. Reflecting a moment, he placed his hand on the letter and said: "The
truth is here." His opinion was unanimously adopted by the
Congregation and a decree establishing the generalate at Angers
was drawn up and signed.

With the good news of the approval of her congregation came
a letter from Father Kohlmann with very prudent advice:

I cannot tell you how taken I am with the grand idea with
which God has inspired your soul to spread, so far as it depends
on you, this great work to all parts of the world . . . this beautiful work which seems to me to be destined to give so much
glory to God and snatch so many souls from hell. The Mother
Superior, assisted by her counselors, ought to be perfectly free
in the government and the disposal of her subjects. Believe me,
that for religious orders which wish to spread, there is no better
superior than the Sovereign Pontiff, and that, under the immediate jurisdiction and protection of the Holy See, they prosper
most.

When the decree establishing the Congregation of the Sisters
of Good Shepherd of Angers was read to the Holy Father for
his approval and they came to the passage where permission was
given to the Superior to found different houses in France, Father
Kohlmann stood up and asked permission to speak.

"That sentence," he said, "appears to me to be incomplete. I propose that the phrase *in the whole universe* be substituted for the word *France*."

"Father Kohlmann," exclaimed Cardinal Odeschalchi smiling, "you wish to make the Good Shepherds a second Society of Jesus." The cardinal was answered with a smiling bow and the scriptural phrase: "Thou hast said it."

When Mother Euphrasia received the papal decree, the Kohlmann amendment was more than she had ever hoped for. In the year since that time, she had reason to be very grateful for all his help. The news from Rome said he had died on April 10. The Sisters would have to be told. Father Kohlmann deserved their undying prayers. She stopped at the chapel.

Epilogue

I

Fifth Avenue in front of the cathedral was black with people. Inside, they were packed solid along the walls. The surpliced procession of clergy seemed endless. After them forty-five bishops and archbishops flanked by deacons of honor filed slowly up the steps. Then a splash of scarlet in the sun. It was America's first cardinal. He considered that May morning in 1879 the greatest day of his life. Some who could remember remarked that he looked that day like the boy-bishop he had been thirty-five years ago. The same Jesuit, Benedict Fenwick, who had baptized him was bishop of Boston then, and had come down to help consecrate him auxiliary of New York. With his mother they had talked about Brooklyn, old St. Peter's, and the St. Patrick's Father Kohlmann had built. This morning he was dedicating the new St. Patrick's. Her Gothic beauty was anchored deep in the property Father Kohlmann had first bought for his Jesuit school. Now he, as Kohlmann's successor, was spiritual head of the diocese. John Cardinal McCloskey, Archbishop of New York, walked slowly up the steps and disappeared inside as the *Ecce Sacerdos Magnus* boomed through the groined vaults of the new cathedral.

Thoroughfare for Freedom

II

There was one more private audience on the schedule. Leo XIII, seated behind his big desk in the Vatican, looked tired and sick. The white cassock clung like a shroud to his skeletal frame. From his stooped neck the pectoral cross dangled free in front of his broad cincture. The skin on his face was stretched taut and had the transparent look of fine china. His long thin fingers clutched the edge of the desk. This man looked much too frail to be carrying the burdens of the Vicar of Christ.

Yet his pontificate, now near its close, was a monumental one. From this frail figure had come some of the great documents of the century. *Rerum Novarum* in '91 was one of his best; like a cofferdam it was already slowly deflecting the stream of modern capitalism. Earlier, by his *Aeterni Patris*, he had dug out and dusted off the works of St. Thomas Aquinas, too long stored in the neglected attic of scholasticism; an intellectual renaissance had followed. And these documents were but two in a long impressive list. He deserved to be tired.

There was still one more private audience scheduled. His chamberlain was ushering in an old papal Zouave, veteran of Pio Nono's service. He had fought well for the papacy and merited the special consideration of a private interview. The Holy Father rose to greet him.

"And where are you from?" The question was routine. Talking about home always put the pilgrims at ease.

"Kaysersberg, Alsace, Your Holiness."

The figure in white leaned forward eagerly.

"Why, that's the place that our old teacher, Father Anthony Kohlmann, came from. He taught at the Roman College when we studied there back in the 1820's. What an inspiration he was to us young students and how much we owe to him."

"Your Holiness, I am Father Kohlmann's nephew."

Routine was gone. A light color stole up the Pope's white face and his small dark eyes were sparkling. The old men chatted like boyhood friends. It was with difficulty that the chamberlain ended the visit. The Holy Father gave orders that a special gift from him personally should be sent back with the visitor to Kaysersberg. It could be used in the parish church in memory of Father Kohlmann.

The old papal soldier knelt for a last blessing. The Pope walked with him to the door and then turned back to his desk. He was still very tired. But the mention of Father Kohlmann stirred the banked fires of his memory. He sat alone in his room in the Vatican and stared into the past, smiling.

III

May Day, 1940, in France was quiet. Too quiet for comfort. The silence was like stillness in an execution chamber. The Republic of France was going to die. She had been cajoled, betrayed, and raped, but what would hurt her most would be the humiliation of final acquiescence. German Panzer divisions were poised along the borders of the Low Countries, waiting for the big push to begin on May 10. With the ease of war maneuvers they would sweep across Belgium, Holland, and France in a matter of days. The French Republic would be history. The quiet over France was ominous.

Down in Rome on May 2 the mood was festive. Forty thousand happy people filled St. Peter's and overflowed into the huge square outside. They were witnessing the first canonization ceremonies of Pius XII's reign. Above the high altar was a massive oil painting of France's latest heroine.

France had been her home, and from Angers she had dreamed of French houses of refuge for delinquent girls. Then from Rome had come the mandate with the Kohlmann amendment that made her vision world-wide. Before her death she was able to say: "I am no longer French. I am Italian, English, Spanish, American, African. I belong to every nation where there are souls to save." Around the world in two hundred and fifty houses scattered in forty-three countries, 10,000 Sisters of the Good Shepherd were awaiting this highest tribute yet paid their Mother.

Pius XII presided at the four-hour ceremony. Before him knelt two cardinals-advocate. Three times they begged the Pope for the canonization. Twice he told them to pray for God's guidance. The third time he declared their petition granted. Silver trumpets blew; the choir burst into a mighty *Te Deum* and all the bells of Rome rang out.

St. Euphrasia Pelletier belonged no longer to Angers, nor to France, but to the universe.

THROUGH *the long days and months, Colonial statesmen put together bit by bit the American constitution. It was not good enough for the people though. They remembered too well how guarantees had died on lips that uttered them; the ultimate asylum must not be promises, but law. A Bill of Rights was added with safeguards spelled out so that the commoner would know his father's blood and his son's blood had not been spilled without avail.*

Lafayette and John Paul Jones were already names revered throughout the land. Washington gave to the struggling nation the leadership it desperately needed, helped fuse the scattered allegiance. Benedict Arnold, of course, had fled by now the land he sought to betray—his name rang like a counterfeit coin, a by-word of contempt and opprobrium.

It was hard to keep abreast of the swift-moving times. The cotton-gin and iron plow, Whitney's assembly-line gun put the country fifty years ahead. Longfellow and Hawthorne and Washington Irving were being read even in Europe. No small tribute to this barbaric land! Commerce was becoming a mighty factor along the Great Lakes. There was talk of the Erie Canal.

A contagious spell of wanderlust began to settle on the whole country. Those were the days when a man could take up his skillet and knapsack and be off for the open country. Out past the Blue Grass Region of Kentucky the settlers moved. They populated Ohio and Alabama; they edged into lower Illinois. Little clusters of Scotch-Irish began burying their stakes in the hill country of Tennessee. Restlessness and growth were everywhere.

* * *

A Dream Went West

Father Peter De Smet, S.J.

by Michael McHugh, S.J.

In 1823 the United States was a nation on wheels, and all the wheels were turning toward the west. Conestoga wagons rumbled up and out of the Atlantic seaboard, winding through the Alleghanies on the newly cut Cumberland Pike. Long-legged pioneers crowded their oxen past the droves of cattle and sheep, grimly swallowing down dust beat up by hoofs and wheels. They were heading west to build themselves a home in the free land of the frontier.

Two of those wagons creaking through the Cumberland Gap in 1823 were making west for more than a homestead. They were piled high with the tools and books and baggage of a dozen Jesuits, half of them still novices, moving out from Maryland to Missouri to set up an Indian mission.

One of these Jesuit novices was a husky young fellow in his early twenties: open-faced, fair-haired, with friendly blue eyes alive to every new adventure in this amazing America. This was Peter De Smet, who had run away from home in Belgium, shipped across the Atlantic, and joined the Jesuits in Maryland because he wanted to become a great Indian missionary in the United States.

Peter's timing was perfect—only a few months after he got his cassock at the White Marsh novitiate, Bishop Du Bourg had arranged for the novices to pack up and move out to his diocese in the Mississippi Valley. Just the thing Peter had hoped for—to ride out west right along with the pioneers. Only he didn't do much riding. The Jesuits had no fare for stage coach travel, so it was shank's mare for Peter and the others over the hard roads of Maryland and Pennsylvania as far as the Ohio.

But travel was free down the river, floating with the big current in hard-to-handle flatboat rafts. Peter loved it—lunging his muscled weight on the stiff steering oar, standing a lone night watch to spot steamboats shouldering their right of way up river, floating swiftly past booming young towns like Portsmouth and Cincinnati, then unloading the flatboats to shoot the rapids at Louisville.

But the river ride was over at Shawneetown, Illinois. There the traveling novitiate took to the open road, across the American Bottom country to where St. Louis, just that year incorporated into a city, stood as the gateway to the Indian country.

Not far beyond, on a farm at Florissant, Missouri, the Jesuits settled down to the routine of religious life again. But first there was building to be done—a church and kitchen and schoolrooms —then they could look forward to some needed years of study before the young novices would be ready for ordination as priests.

Peter liked the building work. He was well muscled for hefting and hauling quarry stone and lumber. But he found in Latin grammar and the syllogistic footwork of philosophy too narrow an outlet for his restless makeup. He wanted work; missionary work was what he had come for. Those poor pagan Indians camped down along the river had no more notion of Christ and His love for them than did the dry grass of the prairie. Why waste the five years before ordination without helping them? He could plant Christianity right away in this desert soil by starting a boarding school for Indian boys.

More than just catechism too—besides Christianity the youngsters would get the seeds of culture—reading, writing, spelling, then tool forging, blacksmithing, carpentry, and farming; also music and good manners and cleanliness and all that goes for civilized living. Fortunately Mother Duchesne and her Sacred Heart nuns were nearby to do the same for the Indian girls. When they finished school, the young men and women could marry, settle in new Christian villages, and raise their children to a proper way of living. Why, in one generation all the ignorance and superstition and savagery of the accumulated centuries would be ploughed under forever.

The plan sounded good to General William Clark, who was handling Indian matters for the government. He got Andrew Jackson interested at the White House, and soon Secretary of War Calhoun had signed an appropriation for St. Regis Seminary.

Peter De Smet and his fellow philosophy students rode out to the tribes around—the Shawnee, Iowa, Sauk, Osage—beating a big drum and inviting the lads to school. The kids came, curious like kittens to tumble about in the dormitories and race through the dining room, but they stampeded like young buffalo at the whisper of work. These young braves couldn't sit cramped over books on the hard benches. Chopping stove wood and hoeing the corn was for squaws. Long chapel prayers hurt their knees. They squirmed away from wearing shirts and shoes and combing the lice from their hair. They grew homesick for their ponies and the prairies—and they ran away.

Their persistent Jesuit prefects chased after and dragged them back, throughout a half dozen years of this double duty of teaching and studying—up to and after their ordination as priests by Bishop Rosati in 1827. But by then St. Regis Seminary was suffering from hard times. Money for food and books and clothes was difficult to get in the hand-to-mouth frontier economy. These young Jesuit priests were finding more satisfying work in the pioneering of parishes, or building up the new college in St. Louis. And so, when the Missouri tribes loaded their ponies and pulled their teepees farther west, to more promising reservation land, De Smet's little log school was left ringing with the empty echoes of once hopeful teachers and their half-hearted pupils.

But to young Father De Smet it was more than just one dream gone dead. It was his failure—a solid, disappointing shock —and he felt it. Peter was a man of moods that change like the weather. When the warm sun shone down on him, there was nothing he could not do. He was strong; he was able; enthusiasms and ambitions electrified his blood. But let the sun get lost in a rain cloud, let a disappointment or difficulty or discouragement wrap him in cold mist, and Peter shivered, got dejected very easily. So far his life had been full of sunshine. His home in Belgium was golden with memories of warm and well-off family happiness; school days had been pleasant—the boys always following his lead—"Samson" was what they called him; then God had blessed him with a vocation to be a priest and up to now had blazed him a bright trail out to the Indians.

But now clouds cut off the sunshine. All he had now was the memory of these ten years spent—wasted rather—in Missouri—ten years of salt pork, mud, mosquitoes, and this empty, mocking schoolhouse. The others had made a go of it—as pastors or college teachers in the St. Louis school. Mother Duchesne and her Religious of the Sacred Heart were successful—but he, Peter De Smet, priest of the Society of Jesus, was a ridiculous failure. And to add to his troubles—this climate was marring his face and hands with some skin disease, eczema it looked like. All in all, this Indian apostolate was not the high romance he had come for. He would do much better to go back to Belguim and help the Indians by sending men and money out to the missions. That's what they needed. And besides the home town climate might clear up his skin. At least, he reflected, he would be on the move a bit.

Father Roothan, General of the Jesuits, gave the go sign and De Smet took a boat back to Belgium. His recruiting agency was effective—he got a library from the University of Louvain, vestments and chalices from the Archbishop of Mechlin, a substantial check from the Propagation of the Faith in Lyons. All of this and five Jesuit novices he shipped across to Missouri—but De Smet stayed on in Europe. His skin disease was spreading; so was his discouragement. He did not feel he was cut out for front-line mission duty and reluctantly asked his release from the Society. Reluctantly, too, Father Roothan let him go—and for the next few years Father De Smet was chaplain at the Carmelite convent in his home town of Termonde.

But the makings of a missionary were in him yet. The quiet

sunshine of a cloister garden cleared up his face, and also perked up his sleeping zeal. So another letter to Rome—could he come back to the Society and go out again to Missouri? Roothan judged he might, and prayed God to bless his vocation with firm, deeply rooted graces. So back out to Florissant again he came, bringing with him other younger novices, among them Arnold Damen, future apostle of Chicago.

De Smet soon had a job ready waiting for him. There were 2,000 Potawatomi Indians recently settled along the Missouri River in the Nebraska Territory. Senator Benton of Missouri and General Clark of the Indian Bureau pushed the plan of a resident missionary. President Van Buren was interested—and Father De Smet was issued passport and steamboat passage up-river to Council Bluffs. Converting 2,000 Indians was also an up-river job, but he went to work this time with a zeal steadied by experience. No more the forced feeding of culture to indifferent Indians. The thing was to get God out there into the villages. The blackrobe should build his log church among the tents, feast with his Indians on roast dog, and starve with them on moss and acorns. He must take them as they were, and by long and hard work make them good Christians right in their own surroundings.

De Smet soon found out that those surroundings were pretty sordid. The poor Potawatomis were going to seed. The men squatted at gambling games all day long; the squaws drudged about the filthy tents; naked children yelped like starving dogs through the shoddy village. Laziness and disease had shattered the backbone of the tribe. There was no fight in the braves; their war-crazy Sioux neighbors rode screaming out of the Dakotas, cutting down the Potawatomis like weeds.

But even worse than the blood-wild Sioux was the white man and his whiskey. When the Potawatomis got their government pension money, they poured it out for liquor. After the cash was gone, they bartered blankets, horses, food—even their own children—for drink. Then they murdered and mutilated— hacking at each other's ears and noses with bloody knives.

It was such surroundings De Smet set out to sanctify. He became the Potawatomis' blackrobe—a doctor bandaging their wounds, nursing them through smallpox and cholera plagues— a teacher encouraging and showing them how to pray to God for strength—a priest baptizing them to Christian holiness as the layers of pagan ignorance and superstition were scrubbed away.

Their blackrobe then went to war for his people. Armed only with his big bronze crucifix, he followed the Sioux war trails up along the Missouri and rode right into the hostile camp in South Dakota. He told them about God who was crucified, how that God wanted all His children to be good brothers—and he brought back to his Potawatomis a pledge of peace from the Sioux.

But when their blackrobe took up the war against whiskey— he was whipped. Nothing De Smet did could loosen the life-choking grip of the liquor traffic. His preaching and thundering threats couldn't kill the maddened Indian thirst. He appealed for protection from the territorial law; he denounced the white bootleggers, smashed open their barrels unloading on the river landing, dumped the liquor into the Missouri. But it was no use: every boat up-river brought in more. He might as well try to dam up the Missouri with a canoe paddle. His only hope was to get his Indians by themselves, away from easy temptation, wall them off from these greedy exploiters. Then he could grow healthy souls in healthy bodies. But here, both body and soul were rotting to death.

Jesuits had civilized such savages before. Just a century ago in South America there was a beautiful Christian Indian civilization in full bloom in the jungles of Paraguay, far up the Parana River, far beyond the greedy reach of exploiting adventurers. Muratori's book told all about those Paraguay Reductions; De Smet carried his own copy, dog-eared from his insistent, pondering study. Could the same be done here in North America in 1838? De Smet wore out his Muratori like a prayer book, praying for the chance to show that it could be done.

In his second dreary summer with the Potawatomis, De Smet got his chance when two strange Indians came paddling down the Missouri and beached their canoe at his mission. They were from the Flathead tribe, way out west in Montana, on the far side of the Rocky Mountains. They had heard about the white blackrobes and were on their way to St. Louis to get one and bring him back to the mountains to teach them about the Great Spirit.

This was not the first blackrobe-begging trip the Flatheads had made. Three times in ten years they had crossed the plains for a priest, and though this "Macedonian Cry" got a lot of publicity in the East, no priest had been available. But this fourth time they had met De Smet, and he was definitely available. The Rocky Mountains would be his wall against white contamination. Behind that wall he could build his dream—an Indian civilization in the shadow of the cross.

De Smet wasted no time weighing pros and cons, but hit the Oregon Trail at a hard gallop. He was like a whirlwind over the prairie that summer of '38—facing west from Independence with the spring fur traders, along the Platte River into Western Wyoming where Flathead scouts picked him up, followed his Indian guides north along the Rockies into Montana, saying Mass under the canopy of massive mountains where few white men had been before, living at the Flathead village long enough to teach them their prayers and reassure himself that here his dream could be born, then out of the mountains east along the Yellowstone and Missouri Rivers, past the gray Potawatomi ruins at Council Bluffs, and back to St. Louis in late fall.

He spent the winter selling his mission dreams to the Catholics of the country. Educating Indians to Christianity beyond the Rockies was an expensive apostolate, when you had to pay almost a hundred dollars for one horse, and his plans were to pack full mission and farm equipment out there. He got his help —Bishop Kenrick and his Philadelphia clergy came through with a big drive—New Orleans ladies tossed gold bracelets and jewels into his mission alms box. The next spring five more Jesuits were fully outfitted and on the Oregon Trail.

The year was 1841. In the same wagon train, led by the famous scout Tom Fitzpatrick, was John Bidwell and his party of pioneers making their memorable overland crossing into the

Sacramento Valley of California, and Joseph Williams, a minister, heading for the Oregon coast. The Jesuits in the caravan were Father De Smet; Father Point, founder of Grand Couteau College, Louisiana; Father Mengarini, fresh out from Rome; Brother Claessens, carpenter; Brother Specht, blacksmith; Brother Huet, jack-of-all-trades.

They followed the Oregon Trail as far as Fort Hall, Southern Idaho, then spurred off to pick and scramble the rocky trial north into Montana. The Flathead Tribe was ready and waiting for their blackrobes on the Bitter Root River in a valley of the Rocky Mountains. It was a beautiful and fertile valley, spring fed off the snow-topped rock ranges piled high on all sides—a natural hub for the Indian trails that crisscrossed through the mountains—yet well off the white wagon roads to the West Coast. Here Father De Smet set up St. Mary's Mission—the first of many in the Rocky Mountains.

Before long a church was built. A lumber mill, the first in Montana, was turning out rough planks with a saw blade hammered flat from wagon-wheel rims. And a flour mill ground ten bushels a day from the wheat harvest. The Indians were awed by it all—especially at the mysteries of gardening and growing. It had seemed stupid to turn good pony grass underground and then bury good seeds in the dirt. But when green shoots poked up from the black soil the bucks gaped and would squat for hours along the split rail fences to watch the garden grow.

God was pouring down His sunshine of warm graces upon these devout folk. Tents mushroomed up around the log church; morning and night the tribe knelt to pray; the braves broke with polygamy; marriages were blessed; papooses were baptized. A little girl going on twelve years lay dying—she suddenly sat up and cried—"Oh, how beautiful! I see Mary, my Mother," and lay back on her blanket dead.

Before long other tribes, like the Kalispels and the Coeur d' Alenes, came in curious crowds to see what was doing in the Bitter Root Valley. They liked what they saw—the church and the big cross, the gardens and cows and chickens. They begged the blackrobes to come to their villages too and tell them about

Jesus, to teach them how to talk to the Great Spirit, to pour water on their heads, to set up an altar and say the Big Prayer for them every morning. They too wanted to be good.

De Smet saddled up at the suggestion and explored along the rivers flowing west from the Rockies. He came into the Kalispel and Kootenai camps, teaching, baptizing, sizing up the ground for further foundations. In Northern Idaho he met the Coeur d' Alenes, then past Spokane Falls, Kettle Falls, and the Okanogan villages. All these tribes were eager for blackrobes. De Smet was willing, but how could he straddle so many mountain missions with so few men?

There were two priests pioneering the Church down by Fort Vancouver toward the coast. To meet them and plan out ways and means De Smet joined a Hudson's Bay boat going down the Columbia. It was spring flood time and he nearly ended his career at the Little Dalles when the light skiff capsized and was crushed in the rock rapids.

His meeting with Fathers Blanchet and Demers, and with Dr. John McLoughlin of Hudson's Bay Company, was a warm encouragement to De Smet. Working together, they could pinpoint the land from the Pacific to the mountains with Catholic missions. They needed more men and more money, but De Smet could get those. He would leave the missions for the missions, go back to civilization, alert Catholic interest and aid, bring back an army of workers to the West.

Back in the States, De Smet spotlighted his mission needs by publishing the diaries and letters home during his Rocky Mountain days. These books were studded with curious details of mission life—the Indian customs, tribal war tortures, geography, descriptive travelogues, and true stories of the natives—like that of Louise Sighouin, an Indian princess, who gave up her father's wealth and like a nun dedicated her life to teaching catechism and nursing the sick. And then there was Victor, the Flathead chief, who sent to Pope Benedict XVI the invitation to come out to St. Mary's Mission in the Bitter Root Valley. There the Flathead braves would guard him night and day from his enemies and the squaws would keep his kettle filled with the best venison.

These stories were read eagerly by Catholics in America, and even by the pioneer missionaries, Mr. and Mrs. Marcus Whitman, at their Methodist church near Walla Walla. And even farther than that, as De Smet found out when he crossed the Atlantic to beg in Europe. He was hailed as a highly famous—almost fabulous—modern nineteenth-century missionary. And, captivating personality and showman that he was, he lived up to his reputation.

Parish school halls were crammed in awed silence as wide-eyed children and their teachers listened in wonder to Father De Smet describing how lumbering bear and dainty deer came right up to his mission doorsteps. And one night he was lost in a mountain snowstorm, alone and far from home. As he had no place to sleep, he crawled into a big hollow stump—and guess what he found—a whole family of baby bear cubs snuggled up inside the stump. Father lay right down with them—and then he heard Mama bear grunting along the forest trail and then right up the stump too, and starting to drop down inside on top of poor Father. What did he do? He just grabbed hold of her tail and pulled and pulled until Mama bear was so scared she ran off into the woods and left Father cozy and warm with the little cubs.

And did they know how Indian boys and girls learned their prayers? There were no books or blackboards or good Sisters to repeat the words day after day. The busy Father can only stay a day or so at each village—so he rings a bell to get all the children, then lines them up in a big circle, and walks from one to the next giving each child one little bit of a prayer like "Hallowed be Thy Name" to learn by heart. That doesn't take long —and then the prayer is recited out loud around the circle with each youngster saying his one memorized line. Before long, all the children, and all the parents too, listen and learn all the prayers by heart.

What did the Indians call him? They called him the "Medicine Man of the White Nation." Why? Oh, just because of a box of matches, like the kind in Mother's kitchen at home. The Indians didn't have matches and they would watch him light his pipe by rubbing one end of a little stick and thought it was magic. Well, once a jealous Indian wanted to show off to his friend that he could make fire magic too, so he begged some fire sticks from the Father—but then, to make sure that they all worked—he went off alone into his tent and tried each one. Yes, they all worked; then he gathered up his box of burnt matches and went out to make magic for his friend and you can just imagine the surprise he got.

Father De Smet enjoyed such stories as much as the youngsters. When it was time to go, he would ask for a list of all their names, so he could baptize the Indian babies after them and then they would have someone special to pray hard for in the Rocky Mountains.

De Smet was just as popular in his talks to adults, though he let them, especially priests and nuns and seminarians, feel a bit of the weight of the missionary's cross. An Indian mission camp was no place for weak souls. If one would follow a Rocky Mountain vocation—he, or she, must be ready to ride for days along the trail fasting on cold water and a handful of dry mush. Even when food was plentiful, the tastes must be trained to the Indian's diet—green moss, crushed roots, greasy meat—there was no bread, no tea, coffee, salt, or sugar. The winters were cold; you slept on the ground in a frozen buffalo hide, or waded wet shod across roaring mountain streams, where one slip might snuff out your life in a second. The guttural language was hard to come by. The customs were too, such as passing a drink of whiskey from mouth to mouth around the camp fire, the last man in the circle getting to swallow it. Underclothes often were a mere memory; a cassock made from an Indian blanket was all one Brother had to wear. Cultured companionship, even the religious comradeship with fellow priests, and daily Mass, and confession—was often part of the sacrifice.

Yet the need for missionaries was staggering, he told them. Thousands of pagan Indians from the Mississippi River in the the middle of the United States clear out over the Rockies to the Pacific were begging for blackrobes. And what did the Church have for them? Two overworked diocesan priests in Oregon and a scattering of Jesuits in Montana. How could that handful hope to reach out and bless every valley and every village? Must his dream of dotting that pagan land with churches, schools, and farms be left to die for lack of willing workers?

There was still need of nineteenth-century martyrs' blood to nourish Christian growth. Did they know how the Faith had first come to the Rockies? Pagan Flathead Indians had crossed half a continent looking for a priest. How had these Flatheads ever heard about the blackrobe? From Iroquois Indians wandering west with the fur trade, Catholic Iroquois whose ancestors had martyred the missionaries, like Jogues and Brebeuf, in the Great Lakes Country. A nineteenth-century mission was the fruit of saintly blood spilt two hundred years before. And there was still need of martyrs' blood.

Such frank appeals opened up budding vocations, and purse strings also, all over Europe. Priests like Father Joset, nuns like the Sisters of Notre Dame de Namur signed up to spend their lives on these missions. And those who could not pack up and go showed their interest by prayers and donations of books, vestments, pictures, rosaries. At the close of this one trip through Europe, De Smet chartered a brig out of Antwerp and sailed for the Oregon coast by way of Cape Horn. Half a year later, after a narrowly safe passage of the wrong mouth of the Columbia, De Smet was back in his Northwest missions.

He went to work. Like a missionary Johnny Appleseed, he planted the seeds of mission church and school wherever the ground was good—along the Willamette River in Oregon, among the Coeur d'Alenes, Kalispels, Kootenai, and Kettle Falls Indians in the mountains. But he didn't stay to watch the harvest; he left other blackrobes behind to gather the fruit, while he rode farther on for new and needy tribes. Wherever he rode the Indians recognized him. He was the "Great Blackrobe," the "Indian's Best Friend"—and at sight of the short and wide figure in his dusty cassock, white hair falling long to his shoulders, with his big bronze crucifix and warm full-cheeked smile, any Indian camp from the Missouri to the Columbia, whether friendly or hostile, crowded round him chanting—"The Blackrobe has come!"

And of course, Peter De Smet loved every bit of it. He kept always on the go, never stopped in any place long enough to learn the language. He moved by canoe, steamboat, on horse and afoot, by dogteam and snowshoe. De Smet on snowshoes floundered and crushed along like a bull moose. On one mid-winter hunt for the Blackfeet, his Indian interpreters made him fast for a month so the northern Rocky snow crust could carry his 200-pound frame.

In spite of his enforced fast, he did not find the Blackfeet all winter and he was packing up for another try on this one-man roundup when he was called in off the trail. His orders were to unsaddle and slip his pack—settle down to an office and desk in St. Louis. Father Roothan had just appointed him as treasurer and corresponding secretary for all the Jesuit establishments from the Great Lakes to Louisiana. Father Joset would take over on the mission field.

This was a bitter dose for De Smet to swallow. Why, he was not yet fifty years old. He could keep up with the best and youngest of them on the trail. There was no one who got along with the Indians as he did. What would all his Rocky Mountain missions do without him? What about his dream of driving Christianity deep into the country's culture? He was still needed out there. His superiors, however, did not see it the same way. Of course, Father was zealous and energetic and hard working, also experienced, and indeed popular. But perhaps his zeal was pushing him too far. He was wonderful for the mission beginnings—to give them a sound start. But he lacked control and perhaps moderation, and what the missions needed now was a steady hand for consolidation and controlled growth. Let good Father De Smet find consolation and an outlet for his zeal in the help he could give his missions from his treasurer's desk.

And every few years, when his money-hungry houses ran low on funds or when a fresh injection of novice blood was needed, De Smet was sent overseas to Belgium, Holland, France, and Germany to tap the European sources. He was born to travel—sixteen times he crossed the Atlantic Ocean—and born to talk, for by his enthusiastic contact he was personally responsible for bringing back almost 100 priest workers for the United States.

At the end of every trip he found at his St. Louis desk piles of mail to answer—Bishop Lamy of Santa Fe asks that Father De Smet come to New Mexico to convert the Indians there. Governor Isaac Stevens up in Washington Territory needed the priest-explorer's help in surveying a railroad from the Mississippi to the Pacific. Lieutenant John Mullan, U. S. Army, would appreciate De Smet's help in laying out the wagon road from Fort Benton to Walla Walla. Bishop Miege out in Kansas, "Bloody Kansas" it was then, writes a sorrowful account of the slave-and-free-staters' fight and the poor Indians caught in the middle of it. From the White House a war-tired President Lincoln was concerned about keeping the Sioux and Osage tribes from taking up arms against the government. Captain La Barge would like his good friend to come down to the levee and bless his new steamboat, the best yet built on the River, and a postscript asking whether Father had the spring shipment of axes and plows and seed ready for the Kansas missions. And another postscript—that Mother Duchesne up at St. Charles Mission sends her regards to Father and would he offer Mass that the cholera doesn't take any more of her Indian pupils. A magazine editor suggested that the Father do a series of articles on his Western experiences—including such items as what De Smet proposed regarding a National Park in the Yellowstone geyser region, an account of De Smet's meeting with the Mormons and how he directed Brigham Young to the Great Salt Lake, and his own reflections on his frontier friends, like Kit Carson, John Fremont, Jim Bridger, and so forth. But the letters De Smet looked for most were the wrinkled and dusty packets in from the Rocky Mountains. He rejoiced at every gain God made in those hills. He could work here, happy, knowing his mission dream was coming true. But that was one more disappointment

—his dream was getting dimmer year by year, and the news the pony express carried in from the Rockies was not good.

Ever since gold had been found in the far West, the waves of seekers and settlers had come crashing across the prairies to the Pacific. Even the remote valleys and backwashes were filling up where De Smet once thought his Indians would be sheltered. His dream of happy isolation was breaking apart. There was left no place to hide. What protection was there now for an Indian's simple way with God? Contact with the frontier whites would rub away the Indian's religion, just as contact with the whites was rubbing up the Indian's fighting temper. The tribes were getting crowded and restless with the constant coming of the wagon trains. There were more and more skirmishes and scalpings and slaughters.

The United States government was alarmed at these touch-and-go massacres of Indian and white, and in 1851 called upon Father De Smet for help. He was saddened at the need, yet glad to help, to get out from behind his ineffective desk and use his influence for peace. 10,000 Indians of the plains—the Sioux, Cheyennes, Arapahos, Crows, Assiniboins, and Gros Ventres—were converging at Fort Laramie, Wyoming, for the peace pow-wow. De Smet was the go-between for the suspicious Indians and the somewhat uneasy government envoys. He did a good job—pleading the need of faith and cooperation and fair play. Fighting was futile—the white wagon trains could never be stopped by arrows and bullets; it was pouring blood into the prairie sands to continue the wars. Lay down your weapons, pick up the calumet of peace, take the money the white man wished to pay, and live on the reservation lands in safety and security. The white man will keep his word, and all, Indian and white, will live together in happiness. The treaty talk was successful. The Indians got the promise of unmolested reservations; the government got peaceful passage along the wagon roads west—and Father De Smet, in his new role of pacifier, went back to his desk in St. Louis.

But seven years later he was called out again. This time the war drums were booming beyond the Rockies. Miners and settlers had begun closing in around the mountain missions, and mixed up in the Steptoe War were De Smet's own Coeur d' Alenes, and Kalispels, and Flatheads. It was hard riding for his rheumatic 60-year-old body to make the winter trip into the mountains—and harder still on his fatherly soul to see the ruins of what had been his rosy dream. Now his Indians were out-laws, crowded into this suicidal war, and St. Mary's Mission of the Flatheads was a sagging ghost town.

His dream was dead now. It was too late to save his Indians in their Christianized culture, but he could still save some lives. In 1867 the Sioux were on the warpath, and Sitting Bull had sworn to cut down every white man that crossed his path. The Army was interested in peace, but Generals Sheridan and Sher-man, Harney and Terry knew of only one white man who could get safely in to talk to the Sioux chief. They called on Father De Smet, and the white haired old man of 68 rode across the Bad Lands into the bristling Sioux camp on the Yellowstone, flying one flag, the banner of the Blessed Virgin Mary, Queen of Peace.

When De Smet rode back, he took with him Sitting Bull's promise to keep the peace if the white men would leave his people alone and keep off their reservation lands. The treaty was signed, and De Smet went back to St. Louis for the last time.

Then gold was discovered on the Sioux reservation in the Black Hills of Dakota. De Smet had crossed that country a dozen years before and had come across the gold deposits. But fearing a mining invasion of Indian lands, he covered the vein and kept it silent. Now, however, his secret was out and waves of gold-mad men poured into the Sioux hunting grounds. Sitting Bull took up his war hatchet, vowing he would hunt the treaty breaking white men to death, and massacred Custer and his whole command on the Little Big Horn.

This time, though, De Smet was not called on to bring Sitting Bull to peace. Peter De Smet was dead.

J EFFERSON *left his mark as few presidents were to do. From Napoleon he purchased prosperous Louisiana. The French blood, the Old World culture of Paris and Marseilles from New Orleans and the lower Mississippi Valley began now to move into the stream of national life.*

When Hamilton and his like-minded confreres might have made America an aristocracy, government by gentry, it was the great commoner, Jefferson, who turned the tide of destiny in favor of plebiscite, of democratic procedures. The times called for stature and strength to set progress in its historic groove. His mind and integrity, his quill were an answer to prayer.

Into the harbors now came the immigrants in ever mounting waves. Long before the Potato Famine, Boston and New York felt the impact of the Irish, a despised lot of ill-clad men and working girls who asked but a pittance for back-breaking hours in mill and factory. The Germans too swept along in vast numbers through Pennsylvania and the great Ohio Valley. Language and Faith held them together, helped them build their clean sturdy townships. Poverty meanwhile forced many a man into the dank mines where he seldom survived.

The great flood of wagons and men moved on. Iowa, Kansas, and Nebraska had been opened. The Swedes, Norwegians, and Finns hit through Michigan up to Wisconsin and Minnesota. Even in the distant Oregon country British claims were being successfully challenged. Boatloads of pioneers were pulling in at Astoria and Vancouver. Some few brave men had made the long trek across the Dakotas and over the Rockies. Signal fires began to burn. Red warriors shaded their eyes as they watched the caravans moving into their land, and they wondered.

* * *

Drums Along the Rockies

Father Joseph Joset, S.J.

by R. I. Burns, S.J.

The soft spring night throbbed to the ominous pulse of war drums. Frenzied chants and high weird yells paced the rapid drums in a rhythmic nightmare of sound. It was a picture out of Dante's hell: paint-smeared Indian braves leaping about their fires like demons, anticipating, like demons, the shuddering wails of the victims they intended for the fire.*

Only six miles away twinkled the bivouac fires of the troops —tired, tense men scattered about a swampy bottom-land, each sleeping on his gun, while a strong sentry-guard listened nervously and a Nez Perce scout fled south in the night to Fort Walla Walla in a hopeless appeal for aid.

The men in the command of Brevet Lieutenant Colonel Steptoe had good cause for the fear which gripped their stomachs and parched their mouths. In this year of grace 1858 not many white men had yet been privileged to penetrate that far northwestern corner of the American republic. The real frontier was back on the Missouri and the Mississippi; the real boom-town was still St. Louis. Settlers were sailing around the Horn in

---

* Parts of this are an adaptation from a previous, more technical article, "A Jesuit in the War against the Northern Indians," *Records of the American Catholic Historical Society,* LXI (1950), 9–54; the manuscript sources from which it is largely drawn will be found there cited. Joset's original narrative I have edited in the *Pacific Northwest Quarterly,* XXXVIII (1947), 285–314.

growing numbers, dotting the Pacific coast with their settlements. But this vast interior, from the Cascades to the Rockies and beyond, was Indian country. The forlorn little outpost of Walla Walla had been pushed forward just recently—and the troopers, all 157 of them, were now 80 miles from even that problematical shelter.

This very morning they had been swinging on a routine march through the great rolling hills of the Palouse country, remarking how the land tumbled in gentle swells off to the far horizon, for all the world like an ocean suddenly frozen. Then all at once there were Indians everywhere. Hundreds upon hundreds of them—Spokanes, Palouses, Coeur d'Alenes, Yakimas, Okinagans, Flatheads, Kootenais, Kalispels. The hills became alive with them. In full war paint and well armed, they were in ugly mood. Strangely enough, they had not attacked at once, but had held protracted parleys with the whites. Howling braves had flanked the soldiers on their mile-long retreat to this lakeside camping-site where the dragoons had sat their mounts, immobile, until the setting sun had ended the parleys and the immediate crisis. Obviously some strange force had postponed the slaughter. Obviously, also, it would not be able to contain the fury of the savages much longer.

Puzzlement in the military ranks would have given way to amazement, could they have seen that "force" in action among the Indians that very moment.

An earnest little Jesuit priest, bone-weary and travel-stained after his frantic ride from the Coeur d'Alene mission, was bustling about among the warriors. These were his very children whom he had baptized, catechized, civilized, married, whose names he had bestowed and had written so often in the church registers. He chided them now until their feathered heads drooped over their painted breasts. Soon he had them assembled for their evening prayers.

Make no mistake about it: these were no reservation Indians, off on an emotional frolic. They were savages, in whose child-like minds the new force of Catholicism was battling against a centuries-old heritage of evil. The Jesuit's heroic effort that night failed, and many men would die before he could stop the War against the Northern Indians. But stop it he would.

The story of his services for the peace of our Pacific Northwestern frontier is told here, not because it is an isolated tale of romance in a prosaic mission history, but precisely because it is typical. We might well have chosen the story of the Jesuits in Chief Joseph's War of 1877, where they localized one of the most famous and costly Indian outbreaks in our history, limiting its participants to a single tribe. Or we might have watched the Fathers at work in the many councils, great and small, where the government required their presence. Had we wanted dramatic contrast, we could have drawn scenes such as that strange spectacle in the Crow War, where the Indians stopped their hostile demonstrations against the Agency long enough to welcome the nuns newly arrived there with their Jesuit guide; first the cavalry officers paid their respects, then the Indians led their guests away toward the Crow camps, and then hostilities were renewed!

Had we wanted adventure, we could have dipped into the lives of the missioners at random. Giorda, for instance, stripped naked in sub-zero weather and hauled into captivity by a Gros Ventres war-party, yet converting his mishap into an opportunity to evangelize the Gros Ventres on a pentecostal scale. Or Hoecken, doing the work of five and six men as he labored to subdue cholera plagues, Indian passions, and hostile neighboring tribes; laboring also to implement in detail a treaty whose promises the American government had found it convenient to forget. Or Ravalli, d' Aste, De Smet, Cataldo—all renowned in their day for repeated pacification of the tribes. Everywhere in the Rocky Mountain Mission, from the Columbia to the headwaters of the Missouri, they used their influence effectively for peace: among the Blackfeet, Yakimas, Nez Perces, Kettles, Flatheads, Cayuses, Spokanes, Palouses, Coeur d'Alenes, and others. Their hazardous services in the cause of peace—many of them forgotten in history books but embalmed in grim tomes of official government reports—would alone insure them a significant place in our national history.

So if only Joset appears on our pages, we must remember this is not his story alone. It serves as a type, an epitaph for all that brave company. Besides this, of course, the missioners' contributions were equally significant in multiple other phases in the building of the far frontier. Had we space enough, Joset might serve here also as their symbol. Joset, the co-builder of Gonzaga University! Joset, the chaplain of U. S. border troops! Joset, the pioneer in agriculture! Joset, the administrator sending priests to the gold-hordes of California in '49, or plodding on snowshoes incredible distances from mission to mission! Joset, the itinerant missioner to the isolated white settlements sprinkled over the prairie lands! Joset, the Tertian Master or spiritual director of young priests who, in turn, would influence the religious and social life of the frontier! Joset, the historian and ethnologist, author of lengthy memoirs on the tribes, flora, and languages of the region! And Joset the Apostle. Above all, Joset the Apostle. This was the aspect of his life which so forcefully struck a visitor, the son of General William Tecumseh Sherman, that the young man decided to abandon all his brilliant prospects as a lawyer, all the ambitions which his famous father cherished for him, in order to become a Jesuit priest. "I'd rather be Father Joset," he wrote to his father, "than Chief Justice of the United States."

In later years, to a query as to the motives which had sustained him in the wilderness, Joset would give blunt answer: "What could it be, but to Christianize these poor benighted ones? You will not think the missioners to be fools. Men endowed with knowledge and self control will always be able to win a comfortable living in this world. How, then, could a sensible one say goodbye to all the advantages of civilization, to go and bury his life among savages. . . . No, the end of the Catholic missioner is no other than to prepare these poor ones for the blissful hereafter. But to make Christians of them the greatest obstacle was their native laziness: they were to be turned industrious."

"To bury his life among savages." Fifteen long years were now passed since the little packet *Chateaubriand* had stood out of Le

Havre to carry him to this New World. Not that he had seen much of the sprawling young republic called America—just a glimpse of New Orleans, and a week's trip by paddle-wheeler up the broad Mississippi to St. Louis. And before that? Before that, the Alps and the lovely meadowlands of his native Switzerland.

The pageant of world events (for Napoleon Bonaparte was master of Switzerland when young Joset first cried his way into the world) had hardly touched the prosaic pattern of his early life, the quiet years of schooling, the quiet days of solidly pious family-life. Of his four brothers, one was destined to become a Capuchin monk, another a Jesuit lay-brother in the eastern United States, and a third the prefect-apostolic of Hong Kong. Joseph Joset himself would discover, after four years in the College of Fribourg (1826–1830), a vocation to join the Order to which his teachers belonged. At one time or another during his thirteen years of Jesuit training in Europe, he prefected boarders, acted as librarian, taught Latin, mathematics, French, and Hebrew. It was only later, in the cloistered quiet of his post-ordination ascetical year at Notre Dame d'Ay, France, that he made known to Rome a long cherished desire to be a missionary. These were the halcyon days when the great Jesuit De Smet was ranging the labyrinthine "Oregon" wilderness and stirring Europe with his colorful reports. Just as Joset in the course of his training had once asked with impetuous generosity to be allowed to sacrifice his ideal of the priesthood by becoming a lay-brother, so with equal impetuosity he now sacrificed a last visit to his parents, disregarding an urgent appeal from his parish priest, permission from his superiors, and probably the legitimate demands of filial piety.

In the New World there had been a year of prefecting and teaching at St. Louis University, then the long bitter trek with an emigrant train, two thousand miles into the wilderness. "We were six weeks," he would recall in later life, "making the first twenty miles." Unmanageable mules, swamps where the motley array of canvas-roofed wagons had to be unloaded and reloaded three times in a day, heavy rains which delayed them near the Kansas river: "our journey was not the gayest possible."

His first years on the mission were not gay either. The language almost broke his heart, and eating moss from the trees in time of starvation surely did not promote his health. He was sent immediately to take charge of the fiercest tribe and most troublesome station of the whole Rocky Mountain Mission chain: the savage, warlike Coeur d'Alenes—Hearts like an Awl, or Mean Hearts. He rode down to his mission, which today would lie in the panhandle of Northern Idaho, with the discouraging instructions from De Smet: "If you suppress it, all right."

We have not space here—no, not in this whole book—to tell the complete story of those next fifty-five years. We must be content to isolate one aspect of his life: his services in the cause of peace. Even here, however, we must focus sharply on the major events in a single one of those services, his attempts to restore peace during the 1858 War against the Northern Indians.

The 1858 troubles did not fall from a clear sky, unannounced. For a decade now the government had been keeping a wary eye peeled over the Cascades. The savagery of the Cayuse and Rogue River wars had been a prelude to a long series of Indian troubles. Just recently in 1855, the Superintendent of Indian Affairs, Isaac Stevens, had gone far into the Rockies on his famous Treaty Tour to placate the tribes, only to have the country behind him explode into the 1855–1856 war. In the latter year even the coast village of Seattle was attacked, while from 1855 the great lonely interior had been closed to immigration by worried military authorities. Now General Clarke was anxiously penning official apprehensions from his Department of the Pacific: "In Oregon and Washington Territories, east of the Cascade Range, I consider it unsafe to remove a man for service elsewhere." The good Père Joset, stationed at Sacred Heart Mission with two lay-brothers, felt he could control the Coeur d'Alenes as long as the whites made no hostile move. Father Ravalli had confided, by letter from the Kettles' mission, that "I fear a general rising among the Indians toward the commencement of spring. Let us pray, and let us engage others to pray with us, in order to avert this calamity." The Coeur d'Alenes were apprehensive all that winter, and the priest had constantly to reassure them. Rumors flew about wildly: that troops were massing along the Snake River, that soon there would be an invasion, and that the Indians would be slaughtered. A military road through the interior was actually under way, and the prospect of this new encroachment heightened the panic. The tribes became more uneasy, then truculent. The Coeur d'Alenes loved their little blackrobe, but they assured him they meant to fight for their lands. Already the Palouse country below was dangerous. Joset could find no brave willing to risk carrying a message of warning through to Fort Walla Walla. While the tribe moved on to the lower plain for their root-digging season, he prepared to go himself.

Three young braves rode with him down from the mountains, over quickening ribbons of thawed brooks, and out into the small seas of Camas blossoms in Paradise Valley. Their message never got through. Chief Vincent headed them off at the upper crossing of Hangman's Creek and warned of a Palouse ambush ahead. Besides, the young bucks were too excited now for Vincent to restrain them longer: that ambush would mean war between the many tribes. "It may very well be," he told the party, "that we shall have to fight the Palouses, who are very sore against us because we will not declare against the Americans." If soldiers did come, Vincent said, "I am sure the Nez Perces are going to direct them upon us."

Joset yielded. But he exacted from the head chief a promise to send for him as soon as white soldiers actually marched. It was on this occasion that the sturdy little priest was threatened by a Nez Perce war-party. He faced them down, advancing dramatically with his crucifix held high: "Here I am! Strike me. Behold my medicine! Possessed of this I do not fear you."

Back at the mission he dashed off a warning to his superior, Father Congiato, who should be arriving in the lower country for a visitation of the missions. The letter had to travel indirectly, far north and around the Palouse lands, while precious days slipped by. In the meantime, white troops marched against the Coeur d'Alene root-diggers.

Vincent's desperate call for aid arrived by courier. Joset paused only long enough to have the lay-brothers destroy all available gunpowder, and to scold some warriors into remaining home. Then he raced to the scene of trouble. Chief Vincent placed the whole mess in his hands. As Colonel Steptoe had advanced, Vincent had retreated north upon the Spokanes (his guests at the root-digging) and upon the Palouse bands in that area. By a masterly effort he and the Spokane chief had prevented hostilities until Joset could arrive. As soon as he dissuaded one group from attacking, he would find Palouses urging on another group. Parleys were held with Steptoe who insisted he was merely passing through to Colville—a route Joset describes as akin to traveling "from Paris through Berlin to Turin." A further headache for Vincent was Steptoe's guide, the Nez Perce Timothy, who kept sending messages: "Coeur d'Alenes, your wives, your horses, your goods shall very soon be ours!" In later years this Timothy would confess to Fathers Cataldo and Joset that he had instigated the Steptoe disaster, directing the soldiers toward the Coeur d'Alene body; yet by a cruel paradox his name shines brightly today on the granite Steptoe memorial, while that of Joset is all but ignored!

It was only with the greatest difficulty that the warriors—now gathered from many tribes—were persuaded to make camp that evening. "I had no rest the whole day," the weary chief concluded; "I feel very tired." Joset looked about him. The savages, whose number he estimated at over a thousand, were "indeed awfully excited." To his mind it seemed already too late, but an effort must be made. Gathering together the chiefs and sub-chiefs "and a quantity of other Indians," he began his harangue. He explained the "principles of war": he stressed their ignorance of the actual motives of the white chief; he reminded them that this was Sunday, a day too holy for talk of war. "Whosoever kills by his private authority," he warned, "is a murderer; whosoever engages a battle without the order of his chief is guilty of all the evil which flows from it; it is the duty of the chief to examine when he has to wage war for his own defense." As soon as it was dawn, they were to have a horse prepared for him; he would lead the chiefs to see the white chief, first entering alone by himself and then introducing them. All would be settled peaceably.

With this the chiefs and more responsible warriors were quieted. But all his exhortations and cajoleries produced "no or very little effect" on the young bucks. He did manage to gather all the fierce warriors for their customary evening prayers, but hardly had the last "Amen" died when a "slave" of the Americans, a Nez Perce guide, arrived to repeat the boasts of the day: "Your lands, your women are ours." Joset told his people not to believe this; "no officer ever spoke in that way; tomorrow I will ask the chief of the soldiers if he has said that."

At daybreak the priest rode out to hold his parley. A swirl of Indians swept behind him in riotous pageantry of war-paint, feathers, and lances. The Americans had begun what they called "a retrograde movement" toward the post, eight days distant. However, a brisk gallop for three miles brought their column into view: a long serpent of blue winding and bobbing in the dim daylight along the three-hundred-yard-wide valley of Tohotonimme Creek, two companies of cavalry in the van, another at the rear, and over a hundred pack-horses as well as some twenty-five tense and subdued infantry sandwiched between.

The parley between the colonel and the priest was carried on from horseback while the retreat continued. Joset then brought in Vincent and some sub-chiefs. Full satisfaction was given on both sides and a council arranged to be held at Walla Walla. When news was brought that the Palouses were again agitating to open fire, there were hasty handshakes, and Joset spurred back to restrain his Indians. They were overjoyed at the outcome and voted to go home. Strangely enough, one influential tribesman became furious at this decision, striking out at sub-chief Jean and then grappling with sub-chief Victor. Joset threw himself between the warriors and tore them apart. Then, after a few last words to his flock, he left to announce his good news to the women and elders at the Indian base-camp some fifteen miles away.

It was during his absence that an influential tribesman, one of the few belonging secretly to the Palouse-Nez Perce party, created a scene in which a few excitable bucks fired on the whites. It was a scene and nothing else—until two of the most popular Indians of the tribe were killed and sub-chief Victor mortally wounded. Chief Vincent later explained shamefacedly to Joset: "I had no intention to fight, but at seeing the corpse of my brother-in-law I lost my head."

The soldiers carried almost no ammunition; their cavalry wore no sabres. On a lonely hilltop refuge they fought desperately, as one of their officers put it, "amid the howling of the Indians, the groans of the dying, and the whistling of balls and arrows." That midnight the veteran Indian-fighter Steptoe consummated one of the most brilliant escapes in the history of Indian warfare, single-filing his entire command through the Indian lines. But it had been a major humiliation for the army of the United States, making them the laughing stock of the Indians, and meriting the tag it won and kept, *The Steptoe Disaster*.

And what of Joset? The whole heartbreaking task must be gone through again. The Indians would be even more difficult to handle; the whites would be thoroughly aroused; and the fate of all his years of mission work would hang in the balance. He felt, he tells us, as though he had a dagger in his heart. At the mission he found fierce confusion. Some hotheads were for burning it to the ground because the lay-brothers had destroyed the gunpowder. The dead Zachary's mother was fanning the embers of war with her continual wailings and cries for vengeance. Braves were returning from the warpath loaded with booty and boasting that they could meet and conquer the whole United States army. A severe tongue-lashing settled Zachary's mother. Scoldings, queries, and rebukes gradually brought many back to their Christian senses.

Two white travelers barely escaped the stake. First, old Brother Francis had made a grueling trip to warn them; then, when hunger drove them into the open, Brother Magean's Irish eloquence had restrained the savages from harming them. With the aid of two chastened ex-combatants, Joset secreted them in his house for two days and eventually had them spirited into Flathead country.

Relentlessly the priest argued with his flock and instructed them. "You are only murderers," he told Vincent, "the authors of the death of your own people." He made especially sure they had taken no scalps and had buried the dead. When they were sufficiently subdued, he gathered them before a map, showed them how insignificant a spot they held in this vast country, warned them that the soldiers would now come in overpowering numbers, shamed them for being bad Catholics, and threatened to abandon them.

They were frightened now. None dared accompany him to see the white chief. Chief Garry of the Spokanes warned that if the whites killed their blackrobe "it will be impossible to control the people." Joset now sadly filled in the names of the fallen in the *Liber Defunctorum*, wrote an account of the whole tragedy to Father Hoecken among the Flatheads (it was forwarded to Washington, D. C.), and circled down the far bank of the Columbia to help his people, if necessary, "with my blood." At Fort Walla Walla, Steptoe received him royally. First rumors had actually credited the priest with starting the war, but he was now everywhere hailed by the military. At Vancouver he convinced General Clarke of the essential innocence of the Coeur d'Alenes and others, but was asked to carry back severe surrender terms. Clarke thanked him "for your efforts in the cause of humanity," and begged him to reconsider his threat of abandoning the Coeur d'Alenes because "you may yet be enabled to save them by remaining among them a little longer."

Joset, now accompanied by Father Congiato, rode happily back into the interior, carrying official passports for the Indian delegates he was to collect. But the two priests were astounded to find the whole Indian country on the brink of "a general uprising." In their absence emissaries from the lower country had unsettled the mission tribes with taunts and bribes. The chiefs had restrained many, so far, such as the Kettles, most of the Kalispels, and a little under half of the Coeur d'Alenes. Relatives of the slain had vetoed the Coeur d'Alenes' peace plans, and now the harsh conditions laid down by General Clarke reduced even Chief Vincent to silence. A few warriors threatened the chiefs and the Jesuits.

For three weeks now Congiato and Joset would ride from camp to camp over the vast Coeur d'Alene domains, detailing with chilling eloquence to each group of savages the number and power of the American forces. The braves stopped their war dances and laid aside their regalia. But they were stunned by Clarke's demands and saw no way of complying; particularly against their tribal ethic was the handing over of war criminals to the enemy. Like the children they were—confused, stubborn, and a little frightened—they promised that if the blackrobes abandoned them, they would retaliate by throwing themselves unanimously into the war.

Among the Kettles in the north the two Jesuits again used their restraining influence. They decided to postpone as well their projected abandonment of the Kettle mission, at the appeal of the few whites in that area. The far-flung tribes of the Flat-head Confederacy backed the Jesuit peace-drive, and one of them (the Pend d'Oreilles) proclaimed that they would kill any Indian combatants who should take refuge on Pend d'Oreille territory.

A report of all this, together with letters from Coeur d'Alene and Spokane leaders, was carried to Walla Walla by Father Ravalli, who had been brought down from Colville to run messages through the hostile territory. By the time the priest's message reached Vancouver, Colonel Wright's punitive expedition was crossing the Snake River. As one officer put it, the Jesuits had courageously "harangued early and late and long"; but this peace effort had also failed.

The whites wanted no collective bargaining. It was to be unconditional surrender and vengeance, or war. Telegraph wires had hummed as troops were rushed in from California, Colorado, and the Midwest. General Harney, stopped in mid-career a thousand miles across the plains on his march to the Mormon War, was ordered to return to New York and sail via Panama to command the situation. The Secretary of War requested the Jesuit De Smet to reconsider his proposed resignation as chaplain for the Utah Expedition and to accompany Harney to aid the cause of peace with his experience of the Rocky Mountain Indians. The low meadow-grounds of Vancouver were lively with the rattle of drums as troops were hurriedly routed through to Walla Walla. In the wooded Walla Walla Valley, against a far backdrop of the Blue Mountains stretching into the horizon, the troopers had sweated in the July heat of the parade grounds in special intensive drills in Indian warfare. Now, while outposts were manned to cover supply lines, 570 regulars, 35 Nez Perce allies, 100 civilians, and 800 "animals of all kinds" pushed off into Indian country.

This is not the place to describe the preliminary skirmishes and overall strategy. Suffice it to say that the coalition of nine tribes fought savagely from the start, harassed the advancing column, and was resoundingly defeated in two pitched battles on the open plains. The latter included, of course, the classic cavalry attack: Major Grier's ringing "Charge the rascals!" as the mounted dragoons thundered by in a rolling storm of hoofs, sabres flashing in the sun. A comic-opera effect is achieved by the fact that not a single soldier lost his life in these engagements. But plains-history was being made. The bewildered savages had tangled not merely with artillery, cavalry, and specially trained Indian fighters, but also with a deadly new weapon: the breech-loading Sharps. The Indian muzzle-loaders could not compare in fire-power, range, or accuracy. Perhaps they would have been consoled to know that their humiliation was being duplicated in a white land that very year, when Colonel Suasue's thousand revolutionaries defeated Mexican government troops with Sharps rifles, killing six hundred with only slight loss to their own side.

The war was far from over. The Indians retreated into impenetrable Idaho forests and into the mountain country. After their initial panic, they were sure to re-form for guerrilla fighting, where cavalry and Sharps would be equally nullified. Many historians, puzzled at their peace overtures now, have mistakenly attributed them to Wright's slaughter of captured horses. Actually these horses were largely the property of a single Indian, Telxawey, and the warriors were not at all dismounted. The secret of the peace negotiations was Father Joset.

While his "youngsters" were still upset at the sudden disaster, he began again his exhortations and sympathetic scoldings. With some difficulty he managed to keep many at the mission, but refused to see Wright for them: "twice you have put me to shame." Finally he relented and sent down to the colonel a plea for peace. Wright accepted on condition of "unqualified submission to my will," and began his exhausting march to the mission. Abandoning wagon and howitzer limber, the soldiers single-filed over a barely navigable Indian trail—the forest becoming "more dense as we advanced, until we could see nothing about us but high hills and deep caverns, with thick woods covering all, through which we wound our way in a twilight gloom." In his diary Lieutenant Kip reflects: "The priests will now be exceedingly useful to us . . . it will be through the agency and influence of their priests alone that we shall be able to reassure them and induce them to accede to the necessary terms."

The impact of the saintly Joset's life upon the hard-shelled American military was remarkable. Captain—later Brevet Brigadier General—E. D. Keyes, who had come up from the San Francisco presidio to command six companies of artillery serving as infantry in the campaign, was never to forget the experience. His account of the influence the former Fribourg professor had upon him at this time is worth repeating at some length. "In Father Joset I found a cultivated gentleman in the prime of life, fit to adorn the most polished society in the world. I was unable to restrain my expressions of astonishment when he informed me that he had passed the last 14 years in the wilderness with the savages. I asked him if he had no longings for a better life and society. 'No,' said he, 'I am content and happy where I am.

In your profession an outward obedience to orders is all that is required of you, but in the Society to which I belong obedience must be internal, and cheerful, and ready. I am happy, and have no desire to exchange situations with any person.'

"Twice every day while I remained at the mission I had conversations with Father Joset, which increased my admiration for his character and my estimation of his self-denial. He instructed me how his Church had preserved the traditions and dogmas of Christianity . . . and it was primarily due to his influence that I enrolled myself, at a subsequent date, in the Roman Catholic Church."

We may dispense with the tedious negotiations which followed, and which Joset stage-managed. He acted as host and interpreter during the council, assisted by Father Menetrey. Then he rode out to round up 107 delegates from the Spokane, Pend d'Oreille, Isle des Pierres, Kettle, and other tribes for a second council. He brought in the Yakima, Kamiakin, one of the chief instigators of the trouble, but that worthy fled again before the council convened. Later De Smet would bring the chiefs, including Kamiakin, to a council at Vancouver, but the latter would again grow frightened and leave at the eleventh hour.

Colonel Wright once more "expressed his satisfaction" to Joset for all he had done, and the officers agreed "that but for the priest's help the affair would never have been brought to so speedy a conclusion." Wright ends his report of September twenty-seventh: "I cannot close this communication without expressing my thanks to Father Joset, the superior of the Coeur d'Alenes mission, for his zealous and unwearied exertions in bringing all these Indians to an understanding of their true position. For ten days and nights the Father has toiled incessantly, and only left us this morning after witnessing the fruition of all his labors."

The episode was ended. Happily Joset returned to the long and arduous years—forty and more of them—of missionary labor left to him; Wright headed off to hang Palouses "in a gallows in a tall pine tree" and otherwise write finis to the campaign. There were dark mutterings yet among a few of the die-hard

Coeur d'Alenes: "were the Black Gowns out of the country, we would begin again." But the tribe as a whole had been won by their military guests and had learned by bitter experience to return to their unquestioning trust of the man Lieutenant Mullan had called their "oracle of Delphos." They would refuse to ally with the Sioux in that tribe's uprising shortly afterwards, and would eject the Sioux envoys unceremoniously from their territory. They would throw their influence on the side of the whites in 1877, narrowly limiting Chief Joseph's Nez Perce War, frustrating the Nez Perce intrigues to bring in the northern tribes, and even caring for the farms abandoned by frightened settlers. These dispositions the Coeur d'Alene chiefs and headmen, in solemn council assembled, declared to be due to the exhortations of their blackrobes—which would mean Joset above all—without whom in 1877 "we would have been numbered among the hostiles."

When young Père Joset rode out of Fort Hall on the last lap of his journey west, late in 1844, old "Oregon" had been a howling wilderness. Poised safely on his home frontier east of the Mississippi, the child of civilization could contemplate Oregon's massive mountain barrier, the Rockies, and barely grasp with his imagination the immensities which stretched from his eastern threshold far and far away to the unexplored waters of the Pacific. Its evergreen forests swept awesomely down to a land of ranchos and adobe missions, Mexican California, while its northern expanses rolled through tangled wildernesses to fields of snow and ice where its limits mingled with the Russian claims. Sturdy pioneers were even then leaving their imprint on the rugged land: the lonely trail of a Hudson's Bay fur brigade, the melancholy grave of an emigrant who had met a war party or a plague, the hardy souls in the little log cabins, the proud but tiny settlements on the coast. Then the tempo of progress had accelerated. Like an amoeba, Oregon had split into territories. Territories became states: Idaho, Washington, Oregon, Montana. A British border cut sharply into its northern pretensions, but an American state, California, stood proudly to its south. The great Mullan military road, which Joset had done so much to help, was forerunner to a spiderweb of roads and highways. Railways had sent their fingers of steel probing through the northwest states, and his fellow Jesuits had donated valuable rights-of-way. Jesuits had evangelized the boom-towns of Idaho during its gold-rush of the sixties, had contributed a handful of high schools plus two universities to its educational frontier, had been religious and civic pioneers in the little townlets which were growing up to be cities.

Joset himself would become a familiar and revered figure during the latter years, taking his privileged free passage on stages or railroad lines, or lost in prayer on the seat of his supply wagon in what had now become the booming "Inland Empire" as his horse wandered freely down the wrong side of city streets; his ingrained prayer customs could never quite be reconciled to this non-wilderness milieu. You will not find his name in the history books; a rare historian will note in passing that he played some minor role in the Coeur d'Alene troubles.

But Père Joset had not lived for the historians. He had lived for his God and his fellow-man. At the turn of the century, June 19, 1900, the old priest closed his eyes on a world vastly different to that he had entered in 1810. He left quietly to join his fellow-men in the eternal enjoyment of God.

I<small>T TOOK</small> *"Old Hickory," Andrew Jackson, to make the West feel it was part of America. On inauguration day great crowds pushed through the White House in wild enthusiasm. Washington was startled by this backwoods invasion. Meanwhile in Europe Metternich was trying vainly to keep the old order together. Kingdoms were toppling, colonies in the new world breaking loose from their mother-land. All South and Central America was in ferment. Leaders like the vaunted Bolivar set contagion afoot wherever they went.*

But America had little time for the ancient world. She scrawled hurriedly, in black and white, pronouncements of hemispheric solidarity. Be and let be—was the scope of her brass-knuckled policy set down by President Monroe. The nation's internal problems alone were more than she could care for. Florida was long a state now. Texas, the lone star, threw her lot with America, and "Remember the Alamo" became briefly a rallying cry for the nascent loyalties of her various peoples.

Then came gold in California. Men died in the rush of '49; but when it was over, America's long arm had reached to the Southern Pacific and the Mexican border. The Santa Fe ploughed its hot sandy route through sagebrush and majesty. By now the Iron Horse was moving farther inland, forging the West to the East link by link.

The distant rumbling of the slavery question grew louder. Harriet Beecher Stowe penned her "Uncle Tom's Cabin" and whipped New England righteousness to a gale. Protestant resentment to the Mother Church began to grow mightily too. The promise of Catholic influence could no longer be ignored. Maria Monk became notorious. Louisville had her Bloody Monday against Romans, and in Philadelphia loyal "Native Americans" rioted against the Church, killed and wounded many, burned the Augustinian library. Men's tempers were frayed with controversy.

* * *

Out of the Dusk

Father John Bapst, S.J.

by LEONARD KOHLMAN, S.J.

Out of the night there came a cry, "Help, Brother! Help, they are coming through the windows." The Brother infirmarian of the old novitiate roused up and shook the cobwebs of sleep from his head. He turned toward the window and saw nothing more than the curtains fluttering in the night wind. "It's all right, Father; they won't bother you, I'm here," he said as he lit a lamp. In its flickering the old priest stared unseeingly at the spot where his tormenters had only this moment disappeared. He was a man who looked a score more than his age of sixty years, and his eyes had the blankness of the empty windows in an old house where no one lives. It was always on dark windy nights like this that Father Bapst saw the mob creeping upon him, and sought companionship to drive away his terrors.

Yes, he was a haunted man who had lost contact with reality. His only reality were phantoms out of a troubled life. There was no realization of time or place. He was reliving the past to the exclusion of all else, and it was an incident thirty years in the past that was haunting him once more.

That night the wind was churning down the Maine coast like a thousand ghostly horses, and their hoofs sprayed sleet from the heavy clouds. It was a choking storm that had spent most of its fury, but the sea still rolled heavily. There was finally a lull when the clouds were pried apart by the wind, and a reflection from the pale October moon showed a slippery and deserted dock in the town of Ellsworth, Maine. On the dock there was only a pile of rotting rope, tarred and white, sea-stained. But it was not rope . . . it began to move . . . it was alive, it moaned . . . it wept. There is no beast with a cry like that. It was a man . . . at least it gained two unsteady feet and reeled away into the night like a blind man who had lost all sense of balance. He was not sure if the mob had followed him. He didn't care, for on this night they had ridden him on a rail, tried to burn him alive, and finally tarred and feathered him and dumped him on the dock unconscious or dead—it didn't matter to them.

There were other things that Father John Bapst remembered, both beautiful and terrible.

Going back to shortly after his ordination in 1847, there was that last night in his beloved country. A night without sleep . . . only dreams. The Jesuits had been exiled from Switzerland, and this was almost more than a generous Swiss heart could stand. It was a choice between God and country. It seemed as reasonable to offer a man his choice between food and drink—knowing that he could not live long without both.

His mind kept turning to the village of La Roche like a bird circling back to its nest . . . here were the Alps; their majesty and their terror had given him his first glimpse into the unknown might of God.

In the beginning of his religious life he had made a contemplation that told him to look on creation in order to know and praise the Creator. Did they think he was blind and dumb? The mountains and the storms were his personality . . . it was shocking to realize now that his Swiss enthusiasm had run away with him. He had been elevated by the gifts of God, and he saw that his thoughts should not have been directed inward but outward, and the outward direction dare not pause with creatures, but must extend to their Maker. He had hung up at mid-point, and even now he could see half madly that he had been selfish. He said a prayer of thanksgiving that he had not perished because of the darkness, that the mist had not covered his face . . . as the darkness in the east was broken by a bar of gray . . . the bar of gray was split by needles of silver and morning lifted itself laboriously over his beloved Alps; Bapst had bowed a humbled head and said, "Take, O Lord, and receive Thy unprofitable servant."

With the majority of the other Swiss exiles, Father John was sent to France. There he commenced the final year of training. It is known as the tertianship, and is devoted to prayer and study of the spiritual life. Its purpose is to reorientate the man after fourteen years of study and teaching—to plant his feet solidly on the ground so that he will be able to march to the ends of the earth for the glory of God.

This Bapst was a young man of character and talent. His strongest talents pointed to a life of teaching in the colleges, for he was brilliant, and his keen mind was bent toward that kind of life. So it was a commonly accepted fact that he had his vocation set out for him at home, and would be ill-fitted for the foreign missions. Father John was open with his fellow priests and enjoyed the give and take of community life; he had always freely admitted a natural aversion to the missions and his fellow tertians had great sport badgering him about his future travels across oceans and continents.

One night he had a strange dream for a student, ridiculous, in fact, he thought, as he awoke. He saw a race of men before him and could not, for all the books he had read, make out what race they were. They were neither white nor black, nor were they Asiatics. A voice said quite distinctly, "John, tomorrow you will set out to work among these people."

In the morning the dream was still perfectly present to his mind. He was eager to tell it in recreation and the Fathers pounced on it and stretched it to the limits of their poetical and practical imaginations. Since they were so well aware of his repugnance for the missions, the humor of the event was all the more pointed. "Prepare ye the way of the Lord, John. Pull down the mountains and fill the valleys with books—you'll have no more use for them." "John, give me a second intention in your seventh shipwreck." "Bow down, ye heathen gods, for here cometh the yodeling Swiss apostle."

When John laughingly told them that he was to set out this very same day, they almost overwhelmed him with exotic and ridiculous requests for various items from the seven seas.

Yes, it was a jolly time they had at the expense of the dreamer and he enjoyed the bantering as much as any of them, but at three o'clock that afternoon he received a letter from his Provincial Superior, ordering him to start immediately for Antwerp and await passage for the American Missions. John was so stunned he sat down and cried. It is a terrible thing to see a grown man cry, but John had received a terrible shock—here was the frustration of all his hopes. Here he thought he had been close to Christ, and now Christ asked a thing so repugnant.

His friends sorrowed with him. "Write the Provincial," they told him; "he surely doesn't understand the situation; he'd gladly let you stay." "No," John answered, "if I am half a man, and if I mean half the things I've been pledging for years, I'll go." So by six o'clock that afternoon he was on his way to America.

It was a dismal journey, but its slowness was welcome in a way. If he were going to be a missionary in spite of his natural revulsion, he had to marshal his forces. After all, what forces did he have? A head full of assorted knowledge and syllogisms. No languages but French and a smattering of German. Latin and Greek and Hebrew were useless in America. He had no practical turn of mind and no knowledge of finances. How could he run a mission and support it? He was a Catholic, a priest, and a Jesuit—three terms of opprobrium if he could believe the frequent stories of bigotry he had heard.

There was one way out—the grace of God; but, he thought sadly, all these years he had been putting his trust in the Sacred Heart he had been deceiving himself. He had not really trusted Christ and his final dependence had always been on John Bapst. Why should God trust him when he had practically denied Him twice? His selfishness in leaving Switzerland and his rebellion against the missions were disgraceful. How serious had his daily prayer, the *Suscipe*, been? "Take, O Lord, and receive all my liberty; my memory, my understanding and my whole will . . . give me only Thy love and Thy grace. . . ."

When he landed in New York, he trusted neither himself nor America, but he was willing to accept whatever it offered. In the grand shuffle that followed the arrival of forty new missionaries, he was offered the Indian Mission at Old Town, Maine. He accepted with some disappointment, for the hardest thing he could imagine on the missions would be a life alone—separated from his fellow religious. He proceeded to Boston with Father Eck, his last friend in this world. After a few days he set out alone, ignorant of the language and country, for his apostolate.

The Penobscot Indians welcomed their priest with a day of rejoicing. He wrote to his Superior:

They led me first to the church, where, after a hymn of thanksgiving, I wished to address them a few words in French; but I soon saw that no one understood me . . . when I saw myself alone on that wild island, three thousand leagues from my own country, my heart still sad with the thoughts which overpowered me when I broke the ties . . . then for the first time I realized the full import of the sacrifice . . . the mission of Old Town was founded by a father of the old Society, Father Rasle. After he had converted the savages of Maine, and had devoted himself to their service during more than twenty years . . . he was at last butchered by the Protestants at the foot of a cross which he himself had erected.

This mission had been fitfully cared for during sixty years, and these people had not had a priest living among them for over twenty years. Bapst continues:

I had imagined on my arrival that all the Indians were still good Catholics . . . my illusion did not last long . . . the Indians are commonly drunkards by profession; perhaps half of them no longer believe in hell, nor puragtory, nor confession, nor Communion, nor Church, nor fasts, nor festivals, nor anything else; moreover, they are estranged from each other by such implacable hatred that they are driven from time to time to the very last excess.

Here the next three years were spent trying to unravel the prejudices and bad habits of these Indians whom he came to love as his own children. He learned their language and at first had great success, but when it became evident that he was not satisfied with professions of faith, but insisted on charity and temperance in practice, the more recalcitrant members of the tribe turned bitterly against him. The division of the tribe that he spoke of was social, political, and religious. His presence brought these differences to a head, and he was fought at every turn. He exercised a remarkable zeal that wasted no motion and lost no time on dreams.

He showed a likewise remarkable prudence in maintaining a neutrality that could give offense to neither side. He tried to make peace, but failed. He tried to start a Catholic school, but they counter-attacked with a government-supported Protestant school—all his efforts were in vain; and since his life had been threatened, he was removed by his superiors to a new and more promising mission field.

He had not been a total failure among the Indians; for when he left, a great number of them came down to the shore with tears in their eyes. This was a rare thing among these wild people who were not known to weep even when their dearest relatives died.

Bapst was already a different man from the one who had come to America. There was a bias that his spirit of fairness had forced him to drop. There had even been a doubtful feeling about his fellow Jesuits, but he now wrote to one of his brother priests in Europe:

About a month ago, when I was worn out . . . from the oppressing influence of a three years' solitary life among the Indians, Rev. Fr. Brocard . . . invited me . . . to seek a little necessary recreation by taking a trip to Georgetown, and visiting on the way the various houses of the Maryland Province. Before undertaking this journey I had formed many prejudices against the province of Maryland, due to the unfavorable reports . . . which I had frequently heard before coming to this country. But this visit has dispelled all my prejudices. I now firmly believe that the Province of Maryland is as flourishing, from a religious point of view, as any province in Europe; I would no longer have any repugnance to casting my lot with that of this dear province, and becoming a member of it.

So it was late in 1850 that Bapst moved from his untenable mission field and established a new one. His duties were undefined and the procedure was left to his own judgment. There were at that time in Maine only four places in the entire state where there were priests to care for the people. In most of these places there were only individual priests who were so busy in their own parishes that there was no time to evangelize the neighboring districts. Bapst was to care for the rest of the Catholics in the State.

The first thing that was apparent was the vastness of the territory to be covered: a territory of over two hundred square miles where there were thousands of Catholics that had been away from the Church for years. Bapst obtained two priests to help in this new undertaking and moved his headquarters to Eastport, which is on the coast just across the river from New Brunswick.

The Catholics were in a miserable state. They were mostly of the lower social strata. They were Irish immigrants and French Canadians. Most of them were not fervent examples of Catholicity, and they were beset with too much liquor for their own good. They were looked down on by their Protestant betters, but despite all this a surprising number of them had held tenaciously to their Faith.

The missionaries founded thirty-three mission stations and covered them by every means of transportation from steamboats to horse-back to walking. At the beginning they had to swallow their pride and beg for enough to keep alive. When they had become established, they immediately began erecting new chapels. These were financed by the simple procedure of having all the money collected or subscribed before any work was done. It was a fool-proof procedure.

For the next three years no one heard much of the missionaries, for such mission work as they had offered little of the exotic or of the unusual. There were heartbreaks and consolations, but it was mostly weariness and toil—day after day. They tried to multiply themselves to care for the nine thousand souls and to be in more places at once than was humanly possible. The people's faith was strong, but in many cases there were too many temptations. These weaker members always appreciated the moral strength that the priest's presence gave their good resolutions, and they needed the grace of the sacraments.

Temperance societies were founded that were successful and even gained praise from the Protestants. Their new chapels increased to a dozen. The Catholic religion was becoming solidly established and even respected. It was a story that was thrilling only in the slowly manifest economy of Divine Grace.

It looked for a while as though the missions might be doomed. The provincial of the Maryland Province was so short of men that he considered removing his three priests from Maine. Bapst pointed out to him that he could not, in justice, leave nine thousand people without a pastor. To this the provincial replied by sending the long requested fourth Jesuit to help on the mission.

It was now possible to move two of the priests to a new center of operations, and Bapst chose Ellsworth, a town about a hundred and fifty miles southwest of Eastport. This saved a tremendous amount of travel and allowed time for more permanent foundations.

A word about the background against which Bapst was working. Protestantism was something that deserved the serious consideration of a priest in Maine in the 1850's. No, it wasn't Protestantism itself, but a bigotry which it had sired. When we look back a hundred years, it is a little more difficult to visualize such things as the burning of convents—committees appointed by the state legislatures to inspect all Catholic institutions and to stamp out the violations of the moral law that were supposed to be rampant there. To them priests were profligates and nuns were "women of ill repute." Convents were "dens of vice" and no respectable person would ever admit membership in the Catholic Church. These were the opinions of a party called the Know Nothings. They were considered a political party, but they were essentially a secret society pledged to the destruction of Catholicism, Popery, Immigration, and Slavery.

The "Popish Priest" was watched with cat-like scrutiny, but "they could find no cause in him." Like their forefathers, the witch-burners, this only confirmed their certainty of his guilt and of his Jesuitical cleverness. They did not yet have the courage to attack him openly, but they passed many a remark at the cross-roads and reviled the Catholic children for their simplicity in being taken in by the priest.

The State Legislature of Maine was controlled by the Know Nothings—bigotry was deeply rooted on either side of nearly any question a common man was likely to consider.

Bapst, fortunately, had enough sense to distinguish between the prudent and the hot-heads, and claimed many good Protestants as his stanchest friends. To his brother priest in Europe, who was Rector of the College of Brussels, he wrote:

For my own part, I can honestly assert that since my arrival in these regions, I have been treated with the greatest respect by the Protestants, although every one knows that I am a Catholic priest and even a Jesuit. Indeed I enjoy an esteem which would certainly not be mine, were I not a priest or a Jesuit. You may think, perhaps, that I am indulging in exaggeration . . . but such is the bright side of American liberty. . . .

In fact, he was forced to pay them a tribute of honesty that it had taken his European mind a long time to realize and accept.

I may be mistaken, but I feel convinced that if there were in this part of the world some zealous and learned missioners, capable of speaking the English language well, a great number of conversions would soon be effected among the most prominent people of this part of the United States. For Protestantism in this region has seen its best days: it cannot maintain its stand before the good sense of the Americans.

The ache in his heart for Switzerland remained, but it was overshadowed by love for his adopted country and its people:

There is still another thing which is worthy of consideration. The United States is the freest country in the world. You believe yourselves free in France and in Belgium: but be assured that you possess but the shadow of the liberty which we enjoy in America. I can establish here as many schools as I wish, and no one will interfere . . . what is more, I could preach the doctrines of the Catholic religion in the most Protestant town, before an audience composed entirely of Protestants, and I feel sure that I would not suffer a single interruption.

Recently an American gentleman delivered a public lecture at Bangor, a town not far from here. He was a Protestant; and what do you think was the subject of his lecture? A strange one indeed! I will wager a dollar that you will not guess it. He chose for his subject no less a topic than the Jesuits; and a Catholic priest, who was one of his audience, assures me that he never heard a eulogy of the Society of Jesus that was more eloquent, loftier and more correct than this tribute from a Protestant.

And in what spirit do you suppose his hearers greeted his remarks? They responded by frequent applause, although his entire audience was composed of Protestants, and the city itself is Protestant. What do you say to such an event as that? Let a like discourse be delivered in your Catholic France or Belgium, and we shall see whether it meet with a like reception.

Yet there was a reverse side to the coin and no better words than Bapst's own narrative can tell it.

When I first came to Ellsworth, I began a course of Sunday afternoon lectures on the doctrines of the Church. These instructions drew to the afternoon service on Sundays a large concourse of Protestants, curious to know what could be said in defense of a religious system which in their opinion had long before been thoroughly exploded.

The results of my labors were most gratifying. Before many months had elapsed I had gathered into the fold a goodly number of Protestants, and among them twelve young ladies, all members of prominent families of the town. Religious feeling ran high in consequence. I was denounced, from the pulpit and in the press, as a perverter of the young. I was warned to stop my work of proselytizing, and of reducing free-born Americans to Rome's galling yoke. All manner of threats were uttered against me.

To add fuel to the already fiercely burning fire of religious hatred, Catholics whose children attended the public schools of the town protested against the law recently passed by the school committee of Ellsworth, whereby their sons and daughters were forced under pain of expulsion to read in the school the Protestant version of the Bible and to join in the Protestant prayers.

They petitioned the committee to permit the Catholic children to read the Catholic version, or else to excuse them from reading any. In their petition they expressly declared that they had no desire to interfere with the right of Protestant children to read any version deemed proper by their parents, but simply wished to protect the religious faith of their own children. I knew that the board as a whole had an intense hatred of all that was Catholic and foreign, but I found some of the committee, as well as the teachers, willing to accede to my request that the children be not forced to act against the dictates of their consciences by reading a Protestant version of the Bible and by uniting in prayers not approved by the Church.

I was the more anxious to ward off these dangers, as I knew on good authority that one of the members of the school board had said openly: "We are determined to protestantize the Catholic children; they shall read the Protestant Bible or be dismissed from the schools . . ." I could not, therefore, in conscience permit my Catholic children to join in the Protestant religious exercises, as such a course would be a virtual profession of Protestantism, seeing that the regulation was insisted upon in hatred of the true Faith. I did not wish to excite our enemies unnecessarily, and did all I could to lower the high pitch to which the public mind had been excited. I held in check the overwrought feelings of my flock, and abstained from all bitterness in pushing the righteous claims of my people. But in vain!

The protest, signed by over a hundred Catholics, which was presented to the consideration of the school board one morning in November, 1853, by Mr. White and myself, was rejected with insult and abuse. Next day Messrs. Tisdale and Richards, two members of the board, went to the school where most of the Catholic children attended, and forthwith expelled all who refused to read the Protestant Bible.

I was therefore obliged to provide means of instruction for these dear little confessors of Christ. I opened a Catholic school in our old chapel, but in thus baffling the plan of our adversaries, who were intent upon obtaining an unconditional surrender on the part of the Catholics, I was much pained to find that I only increased their blind fury against us. The chapel was blown up one night, and we were obliged to transfer the school to the galleries of the new church. To try whether the law could provide a remedy by declaring the cause of the school board unconstitutional, a test case was made in behalf of the son of Lawrence Donahoe, and a suit commenced against the committee, but to no purpose. Bigotry won the day.

An incident that happened shortly before the dismissal of the children from the school added fuel to the flames. I was drawn, much against my will, into controversy with one of the Protestant ministers of the town, and defeated him so completely as to put the Protestants present to the blush for their poor champion. It came about as follows:

One morning business called me to the office of one of the town lawyers, and while I was engaged with him, who should come in but the other powers of the town, the leading minister and the most popular doctor of the place. After I had politely saluted them both, I overheard the lawyer whisper to the minister: "Now you have got the papist priest at your mercy; give it to him!" I saw from the confident smile of the lawyer and doctor that they anticipated an easy victory for their clerical champion. He, no wise unwilling, entered the fray without gloves, and abruptly put forth this astonishing statement: "You Catholics despise the Bible. You have no faith in the written Word of God. How can you call yourselves Christians?"

To this exceedingly ill-timed remark I would have gladly avoided giving an answer, but as I considered that silence would be taken for assent, I quietly and gently proceeded to pursue a line of argument whereby the minister would be put to rout by his own admission. "Well," said I, "supposing, Reverend Sir, that your statement be correct, that we set no value on the Bible, granting this to be true for the sake of argument, may I ask you, with all due respect, do you set any value on oral tradition?" "No, of course not," replied the minister with a deep frown, "that is a popish doctrine." "Well then," I said, "may I ask you why you value the Bible so highly? How do you know it is the Word of God?" "Why," he replied, "it bears the divine imprint on its every page." "Those who have read the Koran and the works of Confucius," I said, "have found them very like in style to the Bible, yet these are certainly not the Word of God." "Well," replied the now greatly excited minister, "our forefathers have always revered the Bible as the Word of God, and have so taught their descendants."

"But how were your forefathers able with certainty to hold the Bible as from God?" "Why, my dear sir, how simple you are! They had the testimony of their ancestors to that effect, and these ancestors had the testimony of theirs, and so on up to the time of Christ." "Well, Reverend Sir, excuse me if I ask one more question. What do you call that, oral testimony? I am sure you are too honest to deny that this is oral tradition under another name, and therefore your Bible has no intrinsic value without the aid of tradition."

The expression of the minister's face was terrible to behold. It was one of baffled hatred and shame. He did not venture a reply, but turned from me abruptly, and sought the fellowship of the two spectators who had been in full sympathy with him from the opening of the tilt. When I was leaving the office, I overheard the lawyer mutter the following words expressive of his deep chagrin: "Well, I could have stood our parson's being overcome by an enlightened American, but to have had him completely routed by one of these Romish foreigners—a man who can't speak two words of English correctly—it's a crying shame!"

The fanatical fury of the Know Nothing party increased with time, and at length reached such a pitch that, after destroying the old church, they broke the windows of my dwelling. This happened on the evening of June 3, 1854. From the early part of the preceding November the agitation was kept alive by the Ellsworth *Herald* in its daily attacks on the Catholics, and on Sundays by the tirades of the minister. On June 6, the mob broke the windows of our church, and then went to the nearest tavern to muster up courage for further outrages, threatening all the while to inflict all manner of injury upon the Catholics.

At this stage of the excitement I was directed by Bishop Fitzpatrick of Boston to take up my permanent abode at Bangor, which I had previously cared for as its temporary pastor, pending the appointment of a secular priest as successor to Father O'Sullivan. I was ordered by the bishop not to return to Ellsworth even for the Sunday services, but to send another Father who was not connected with the school trouble.

On the morning of July 16, word came to Bangor that the untiring mob of Ellsworth had attempted to burn down the chapel at one o'clock that morning. The fire was luckily discovered in time by Amory Otis, one of the right-minded citizens of Ellsworth, and put out before any damage was done except to the cellar.

After blowing up the school-house, the Protestants feared reprisals and the more level-headed called a public meeting to denounce the affair and declare it the work of "ignorant bigots."

When they arrived at the meeting, they found that the Know Nothing element had taken possession. The good gentlemen withdrew for fear that their presence might be taken as an approval of the proceedings. Their doubts about the sanity of the meeting were correct, for here is the resolution that was passed without a dissenting vote and was cheered to an echo:

July 8, 1854.

Moved by George W. Madox—That if John Bapst, S.J., be found again on Ellsworth soil we will provide for him, and try on an entire suit of new clothes such as cannot be found at the shops of any tailor (*sic*), and that when thus apparelled he be presented with a free ticket to leave Ellsworth upon the first railroad operation that may go into effect.

Voted, that the resolutions adopted at this meeting be published in the Ellsworth *Herald* and *Eastern Freeman*.

Voted, that we now adjourn *sine die*.

W. A. Chaney, Town Clerk.

The declaration of hostility was now formal; and after the attempt to burn the church had failed, the mob seemed to be pacified by their victory in having the priest moved out of their city to Bangor. It was only by the efforts of Bapst that the Catholics had been restrained during these violent times. It now seemed that things would quiet down and be forgotten.

On October 14 the storm finally broke. Father John had received a sick-call from a village some miles on the other side of Ellsworth from Bangor; when he was returning through Ellsworth that Saturday evening, he thought there would be no harm in stopping over to hear confessions that night and in saying Mass for the people the next morning.

He went to the house of an Irish Catholic named Kent—for it would have been folly to show himself at the rectory. When darkness set in, the house was surrounded by a mob dressed in white with faces securely masked. They blasphemously demanded the priest. Mr. Kent had induced Father Bapst to crawl through a trap-door and hide himself in the cellar. Kent then opened the door and attempted to reason with his townsmen. They became more violent by the minute and threatened to burn the house if the priest were not produced immediately. When Bapst heard this, he came out and gave himself up to save the good man's property. He still thought these people had too much humanity to carry out their threat.

Out of the Dusk

With a yell they rushed upon the priest and dragged him out
of the house and up the road. He was mounted on a sharp rail
and borne along to the accompaniment of hooting and cursing.
They carried him out of town into a back field and robbed him
of his money and watch. He was then tied to a tree and brush
was piled around him; but they did not succeed in burning him
because it was damp and a violent storm lashed at the flames.
Some wanted to kill him and have done with it, but others insisted on carrying out the threat they had published. So they
dragged him into town and built a fire in the shelter of the
buildings to heat their tar—it was plastered over his naked body
and the feathers applied. One blasphemer cried, "So they persecuted Jesus of old." Another, "Call on the Virgin to help
you, you papist demon." Every obscene invective they could
lay their well practiced tongues to was heaped on this man who
loved purity. They tauntingly lifted the edges of their masks
and said, "Prophesy, O Forgiver of Sin—Who is your tailor!"

There was another "railroad journey" to the wharf, where
they dumped him totally unconscious from his sufferings. It
was again suggested to hang the priest, but someone thought it
was better to leave him. If he recovered, he would be forever
disgraced and his presence would add strength to their cause.
They went happily away savoring the taste of victory.

Father Bapst recovered consciousness sometime after midnight, wrapped a piece of matting around himself, and staggered
away from the wharf. Fortunately, he met an armed group of
the decent townsmen who were searching for his body. They
had not even dared to hope that they would find him alive.

They took him to a place of safety and attempted to remove
the tar and feathers as best they could. They tried hot water
and soap, but finally had to shave his hair and scrape his skin
raw. They then formed a guard to protect the priest for the
rest of the night.

On Sunday morning Bapst had the people assembled for Mass.
It was perhaps a foolish thing, for the Know Nothings had
warned him that if he was again seen alive in the town of Ells-

worth—he would not live long. This did not deter him in the least—one of the Protestants said, thirty years later:

Father Bapst preached the next day in his church, for although of a very mild disposition, he had the heart of a lion in the cause of duty.

It was his duty to calm his parishioners, who were so aroused they would have fought to the death to avenge the disgrace of their pastor.

He begged them not to act like a mob of bigots themselves, and not to disgrace their religion by their bitterness. He reminded them of Divine Justice, "Revenge is Mine, I will repay, saith the Lord."

To this he added the argument of charity—that stumbling-block of nations, "Bless them that persecute you: bless and curse not."

This is the kind of heroism that one associates with the saints, but to Bapst there was no reflection of heroism connected with it: it was simply his duty as pastor. If he had reflected, he might have gone one step farther and applied the justice that charity itself contains: "Do good to those that persecute you and you will heap coals of fire upon their heads." But it was not in his character to seek even the revenge of the righteous; he was simply attempting to do away with the bigotry that stained the American spirit of freedom which he was coming so to love.

He stayed over Sunday and said Mass again on Monday morning and one of his Protestant friends drove him back to Bangor in his own carriage. The citizens of Bangor had heard of the events that preceded him and turned out almost to a man to welcome him.

Later the whole town held a banquet in his behalf, and Bapst was amazed at the tribute some of his former enemies paid him in public. They presented him a purse of money and the best gold watch that could be made in reparation for that which had been stolen from him by the mob. There were praises of his bravery and charity. He wept with joy—the reward of his forbearance was so sudden that he was overwhelmed and could scarcely utter a word of gratitude.

The quasi-martyrdom of this priest fanned the spark of faith that he had been nurturing in Maine to a brilliant fire. Confidence in the Catholic Church sky-rocketed, and Bapst became the friend and counselor for the whole countryside.

It may seem strange, but the Jesuits were removed from Maine in 1859. Just when things began to look promising they were moved. Well, the Jesuits have a double apostolate—the missions and the schools. When a mission territory becomes established, and the local bishop has enough priests to care for the parishes, they willingly hand over their work to other men. They seldom lay further claim to the territory.

So Bapst was on the move again. He was spiritual director in one of the Jesuit houses of study, and he then became the first rector of Boston College in 1860. When it was closed three years later because of the Civil War, he became pastor of the Jesuit Church in Boston. He was thus employed in positions of trust until '69, when he was made superior of the New York and Canadian Mission. This territory was independent but not self-sufficient. It required resourcefulness and keen judgment in its superior to recruit and deploy his men to the greatest benefit, and there was no end to its financial problems.

There was a peculiar thing about this superiorship. The Society of Jesus is ordinarily run as a monarchy, and all important superiors are appointed by the General in Rome. Not so with Father Bapst. He was so popular and so exhibited the wisdom of a genius and the humility of a child that the Fathers of his territory wrote to Rome and asked to have him appointed as superior. It was a rare event in the Society and a most unusual tribute.

By 1873 Bapst's health began to fail, and he was relieved of his job as superior. His work was not finished, though, and he kept giving retreats for six more years.

His specialty, for some time, had been in conducting retreats for the diocesan priests. He had given these retreats from the Gulf of Mexico to the St. Lawrence and beyond. He came back to the same places and to the same men year after year, and they never wearied of him.

Now, a retreat is eight days of prayer, silence, and meditation. The director's job is to give the points for meditation and conferences on various phases of the spiritual life. Priests are not beginners in spiritual matters. They know all the answers. It takes more than a glib and clever man to interest them and compel them to attack their pride at its roots and surrender to grace.

The Yankees have a strict code of individualism, and the Maine Yankee is probably the most self-sufficient of them all. His code could be summed up:

> God bless me and my wife,
> *My son John and his wife,*
> Us four,
> No more.

But the Yankees saw that Bapst's code was charity—a love that knew no bounds. He was accessible to old and young, rich and poor. The sorrows of others became his own. The poorer, the more obscure the applicant, the more claim he seemed to have on Bapst's sympathies and assistance. Simple and childlike in his nature, he knew in his priestly character no difference in talent or rank. The Yankee axiom, "God helps him who helps himself," collapsed. His life and teaching were summed up in "Love thy neighbor as thyself," and it was a strange truth to these people whose hearts were as rocky as their soil. But there is an insistence in love that will not be denied. Life, liberty, and pursuit of happiness is another way of saying the same thing, but it is cold and impersonal when compared with Bapst's creed.

He left a tradition of a true Americanism in the whole of New England that is not written on paper but in the hearts of its children. He was no different from the scores of Jesuits and brother priests who were working with him to the same end. He is remembered only because of the one incident that happened in Ellsworth when he proved his mettle. His whole life is otherwise hidden in the rush of progress, but his spirit remains.

It remains in the small hamlets of Vermont and New Hampshire, in the great and flourishing faith of Connecticut, Rhode Island, Massachussets, and New Jersey. This was the field God gave John Bapst to sow and today reapers are at work on the abundant harvest with which He crowned the labor of His pioneer priests.

There are many things easier to write about than the next and final scene of Bapst's life. Many Americans have a warped psychology, a psychology divorced from truth when we come to the question of insanity. It is hard to say where we picked up these distorted impressions. It may be from a gibbering materialism or a fatalistic Puritanism—the fact remains that we are insane in our judgment of insanity. We consider a person who loses his mind as one lacking in mental discipline or one who is seeking to escape from reality. We attach a stigma that is not just.

Bapst had lived an intense life that would have snapped the spirit of less generous men. He faced crises that we would have turned away from in shame. Many times the prospect of martyrdom hung over his head when he was among the Indians, and he admitted that he could not face such an end and would probably abandon his post without warning. He finally grew in stature enough to endure anything that could be offered in suffering or death when it hinged on his Faith. He did suffer, but his total offering was not accepted—then there came a day when he realized that he was walking in the valley of the living-dead. Shame and despair walked with him.

There now came to Bapst a humiliation that few Christian ascetics ordinarily consider. The loss of his memory and understanding.

Again he said, as he had so many years ago in France, "If I am a man, I will accept. I have been saying my *Suscipe* daily for years and I never realized the meaning of 'Take, O Lord, and receive, my memory, my understanding and my will.' Mine is to pray with Job. 'God hath softened my heart: and the Almighty hath troubled me. For I have not perished because of the darkness that hangs over me: neither hath the mist covered my face.'"

I Lift My Lamp

Out of the dusk a shadow,
 Then, a spark,
Out of the cloud a silence,
 Then a lark;
Out of the heart a rapture,
 Then a pain;
Out of the dead cold ashes,
 Life again.

(*Evolution* by John B. Tabb)

THE NATION *entered on travail. Crisis was in the offing. Storm clouds gathered at the Dred Scott Decision. There was John Brown with frenzied eyes at Harper's Ferry. Each territory seeking entrance to the Union was victim to the strife. Southern gallantry bridled at insult from the North. Northern wrath pilloried the real and fancied wrongs, the brandished whip.*

Into the White House strode the tall gaunt Lincoln, heir to these fears, the rampant indignation. Greatness flowed in his blood. Only the lean supple shoulders of a mighty man could assume these burdens: free the slaves, hold the Republic together, preserve the Union. The shoulders would sag, the head bow.

War broke, national fratricide. "Dixie" and "Yankee Doodle" blared on every battle-field where the blue and the gray fought tragically for honor and right. Brave generals struggled up and down the land—Jackson and Robert E. Lee, Grant and Sherman. No man could tell how it would end.

But the will of Lincoln, steel-wrought, warm with compassion, presided at America's darkest hour. At Gettysburg his name was writ in words of gold and fire. They would not be erased. Then one night his assassin stole from him his life just when the man was needed most to heal the wounds, to reconcile and assuage the bitterness.

Still the wheels of progress turned. From across the seas came the Russians and the Poles to fill the foundries and split the rails. Hardy miners pushed into the mountains beyond the Black Hills. Brigham Young's colony flourished in distant Utah. And the country was glad now that Sacajewea had opened for Lewis and Clark those long years ago such promise in the Far West. Time would stanch the flow of strife.

* * *

The Builder

Father Arnold Damen, S.J.

by John P. Leary, S.J.

It is fascinating to watch twilight settle on a great city. You notice the way flickering neons mingle with the sunset, and how night comes stealing out of the east to muffle the roar of the throngs. You see the lines in weary faces begin to loosen, the tired constriction of forehead and eyes gradually relaxed. You think how merciful the night is when stillness washes the world of its heartache and when the dark hides the anguish and the anxiety of the day.

I remember once sitting at a hotel window looking down on just such a city, that great establishment they call Chicago. It was evening, just the time of day when her vast skyline had flung itself against the dusk, etched sharp and proud above the turmoil. Eleven stories below me were the sidewalks buried in humanity, the careening cabs, the subterranean roar of trains and tunnels scooping workers miles away to the suburbs, the jammed doorways of the Owl Drug and Sears-Roebuck, the pale tiny lights starting to flash from the windows of the Trib down the way.

It was like any American city at closing hour, I suppose. All of this excitement, the noise and rush, the cry of the newsboy had become part and parcel of the national scene. All of this was going on daily in Boston and Baltimore, Kansas City and Seattle. All of these American cities were phenomenal. They were like small boys grown into giants over the weekend.

The ancient cities of the world, Paris and Bombay, London and storied Rome could look with arched eyebrow and disbelief at this upstart civilization, this youngest of man's children with its shattering energy and its dreams. But America seemed to give little heed—the march was in her blood. She would take all the old could offer, all that was good from the past, the beauty and wisdom, knowledge of the deep things of faith, the sure hand made steady by miscalculation, defeat, and want, the love of freedom, home, and the land. All of these things were hers from of old. And here in this new virgin country she would make the dream all men had always nurtured come true. She was doing precisely that.

One might take the story of any of her cities, save a few along the eastern seaboard, interchange the names, and the tale told would be the same. A wilderness, a lone cabin or general store, then the clustered group of log houses, the muddy streets, the first spigots of steel as the iron horse moved west. Then came a boom and wild growth, then calamity, fire, flood, or quake, then rebirth and a rate of progress that made even the natives rub their eyes as dawn at times caught the vast array in a burst of morning glory.

I like the story of Chicago because it, perhaps better than any other, shows the impact of mind upon matter, more specifically of an American mind, a man, in other words, with vision and with fire in his blood, set loose on a prairie by a lake and told to live and to fan the flames of faith. The time was limited, a hundred years perhaps to do what it had taken others a thousand years to do. Competition was stern. A whole continent was beckoning the venturesome man, and for the non-venturesome man in those days Ohio was the border of civilization. Go farther and you might have to reckon with the tomahawk and the stake.

It was about three centuries ago that the first white men hit Chicago; they were French on their way south from Canada: the young explorer Jolliet and the Catholic priest, Père Marquette. It looked to them for all the world like flat vacant land forked by two rivers, margined by an immense lake, a camping grounds for nomadic redmen now and then, but that was all.

That's the only thing we hear of Chicago for one hundred

years, just those scrawled details in the hand of the Jesuit priest. The Revolutionary War was in full flare when a Negro from San Domengo named Jean Baptiste au Sable built a cabin on the plain. A single lone cabin in all the prairie! That was Chicago in 1777, population, 1.

Just after the turn of the century, in '03, John Kinzie bought the Negro's house. He had trader's fever. This would be a good spot to carry on with pelts and beads. Before that time Governor Patrick Henry of give-me-liberty-or-give-me-death fame had sent an expedition into this western wilderness. Virginia claimed the whole Illinois territory as a county. Conquest, they said. New York was claiming it too. The result of a treaty with the Iroquois, they said.

Both states forewent their questionable right. The territory grew prodigiously. In 1818 Illinois was admitted to the Union. But where was Chicago? Just where it is now, only a hamlet by a lake. There were not 100 people there in 1830. No signs anywhere of what a future lay before it. Even to the neighbors, a complete nonentity. It was bandied around from county to county. No one seemed particularly to want it. Wayne County had it for a while (Detroit, too, by the way), then Madison County, then Edwards, Crawford, Clark, Pike, Fulton, Peoria, and finally Cook County.

In '31 boundary difficulties were cleared up in the Senate. Wisconsin would be sorry, and Illinois had no idea what it was getting for itself. But that was all to come.

And now a man comes into the story. Strange to what simple terms great and complex situations can be reduced. The world would know America better if it knew a Chicago. And to know Chicago, all one had to do was take it apart, find its elements in a breakdown, the moving spirit of the place, the men who drove it to greatness, slaved to make the vision real, the *man* who towered above his fellows and showed them the way.

In the fall of '37 a young Dutchman got his first look at the sidewalks of New York. He had just landed, but no one paid any attention. Shiploads of immigrants were landing so often, it was commonplace. New Yorkers did feel glad in a way, though, for they needed the people, and they needed droves of them out west too in Kansas and Indiana and Missouri. They needed cheap labor. These foreigners would serve well in pushing the frontiers.

The young fellow with the uncomfortable stiff collar was also going west. He had been recruited by a Jesuit priest named De Smet. The Father came one day to his school at Turnhout in Belgium and told the boys about what might be done in this new land. In fact, he quite set afire the whole establishment with his tales of America. The Dutch lad, Arnold Damen, decided he would become a priest too. He was old enough to make up his mind, 22 now, and he had had a longing for the altar since he was a boy.

There were Jesuits aplenty in the East in those days; their work and organization was ingeniously split into regional divisions—ranks were formed, then spread out; soon a new group formed itself in a new land. A band of the blackrobes had followed the early pioneers far into Missouri. Now the old missioner De Smet headed for the west with the glee of a miner who had struck it rich. These fine solid Lowlanders would help start a province; they would be the bulwark of the Church in this New World.

The train moved on with its smoke and terrible noise, along the flat Ohio farmlands, through Indiana and Illinois. No one even thought of mentioning Chicago with its pitiful frame buildings, its squalid poverty there by the lake. The engine roared on, past the covered wagons and schooners, the half-built houses, the bewildered Indians clustered in groups of awe by small stations. Late one afternoon they snorted close to St. Louis. Then by wagon they covered the last lap.

In rolling flat farmland near the little French settlement of Florissant in Missouri the Jesuits had set up their training quarters, a sort of West Point for the Order, where the men learned discipline, fidelity, and honor. It was a secluded spot, only a few miles from the great river.

The long grind began. The setup was one to try the calling of the most austere. Log cabins served for everything, chapel included. The novice-master who traditionally undertakes the stern task of shaping newcomers to the ideals of religious life did not tone down the doctrine he was expected to give.

The Church had one mission, he told them, the salvation of souls. This and this alone was paramount. It was an objective so impelling that men quite literally lived and died in every clime and under every appalling circumstance to promote the cause. No land was alien to the message of Christ; there was no such thing as a soil foreign to the teachings of the Church.

The Jesuit Order as an arm of the Church shared in this divine purpose. It set itself to adapt, to deploy, to influence those in high places and low places, to master language and custom and tradition, to use "every legitimate means that worldly men use in achieving their ends," but for a more lasting and valued ideal. Bit by bit the young men had unfolded before them the mystery and glory of the Order, a practical asceticism, a highly organized and competent spirituality that strove for results here and now, but was satisfied if they came a little later on.

For two years each man who entered and stayed, went through the training. And though it was hard, still the native vigor of youth was always at hand: ideals of the highest calibre were as native to them as blood to the arteries. And then, too, even in Missouri there was a God who shoved when the going was difficult and showed them the worth of it all, the things to laugh at, the aims to strive for, the hopes that beckoned in this new land.

Up every morning at 4:30 and to bed after 9, this was no life for less than a hardy soul. Woods to cut, fields to plough, water to draw, endless crops to care for, and with rude tools too. Through all of this and more young Arnold Damen conducted himself with thorough facility. He brought to all he did a zest and quiet strength that boded well for later days. He showed perhaps a rigor that needed tempering in those days. But it was an excess toward which any strong will would tend. His folks in far off Holland probably felt a little empty and sad when they received his rare letters filled more with exhortation and strong-headedness than the words of tender affection which they

needed. But time has its own way of ironing out wrinkles and
bending steel with the warm flame.

Before too many years Damen had passed successively through
the stages of training the Order demands. It was relatively short
in those days when the needs were overwhelming. A student, a
teacher, a priest. Seven years after he arrived, the Bishop in St.
Louis made him a priest one morning. It was a day of great joy
for him. And he began his new work almost at once.

In those days St. Louis was a wide open frontier town; the
liquor flowed and the dice fell, pretty much as we might think
a Laramie, Wyoming, or a Virginia City, Nevada, were at the
turn of our own century. But there remained, however, a fairly
representative segment of ancient French culture. It had been
under Spanish rule, too, for that matter. So one could find here
and there elements of Old World gentility. And devotion to the
Faith among the aristocratic element was strong. It was the men
coming in, the thousands of Walt Whitmans in search of adventure, who were sending its census a rocketing. This vanguard of American progress was what appalled him.

For the next thirteen years Father Damen set himself to the
task of a pastor. By this time he had grasped the idiom fairly
well, but was no preacher—yet, anyhow. What vigor the man
had though! There seemed to be no end to the work he could
do, the vast supply of energy that was stored up in the now
large and expansive frame. He went to the rich, where the
money was; he got the money and he used it, never on himself.
He was criticized for that . . . because he took money from
the rich and gave it to the poor. He didn't care. For he knew
that the first of all priests had been criticized quite literally to
death. He learned quite young that to do things and have everybody approve are mutually exclusive ideas in this man's world.

So he went on with amazing imperturbability . . . doing. Hard
times, and he opened soup kitchens; good times, and he went on
collecting funds, planning to build. Meanwhile he began to improve mightily as a preacher. He could tell how much more
effective he was becoming. God knows there was little competition, so little that by 1856 Damen found himself a man of pulpit

stature. His own inner response was immediate and he was not too proud to admit that his desires to convert great numbers of people could hardly keep within the pace provided by his limited opportunities.

A fellow priest of his, a hearty Irishman by the name of O'Regan, had heard Damen talk and liked him. One day a letter came from Rome telling O'Regan he was to be Bishop of Chicago. Before long, old friend in the East called on old friend in the West. Would Damen come and give a mission in Chicago? The problems in the place were immense. National differences, language problems, hypersensitivity, simply enormous waves of immigrants that no church could hold or to whom scarcely any priest could make himself understood created serious difficulties. Many of the people did not like the Bishop. Damen, when he went there, saw with what sullen disrespect they greeted him in procession to the church. He scolded them severely. No doubt about it, there was work to be done here. He was glad he had come.

Of course, Damen made a hit in Chicago; the people were drawn to him like nails to a magnet—some of them hard nails too by this time.

He left; nothing would do but for him to return. The Bishop begged and besought his superiors. Before the year was out, the man who helped make Chicago entered late one afternoon, inauspiciously, it is true, rather with the quite clerical and quite sombre dignity that his mission required.

The 1840 census of 5000 souls had twenty-fived itself by this time. A surge and roar of activity that would have stunned the Negro Jean Baptiste or the hardy American trader Kinzie seemed to make the great shore line of Lake Michigan quite alive; even in the dark it was bright with little boats and barges, flickering bobbing gas lamps, the flames of a forge dotted here and there along the land.

So here, then, one block west of what is now the corner of Roosevelt Road and Blue Island Avenue, Damen built the first log church for his parish, a mere matter of some 50 square miles, the whole west and southwest of Chicago. He offered Mass, the great Sacrifice, where, almost two centuries before, his brother Jesuit, Marquette, had done the same thing. What a linking of hands across centuries; this was indeed a welding together of purpose and brotherly endeavor. No time for fond recollections though. The builder had arrived. Chicago had found itself a dreamer with his two feet on the ground, this man with the gentle serious eyes, the voice of a lion, and plans for the future that would make any Chamber of Commerce blush with the thought of it.

In no time at all he could see this small church would not do. This prairie parish of his wasn't going to be that for long. The Poles and Germans were moving in by droves, most of them Catholics, looking for anything in their heartsickness that would help recreate the old world in the new. They flocked to the few bare churches. Over in Holy Family Parish, where the priest Damen worked, it was the Irish who swelled the district until he began to wonder how anyone could be left on that green isle across the sea.

And strange to say, they struck it off well, the bruising, big hearted, toe-to-toe Irishmen and the shrewd kindly Hollander with plans in his pocket. The first thing would be to build a church, so large that it would challenge a St. Patrick's and rank with the best in the country. He chose the spot, not a house around, only the flat land running into the sky, and there it was begun. His fellow Jesuits thought he had gone quite mad with his dreams—such an apparently sensible fellow too, and here he was building a church to hold thousands in a wilderness.

Then there was a little matter of financial panic sweeping the country in '57. Where was the money to come from for godfather's castle on the plain? How deep could one go in the cookie jar? Would there be no end to his imperturbable begging? No, there wouldn't. The people had a little, all of them a little, and he was going to see to it that they gave to build God a decent house, one in which they themselves could take honest pride.

Irish blood and sweat went into the church. The great pile began to rise, its solitary hulk a landmark in the emptiness.

Crowds began beating a muddy path to its door. And after a few months, little houses, old frame affairs, began to mushroom here and there. Damen's eyes had that told-you-so twinkle as he fingered the stem of his old pipe and marched out to collect the wages to pay the workers.

He barely kept ahead of his creditors. Letters to St. Louis asked for more money. Letters to Rome asked for money. He simply had to have it; his plans were too far along to change. It could be done so cheaply in these hard times. It would all be paid back. The funds still ran short. He determined to auction off his horse and carriage. He did that. And there was many a laugh at the dignified black soutane with the man in it picking its way gingerly along the broad avenues of mud that flanked his "cathedral." But somehow it hurt the self-respect of many a townsman: before long, the saloon keepers, the butchers, and the tradesmen had taken up their own collection and Damen went a-riding once more.

There just never was such a businessman. He would saunter up on a Monday morning to one of the foremen.

"Is your gang in charge of the roof?"

"Yes, Father," came the County Down reply.

"Well, now, I examined that roof myself yesterday afternoon; there's many a slate with only one nail to hold it. Have that fixed at once."

"Yes, yer Reverence," came the awed answer.

"And furthermore, you are using here and there nails without heads. They won't last. We'll have no roof at all with that kind of work and the wind in these parts and the rain. I am paying for the best, Mike, and I want it."

The little clusters of workmen would clear the way for him on those days. The bright fierceness below the eyebrows should not be tampered with. Common men always have a sense of propriety; frequently, even when they're drunk, they know when to steer the other way.

Up before dawn every morning the builder had said his Mass in the log church, mulled over in his mind for an hour the deep thoughts of faith that pounded for his attention along with several hundred distractions, then eaten his breakfast, and was out to make the most of another day before the workers arrived. That was a good chunk of business right there. One day he would pick up an old disillusioned artist about to return to Germany. Would he do some carvings, woodwork, communion rails, and so forth over at the new Holy Family Church. He would. The bargain would be struck, the grip unpacked.

Next day the portly figure would take pen in hand and ask in a choice flow of uninhibited American eloquence if His Paternity (the General of the Jesuit Order) would not like to furnish Stations of the Cross for this beautiful church in the New World . . . stations worthy of the General of the Society of Jesus. The General was sorry and undoubtedly somewhat amused. There was nothing he could do.

He was to find out that this frank priest out in the midwestern United States, in a place called, was it Chicago? should be named Arnold *Ask* Damen. Never any misgivings, or apologies. For a half century he went on asking. Never for himself, of course; that was what made the difference. He really knew how to appeal for churches, school, convents, and general facilities with magnificent detachment. His contemporaries noticed in him the round-eyed steady humility of a child who does not take NO for an answer, and who would never think of asking if it were not necessary.

Finally the church was done. It made an unprecedented sight, the dedication of this monarch on the plain. It was in August, and the ecclesiastical gentry from all over the States lent their presence to dignify the work of their friend. Damen was quite literally a friend to at least half of the American hierarchy. The muddy canals were dry then; cattle grazed for miles around; chickens and turkeys set up a great chatter and screech as the long procession made its way into the church.

The Irish thought that even His Lordship of Armagh could scarce be surrounded with more glory than this. And all through that day, as the stout flowed and the good cheer mounted to almost scandalous proportions, said many a Pat to many a Mike,

"You've got to hand it that Dutchman. Here he's gone and built us all the grandest church in this part of the world."

Damen had only begun. They didn't know that. And while they quaffed their "ale," neither did they know that a temperance crusade would be in full swing from the new pulpit before long. Not the Carrie Nation appeal, but a stolid, determined effort to save the Irish from too much celebration and the tragedies that sometimes followed. The organizational powers of the man were immense. In a few short years, he had from 15 to 20 large groups active in parish affairs.

Now the people came by droves. There were children. There must be a school. A Catholic school in those days was a novelty. There was no taken-for-granted principle that people who wanted their children to have a religious education should ignore the public schools and build their own, staff them, furnish them, and keep them going.

The priest had not only to do and take the lead in all these things. He was quite literally a pioneer who had to transmit his own vision, convince these people of the value of their own school. Well, by '65, he had almost 1000 boys in the parish school and there were 500 girls under the Religious of the Sacred Heart right near. Those were real numbers in any man's directory.

One day the school plant, old frame affair that it was, burned down. The undaunted pastor began all over again. Just when the Civil War was at its height. But he had 2000 families in the environs of Holy Family by this time. The school he built was the equal of any public building of its kind in the whole region. It held more than 2500 students and was always full.

They used to call it the Brothers' School. The first teachers were Jesuit Brothers Corcoran and O'Neill. No one who had them could forget them. And here it was the kindly hulk of Damen, the father, who superintended the sports, the bands, the swims, the picnics, the hikes, the study at night, the processions, the prayers.

The Irish had always loved to get up and speak their piece. Oratory flowed in their blood. Every St. Patrick's night, for example, the halls and grounds were jammed while the kids performed, ran off their come-all-ye's, danced the reels and jigs, and left the old-timers in laughter and tears. With all the dignity of middle age now stealing up on him, "the builder" would sit in row number one and chuckle with the sympathy that one Old Worlder has for another.

One almost has to check himself for possible optical illusions when he reads from the records that in the seventeen years of his administration there now stood eight schools with 5000 pupils; it was the largest parish school setup in the world. An association of 75 faithful lay teachers plus the nuns and Brothers helped carry on the vast work.

And the parish in that time had grown to such proportions that it needed 12 Jesuits full time to handle the work. The whole plant was a staggering monument to the energies and stimulus of any man. The city had soared from its meagre 90,000 upon his arrival to 280,000 by 1870.

Three-fourths of the population was immigrant. They might have gone any place, farther west, back east again, or home, but they stayed, and in Chicago. The fact was that an immigrant like themselves was showing them how it could be done. Even the simple and unlettered, stripped suddenly bare of their whole past in this new country, found solace and strong spiritual kinship in the Church. The Church helped them survive, to cement their differences, to fuse this new blood into a force that would do much good.

Whether he knew it or not, Damen was in many people's minds quite synonymous with the Church in those days. The Pope was far away; Bishops frequently overawed them; but Damen was of the people and yet sufficiently aloof to command their respect, sufficiently ingenious to win their admiration. He had some of their flaws, too, very obvious ones that the people could pick up and gossip about after he called on them or found their husbands in the saloon or gave a tongue lashing to one of the building bosses.

He was stingy at times, didn't always pay the wages he should, looked at every dollar twice before parting with it. And he was overly blunt, seemed to lose his temper too easily, and used his position to enforce his own ideas. The young Irish teenagers didn't like his mimicking the brogue either.

But he knew these things himself, and it was food for humility to a man who must needs be shown the frailty of the flesh in some way. He knew quite well that no one in God's world, least of all His Son, met with success at every turn. And this priest was getting more than his share of tangible satisfaction. There was always enough error and raw defect in Damen to keep him in his place, a very human man with natural flairs needing control.

Before long he wanted a college, got the letters in the mail to Rome for permission, and got a qualified answer in reply: if you have the money, you may build. One of his fellow Jesuits, a Father Van Goch, had a brother in Holland who would be glad to lend Damen $100,000, if, the brother added slyly, the two could come to the native land, talk it over, and give guarantees. Out of that trip came the wherewithal to finance St. Ignatius College, today's Loyola University. That made his educational plant complete. He was installed as president; and just as 1870 was being tolled in, it looked as if, in spite of himself, he would be named Bishop of Chicago, too, with Bishop Duggan so ill, and he himself a popular figure in every circle. But, no.

The builder was in Brooklyn in '71 giving a retreat when the cow kicked over the lantern in Mrs. O'Leary's barn and the great fire was under way. The city was like tinder after three months of hot wind and no rain. That night, as the city he loved went up in smoke, the large figure in black knelt through the dark hours in church and vowed to his Lady that seven lights would burn before her image always if she would save the parish. The fire veered east and, as if by a miracle, his prayer came true. He rushed back home.

There stood his church and schools in the midst of charred ruins. For months Holy Family was an asylum to thousands. Tragedy, the great leveler, brought Chicago together: the Poles began to like the Germans; the Germans could see the French more now, notwithstanding the enmities Bismarck was sowing; the Irish thought the Italians weren't so bad after all. A vast new surge of life coursed through the veins of the city by the lake. The nation had responded sympathetically to her distress, but that would not last. She must again show the resourcefulness and genius that had made her great. So the rubble was cleared away, and what might have been a lumbering, frame-buildinged city of a half million turned out to be a metropolis.

The complete turnover of population brought thousands into first contact with the west side of Chicago where the Dutch priest had erected a city within a city. There was no getting around it: Damen was phenomenal; it wasn't unusual to have 2000 people in the church for Sunday Vespers, and that after a morning when from five o'clock on crowds equally as big had packed the place for Mass.

Then there were the picnic days. His great parish band would gather at the church, and the parade would start, a jolly round priest leading the way with amused dignity and thousands following in his footsteps to the tune of Killarney and the songs of Erin's Isle. A train would be waiting and off it would chug to some wooded spot or up the lake a ways where a full and vigorous day followed. He mixed with everyone; age was giving him a mellow leisure that helped people love him even more.

What was really remarkable was that through all of this torrid struggle with administrative details, Damen had still other chores. For he had become a great preacher. From all over the country requests poured in that this priest be sent out to reclaim the thousands who were falling away. The growth of the country was prodigious. Hundreds of thousands of Catholics from foreign countries were flooding the nation, but they did not bring their priests with them. *They* would remember; the crucifix, the old framed Angelus, the ikon perhaps: these things would mean something to the older folks, especially the women. But for the men, rubbing elbows daily with those of other faiths or none at all, the pull of spiritual ideals was not there. Gold, getting along, getting ahead, the rainy day, the kids when they

grew up: these were the stirring and immediate problems which
occupied their days. And for the children, well, who was there
to train them?

So for weeks at a time, even when he was faced with mountains of domestic responsibility, Damen would slip away. By
now of course he had mastered the tongue. He needed no loud
speakers. And his mind was clear always. The result was as great
a pulpit orator as then was abroad on the continent.

Just after the first election of Abraham Lincoln, he was able
to write in his report to the Jesuit General that in the past year
he had brought back to the Church 30,000 souls who had been
away for from two to fifty years. He had made 260 converts,
including several Protestant ministers. The following year he
reported 40,000 returned, over 600 converts. And that went on
year after year.

He considered the work in the confessional even more important than preaching. In Milwaukee at one time he stayed
almost continuously in the box from five in the morning to
midnight. The lines never seemed to recede. Across the waters
in France the Curé of Ars felt also that the confessional was *the*
truly fruitful apostolate. Here humble men knelt in the darkness. For the most part their simply being there testified wonderfully to their dispositions. All a priest needed to do was counsel,
exhort, absolve from sin with the power Christ had given to His
apostles, and the Holy Ghost, of course, "with warm breast and,
ah! bright wings, hovered over the bent world."

You could put your finger on a map of the United States and
trace the zigzag path of the thundering priest across the country. The names of those places are part of our national vocab-
ulary by this time: Waukegan, Battle Creek, La Crosse,
Dubuque, Louisville, Toledo, Milwaukee, Missouri and Indiana,
Philadelphia, Jersey City, Ottawa, New Orleans, Boston,
Brooklyn, New York. But in his time many of these spots were
outposts of civilization, the edge of a continent, the Far West.
And from all this Chicago—gained. The table talk in a million
homes strung like a necklace around the city by the lake was
that the famous Damen of Chicago would be in town to preach

The Builder

next January. It was that kind of an event, the kind where you looked ahead for seven or eight months to seeing and hearing an almost mythical figure in middle nineteenth century U. S. A.

The Dutchman thought his confrere in preaching, a Father Smarius, was greater than he. But the esteem in which he himself was held and the evaluations of competent critics seemed to give the lie to much of his opinion. There was no invective in Damen, no frenzy, but lots of thunder, reason, drama, pathos. He liked to re-enact conversations, made a great play of fair analysis of issues with the non-Catholic brethren in mind. And he succeeded to the extent of 12,000 souls which he and the Holy Ghost had a large part in bringing around to the Church. That would be about two converts a day every day for 22 years of missionary activity.

After the mission was over, the shrewd old pastor would give a final lecture in the basement of the church or the town hall, and he would charge. Money needed to help defray the expenses of the huge building program in Chicago, he would say. And he was right. But the General got wind of said commercialism, and despite Damen's protests, distinctions, and general defense, told him there would be no more lectures given for money. It might be all right, but the superior saw the danger of scandal, and naturally Damen complied.

He was always a most obedient priest and that is more difficult for a man who is himself in a position of great authority. The submission that Ignatius asked of his men if the whole strategy of Redemption were to be carried through was a cardinal idea in his life. Once, in fact, he made a special promise to follow in every detail even the slightest indication of his superior's will.

So gradually his hair turned white, the strong, fast gait slowed down to a half trot, the mind became less clear than it had been. The assistant pastors had to do a lot of fast talking to convince him in the late '70's that the streets around the church and school were no place for cattle, ducks, chickens, and turkeys. A new city had no place for animals and fowl abroad. Reluctantly he submitted to the swiftly moving times.

But still the voice held out, and the heart. So he went on from diocese to diocese, back to Chicago, out again, back again. Up at 4:30 with a "Let us bless the Lord" and a pounding at his fellow missionary's door, he kept at his work all day. Whenever you saw him alone, he had the beads in his hand. He knew how sterile his work would be without prayer. He ate lightly, fasted a great deal for a large man, was austere in his own personal life: a bare room, the penitential scourging taken frequently, remarkable docility in seeking permissions, and so forth.

In '87 the old man realized in more ways than one that he had been 50 years a Jesuit. That was a milestone relatively few men in the Order lived to see. Chicago, Damen's Chicago at least, spent three days celebrating the event. High Masses, banquets, assemblies, great crowds of students waited on the pleased old man. He was old enough now, he knew, to take bouquets without a flinch and simple enough not to conceal his delight at all of this for him. God had indeed been good to this Dutch boy come to a new land a half century ago.

Where only a few hundred once lived in that parish of fifty square miles, now more than a million teemed along walks and expanding highways. The papers ran pictures and bold-faced stories about this "wonder priest" who so profoundly typified Chicago and America. Hundreds of thousands read about him who had never heard of him before. And most of them probably forgot about him as soon as they put the paper down. But not those who had known the man. They could never forget him. They who had lived with him knew that this roaring, bawling wilderness of steel and hogs and the low moan of fog horns upon the great lake might all very well have been a different story if this American-souled priest had not with his vision and energy welded the tongues and temperaments into a strong force.

Sometimes all that changes the tides of history and sets progress in a different groove is the stand of a solitary man. A thousand sentiments and convictions are crystallized in his own mind; he resolves to stroke against the current. His doing that is in-

The Builder

fectious; others are caught up in the same spirit; a movement is afoot. Cities just don't roll from five thousand to five million in a century. Someone must give incentive, charge the blood of a people with dreams and enterprise, give substance to their hopes.

Damen did all that. In a quick moment of history he captured the imagination of floundering immigrants, fused their allegiances, made a home for them out of this alien land; he gave focus to all their confused hopes for betterment.

But even after his jubilee he wasn't done. Slowed down a lot, yes, but still trumpeting and perhaps even a bit more impressive in his declining seventies. By June of '89 he had worked his way out to Wyoming, a real rootin'-tootin' frontier territory in those days and difficult of access. One bright June morning he was giving out Holy Communion at a little church when he staggered. It was a stroke. Somehow he made it back to Cheyenne, then on to the Jesuit College of Creighton in Omaha. For six months he sat up in anguish and, as the new year came in, Damen went home.

He was indeed far from the madding crowd. None of Chicago was near him. They buried him out at Florissant in Missouri where so many years before he had learned how to be a Jesuit on the flat rolling land near the river.

Chicago and America generally pretty much forgot about the "wonder priest." The country was lucky to remember the names of its presidents, a few generals, Mark Twain, Emerson, and Longfellow. But a Catholic priest in a Protestant country could lay little claim to statues or salutes or a choice spot in sixth grade history books.

Much of the district where Damen labored lies now in shambled glory, dark streets, poverty, age. It is almost as if history were always determined to efface ultimately the vestiges of men's achievement, to wear away their monuments until only names on tombstones remained, then only the stones, then dust.

But still the fog-horns are moaning on Lake Michigan. The rain splashes in puddles along the sidewalks and little eddies of light ripple to the dark corners of her streets. Like a jeweled queen Chicago sits in the night quite oblivious of her past, thinking of the game at Comiskey Park tomorrow, or when the strike will end, or the wheat market and Pullman sleepers. She is wondering about the future which stretches before her everywhere. Her steel rails are pounding like arteries, warm with expectation.

THE BOOMING 'seventies saw no letup in the onward rush. Already the last spike had been driven and the Union Pacific now lay across the land, a winding ribbon of steel from shore to shore. Alexander Bell was startling the world with the miracle of a voice on wire. Edison let men listen to his phenomenal music box. A few years later, and his incandescent light lit up the contemporary scene. This man was a genius towering among whole generations.

Little Nevada had its spot now in the Senate, close by New York. Nebraska was in the Union too, and beautiful Colorado took her place in the nation one hundred years after the Declaration of Independence on historic July 4. By now people were more accustomed to thinking of Alaska as their own too. Seward had engineered the purchase, seven million dollars to Russia for 580,000 square miles. Only time would break open the secrets locked in the icy north, the grandeur and wealth sealed beyond the glaciers.

Working men had begun meanwhile to chafe beneath the yoke of economic serfdom. No one had an answer for the cries of numberless tubercular miners, legions of children set to labor long hours, deprived of schooling, growing up stunted. Powerful combines formed to snatch the wealth lying fallow everywhere, plunder the forests, gouge out the bowels of the earth, make the wheels of industry spin faster. Exploitation lifted its ugly head.

Carnegie Steel and Standard Oil manipulated power in high places. John Jacob Astor and his twenty million were small change now in this new gargantuan empire. Bryan's Cross of

Gold Campaign could not turn the tide. Common men began to organize, wildly, rebelliously at first, but the ominous rumblings of sympathy throughout the land gave promise of eventual success.

* * *

Whom the Lord Loveth

Father Frank Barnum, S.J.

by LEO B. KAUFMANN, S.J.

It was Seattle in 1898 tossing with fever, the yellow contagion brought down from the Klondike. A steamer from the Northland pushed silently in from the Sound, adding only the periodic dull blasts of its whistle to the sharp unpleasant cry of the gulls. Its bulk had hardly emerged out of the fog before its nose seemed to be nudging the wharf. Only then with the reversed propellers churning dirty foam and water did it fit into character with the hustling city that welcomed it.

Seattle was sweating to seek and gain its place on the map as the miners poured into its port and out, over the Chilcoot, on to Dawson and the gold fields. Some made fortunes; some made nothing; many, for whom the fever had run its course and taken its toll, were already coming back.

The English steamer *Goronne* had sailed from St. Michael's, Alaska, with 600 passengers on board, "mostly disappointed gold-seekers and adventurers from all countries. Quite a number were sick with typhoid, scurvy . . ." They were orderly now, but they had been an unruly lot making the few quiet passengers aboard "uncomfortable by the constant rows and fights that took place."

Whom the Lord Loveth

Among these passengers was the missionary who left us a description of the voyage. His face was weather-beaten, his teeth discolored, and his clerical clothes shabby and soiled from rubbing elbows with a none too fastidious flock. He had first gone to Alaska in '91, the year that had already become "the old pioneer days or the fur period."

At first sight a loiterer on the docks could easily have passed him off as one of those very foreign missionaries with their faltering English and old-country ways.

But only a second look as he heard him ask for directions would have given pause to even the most undiscerning.

For neither membership in the Jesuit Order, that root of all un-American activities in the nineteenth century, nor seven winters in snow-buried shacks on the tundra had obscured the distinctive American background of Frank Barnum. And of those strange and contradictory requirements that went to make up an American among Americans, little more could be asked of him.

Born of wealthy parents in a land of equality, he was the scion of an old Southern family that was proud to trace itself back to older England where "Barnum" broadened into "Barn-ham"; he was tutored at Miss Sellar's private school, with finishing touches at Paris and a year at Virginia's Medical School. It was no wonder, then, that there were those who could not believe that Frank Barnum was a bona fide Jesuit.

For in many quarters prejudice would not permit the Jesuits to be accepted as part of the American scene. Even an old native woman remembers with a chuckle the consternation of a Protestant missionary as he realized that this pleasant and witty conversationalist had been all along a Jesuit disguised as an American.

But now as he trudged up Seattle's hills to the Jesuit residence at old Seattle College before boarding the Canadian Pacific for the East, he must have suspected that he would never go back to Alaska. Before coming down, he had given his Mass kit to a young Italian Jesuit—an act which, for the initiated in the ways of missionaries, carries all the finality of a worn out knight's deeding his sword to a squire. But Barnum was still a young man, as missionaries go, and far from through. Just why his superiors would never send him back to Alaska remains somewhat of a mystery, especially when we consider the talents which seemed to fit him so well for mission life. In a land where monotony and frozen boredom were the chief trial of the missionary, fascinating Frank Barnum was often the spark rekindling a smile on a drawn frost-bitten face. Barnum, the letters of contemporary Alaskans testify, had many facets that travel and education had polished to brilliancy: coldly exact in scientific observation, yet warmly sympathetic among his fellows, a restless adventurer, yet author of an accurate Eskimo grammar, casually at home in a plush mansion or squalid hut. But above all, there was the human Father Barnum, loving travel, a witty story, a practical joke, who, after seeing half the world, inconsistently fell in love with one bleak and icy corner of it nicknamed "Seward's Icebox."

He notes in his private papers that he was converted to the Catholic Church when eighteen, but next to nothing about the why and wherefore.

We do know that he was born in Baltimore on January 23, 1849, where his father owned Barnum's Hotel, one of the great hostelries of the South in the middle of the nineteenth century.

These white-collar Barnums of Baltimore had some shirt-sleeve cousins in New England, whence originated P. T. Barnum of circus fame. Just what the precise relationship was it would be hard to say. But on what must have been otherwise a very dull day, Frank found time to work out an elaborate genealogy in which P. T. receives honorable mention.

During the Civil War young Barnum was at Hagerstown, Maryland, attending St. James School until it was dispersed when Lee set up his headquarters in the vicinity shortly before the decisive Battle of Antietam. Throughout his life he retained a facility of being close by when things were happening, and not always, as in this case, on account of "pure fate."

From Hagerstown he enrolled at Loyola College, where three years later he was baptized by a Jesuit, Father Clarke. In three more years his application had been accepted by the Jesuits for admission into their Novitiate at Frederick, but not before he had spent his last year of freedom traveling all over Europe. The 20-year-old Barnum had already been abroad several times with his family. Now he continued on to the Holy Land and through Egypt, following the Nile from the delta to its source, a trip painstakingly recorded in his journal.

In entering the novitiate at Frederick he gave up a fortune and that at a time when becoming a Jesuit was decidedly unfashionable. But he had been there not quite eleven months when his mother's death forced him to withdraw. He had to take care of the younger children and manage the estate. He was not to return to the Jesuits for ten years, and the two reasons for which he had left the novitiate far from occupied all his time. Within a year he had taken up his travels again. He was to go to Europe three more times, once via Quebec and once via Buenos Aires on a sailing vessel, a barkentine, as he recalled. As an old man he was able to count 58 trips by boat alone, 24 of them full length ocean voyages.

Since he had left the Society in good graces and with the intention of returning, he was easily able to get letters of recommendation from the Provincial of the Maryland Province to Jesuit superiors in Europe. He took advantage of this unique position to visit Jesuit houses almost everywhere on what he later called his "visitation" of the Society. At the same time he sent back to his former confreres in America whatever he could get his hands on that he thought would be useful, including books and pamphlets from Russia and a Hebrew parchment roll of the Pentateuch from Jerusalem.

But he may have wavered in his first intention or given up hope of being able to re-enter the Society. For after some time at the University of Virginia's Medical School, he tried his hand at orange-growing in Florida.

But this enterprise burned out and his "itchy feet" sent him forth again, this time in America itself. He wandered on foot through Louisiana, made his way back up to Baltimore, and finally out to Leadville, Colorado. His native wanderlust and the restless American spirit of the expanding 'seventies seemed to have joined forces to claim him permanently for their own. That is, until at Kansas City, as he carefully notes in his personal record, he resolved to return to Frederick.

By this time he had become, to all outward appearances at least, a most advanced type of nineteenth-century American gentleman, which income and inheritance taxes have almost made an extinct species: a man of leisure with the most universal and boundless interests, especially in things scientific, whom more modern specialists might look upon as a dabbler; a seeker of information and a compiler of notes, almost for the sheer joy of seeking and compiling.

But surely no Jesuit novice could have known better the world he was leaving nor the Society he was re-entering than Frank Barnum.

Probably never before or since have Jesuit superiors had a longer period or more opportunities to observe a postulant. We can be sure that they did not try to fool themselves. They knew him for a rolling stone that in ten years had gathered momentum rather than moss. But momentum they could harness—as for moss—it is neither here nor there.

The Society of Jesus demands talents tempered with good sense and zeal forged by obedience.

On these criteria its superiors judged Frank Barnum and decided that he would do great good and fulfill the purpose of his vocation.

And when forty years later his brethren sat down to write his obituary, even were the incredulous to discount 50 per cent of it as pure edification, there could remain no doubt that the original judgment had been fulfilled.

But had it not been for his adopted Faith and the Jesuit Order, he could not have equalled his contemporary Henry Adams in the pursuit of the greater glory of God. Adams, unlike Barnum, was too discerning to be swept away by scientific progress, but too skeptical to be anchored in Christian tradition. Hence Adams was fated to wander throughout the world adding only wistful commentary to his changing generation.

Barnum, for his part, was too much taken up with things and enamored of science to see through them all directly—rather, he saw around them. As a Jesuit trained in the Spiritual Exercises of St. Ignatius, Barnum acquired a grasp of reality that more than made up for this lack of natural insight and discernment. While always in contact with the eternal truths, he embraced his natural interests with all his native zest, yet only as a means to the one great end, the salvation of souls. But Adams, seeing through the nineteenth century much better, saw nothing clear beyond, and there his vision stopped.

Once back in the Society of Jesus, Barnum's life was, comparatively speaking, uneventful for almost ten years. He did, however, receive honorable mention in the same will with the Mayor and City Council of Baltimore.

Two years after he re-entered the Society, his younger brother Dr. Zenus Barnum died. The doctor's will read in part as follows:

> If, within twelve months after my decease [i.e., a year to think it over] my brother Frank Barnum, shall withdraw from the priesthood in the Roman Catholic Church . . . and from any and every order and society connected with the said Church, . . . I direct that the net income of said rest and residue of my estate be paid to the said Frank Barnum. . . .
>
> But if within twelve months after the time of my death, my brother shall not have withdrawn from the priesthood aforesaid . . . and from any and every order or society connected with said Church . . . I give, devise and bequeath the said rest and residue of my estate to the Mayor and City Council of Baltimore, in trust, for the McDonough Educational Fund and Institute, to be applied to establishing a chair therein, to be called the "Zenus Barnum Chair" . . .

Needless to say, the said Frank Barnum did not withdraw, and the said "Zenus Barnum Chair" was established with all the other aforesaids.

One at least of Barnum's sisters did not seem to share all the Doctor's sentiments toward the errors of their brother. As one of Barnum's fellow missionaries described it:

> Father Barnum's sister was in Paris when the news reached her of the departure of her brother for Alaska. Immediately she crossed the ocean and the whole of the United States, and arrived at San Francisco a short while before the departure of her brother; and as she is very rich, she provided her brother very liberally with all the necessaries for Alaska.

After ordination Barnum had a year perfecting the small boys at old Georgetown College. Then he was assigned to the home mission band. But after he had part in preaching twenty-four missions throughout the eastern states, he resumed his travels. Mexico was his first conquest. His job was to accompany some young Mexican students home from Georgetown for vacation, pick up some books for the library, and after three months bring books and students safely back. In the meantime he observed about as much of Mexican life as was observable, especially that which pertained to the Church and his Society, from the fact that every altar had two missal stands to the crackers on the menu of a Jesuit College.

In two letters home, both crammed full of interesting details, taken from his ever present diary, he describes, in his own casually observant way, a holy picture painted by an Indian artist:

> A stream flows through the foreground, and the Blessed Virgin is represented engaged in washing, exactly after the manner of Mexican women. She has a great wooden paddle, with which she pounds the clothes upon a flat stone at the water's edge. There is an extraordinary amount of "wash" in various piles, and a number of Angels are busily engaged in hanging the garments on the branches of a very high tree. One Angel is just on the point of flying up, with a great armful of wet linen.

But it was not only the incongruous that caught his eye.

> . . . I met an old Franciscan Friar nearly ninety years of age, named Father Alvarez. . . . Years and years ago, he had labored in the distant California missions . . . his early life had been spent—spent in months of weary marches, years of weary toil, in privations and self-sacrifice, known only to the Divine Master, Who bade him "Go and Teach." As we walked along the great stone corridors of the convent, and through the silent cloisters, it was sad to hear the good old man whisper mournfully of the times when three hundred of his brethren lived here in peace, beloved and honored. He saw them rudely driven forth, and scattered far and wide. Now burdened with his weight of years he has crept back again to his cloister home hoping to die within its beloved walls.

In fact, a fellow Jesuit thumbing back over Barnum's files in the archives finds a great storehouse of information, everything from how coffee trees are haphazardly planted all over a hill to the price of ferry boats on the Nile. He retained always a passion for details, both relevant and irrelevant. Unhappily, the irrelevant and seemingly irrelevant in all his work was disconcerting to some of his more practical-minded superiors and eventually the source of much misunderstanding.

Back in the States, Father Barnum resumed work on the mission band, but within three months he had started on the way to Alaska. A fellow member of the mission band describes how he received his orders:

> Here it was that Father Barnum received from the Indian missionary, Father Van Gorp, who came down to Petersburg to see him, the news of the permission to go to the mission of Alaska. He was overjoyed, and left, on the day after the mission, for New York, there to make his preparation for his long journey to the far and desolate North. His wonderful perseverance in the beginning of his vocation and his many sacrifices cause this heroic resolve to occasion

no surprise to those who know his generous nature. . . .
When Archbishop Seghers visited Boston College some
seven years ago, Father Barnum, ardently desirous of the
Alaska Mission, which was under the spiritual control of
the Archbishop, spoke on the subject to the saintly prelate,
and was urged to accompany him on his homeward journey.
He sought the permission of superiors, but it was refused.
The late Father Dompieri, a man of great holiness, consoled
the disappointed aspirant for missionary hardships, by assur-
ing him solemnly that he would certainly obtain permission
in time. After a while Father Barnum urged his petition
again, and met with another denial. He then resolved to
leave all to God, and for over four years never renewed
his request. Father Dompieri died in November, and about
one month after his death, the permission to proceed to
Alaska came unsought and unexpected.

As Barnum, who was later to become something of an authority on Alaskan mission history, wrote about Seghers:

> The foundation of the first Catholic Mission among the
> natives of Alaska is due to the efforts of the Most Rev.
> Charles J. Seghers, whose saintly life was sacrificed in the
> prosecution of this apostolic work.

Two Jesuits, Fathers Tosi and Robaut, had accompanied the
Archbishop on his fifth and fateful trip to Alaska. They stayed
in the interior while the Archbishop, making his way down the
river, was murdered by a half-crazed attendant.

When the two Fathers heard of the Archbishop's death, one
remained in Alaska, while the other came down to San Francisco
for reinforcements, thus taking over the mission field in Alaska
in charge of which the Jesuits have remained ever since.

Now five years later Barnum was to be the eighth Jesuit priest
sent to Alaska, the second born in America. As such, he got in
on much of the spade work and a full share of the privations.

Volunteering for Alaska was so much in character with the
adventure-loving side of Frank Barnum that it may lose a bit on

the heroic side. But the first years were to test his mettle and hear it ring true.

His own accounts of Alaska written down to his fellow Jesuits overflow with cheer and humor. But one has only to read between the lines to appreciate what he later wrote in a brief history of the missions:

> It is simply impossible to convey to the minds of those always accustomed to the conditions of life in a pleasant climate, and to all the thousand comforts and conveniences of civilization, any adequate concept of the innumerable miseries, which at that time, were endured by all the members of the Mission.

Many of his letters from Alaska were written to his friend, Father Richards, at one time president of Georgetown. Their interests had much in common—especially as regards things scientific in true nineteenth-century fashion.

His first letter was from St. Michael's, the old Russian trading post on Norton Sound:

> I send you, according to promise, my first batch of notes. . . . You would be delighted to witness the mirages up here. At Nushagak we had the inverted image of a ship. . . . We are camping ashore and cannot start for a fortnight. I am to go down in the Delta to Cape Vancouver, which is considered the "Siberia" of the Missions.

In notes added later to the letter he describes the arrival of Father Treca, who had come up from the mission "Siberia" to meet him:

> He came up in a bidarra [an open canoe made of walrus hide] from Cape Vancouver, a journey of twenty-one days. He was half starved and had been living on putrid fish. When he reached our tent, his exhaustion was so great after his journey of 500 miles along the sea coast that I felt alarmed.

Barnum later remarked that this was his first object lesson in

Alaska travel. All in all, Father Treca's appearance did not give his new companion a too propitious preview of mission life. And their journey back to Cape Vancouver was to be more fore-boding still.

Cape Vancouver is on Nelson Island, on Bering Sea south of the mouth of the Yukon.

The map of Alaska is frequently caricatured into a pudgy face glowering over at Siberia, with Seward Peninsula as the nose, the Yukon as a toothless mouth sucked in above a menacing beard and chin formed by the Aleutians jutting out below Bering Sea. In such a picture, Cape Vancouver is about half way between the mouth and chin, while the island port of St. Michael's, the general rendezvous for mail and supplies in the early days, is about half way between the nose and the mouth.

There were then only two gateways to the interior—the delta of the Yukon via St. Michael's and, 2000 miles away, the head-waters of the same river via Chilcoot Pass near Juneau. The mouth of the Yukon was too shallow for the vessel the Alaska Commercial Company sent up once a year, and the closest place where it could land was St. Michael's Island, 80 miles to the north. There supplies were transferred to the river boats that had to come out of the Yukon and take their chances on Norton Sound.

Before accompanying Father Treca back to the mission, Father Barnum had an opportunity to display to all concerned the patriotism of the "foreign" Jesuits:

> For the next two weeks we have to camp on the shore here. There are about two dozen tents erected around the agency. Most of them are occupied by traders and miners. On the 4th of July everyone who had a flag hoisted it. We had a fine one which I brought up with me. Then I strung up six large Chinese lanterns in front of our tent so that it looked like a Mongolian laundry.

Since the annual steamer was the sole means which the Fathers had for communicating with civilization, Barnum was not heard from again for a year, but by the next summer he had

prepared an account of *Life on the Alaska Mission* for Father
Richards and the rest of his confreres in the States. It was a kind
of Jesuit Relations combined with witty remarks and reflections
based on his early travels.

He gives his opinion of the Alaskan egg as being more
"gamey" than any other, expressly selected just at the period
when mother goose is considering her sedentary labors almost
concluded.

The melancholy howls of the sled dogs when they observe
preparations for a trip recall the wailing camels in the Orient
when they first feel the load. An approaching storm lashing a
great cloud of snow along the tundra reminds him of the Si-
moom whirling the red sands of the Nubian desert.

The first installment started off with a history of the mission,
for Barnum had immediately devoted himself to collecting all
the information he could on the years prior to his coming. The
descriptions of Eskimo life and Alaska geography are rich in
details, while his own sufferings are frequently smothered in
humor. Almost in passing he mentions the difficulties of his first
trip in which he accompanied Father Treca and a Brother from
St. Michael's to his new home:

> From our place to St. Michael's is a sea journey of 400
> miles. [He had estimated it at 500 before making the trip.]
> Often we are far out of sight of land, so it is really a most
> dangerous journey for amateur navigators, with a very ill-
> equipped boat. It requires at least one month to make the
> round trip, as there are so many delays on account of
> storms and we have to double two formidable capes on
> the way.

But in his private records probably compiled later from his
diary he gives the full story:

> Very few of ours [a quaint way the Jesuits have of refer-
> ring to themselves] who were interested in the letters from
> Alaska ever realized the difficulties and dangers which at-
> tended the journeys of the missionaries. Those who wrote

rarely attempted to describe the details of their various expeditions. . . .

Before going into the details of his first trip, which he now intends to leave on record in full for posterity, he gives some necessary background:

In order to obtain a clear idea of our work in Alaska, it must be understood that it consisted of two totally distinct missions, one devoted to the Eskimo, and the second to the Tinneh Indians. These two races are entirely distinct in language and customs, and there is little or no intercourse between them.

The Eskimo are coast dwellers in the strictest sense of the word. Their villages are always situated along the sea shore, or along the lower reaches of the numerous rivers emptying into Bering Sea. There is no such thing as an inland Eskimo settlement, that is to say, one that is not accessible by water. Our second mission was among the Tinneh Indians, a branch of the great Athapascan family, inhabiting all the region along the upper Yukon. . . .

. . . The Fathers usually remained in whichever mission they were first appointed, as the difference in language rendered it inconvenient to change around.

As I had volunteered for the Eskimo mission, I was ordered to proceed to Tununa with Father Treca and Brother Cunningham.

As the journey was by sea, Father Tosi [superior of the whole Alaska mission] had purchased a boat from one of the traders, which was to serve us on that mission. The boat was a large yawl about 18 feet long, which had been decked over by Brother Cunningham, who was a wagon builder. As it had been designed as a row boat, it was not at all adapted for sailing. There was no center board or bowsprit, neither was there any sail or rigging.

I received orders from Father Tosi to prepare this boat [a far cry from the three-masted barkentine to Buenos Aires] for our journey, so I set to work at once to make a sail. As he would not allow me to get any canvas, I was obliged to use the common unbleached cotton cloth that we had for trading. . . . Meanwhile Father Treca and the Brother were engaged in loading the boat with our supplies for the coming year. The sail was not completed when Father Tosi ordered us to start. I went at once to him to explain that the sail was not finished, but he . . . said we could finish it on the way.

There was nothing for us but to obey, and accordingly we set out on a long and dangerous sea voyage in a very poor and unequipped craft. Poor Father Treca knew nothing at all about a sail-boat, and so he did not fully understand how essential the proper rigging was.

The mission river boat towed their "yacht," as Barnum named it, for the first leg of the journey. It took them into the Yukon delta whence they were to drift out to sea again and sail on their own along the coast to Nelson Island.

Barnum continues:

We passed a very miserable night crowded in the little cabin, and as the place was infested with mosquitoes we had no rest. As soon as it was light, we started to finish the sail and fasten it to the gaff and boom . . . all that we could do was to run what rope we had through a hole in the top of the mast, and fasten the end to the gaff. This caused all the weight of the gaff and boom to bear on the thin cloth sail which not only stretched it all out of shape, but caused many of the seams to rip.

Hoisting or lowering the sail in this primitive manner proved to be a most awkward and slow proceeding which required all three of us in lifting and pulling. We were occupied nearly all day in getting this miserable sail fixed and then we started to drift down to sea. . . .

The weather was fair with a light wind, and after a good deal of trouble we succeeded in getting the sail up. . . . All that day and all the next night we crawled along far out of sight of land, with only the vague direction to keep

South and a little West. . . . On the fourth day there were signs of a change. It clouded up and began to rain. . . . Later in the day the lofty headland of Eskinok loomed up ahead of us. . . . Rounding a cape is always an exciting incident in sailing, and I heartily wished that this one was astern of us.

It was a formidable undertaking indeed to attempt this dangerous passage in our condition, but as it was we had no alternative. As we drew nearer we could see the breakers pounding on the various rocky ledges, and it was only with the greatest difficulty that we managed to steer our miserable craft safely through them. After several very exciting escapes, and one in particular when we gave ourselves up as lost, we succeeded in getting past the outer reefs and were trying to make our way into one of the little inlets between the capes. Just then, unfortunately for us, the storm burst upon us in full force. The boat became unmanageable and threatened to founder so that we were obliged to anchor at once.

We were in a very bad place directly between two reefs, but we could not help ourselves. We then made all haste to get the sail down, and a most exciting time we had lowering it in the face of the gale, and saving ourselves from being washed overboard at the same time.

Meanwhile the boat was plunging about and pulling furiously against the anchor; had the poor old rope given way we would have been dashed at once on the neighboring reef . . . a lot of our precious supplies had been washed overboard. There was a great quantity of water in the hold and while we worked as hard as we could, it seemed to come in as fast as we could bail it out.

For two long dreary days and nights we remained in this most wretched and dangerous situation utterly unable to help ourselves in any way. It was truly a doleful time; the roar of the breakers on the reef right along side of us, the noise of the waves beating upon the boat, and the howling of the storm wind prevented any rest or conversation.

The certainty that, should the anchor rope give way, we would in a few moments be dashed upon the rocks and meet our death in the raging surf made every hour seem unending. We commended ourselves to the Mercy of God and prayed that the anchor would hold.

On the third day the storm abated. . . .

That this was not the last time Father Barnum would be in peril of his life we know from his spiritual notes where he enumerates under *Graces Received* the exact dates of several other like situations among which are: June 13, 1892: Blown out to sea . . . Dec. 1, 1892: Lost on the Tundra, three days in a storm and half starved . . . Sept. 4, 1893: On the Yukon, half starved and alone . . . Dec., 1897: Adrift on ice floe in Norton Sound . . . Jan., 1898: Almost shot . . .

At the end of his first journey Barnum was to experience something that perhaps bothered him more than the storm they had encountered.

It was early dawn when we landed, a travel-worn trio. Our coming awoke Father Muset, and he came out of the little hut. He bowed gravely to each of us and shook hands without a word! It was the time of *"la grande Silence"* [time of silence observed by religious communities] so having witnessed our arrival he retired at once. . . . It was very edifying, but still I felt like throwing something at him.

Certainly neither of Barnum's two priest companions, though excellent religious and undoubtedly heroic, were any too practical from an American's point of view.

Sister Calasanctius, a pioneer Sister of St. Ann in Alaska, describes in her memoirs what she heard of their first winter in the North.

. . . Their bedding froze so hard to the side of the hut and ground that they found it impossible to detach it until summer should thaw it out. For three months these Fathers had been trying to get a little sleep in those icy, vermin-filled beds. No matter how great was their fatigue after their visits to the neighboring villages, sleep was utterly out of the question. At this point their Superior, Father Tosi, arrived. He had mushed the thousand miles from Holy Cross (the mission headquarters) to visit these newly arrived priests whose inexperience might put them in danger. He grew pale when he saw the almost complete exhaustion of the men. With all the strength which fatherly love and compassion can inspire, he chopped until he had succeeded in freeing the furs and bedding, and then thawed it by the fire. But the vermin? What a martyrdom these holy young missionaries had endured!

What the charitable old nuns glossed over was the fact that most of their trouble could have been prevented by a decent fire.

In his *Life on the Alaska Mission* Barnum describes the little hut as "a hastily constructed edifice in the home-made style" put together from drift wood by Father Tosi as architect and Father Treca as "consulting engineer, log roller, and cook." He continues:

The result of their combined efforts, impeded by several good-natured natives, is our extraordinary domicile, which partakes of the features of an old Virginia smoke-house, a Harlem shanty, and a native barrabora. The plans and specifications called for a building eighteen feet wide by twenty long. Two of the sides of the house may agree with the measurements of the original design, but the other two surely differ. Furthermore, one gable leans inward, while the corresponding one projects to such an extent, that no less than four large props have been required to be placed against it to hold it in check. . . . The spaces between the logs are caulked with moss. Sometimes during a storm, pieces of this stuffing will fly out. When this occurs, it produces a panic just as an alarm of fire; for the rush of cold air comes in with a force like that of steam from a boiler. The roof is composed of split logs . . . covered with tarred paper, and over this is placed a covering of sods, and finally a thick layer of earth. Every spring the vegetation on the roof is greatly ahead of the other. In spite of the immense weight of this roof the furious winter gales make the poor little shanty almost rock. Sometimes, on account of its exposed situation, it has been so completely buried in the snow, that the Fathers actually could not get out, until the natives kindly came and disinterred them.

. . . The crowning glory of the domicile is its great west window. It is the handiwork of Father Treca, and fashioned after an antique model, if I remember rightly, the Hotel de Ville at Douay. Six photographic plates were sacrificed for the purpose.

Barnum later remarked:

The native abodes were in every way more comfortable and far warmer than our miserable hut, and I have wondered since why we never had sense enough to make use of them.

His appreciation of the natives was not only sympathetic but extremely frank.

These poor creatures are probably the dirtiest race of beings on the earth. In their dress, habitation, and diet they are utterly filthy.

. . . Their food alone will afford a slight clue to the rest, when you learn that their daintiest dishes consist of putrified matter reeking with maggots. . . . They are always covered with dirt and vermin, and their houses are truly like pig-sties.

. . . None of them can approach you unawares, as you are sure to smell him from afar. After Mass the atmosphere of our little chapel is sickening, while in the cassines it is actually overpowering. Father Muset, who has become somewhat accustomed to it now, does not experience any greater annoyance, after a night passed in one of these filthy holes, than merely a tendency to faint on emerging into the fresh air. . . .

After Barnum had gone over the Chilcoot Pass to Dawson on his second trip to Alaska, he remarked in defense of the Eskimos:

> . . . I have known cases where white men camping in the Klondike rush . . . with far less excuse surpassed the Eskimo completely in being filthy.

In describing the Alaskan louse in detail, Barnum made sure that no future missionary would come up unwarned.

> In Alaska, the louse and the missionary are "one and inseparable"; of course this intimacy is entirely due to the obstinate infatuation of the louse. In the beginning, the missionary rejects the overtures of the insinuating insect, and seeks to avoid companionship, but his efforts are in vain, the louse will not be repulsed; the intimacy is inevitable. Humiliating as the confession may sound, it is sad but true. We are all lousy, and we are lousy all the time. When I landed at St. Michael's . . . I noticed a little rash that broke out on my neck. . . . I became convinced that I had caught the itch . . . but determined not to say anything about it to Father Tosi, until after the steamer had left the port, for I did not want to be sent back. Keeping quiet when the other Fathers were about was a trial too hard to describe. One day, however . . . a Father remarked, "So you have gotten some already." . . . That settled it, I could scratch freely, morning, noon, and night. . . . You may say, "This is perfectly horrid, why don't the Fathers wash?" It is horrid I know . . . but these are facts Alaskan; now about washing, there's the rub! Their apparel, which consists of a fur "parki" and a pair of long boots, is never subjected to the ordeal of the wringer and mangle.

Concerning the Eskimos' own attitude toward lice, Barnum

noted that "the first thing the men do, on entering the cassine, is to disrobe and search for vermin. . . ."

He himself tried pouring coal oil down his back with excellent results, but there wasn't enough coal oil. He does not tell how seal oil might have worked, but he describes its use by the natives for food and light in reporting a native social affair.

> . . . I noticed Madame de Kashunok comfortably seated on a bundle of dried salmon, with Kukuyak [her son] close beside her. The body of an old frying-pan, which was used as a lamp, was hanging exactly over the lady's head. Someone, on the third tier, happened to kick this lamp, and about a pint of the rich warm oil flowed directly down upon Madame de Kashunok's head, and over her "set of furs." Such a contretemps, occurring in a drawing room elsewhere would certainly have been attended with apologies, condolences, and hysterics, but not so here. The Madame's serenity was not disturbed in the least degree, in fact she paid no attention to it whatever; but Kukuyak, as a dutiful son, seized a dry salmon, with which he briskly rubbed the head and shoulders of his parent, and then calmly proceeded to eat the improvised handkerchief!

But Father Barnum insisted that his "primitive simple-minded race" were really making great progress.

> All of our little flock here at the mission know now that it is highly unbecoming to disrobe themselves in the chapel, or to massacre vermin during the time of service. Nevertheless I should add, that *one notice* did not suffice to produce the desired effect.

Of the famed Alaska mosquito he says:

> No description of the Yukon country is complete without some allusion to the insect plague, and it may be added that no description can do justice to this subject.

Barnum himself found the silence of the Arctic winter far more impressive than the cold, when a man has only his own voice to prove his hearing and his own limbs to belie the final end of all motion.

> . . . the universal death-like silence of the dreary Polar winter is something so gruesome and unnatural, that it immediately attracts attention, and is most profoundly impressive. . . . The eye wanders over the gloomy motionless landscape, wherein Nature's thousand voices all are hushed, far away stretch the frozen miles, lakes and islands, rivers and plains, all indistinguishable beneath one unbroken covering of snow, and all so profoundly silent, that the ear actually suffers from the excessive stillness, just as the eyes ache from an excess of light. One feels as a wanderer in the silent region of the shades, a trespasser in some forsaken world, where all nature is enclosed within one glistening tomb.

And when in Barnum's diary are found the sad events that helped bring forth this description, Jack London's *In a Far Country* has more than an equal in pathetic realism. London called it "the Fear of the North." "This Fear," he said, "was the joint child of the Great Cold and the Great Silence, and was born in the darkness of December, when the sun dipped below the southern horizon for good." Barnum called it more simply "polar dementia" or "polar anaemia." Whatever it was, it hit the missionaries too. He describes it all very intelligently and objectively without straining after supernatural causes or stooping to the amateurish agnosticism that mars some of London's atmosphere.

It was Barnum's third winter in Alaska.

> The long dark winter dragged slowly on and toward its close, poor Father Treca who was always so kind and energetic grew taciturn and listless, and began showing signs of Polar Anaemia. He would ring the bell at all hours, rousing us up at one or two o'clock in the morning. Then he would start to vest for Mass, but as soon as he arranged his amice he would suddenly tear it off and rush to Father

Parodi for confession. After this he would resume vesting and when nearly finished he would tear off the vestments again and make another rush to Father Parodi. Some mornings he would vest and unvest in this manner six or seven times before he finally turned to the altar. During the day he would frequently go out and walk around and around the house talking wildly to himself until he was half frozen. During his quiet periods I would urge him to go to Holy Cross, but he would not hear of it. . . . I determined to go to St. Michael's where I hoped to meet Father Tosi. My difficulty was to obtain permission as I did not want to excite him by leaving against his will. Each time I requested to go he would say yes, and then just as I was ready to start he would change his mind. Finally I arranged with Father Parodi to engage his attention under some pretext and while he was thus occupied I succeeded in getting away.

Father Tosi rushed back with Father Barnum only to find that, as Barnum says:

> The novelty of his visit enlivened Father Treca so much that he did not display any symptoms of the disease. Father Tosi was vexed . . . and so he promptly departed after expressing his opinion of me as an alarmist.

Father Tosi can hardly be blamed for wondering just who was affected in his coast community, but the opinion he was gradually acquiring of Barnum was eventually to mean the end of Barnum's work in Alaska and his life's greatest cross. But Barnum found his consolation in the service of God and a natural escape in the study of the difficult Eskimo language,

> . . . cut off entirely from the outer world. . . . with no books or opportunities for any intellectual work. . . . without any of the ordinary appurtenances of civilized life. It was only the knowledge that we were endeavoring to extend the Kingdom of Christ, and doing what little we could to make His Holy Name known, that rendered our

existence endurable and gave us patience to support these trials and privations.

Our chief mental relaxation was derived from the study of the language, and in discussing the many problems it presented.

Barnum, who started almost immediately to write a grammar and dictionary in Innuit, described his first efforts with the language for his fellow Jesuits in the States.

. . . Let us take an example. Suppose we are in a boat, you pick up an oar, point to it, and say, "Cha"=what? The native whom you address gazes placidly at you, and says, *Chuya-ugeeakoa*, which means, "I would like some tobacco." You proceed to write in your note-book, Oar= Chuya-ugeeakoa; you feel that you have a start, and so you endeavor to obtain the verb. Therefore you row a few strokes, and then you "cha" again. Probably by this time he is sulky at not receiving the desired chew, or he is somewhat suspicious over that mysterious proceeding of yours with the pencil, so he pays no further attention to you. If he is a very intelligent fellow, he will say "Thou *hast been* rowing." Splendid! Down it goes in the note-book. You notice that there is no similarity between the two words; well, after all, there is none in English either. Next you point to one who is rowing near you, and "cha." The answer comes, and *it is in the dual*, but down it goes as your "third singular." Now you brace for a mighty effort, the hardest of all, to obtain the first person singular. "How do you say, I row?" is what you express as clearly as you can. *Thou rowest* is the invariable reply. Or he may suppose you wish a friendly criticism on your stroke, and with native simplicity says, "Thou rowest very poorly." For the first plural you designate yourself and others, and the reply is "Ye row." When you get to the third plural and point to all-rowing, you promptly get the word, "We are tired of rowing." They wish to rest and to have something to eat.

Whom the Lord Loveth

When you have made out your paradigm at the mission, it will run, in English, somewhat as follows:

Oar = I would like some tobacco.
1st person Singular—Thou rowest very poorly.
2nd person Singular—What do you want?
3rd person Singular—You both are rowing.
1st person Plural—Ye row.
2nd person Plural—Thou hast been rowing.
3rd person Plural—We are tired of rowing.

Henceforward Barnum devoted most of his time to this grammar.

From various letters of fellow missionaries there can remain little doubt that Barnum was not only well liked but was doing a good job. Father Parodi wrote to the superior in the States, "Father Barnum is always as gay and jovial as ever."

Brother Power, the engineer of the mission boat, wrote to a priest friend in 1893:

> Father Barnum . . . is doing in Alaska an immense amount of work for the glory of God. As he has already said in his letter, he will have to travel much this year. . . . His ways are very taking, and one cannot come into contact with him without loving him. He is not only a good missionary but an excellent scientist. Wherever he goes he maps out the country with great care and correctness. . . . Besides all this he has written up some exhaustive descriptions of the country and its resources. . . . Neither is his work on the country limited to paper. He has in truth, rendered an important service . . . by cutting a trail across the mountains that lie between . . . [Kozyresvsky and Kuskokwim]. This trail is now known as "Barnum's Pass."

In fact, Barnum and Treca explored all the great interfluvial tract extending between the Yukon and Kuskokwim rivers in search of possible mission stations. It was while on these trips that Barnum encountered most of the trying experiences of travel by dog sled described in his historical essay.

His writings, which were first published in the *Woodstock Letters* for circulation among Jesuits only, were reprinted in pamphlet form. They met with considerable success.

In the summer of 1894 he wrote down to his friend, Father Richards:

> I hope that you will not mind it much if I have not written any long letter this year; but the fact is that I have not been able to gather any interesting facts, and I have devoted myself solely to Innuit. You will be delighted at the amount of Innuit I have for a grammar, and if I come down next year it will be ready to be printed for our own use. . . .

In 1895 he was called down to the States by the Jesuit General himself, as Barnum understood it, not only to collect funds for the missions by lecturing, but to publish some of his works. But his superior, Father Tosi, understood otherwise.

Father Tosi, who had come down with him, wrote in his faltering English to Barnum's friend, Father Richards, at Georgetown:

> . . . I recommend to your kindness not to let him print anything . . . I don't think proper at present to have printed his Malemute catechism as it is not complete and theologically exact. So also the grammar or dictionary, it will take yet two or more years before it will be worthy of having it exposed to the public. It is true that the good father worked very hard, and what he had, is good, but very deficient and incomplete particularly in the way of writing.
>
> . . . and besides the permit of our Very Rev. Father General is only to try and employ all time to collect material means . . . and so he will have no time for the printing.

It would not be hard to decide where J. Havens Richards' sympathies lay in this controversy. But Jesuits are men who obey and in such a case the benefit of the doubt lies with the immediate superior.

Whom the Lord Loveth

The inability of Father Tosi and Barnum to understand each other was evident from the first, but in some ways, hard to comprehend. From unimpeachable sources there can remain no doubt about Father Tosi's virtue, while Barnum's reputation as a good religious stands unshaken even today among those who knew him best.

Barnum himself remarked in his first letter to Richards how the captain of the ship to Alaska, a man not easily swept off his feet by missionaries, was "an ardent admirer of Father Tosi." The same captain later congratulated Father Tosi on receiving such an excellent man as Father Barnum.

Sister Calasanctius, who had Father Tosi for spiritual director and confessor, described him as one who

> . . . always made an indescribable impression. . . . His whole personality radiated the tenderness of his charity. Everywhere we went we heard him described in terms that varied little: . . . self-forgetful, patient in waiting on God and bearing the faults and limitations of others. A model priest, he graced the Catholic clergy, the religious order of the Jesuits, and the missionary land of Alaska.

But Barnum and Tosi were totally different types. Tosi belonged to an old school of European missionaries who, though they spread the Faith in America, were seldom really in sympathy with the country and its ways. Tosi did not bother to learn English well and read little or nothing in it. Barnum was not only an American and a convert, but a scientist. He had many enthusiasms—his notes and his maps and his interesting facts—the legitimate ones Tosi could hardly understand; for the irrelevant he had no sympathy at all.

On the missions Tosi's work was eminently practical. What he wanted from Barnum were funds and then a grammar for the missionaries. Barnum's hope was that his work, though undertaken for personal use, should be, as it actually turned out, a contribution to the scientific world. In this Barnum was surely closer to the ideal of St. Ignatius who preferred the more universal good to the immediately practical.

Tosi was shocked, as would be many another European Catholic today, at Barnum's evident desire to be on good terms with people of all religions, Protestant and Orthodox alike.

In any event, it would be hard to find two Jesuits who were opposites in more ways than Barnum and Tosi. It was not a heretic or a no-good that was St. Peter Canisius' hardest cross, but a fellow Jesuit who had been given authority in Germany. The saintly Brother Alphonsus and the saintly priest, Francis Regis, both found some of their superiors far from understanding. If such is the case, one ought not to be surprised that Sister Calasanctius' patient and self-forgetful Father Tosi was not always so where Father Barnum's faults and limitations were concerned.

Yet Tosi had no desire to lose Father Barnum for the Alaska Missions. While they were both staying at St. Ignatius College in San Francisco for a few days before sailing back to Alaska, a rumor reached Tosi that Barnum might be recalled to his province. Without any explanation to Barnum, Tosi, as was his right, ordered Barnum to leave the house immediately for Alaska without even saying good-bye to anyone. The Society's enemies would consider such a procedure as most usual, but no Jesuit would, nor did Barnum. Yet good Jesuit that he was, he obeyed, and it was perhaps the greatest single trial of his life to be treated so strangely by a superior. He could not imagine what he might have done to excite Father Tosi. The incident was to weigh on him for a long time until he heard about the rumor and discovered that he had personally no responsibility in the whole affair: Barnum was later to excuse Tosi on the grounds that he was a sick man with not long to live.

On the way back to Alaska, Barnum took the southern and only other door to the interior, i.e., by way of Juneau, over the Chilcoot Pass into Canada and down the head waters of the Yukon. This was the route made famous by the "stampede" of '98 to the Klondike. Barnum seems to have gone through before the big strike. He went in with the group in '96 that was making the first attempt to send United States mail into Alaska by special carriers. Barnum's descriptions of Miles Canyon, White

Horse Rapids, and Five Fingers in his notes and letter to Father Richards could hardly be surpassed.

The explanation he gave Father Richards of why he took the land route was that Father Tosi had given him permission to return by whichever way he found most convenient. It was a very charitable way of describing his premature departure from San Francisco.

But nothing could make Barnum lose his sense of humor, as the stories with which he regaled Father Richards show. He describes the landing of the tow boat he took from Juneau to Dyea:

> The captain managed to get ashore in a skiff, but on returning he was upset in the surf and nearly drowned. At this exciting juncture the mate appeared to be at a loss to know how to act. His early life had not been spent at sea, he drove a milk wagon in San Francisco, a respectable occupation indeed, but one which had not particularly qualified him for marine emergencies. A very forward youth, who served as cabin boy on the tow boat, but whose general deportment was that of owner of the earth, sprang forward and shouted, "Man the life boat." Under the circumstances the order was the proper one, but the "Rustler" had no life boat to man, so after struggling for a long time in the surf, the poor captain finally got on a sand bar. . . . Although he was warmly welcomed after his mishap, still he seemed to show slight regard for sentiment, as he at once began to collect ten dollars apiece passage money.

At Forty Mile, Barnum stopped to see his fellow missionary from Baltimore, Father Judge, but missed him. Judge was the only other American-born priest working in Alaska. Two years later he was to die a hero's death after exhausting himself taking care of the sick in Dawson. Barnum wrote of his hastily constructed hospital:

> Many poor creatures, utterly exhausted by that terrible march over the Chilcoot trail, reached this humble little

hospital just in time to die, expiring at their very journey's end.

Judge seems to have been better understood and appreciated by superiors in Alaska than Barnum. But Barnum must have felt a little less suspect when word reached them that the Masons had insisted on marching in a body at Father Judge's funeral.

Barnum also was to have only two more years in Alaska until in '98 he was called back for good by the Provincial of Maryland. Father Tosi was dead. There was a new superior in Alaska now, but he seemed to have inherited Father Tosi's opinion of Barnum. Whether at the time Barnum felt certain that he was leaving Alaska for good or wanted to, we are not sure. Perhaps under the circumstances he didn't care.

In any event, it was impossible for him to complete his grammar in Alaska and make it, as he conceived it, an ethnological investigation. In Alaska he had neither the time nor the means of making researches necessary for comparing Innuit with kindred languages.

Back in the States Barnum took over as librarian at Georgetown University while finishing his grammar.

It was typical of his life and work in general that the importance of this contribution in the field of comparative philology and ethnology should not be fully appreciated by his contemporaries. Moreover the book, as composed, is not too usable for Alaska missionaries today, and it is easy to lose sight of the honor accruing to the Church from such a work.

However, he received recognition and high praise from a leading literary review in Germany, the *Allgemeine Literaturblatt*. A member of the Royal Danish Geographical Society, himself an authority on the Eastern Eskimos, wrote to Barnum:

> . . . your book . . . seems to me to be the most valuable contribution to our knowledge of the Eskimo language outside of Greenland.

That the work was not more widely recognized has been explained in information supplied by Doctor John P. Harrington, linguist on the present ethnology staff at the Smithsonian Institution.

> Father Barnum's book was not much reviewed simply because no one was competent to write a detailed review of it.

The same authority continues:

> Father Barnum's book is the most complete to date on the Alaska-Eskimo language. He has published many splendid texts, each with notes following (pp. 271–296), and at the end of the book is an Eskimo-English dictionary (pp. 319–376), modestly called a mere vocabulary.

Barnum's genius becomes all the more evident when we remember that he had only seven years' actual contact with the Eskimos and that under the circumstances described in the book's preface as an apology for "its many deficiencies."

> Much of this work has been done in the gloomy underground abodes of the Innuit. Many words were taken down while traveling by dog sled over the ice fields. . . . Frequently have I risked having my hand frozen by removing the mitten in order to make a memorandum of a chance expression which would help to elucidate some point which till then had seemed hopelessly obscure.

Whatever Barnum may have thought about leaving Alaska, he applied to go back already in 1900, even before his grammar was published. Father René, the new superior, wrote back that he had long ago transmitted his request to headquarters, and this was true. But one of Barnum's old fellow missionaries gave him the full story.

> Rev. Father René spoke to us about your desire to come back to Alaska. He is opposed to it for the present, but I have spoken to him in favor of your return and I do not despair of helping you a little.

Evidently Barnum had picked up the reputation with higher authorities in general as not being a fit subject for Alaska. This seemed to have been the final blow. Only one who has seen the hold that the Alaska Missions can have on a man could understand his feelings.

For example, there was an old Alaskan missionary who had been a Count in Italy. When he was an octogenarian, superiors called him back to the States for a rest, so they told him, but actually to die. He would never admit even to himself that his Alaska days were over. And to show to all concerned that he belonged to the Northland, he refused to wear his biretta, insisting on the Jesuit rule that exempts visitors from so doing.

Brother Power, who had been one of Barnum's companions in Alaska, wrote to a priest friend after he had been recalled to the States:

> I am once again in California, yet my heart is in Alaska and I long and pray for the speedy coming of the day when my superiors will permit me to return to that beloved mission.

And in this regard Barnum was no exception even to his last days. Alaska is a "magnetic land." Its memories will always haunt those especially who have tasted its "spiritual possibilities."

He could still see and feel the terrible privations he had undergone, particularly in traveling, and knew he was not exaggerating when he wrote an historical essay on the Catholic missions in Alaska:

> In those days travel in Alaska whether by dog-sled or sail-boat meant a test of endurance; alone in that boundless, desolate, storm-tortured waste, with but just the scanty food which could be carried along, there was no hope of relief in case of sickness or accident. The constant risk of being lost in the furious storms, the hazard of getting adrift on a floe when traveling on the sea, of perishing while running some of the rapids, of freezing in that overpowering cold, the agony of snow-blindness, all these and more be-

Whom the Lord Loveth

sides were the risks and vicissitudes that confronted us on every trip we ever undertook through the great frozen Northland.

Yet his soul yearned to be back there—where he knew he would be, were it not for the higher call of obedience—in the great work he had helped to pioneer. For as he wrote:

> The vast polar empire of Alaska was the only remaining region of the world in which the Gospel of Christ had not yet been preached. The midnight sun had never shed its pale beams upon a cross, nor had the Angelus bell ever echoed over the frozen tundras of the North Land.

Hence, it was impossible that Barnum should ever lose contact with the missions—writing always for news of his old friends, collecting and preserving what he called his Alaskana. From his former fellow missionaries he received many affectionate letters which are proof enough in themselves of the high regard in which he was held by those in Alaska who knew him best. He saved over fifty of these letters, a considerable number when we realize that there were only about 18 missionaries when he left—most of whom could write only once a year.

Some wrote to him as fellow sufferers in exile. Among them was Julius Jette, son of a Governor General of Canada.

> I have been sent to Canada for a year under the pretext that my health was failing. . . . I do not [sic] give up the hopes of returning, and would to God that I could have you along on my way back.

When his old friend and fellow classmate from student days, Raphael Crimont, had become superior of Alaska, and later bishop, it was too late. But they carried on their correspondence. Crimont wrote:

> . . . Your letter of Dec. 1st was a real treat to me, an oasis of rest and pleasure in the desert of my troubles and worries. . . . I am sending your good letter to Father

Robaut [one of the two original Alaska Jesuits]. The old man will be so happy to have this fine visit from you!

This was the same Crimont who outlasted them all, whom Barnum greeted when he arrived in Alaska, as Crimont loved to relate.

> Is it you, poor little Crim? Oh my, we don't want you. You aren't made for this kind of country. In a few weeks you'll be dead. Stay on the boat and go back. It's the only way to do.

If Barnum remained peculiarly attached to "things Alaskan," he was not embittered nor was his life's work through. Far from it. In the next twenty-three years he was to have seventeen different assignments, going from place to place, doing whatever his superiors put him to. So much so that Alaska looks only incidental in a catalogue of his occupations. From librarian at Georgetown to chaplain on Welfare Island, to librarian and pastor at Woodstock, to working with the Spanish Catholics in New York. Nor were his travels through. He was sent on business for his Order to Jamaica, to Cuba, to New Mexico, to Florida.

His last six years were spent taking charge of the museum and and archives at Georgetown. He had started this work while librarian just after he came back from Alaska. One of the first treasures he secured was the bear skin that had been used for a bed by two heroes of the North, Archbishop Seghers and Father Judge.

His method of establishing the archives was simple enough. He merely gathered everything into his own room until he found another place vacant. Twice he was evicted to make room for something else, but he persevered, and is responsible for much of the excellent collection at Georgetown today.

His pleasant wit and disarming playfulness removed him so far from the picture of a frustrated old man that his confreres would have had difficulty in identifying him with the deep pathos of his private writings.

So much so that it could almost be said of him what P. T.
Barnum wrote of himself in the person of one of his grand-
fathers: "He would go farther, wait longer, work harder, and
contrive deeper, to carry out a practical joke, than for anything else under heaven." One would not have to work out a
genealogy to prove a similarity of spirit in all these Barnums. It
would be enough to listen to a few of the stories the Visitation
Sisters tell about the time Father Barnum was their chaplain.

> One day Mother Superior was having a feast day. Father
> Barnum made up some rolls of raw cotton, soaked them in
> butter, and put them into the oven until they were nicely
> browned. He took them to the convent and presented the
> Rev. Mother with a bag of cruller. She passed them around,
> and in a few minutes the Sisters were pulling raw cotton
> out of their teeth.

In the museum at Georgetown he put a football helmet between two bishop's mitres. When asked the reason for such an
arrangement, he said that it was to stimulate interest.

Genial and alert at seventy, he spent his spare time writing
some memoirs and with his sense of history leaving them in the
archives. Some of the more personal things he wrote would have
been unkind had they not come from so kind a man. But then,
who can measure what his removal from Alaska cost, and who
can blame him for acquiring somewhat of a fixation on the
affairs that brought about his exile from the land of his heart.

And when he died a confrere wrote his obituary—"At
Georgetown College, Father Francis Aloysius Barnum died
piously in the Lord on Thursday, November 31, 1921. . . . A
polished gentleman, an extraordinary linguist, an apostolic man,
a man of boundless wit and humor. . . ."

To say that a Jesuit died piously in the Lord is rather trite, but
for this Barnum of Baltimore to have lived and died a pious
Jesuit was certainly not.

As the *turn of the century approached, the tempo of life trebled. In four score years the U. S. had upped her peoples by sixty million. Progress seemed too rapid for normal assimilation. Yet the wheels rolled on. The Dakotas, Washington, and Montana climbed to sew their stars on the flag. A year later Idaho and Wyoming pledged allegiance.*

Schools spread everywhere. More people could read and write. Small towns began to build their own libraries. And on the shelves one could find Americans who wrote: even in the tide of high-geared immediate frantic pursuits there were those who stood off from the scene and sketched the wild meanderings of this Paul Bunyan civilization. Walt Whitman and Bret Harte, Mark Twain's Huckleberry Finn and Tom Sawyer became classic figures.

Thoreau and Louisa May Alcott, Emerson and Whittier, Horace Greeley, Ryan and John Bannister Tabb: all of them were great, doubly so amidst a nation's rife preoccupation with strictly business endeavor. Harvard and Yale were old now, so was William and Mary; the famed Johns Hopkins of Baltimore was rated with the best in Europe. Georgetown and St. Louis grew old with the cities in which they were founded.

And great cities were in the making. There were more than covered the face of the Eastern seaboard now, Cleveland and Pittsburgh, Detroit and Memphis, Minneapolis and San Francisco. A short hot skirmish with Spain in '98 settled the future of Puerto Rico and the Philippines. American imperialism lived, however, a brief span abroad. McKinley's assassination brought to the national scene Theodore Roosevelt, the Rough Rider, a very different sort of president. His life itself was an epic.

* * *

A Nickel for Carfare

Father Albert Biever, S.J.

by Charles T. Miller, S.J.

His shoes clicked a little in the quiet corridor. Outside it was a warm day, somewhat hazy, a day for dreams under a tree. The superior sat reading the good book, waiting for his visitor.

"Now I wonder what the Provincial could be wanting with me," thought Father Biever as he hurried down the hall. He knocked expectantly at the superior's door and was somewhat relieved to hear a *cheerful* greeting.

"Come in, Father Biever." He noticed the twinkling eyes. "How was class today?—the little shavers give you any trouble? Have a seat." All this before he could answer.

He sat down, but didn't bother to comment on class; it was something else his boss had in mind. Was he trying to soften the blow that was due for some negligence—or was this the prelude to some onerous job about to land in his lap?

"Come on, Father—out with it, whatever it is. I'm ready for the worst."

"The worst?" chuckled the Provincial. "Why, man, this is your chance! I want you to go downtown and found a university."

The Provincial smiled. "I'm sending four good teachers along with you. As for the buildings, that's your job. You will live at the Holy Name Rectory—you'll be pastor there, and in charge of their fine grammar school, incidentally. But you'll probably need a temporary classroom building to start with. Buckle down and see what you can do. You have my blessing."

He knelt for the blessing—ready to take anything that was

free—then headed back toward his room to start packing. On the way he dropped in at the little community chapel to tell the Lord about it—as if the Lord hadn't had him picked out for the job long since. And this time he actually got a real mountain-moving blessing. For he came out with a lot more courage in his heart and a sureness in his step. If the South depended on him for its university, then it would get it. He would see to that. He never thought that might be the very reason he was chosen.

A few mornings later, the Brother Porter had a hired buggy waiting at the front door by the time Father Biever had finished Mass and breakfast. His trunks were loaded on, and he squeezed in beside them, waving farewell to the several priests who were there to see him off and wish him success.

The fresh morning air and bustling streets, the stores opening for business, were all invigorating and fitted in with his mood. Baronne Street was getting to be quite a center for trade, he thought.

The steady trot of the horse, the gentle rocking of the buggy, lulled the priest into a mood of reverie.

"The Provincial was right," thought Father Biever; "this is my chance to really do something. Coming at forty-six, though, seems a little late."

He had spent so much time knocking around in odd jobs since his ordination in '91—minister at Spring Hill College; a year of fretting over details of food and clothing for the community; teaching chemistry and rhetoric at the Galveston College the next year; then the tertianship year in Canada to finish off his Jesuit training; following that, a year on the coast of Florida, shepherding a scattered flock of immigrants and vacationers, only to be recalled and rebuked for what seemed a hopeless job in the first place; then these last six years at the Immaculate Conception College in New Orleans, where he started out teaching the lowest grammar preparatory grades. It had been nice teaching the little tots, leading them on to the knowledge and love of God in between their spelling and arithmetic drills. But it was quite a comedown. Why, he had done better than that in his seminary years—he had taught the classics and sciences for six years in the college at Spring Hill when he was in his early twenties. And then in his forties he had been demoted to grammar school. Well, c'est la vie!

But that was all long past. In the last few years he had worked back up to the college fields where he was more at home again. But still, the drudgery and martyrdom of the classroom life was not exactly the cherished dream of a spirited, battle-loving son of the shock-trooper Ignatius. He longed for bigger things. Here, now, was a challenge!—found a university! His classics and science, and anything else he had, would stand him in good stead now.

They swung out of Baronne, and into the drive that circled the monument to General Lee, still fresh and dear in the memory of so many in the city. A third of the way round the circle, the colored boy headed his horse into St. Charles Avenue. It was smoother here, though still unpaved.

They crossed in quick succession the streets named for the nine Greek muses, goddesses of poetry and song, arts and dancing, history and astronomy—Terpsichore, Clio, Calliope, Melpomene—yes, all were there—

On past Jackson Avenue, and then Washington. This was the Garden District—site of many a colonial mansion, not so old yet in 1904. It was the second part of the city to be settled, mostly by the Americans of the pre-Civil War years, who were socially ostracized by the Creoles of the uptown French Quarter. Those were beautiful homes—stately columns and iron lacework set back among the moss-draped oaks and magnolias, their interiors lavish with marble mantels, bronze chandeliers, huge mirrors, canopied beds, spiral stairways. He hoped they would last through the ever changing times.

On down St. Charles, following, at about a mile's distance, within the big bend of the river which gave New Orleans its nickname of Crescent City. On past Louisiana Avenue, and then Napoleon. Things were more recently settled out this way. And a little beyond there was still a remnant of a plantation here and there, with small dairy herds or rich farmlands. But the city was making inroads a-plenty.

A Nickel for Carfare

Round another bend, and there ahead stood the white frame "country" church and rectory which the people called "the Little Jesuits"—to distinguish it from the Fathers' well established Immaculate Conception Church back at the college, just off Canal Street in the heart of the old city.

This was to be the site of his work for the coming years. "How long does it take to found a university?" he asked himself. Well, the city was certainly growing in this direction, and he figured he'd have his school up and ready when the time came for it to take over the lead. He'd have to start with the young boys of the neighborhood, build up a student-body from high school to college level, draw graduates from the uptown area—then at last he'd be ready to function as a genuine university. Only time would show what measure of success or failure was in store for him.

Months later, when the first temporary facilities had been prepared, the opening day of the new school—to be called Loyola—was duly announced throughout the city. When it arrived, it brought but six lonesome-looking students. Father Biever was crushed. He had thought that surely out of all the families he had visited nearby there would have been more than these six to take up his offer. They had all seemed so nice at the time. And the old school had even let him campaign among their students in hopes of getting the ones that lived out his way. But no luck! He peeked at his bank account. One hundred dollars! That wouldn't last very long. He already had something of a debt from this initial investment. What would he do? It's in times like these that a businessman would feel like closing shop and skipping town. He laughed at the thought of how far a Jesuit would get trying that.

Well, anyhow, he decided to go over and see how his "university" was making out. He had left the students with their professors while he retired to his private room where he could pull out his hair in peace. He glanced into the mirror to make sure it hadn't turned completely white in the last few hours. Then he strolled across the yard to go pay his first official visit as president.

He found them—swallowed up in the corners of the rooms—six students and four professors—almost one apiece. They all seemed strangely happy. Of course!—they didn't have to take the blame for this flop! The boys had all learned several of the Latin declensions already, and were in the process of practicing their new knowledge in rapid drill. Father Biever was pleased—then the idea occurred to him. With the almost private tutoring these boys were getting, they should advance very rapidly. They would be his salesmen; that would be it! He gathered the professors together and gave them his plan. They wouldn't tell a soul how the first day had gone, and how few students they had. They'd just go on quietly about their business, and let the progress of the boys speak for itself. They might even send them out as apostles to round up a few more willing students—they could convince their friends easily—a boy's main criterion would be whether or not he had friends there. Then maybe he'd enter them in competition against the freshman classes of other schools, and rope in a few more that way.

In a few weeks the plan was already working. The air of secrecy about it had helped to keep them cheerful. And the president began to be a little optimistic again. It would be a long time, he realized, but they'd get there eventually. He had just expected too much for the first day, that's all. The students were doing their part wonderfully. In a few months' time they had made remarkable progress under the undivided attention of their learned masters. Word began to leak out now, and spread quickly. Soon there were others eager to benefit by the small size of the classes—now that they saw the Fathers' earnestness of purpose and felt that the new school would not fold up on their hands. For some it was nearer home than the uptown college; for others it was more within their present means. In one way and another, the enrollment steadily climbed, until eventually it began to give a hint of future competition to the older school.

Father Biever, meanwhile, had left them to their declensions and conjugations, and was out roaming the streets seeking friends and patrons for the new institution. He made contacts throughout the city and the state, proposing his plans, arguing, persuading, pleading, convincing men of their religious and civic obligation, selling them the idea of all the merit they would receive for aiding such a work for the Church and souls, everywhere firing others with his own determination.

In the process, too, he had to suffer the usual line of abuse—the ridicule of the worldly-minded, the hostility of certain Protestant groups, the stinginess and skepticism of some Catholics who taunted: "No wonder you Jesuits are so rich!—got your beggars making the rounds all the time, huh?" He just swallowed it and passed on.

Before long he had founded what he called the "Marquette Association" from the most interested of his contacts. Its officers were leading men in the city, and its members included many of the most influential men of Louisiana, with the Archbishop of New Orleans at their head.

With such excellent backing from the many fast friends that the genially overpowering Father Biever made so easily, Loyola grew quickly. After seven short years, in 1911, the main building of the University was erected—an inspiring four-story structure of red brick, set far back from the avenue, with sixteen handsome turrets to impress the eye. It was named appropriately for the Jesuit, Marquette, who had been first to explore the great river which was to mother New Orleans and its world-trading port.

Building had been somewhat of a heckling job—poring over blueprints, haggling over prices, waiting for materials. Then there was the noise and disturbance of classes that the teachers complained about, even though they wanted the building, of course. Father Biever himself watched every detail—was in the thick of things, full of the usual questions and observations.

Then, finally, came the day of the dedication ceremony. It was a gala event. Archbishop James H. Blenk, who had himself broken ground for the building and had shown great interest in the institution from the very start, was there in full episcopal array to bless the cornerstone. The members of the Marquette Association who had collected the building funds were in full attendance. And a vast crowd from the city, contributors and well-wishers alike, turned out for the ceremony. The ubiquitous Father Biever was one triumphant smile—happy as a kid at a football game, as he mingled with the people who came to see this promise of the future.

Encouraged by this impressive beginning, the Fathers soon saw fit to merge the college division of the older school on Baronne Street with this new foundation, pooling their efforts in a bid for the educational leadership of the South. Faculty and student-body were thus doubled, and Loyola fast began attaining the full prestige that her type of education warranted.

Father Biever's building program kept pace with the rest. Soon a second spacious hall was erected immediately behind the first, and a comfortable faculty residence arose to one side, in the foreground right on the avenue.

Meanwhile, work was piling up on Father Biever's desk. This president's job was no bed of roses—or if it was, nobody had bothered to pick the thorns off first. There was the constant juggling of teachers and classes, introduction of new courses, and all the myriad details of textbooks and the like. Then, too, they ought to get more school organizations going. He spread the work around among his growing faculty, and tried to hold his presidency job down to that of a sort of general moderator.

Every year now saw the opening of new college divisions, new courses—dentistry, pharmacy, pathology, pre-med, pre-law. They followed one another in swift succession.

An amusing incident occurred in connection with the founding of one of the chairs of science. One of Father Biever's fund solicitors called on the wife of a rich Italian philanthropist to secure a contribution for the science chair. "Well," asked the potential donor, "how much does the chair cost?"

"Ten thousand dollars," was the reply.

"Ten thousand dollars! Why, I am a rich woman, and the chair I sit on costs only two dollars. You go and tell Father Biever to be satisfied with a chair like mine."

With the opening of the various colleges, Loyola had at last become a genuine university. Its official university standing, with power to grant literary honors and degrees, was granted by the state legislature in 1912. The job was done at last.

There had been more times like that first day, when it looked as if the only thing to do was to give it up as a bad job, and be content with the college they already had uptown. There was the perennial money problem—the second embarrassing rounds to those who had already given generously. There were the organizational headaches, the blind alleys that such affairs run into every so often, when he couldn't see his way through.

One might imagine Father Biever in his regulation report to the provincial that year saying in a mock-bragging tone: "Well, your university is up! What do I do now?"

At first one would question the wisdom of the superior who would move a man from such a position at a time like that.

But the gold mine that was this man had not yet been worked out by any means. Superiors saw that he was too valuable to tie down to one house and one job. Why not turn him loose upon the whole South and see what marvels he could accomplish?

In a short time, all of Dixie would feel the impact of the man.

For it was in the providence of God that superiors should appoint Father Biever, in the spring of 1913, to the mission band. His assignment henceforth was the whole southeastern quarter of the United States, and then some!—from Georgia on the Atlantic, and the sunny vacation land of Florida, through the hills of Tennessee and Arkansas above, through Alabama and Mississippi below on the Gulf, through the bayous and little French towns of Louisiana, to the wide open spaces of Texas and Oklahoma—a territory of over a million square miles.

So his next great work began.

The little group of three or four missioners—of which he was made the head the following year—kept constantly on the go, singly or in pairs, making the rounds of practically every parish and mission station in the South—wherever they were invited—preaching, dispensing the sacraments, revitalizing the Church and its members. Father Biever—hardly stopping long enough for a breath—grabbed his meals frequently on the go. There was comfortable lodging in the city rectories; not so comfortable in the country: sometimes with the pastor, when he had food and a bed to spare, sometimes with the parishioners, making the rounds to different homes for each day of a mission.

There was traveling in the slow, creaky milk trains of the day between the sizable cities, and for the country parishes and outlying stations using what conveyance was at hand—a horse and buggy over hot, dusty roads or sloshy, muddy ones—a slow bayou trip on an ancient stern-wheeler—rarely the comparative luxury of an automobile of the 'teens. There was living out of a suitcase with what little it could hold, having to do a good bit of his own laundry, at times having to impose on some good lady of the parish to starch and iron a shirt—rejoicing at the occasional trips to the cities, and a chance to get the well-sweated cassock and dust-coated suit cleaned again.

Preaching was the main task, and Father Biever early showed his prowess in that line. His years of study of the classics and teaching of rhetoric had not been wasted, but furnished him now with many a rolling period and eye-catching figure to put over his point. That was the kind of talk people liked in those days. And he had lots to say, most of all.

Strange to say, his scientific training stood him in almost as good stead on the missions as the humanities themselves. He was able on several occasions to use his illustrated chemistry lectures as a drawing card for a crowd, or to help some parish drive for funds. His general scientific knowledge, too, gave him many a chance to contribute to the physical health of some community when there was need and he had time. Indeed, in certain poor areas he acquired something of the reputation of a traveling medicine man as well as missionary.

On reaching a new station, his first job was to advertise for an audience. In the cities it was fairly easy—announcements in the daily paper and at all the Masses the previous Sunday. But in the little country towns that had no newspaper he often had to resort to handbills that he would have posted around the town and distributed from the general store. Sometimes, when a country priest had been waiting his turn for several months and did not know just when the missioner would get around to his

A Nickel for Carfare

parish, he would ring the church bell at Father Biever's arrival, as a signal that the mission would start that night. Once when a certain pastor did that, it just so happened that it was two o'clock in the morning when Father Biever got there, and all the good farmers, thinking that the church was burning, jumped from their beds and came running with whatever equipment they could find to help save the house of God. Sweating and panting they reached the church—only to find the pastor and Father Biever standing in smiles on the front porch to announce the beginning of the mission. Not the best practice for rendering the audience benevolent, one may be sure.

Generally the missions ran for two weeks, one for the men and one for the women. But often enough, too, he preached to mixed congregations—the whole family showing up, because they didn't know when they would be able to have a mission again.

The missioner preached several times a day—at night for the big crowds; in the morning after Mass for the fervent and generous who came; in the afternoons to the children; and sometimes an extra talk for the farmers in the less busy seasons. He threw himself into the task with all the zeal and sincerity and eloquence he could muster.

He preached the eternal values over the temporal. He showed them the beauty of the paradise on earth that God had planned for man, unveiled to them the hideous spectre of sin in all its forms, conjured up at their very feet the yawning pit of hell. He took them to the bleak crest of Calvary to show them the abundance of God's loving mercy. He taught them the wonder of the glorious redeemed life they were leading—how God had given back to men, insofar as His infinite Justice would mysteriously allow His Infinite Mercy, all the joys of the original paradise—divine sonship by grace, eternal life, the simple joy of the children of God; the seven sacramental fonts of living water; sickness and even death transformed into a thing of beauty when borne for love of Him Who had first shared them Himself. The good priest saw their trials and crosses, their weakness and discouragement, and he lifted them

· 281 ·

up with this supernatural outlook to a new life of peace and joy and virtue, insofar as they could achieve it.

Then there were the long hours of confessional work before and after the evening talks, and at the Mass hours in the morning, to reap the fruit of his labors. The number of confessions was always a good indication of the success of a mission.

And when the two weeks came to an end, there would be the usual impressive closing ceremony—thousands of communions, renewal of baptismal vows, and imparting of the Apostolic Benediction and plenary indulgence. At the close of one of the missions in Thibodeaux, Louisiana, situated on Bayou Lafourche below New Orleans, one thousand children received communion in a body, bringing the total number of communions for the two weeks to five thousand. The immense square in front of the church was filled from early dawn till late at night, flatboats and dugouts plying the chocolate bayou waters all day long bringing the farmhands to the mission. When dusk fell, 3,500 people bearing lighted candles marched in procession beneath a long avenue of century oaks to the foot of a Calvary that stood behind the church. The priests ascended the mound and, standing beneath the cross, led the faithful in the renewal of their baptismal vows. That vast throng in the candlelight with swelling voice pledged their loyalty to Christ Crucified, then with full hearts and brimming eyes climbed back into their little boats, and softly singing a hymn to Mary, wound their way into the dark until their song and flickering lights had faded away. It was a closing that all would long remember. There were many like this.

That, then, was the missioner's life—preaching day after day and night after night, hearing confessions at all hours, searching out individually those too sick to attend the talks and those too hardened to be persuaded to come.

He worked the coast of Florida—booming with the new vacation towns, fast becoming the winter residence of the wealthy and the year-round residence of many who had heard tales of its wonderful climate. There were groups of Irish here and there, and a goodly sprinkling of Cubans that had begun to drift in in large numbers to work the tobacco factories.

From Jacksonville, in the northeast corner of the state, he moved down the coast to the old Spanish Catholic stronghold of St. Augustine. He and the bishop must have had a good laugh over the incident that had occurred when he was here years before. During his stay he had been asked to give an illustrated lecture for the benefit of renovations to be made on the old cathedral. The afternoon lecture would be for the Sisters and children, and the night for the general public. Unable to obtain the hydrogen for his limelight lantern, he substituted 80°-proof gasoline. It worked superbly well for the first few pictures. The children sat spellbound, the nuns "awed" delightedly. Then suddenly there was a loud report like a pistol shot, and a huge hissing flame leapt for the ceiling. Pandemonium broke loose among the children and Sisters, screaming and running for safety. Father Biever kept his presence of mind—ripped open the oxygen bag and extinguished the flame with sand. When it was all over and the smoke cleared, the hall was empty—except for the bishop still sitting in the front row, doubled over with laughter and tears streaming down his cheeks.

The afternoon was ruined, for all but His Excellency. But Father Biever obtained better gasoline and tried the lantern again. All worked smoothly this time, so he went ahead with the night lecture. He showed them first some of the natural wonders of the chemical world—changed one substance into another right before their eyes, with explosive sound effects and colored smoke clouds to add to the mystery. He illustrated the spontaneous combustion of liquids, and the formation of a liquid from two gases rushing together with a crash that shook the hall. Then with his lantern slide he told of the interesting life and habits of the honey bee—and showed colorful scenes of them at work among the flowers. It was all quite a performance in that day when so little science was known to the public. No doubt about it, the man was a born showman.

From St. Augustine, the missioner moved south to West Palm Beach. It was quite a resort now. In his earlier stay there he had lived several months in an unfurnished cottage, his only apostolic work to carry his little folding altar across the long railroad trestle in the early hours of Sunday morning, to say Mass in the ballroom of the Royal Palm Hotel after the dance.

From there, down the coast to Miami, then out the little island chain to the very tip of Key West, and up around the boot, circumventing the impenetrable crocodile heaven of the everglades, to St. Petersburg and Tampa.

He covered Georgia—rich in Southern colonial traditions, and with just a touch of Old English—its best energies concentrated in its beautiful cities of Atlanta, Savannah, Augusta. Here were strongholds of the few Catholic groups of the state, who were necessarily fervent in the face of daily contact with the hostile Baptists and Ku Kluxers, but who could always use a little spiritual reinforcement and encouragement for that same reason.

On to the rolling mountains of Tennessee and Arkansas, and their scattered dwellers—so ridiculed by their Northern brothers, so religiously exploited by the wandering Baptist revivalists. He visited all the big cities, where life's pleasant pace is set by the people's leisurely twang and friendly manner—preached in Nashville's cathedral and several of its parishes, in the churches of Memphis, Knoxville, and Chattanooga—gave missions in the diocese of Little Rock, in the capital city itself, in Helena, Hot Springs, and many smaller towns. Here there was a lot of apologetic work to do—to counteract any doubts that the Baptist atmosphere might have caused, to give the faithful the answers to the Protestant objections they would have to meet, to bring back to the Church those whom economic and social pressure might have alienated.

Then farther south he met the undulating terrain of Alabama —the soft green of its stately, thick-growing pines broken by the jutting red and orange clay banks—the whole criss-crossed with many a sandy-bottomed gully that is full and roaring after the rains wash out the soft roadbeds.

Alabama presented the same problems as the two previous states—always the counteracting of the propaganda and pressure of ignorant Protestants. He fortified the beach-heads of the

Faith in the heart of the state at Montgomery, and in the industrial center of Birmingham. Then he visited Mobile—so different from the rest, like a smaller replica of New Orleans in its French origin, its predominance of Catholicism, its oak-shaded avenues of colonial homes.

Everywhere there were large groups of Negroes for whom Father Biever felt deeply. There were so few priests to evangelize and convert them—hardly enough to attend to the whites already in the Church. It hurt him to see those naturally sensitive religious sensibilities of the colored folk going untended. But he remembered St. Pius X, who had once said, "we are not Divine Providence." So time and patience and prayer would bring more missionaries to care for the Negro.

Then on to the Gulf Coast of Mississippi—dotted with its many friendly fishing towns—Gulfport, Biloxi, Pass Christian—each with its own small share of French Catholic tradition that had spread along the coast between New Orleans and Mobile. Then up to Vicksburg of Confederacy fame, and west to where the state meets the Mississippi River at Natchez—the queen city of the Southern colonial days.

Down the river into the boot of Louisiana, to the heart of all the French Catholic tradition of the South—New Orleans. It was good to get back occasionally and see old friends. He gave several missions in the city at different times. Then he moved on—south into the delta country with its plantations and little villages of French and Negro sharecroppers—west into the bayou country and the French shrimping towns built along the banks of these winding watery highways—further west into the rich, flooded rice fields of the Lafayette area—then north, through the fluffy-topped cotton fields, the long straight rows of corn bending to the summer breeze, the tall sugar cane that his own brother missionaries had introduced a century and a half before and which had proved so successful in the state's semitropical climate—on to the widespread Alexandria diocese in the north of the state, with its sulphur and salt deposits, its oil and farms and dairy herds. This was Louisiana, scattered through with little French towns of simple loyal Catholics, living in an

· 285 ·

atmosphere that took the supernatural completely for granted—no prey to the wandering Baptist preachers who tended to "whoop up" religion in other unfortunate parts of the South. It was the missioner's most fruitful field, and he exploited it to the full.

Father Biever, native of Luxembourg that he was, spoke fluent French; he was better equipped than the other missioners to handle the Louisiana calls. He loved the good people—so childlike in their faith, yet often also childlike in their lack of will power. They were fond of him and loved his sermons for their charming combination of simplicity and elegance—the natural result of a mind that understood their problems and a heart that longed to solve them all. How often it happened that at the end of a mission, when the good country folk brought him an offering of gratitude from their own small earnings, they would plead with him to stay longer with them and minister to their hungry souls.

He loved them when they packed into the church in large families—often having come long distances in covered wagons, to camp nearby for the fortnight. It would mean that he had to run competition to the voices of 20 or 30 babies complaining at the length of his sermons. But that was all compensated for on many an occasion. It was his practice to bless all the little tykes toward the close of a mission. And often he gave rosaries to the mothers with the largest numbers of children. At the mission of Larose, the babes all blessed, he stood up and said: "Now for the mothers of these beautiful children—every mother of seven children or more may now come to the altar and receive a rosary." He goes on to relate: "I had only thirty-five rosaries, thinking that this would be ample. But, to my surprise, instead of thirty-five mothers, two hundred came, all saying: 'I have seven children.' 'I have eight.' 'Ten.' 'Twelve.' 'Fifteen.' 'Eighteen.' One mother claimed three rosaries saying: 'I am the proud mother of twenty-two living children.' "

There was poverty a-plenty along his mission trails. Here is one of the stories he tells. "Bayou Pierre was about eighteen miles distant from Cloutierville. A colored man took me there in a broken-down buggy that we often had to leave to enable the poor horse to pull it along through a very sandy and unfrequented road.

"We reached our destination toward evening. My lodging was to be in the house of an old couple. Its furniture was of the most primitive kind, and its bath and lavatory accommodations did not exist.

"At that time the temperature was freezing. Early in the morning I left the home for the chapel about a mile distant. On my way (it was still dark) I stepped upon what I thought to be terra firma, but found out, to my discomfort, to be nothing but a pool of water lightly frozen and covered with leaves.

"Wet to my knees I moved on and at last came to the little chapel. I opened the fence gate; it collapsed. I pulled the bell rope to give a warning to the people that the missionary had arrived; the rope was rotten and fell down.

"There was, however, plenty of work. Marriages had to be validated, babies were baptized, children were instructed for First Communion and the grown people for the reception of the sacraments.

"About one hundred and fifty Catholics lived in this small settlement."

In Grand Coteau, Opelousas, Church Point, and Rayne he found the colored Catholics extremely numerous—a fact ascribable to the attention given them after the Civil War by the priests of Grand Coteau. In other places he tells of large numbers of confessions of the Negroes, and bemoans the fact that he had no time to give them the instructions that they needed so badly.

He visited St. Martinville, once called "le petit Paris de la Louisiane," and had to hold night services by candle light alone, there being no electricity available. He looked for the famous oak tree on the banks of the Teche where the legendary Evangeline awaited her lover Gabriel, but on examining (old scientific Biever!) the several trees that were claimed to be the original Evangeline oak, he concluded that none of them was old enough.

Everywhere he kept the old scientific eye alert to be of what service he could to the people.

At Patterson, he diagnosed the sickness of many children as typhoid fever, and at the close of the mission suggested that the people examine the water supply at the school. The bottom of the large cistern was found to contain dead rats, cats, sparrows, bats, and mice.

At the close of another mission in Larose, on Easter morn, a Presbyterian minister was discovered to have set up a gospel tent right opposite the church. It was beautifully arranged, and illuminated with acetylene lamps. The public was cordially invited, and the minister was expecting a large crowd. Father Biever rose to the occasion, announced a lecture for that night in the parish hall on "How to Make Larose Healthy, Wealthy, and Wise." He entertained the people with a semi-scientific lecture and what chemical exhibits he could gather. The priest drew all the crowds, and the minister was left with but one family of three.

At the Jennings oil fields, a former seminarian, who had apostatized and become a Protestant minister, had won over nearly all these people into heresy. So Father Biever put out handbills advertising another lecture on health and wealth. It was interestingly illustrated, as he says, with homely but striking chemical experiments. Then giving them some good advice on preserving their bodily health, he announced that for three days he would give them some splendid counsels about the health of their souls. His tactics and sermons won them back.

Back he went to Galveston where he had been stationed for a short time in the earlier years of his priestly ministry. He recalled with a laugh the night he had spent in a little shack on the shore of the Gulf to prove to the people that it was not haunted. The ghost had turned out to be a wandering cow seeking shelter there every evening, and one more myth died the death.

He had spent one summer as pastor in a Negro parish there, too, and along with his care of their souls he did what he could to teach them a little about how to keep well. When called once to give the last sacraments to a dying man, he tried to bring him out of a coma with a bottle of ammonia that he had sent for from the drugstore. By mistake the ammonia was undiluted and proved so strong that it made the poor Negro jump from the bed and vomit some vile black matter. The next morning the man was cured, and ever afterwards the good Negroes looked on the priest as a great medicine man, and came to him with all their ailments.

He had left Galveston that time just a few days before the awful hurricane of 1900, which had completely destroyed the town and many of its 40,000 inhabitants. To the friend who took him to the train, and in farewell had told him to come back soon to stay, Father Biever jokingly replied: "I am afraid, for one of these days you will be washed away." Unwittingly he had prophesied the impending doom.

Then to broad-shouldered, swaggering Houston. During his mission there some Protestant ministers mingled with the congregation to hear his sermon on "The Catholic Church, Champion of Liberty," and gave the story of his sermons to a hostile publisher. His paper next day carried a vile denunciation of these Jesuit liars, and accused Albert Biever, "a papal bachelor," of "rejoicing Beelzebub greatly" by his sermons. Despite the incident the mission was a real success.

On to San Antonio, where he collaborated with a Dr. Campbell on ridding a Mexican settlement of the mosquitoes that were causing their malaria. They had discovered that bats live on mosquitoes. Therefore, they built a bat tower in the desired location, chased the bats into it from a cave some distance away by playing jazz music which they had found the bats disliked. (Strictly "long hair," these bats!) The mosquitoes and malaria disappeared, and Father Biever proceeded to publish several scientific articles on bats, advocating the building of similar towers in other places throughout the South.

On to El Paso, the western limit of the mission run, where he helped to console the Mexican Jesuits driven out by the recent persecutions.

Then back to Dallas and Fort Worth in the north of the state, and all their outlying missions.

Then, finally, up to Oklahoma, and its many small Western towns, with their mixture of Irish, English, and Indian names—a well disposed mission field where he was invited often—to Tulsa, Purcelle, and Oklahoma City. His particular delight there was the little orphanage of Indian children at Purcelle which he grew to love.

That was the missioner's life—full of the consolations that must have overflowed in the heart of Christ in His missionary tours of Palestine, but with a good share, too, of the same trials and hardships that the Master Himself had suffered—having no fixed abode, no place to call home, plenty of poverty and weariness, and the opposition of hostile factions, misrepresentation, backsliding, discouragement.

He gave as many as fifteen missions a year, which, when one allows three weeks per mission—two for the talks and one for extra work and traveling—doesn't leave many free weeks. Yet he found time also in his nine years on the mission band for thirty retreats to the secular clergy of the different dioceses and states; besides that, he must have given a retreat to practically every religious house in the South.

But the old missioner was growing tired now—65 was a pretty advanced age for such an active life. His voice and his knees had got just a little shaky whenever he worked overtime. His throat, particularly, was in bad condition. The three or four talks a day through the years would often cause his throat to be gushing blood when he finally stepped down from the pulpit. He wouldn't be able to stand that strain much longer.

So it was that in 1922 he was called back to his beloved New Orleans. His many friends were glad to see him back, and he was just as happy to be among them again. They had thought of him so often during his missionary years. His reputation had grown greatly by now. "See that priest over there?" they would say; "he's the one that founded Loyola. They just told him: 'Here's a nickel for carfare—go downtown and found a university.' And he did it—almost overnight."

When he was rested again and able to carry on, he was assigned as pastor of the Immaculate Conception Church. He would be centrally located there, easily available to the people that would be constantly seeking him out.

Though it was a mighty popular church, you couldn't call it a normal parish with the location it had. It sat just off Canal Street, which divides the business section from the old French Quarter. It was on the business side, and open for business all hours of the day. There was a constant stream of shoppers and office workers dropping in for a moment's rest and prayer. The vigil-light stands, that the people loved, went far toward the church's upkeep. And St. Anthony's poor-box at the door did a good business for feeding the breadlines that trailed down the street from the rectory each morning. The noon Mass every day always had a packed church of office workers and business-men who chose to spend part of their lunch hour with God, and the altar-rail often filled several times with those that came fast-ing, in order to receive.

The old Jesuit was fond of the landmarks thrusting them-selves on him everywhere when he got out for a stroll. Above all, so close, the French Quarter or Vieux Carré. It was some-thing right out of the pages of history, comparable in its colorful lore to the Latin Quarter of Paris itself. Its aged and shriveled appearance lent an almost human air to the buildings that had been rubbing shoulders there for two centuries—like reverent old couples standing on the sidelines watching the parade go by. Its quaint antique shops, the balconies of iron grillwork, the lantern-shaped lamps down the narrow streets, an occasional patio and fountain—all remained unchanged. The picture was completed by the open pavilion of vegetable stands of the French Market, and the Negresses walking the streets, melodiously hawking the fruit in the baskets carried proudly on their heads. Dominating the scene, facing on Jackson Square and its equestrian monument to the hero of New Orleans, stood the venerable old St. Louis Cathedral, the next nearest church.

After sizing up his parish, Father Biever settled down to his work in earnest—glad to have a position that offered such a fruitful ministry, without all the wasted energy of traveling as on the missions. There were hundreds flocking back for the spiritual advice of this wise, gentle priest on whom they had once depended. Confessional work there was practically an all day job because of the constant visitors dropping in during their spare moments. The church's novenas and missions, too, always had a devoted following from all parts of town—people who had come to love the atmosphere of the old church before their own parish had begun. Father Biever would be preaching again and packing them in—and the crowds had long waited to hear his earnest eloquence once more.

Along with the listlessness that resulted from his settling down after the active mission life came one of the first signs of his real age. In between, when there weren't confessions to hear or sermons to prepare, and when someone else was answering the parlor calls, he began to dream of all the days that had been. Somehow he must have realized the terrific story value of the things he had lived through. And he had so loved the men of the Society whom he had known all along the way— he hated to see their memory die now that they were gone. So he began a book of memoirs, much of the material taken from the diary he had kept in his native French.

He wrote of his boyhood in Luxembourg, of the days there in the minor seminary and the sickness that came on him from overwork; and it is only now that one learns that that pain never left him. He had been advised to apply for the foreign missions in America in hopes of a better climate, and soon found himself on a thrilling bayou trip to the Jesuit Novitiate at Grand Coteau.

He recalled the full days of his six years teaching at Spring Hill, and the happy days of his philosophy and theology study in England, where he delighted in visiting the shrines of the Jesuit martyrs.

Not indulging merely in thoughts of himself, he paged through the records of the archives at the old church, and began a short history of the work of the Jesuits in New Orleans and the Mississippi Valley—which he published in 1924, in commemoration, as his preface states, of "the 250th Anniversary of the discovery of the Mississippi by Father James Marquette, S.J., the Bicentenary of the founding of the first mission of the Jesuits in Louisiana, the 160th Anniversary of their expulsion from colonial France, the Centenary of their return to the Mississippi Valley, the Diamond Jubilee of the beginning of the church and college of the Immaculate Conception in New Orleans, the 50th Anniversary of the enthroning of the historic statue of the Immaculate Virgin along with the erection of the glorious bronze altar in the church, and the twentieth Anniversary of the founding of Loyola." Some jubilees for one little, old preface.

He wrote of the early days when the missionaries had trudged through the dense forests after the Indians, blazing their way by carving the name of Jesus upon the trees—of the cruel slaying of several of them while saying Mass or carrying the Blessed Sacrament to the sick—of the happy days on the plantation in what is now the heart of New Orleans; of the sugar cane, oranges, indigo, and other crops that his Jesuit forebears had started there; and of their care in instructing and baptizing their Negro and Indian farm hands—of their cruel and unjust expulsion in 1763, and the confiscation of all their property—of their second coming years later, and founding of the church and college on the old plantation site.

But time was always pressing—he could not devote much of it to this labor of love. The old church had had its foundations weakened by all the big buildings going up near it through the years, and had been condemned as unsafe. He would have to rebuild it. The devoted parishioners were shocked at the news, and afraid they would lose their church altogether. The president of the bank across the street offered Father the use of the ground floor of his building during the time of the reconstruction. All the city was sympathetic at the loss of the church that had been such a landmark for over 70 years. It had once ruled the downtown area, but now was all but swallowed up by the huge buildings on all sides.

Under the circumstances, the only thing to do was to build again to the exact specifications of the former church. Nothing else would be able to fill its place in the hearts of the people. And so the dismantling began. It meant a lot of detailed checking of blueprints with the contractors, the daily pounding and crashing of tearing down and reconstruction, the inconvenience of their temporary quarters. But Father Biever was an old hand at that sort of thing. He had witnessed every detail of the buildings that went up at Loyola, and was again in the thick of things making his comments and asking questions.

Finally the job was done, and the beautiful statue of the Immaculate Conception could be replaced in its niche high over the altar. It was a very special statue, carved of white marble at the request of Queen Amelie, wife of Louis Philippe, King of France, for the royal chapel in Paris. Somehow it had not reached its original destination, but was brought to New Orleans, where it had been bought by the Jesuit Fathers. With Mary back in control, now, Father Biever could rest easy.

Two years later, when the new church was just well broken in, he was moved again—this time back to his old job as pastor of Holy Name. So once again he packed his trunks and made the trip down St. Charles Avenue.

But things were different now. The broad avenue was paved all the way, and a bank of green ran down the center. The oaks planted along both sides had grown to nicer proportions, and had acquired more of the essential Spanish moss. The buggies of the former time were out of date now, and even the streetcar fare had changed—from a nickel to seven cents. But it was the same gently-curving, beautiful drive. On the way, the memories of that first trip down to found the university swarmed about him—and he relived all the fears and uncertainties that were his at the time, and the determination and youthful courage with which he had tackled them. Names, faces, scenes swept before him.

When he reached his destination, his mind was still in the past—like one long lost in a state of amnesia, and now approaching home and beginning to recall. Was this the Loyola he had known?—the Loyola he had been sent to found? What were those majestic buildings there?—where did they come from? Look at that long beautiful lawn in the hollow of the inverted "U" formed by the buildings—and the drive that circled within it behind the welcoming arms of the Sacred Heart statue. Was that Marquette Hall in the middle?—its turrets rising higher and higher toward the center, lifting your eyes to heaven. There on the left!—that was the new church he had planned but had been unable to put up before he was sent on the missions—what a magnificent job they had done while he was gone—its parapets, spires, buttresses—you'd never dream so much could be done with ordinary brick.

He stood there on the sidewalk amazed. Of course, he had been back several times when passing through the city on his mission rounds, and from his church on Baronne Street these last few years. He had followed every step of the university—his university. It's just that, on this second assignment to Holy Name, his mind had wandered back to that first trip downtown, and he had almost expected to find there only the little white church of the early days. The sight of the university took him by surprise. He saw it suddenly in a new and detached way. He was amazed at the thought of the good that one man can do in starting a work like that, that carries on its apostolate for years after he is gone. It works with a sort of geometric progression, he thought—or like interest reinvested that keeps increasing over the years. He wondered humbly if he'd be getting small dividends from the university's merits that way—long after he had reached heaven—when the little pebble he had loosened had become a tremendous avalanche, each stone freeing several others, and they in turn setting yet others in motion, until the myriad stones and their far-reaching effects could hardly be counted even by the recording angel.

He dropped into the church, told the Lord how glad he was to be back here again, and how grateful he was for the success of the university he had founded.

He had thought surely that by now his building days were over. But that grammar school was in bad shape—they just needed a new one, that was all. So he got busy again and had a new one up the next year.

When that was finished, life moved on at a very easy pace, it seemed. He worked a little more on his memoirs, said his Mass and Office every morning, heard a few confessions, maybe, or visited some of the parishioners. Life was almost like heaven for a priest his age—he was ready whenever the time came—his work was done. Actually there wasn't much use hanging around here any longer. When the call did come, it was very sudden. He died on the morning of November 14, 1934—he was 76 years old.

The notice that day in the paper said that he was mourned by thousands, Catholics and non-Catholics alike—he had won their esteem as a priest, scientist, preacher, writer, founder of Loyola, and rebuilder of the historic church of the Immaculate Conception—that he was one of the most noted Jesuits in the Order's history in New Orleans.

It was hard to list all his accomplishments. As a preacher he had spoken in English, French, classical German, and halting Spanish. As a scientist he had distinguished himself in chemistry and physics, and on his own had studied and lectured on bees, ants, termites, mosquitoes, bats, and what-have-you. As a priest he had brought a glimpse of Christ to countless souls throughout the South—from the pulpit, confessional, bedside, and on the street. But it was as a builder he would be longest remembered—for the magnificent university he had founded.

Was there no end to the talents this man Biever could draw out of his bottomless grab-bag? He had seemed to produce things from nothing, as if by magic—like the wonders he worked before your very eyes in his good old lantern lectures of the 1910's.

When suddenly they handed him his ticket for the trip to heaven, well—he probably found himself inquiring about the health of some of the less eye-stunning angels and saints, and when they had been to the sacraments last, before he realized what had happened and where he was—that he had just had his last joy-ride, that this was the end of the line—and home.

OIL HAD *come to Oklahoma, and Tulsa mushroomed over-*
night. Wherever there was money or opportunity, Americans
flocked like gulls to a seashore. By now Henry Ford's horseless
carriage was revolutionizing industry and transportation. The
old trolley cars surveyed with awe the puffing, snorting monster
with its high seats and proud, self-conscious occupants.

Thoughtful men had begun to see the need for planning in
this turmoil. Space and time were no longer remote dimensions.
Other peoples, their problems and grievances, were felt with
greater impact. Italians were leaving their homeland by the
thousands; so were the Slavs and the peoples of the Balkans. For
a generation they would be the whipping boys with their poor
English, their poverty. Only time would reveal what resource-
fulness they brought, the native drives and sensitivity that lay
harnessed in the tenements.

It was a different Europe that America saw now across the
waters. Germany became a giant under Bismarck, Italy united
under Garibaldi and anti-clericals, the Pope strangely began
to exercise ever more influence in men's councils now that he
was no longer a king among kings, freed from his historic re-
sponsibilities. When Leo spoke, the world listened. Many heeded
his words.

France had meanwhile spurned with fine contempt Bernadette
at Lourdes and Theresa of Lisieux. She demanded the expulsion
of many of her fairest children. Parnell was leading Ireland one
more step to freedom, down the road O'Connell had mapped.
Victoria was Empress of India and truly now the sun did not
set on British soil, with Australia hers, the Boers beaten in
Africa, the Chinese coast pried open, Canada still loyal.

An amazing world, indeed, riding superbly high, flaunting its glories for the past and future to behold before they vanished.

* * *

Interchangeable Terms

Father Richard Tierney, S.J.

by JOHN L. MADDOX

The tall, powerfully framed cleric shifted uneasily at his desk in the flats on East 83rd Street. It was mid-January in New York, but the frost on the windows was hardly more biting than the nervous pencil etching out next week's editorial. *Another Remarkable Invention*, the lead snapped.

> Wonders will never cease. Inventions will never come to an end. A new one is on the market, the strangest of all yet devised by man. It is not a mechanical toy either, nor a machine for making bread. They are common-place and quite unworthy of aesthetic Boston, the Alma Mater of the inventor. This remarkable invention is nothing less than a new religion, "The Christianity of the Twentieth Century." Its author is Charles Eliot, President Emeritus of Harvard. This is the second time the venerable gentleman invented a religion. Last year he fabricated "The Religion of the Future"; this year he gave to the world "The Christianity of the Twentieth Century." In view of the fact that there is no trace of inspiration or revelation in either, this is remarkable fecundity. We trust Dr. Eliot is not exhausted by his efforts. Next year would be dull indeed without another new religion.

Something had happened at *America*. Now in 1914, its fifth

year of publication, the Jesuit weekly review had suddenly stopped cutting its editorial teeth and had started baring them. Richard Henry Tierney had arrived.

It was not exactly a case of dreams coming true. When the thin, handsome, almost aristocratic John J. Wynne, S.J., had fathered the magazine into existence, a new kind of ground had been broken. Editor of the cultural monthly *Messenger* and driving power behind the Gargantuan venture of the *Catholic Encyclopedia,* Wynne had wanted to replace the *Messenger* with a weekly built on the blueprints of the London *Tablet.*

The hundreds of Catholic diocesan weeklies already scattered across the country necessarily served only local readers. What Wynne visualized was a national review that would transcend provincial worries and "discuss questions of the day affecting religion, morality, science, and literature; give information and suggest principles that may help to the solution of the vital problems constantly thrust upon our people." In the autumn of 1908 he probed Europe for a corps of foreign correspondents, collected seven Jesuit associates from deliberately scattered locales throughout America, and with fingers crossed launched the magazine into the unpredictable sea of journalism in the following April.

On the whole it took to the water well. There was actually little of the storm in its make-up. Readers found it leisurely and broadly intellectual. Literary criticism, art, history, science, sociology, education, foreign politics, and international relations got between its covers in an urbane and scholarly fashion. Cultural and cosmopolitan rather than controversial, it endeavored to equip the intellectual with an orthodox point of view.

The paper well under way, Wynne vacated the editor's chair in a year's time to tend to other irons in his multi-ironed fire, and sixty-two-year-old Thomas J. Campbell, a granite-like scholar, author, and former Provincial of the Maryland-New York Province, took over. Under Campbell *America* preserved its high standards of scholarship, but still lacked battling blood. Preferring light skirmishes to frontal attacks, it kept its intellectualism high but its circulation low. "Too academic" was the criticism frequently leveled in its direction.

But if the circulation was languishing, few might have gambled that a young professor of philosophy down at Woodstock College, Maryland, was the man to administer the right sort of adrenaline. Providence sometimes seems partial to paradox and when Father Dick Tierney, metaphysician turned magazine man, quietly joined the staff as an associate editor in January, 1914, it was quickly obvious that his pen might in fact turn out to be the needed hypodermic needle.

What followed in the next ten years is a story highly charged with explosives. For *America* grew under Tierney into something hugely more than a mere magazine. It became a power, a tightly knit force spearheading into unexplored areas of influence, a clearing house for militant, sometimes bellicose, Catholicism in the U.S. For ten electric years Richard Henry Tierney played the human dynamo to the danger point, and ended, characteristically enough, only when he had burned it out.

But success stories never start with the success. They are always hammered out of a background of carefully forged details that shape the event.

There was Tierney's father. Richard, Sr., Tipperary-born, had settled in the States as a young man. In those days Spuyten Duyvil, for all its romantic sounding name, could not make the serious municipal boast of being even a village. A quiet rolling strip of wooded land bounded on the west by the Hudson River and on the south by the Harlem, it was checkered with few homes, most of them tenanted by workers in Johnson's Iron Foundry. Here the tall emigrant rose to superintendent of the plant and at thirty-four wedded a blue-eyed, dark-haired girl of unmistakable ancestry named Bridget Shea.

But Richard, Sr., a big man inside the foundry, was even a bigger man outside of it. He wielded a gentle paternalship over his men that could take such charitably practical directions as arbitrating domestic tiffs or steering wage earners home on Saturday night, wages still unquaffed. The cornerstone of lay activity in the mission district, it was Big Dick who saw to all the arrangements for the Sunday Mass that the two Jesuit Fathers, who had buggied out from Fordham College the afternoon before, would offer in the local public school. Confessions were heard Saturday evening in the parlor of his rambling country home, and the vestments and chalice intrusted to his care.

When, in later years, near-by Kingsbridge boasted a mission church served by the pastor of St. Elizabeth's down at Fort Washington, Msgr. Brann could write in his memoirs that the congregation was "good and generous, and knew their religion well," and that the "best of them was the superintendent in Johnson's Foundry at Spuyten Duyvil, Richard Tierney." Dick, Jr., born in 1870 the sixth of eight children, had done a remarkably felicitous job of picking the right parents.

Educationally, he was fortunate too. After the grammar grades at the local country school-house and later at the larger public school at Kingsbridge, his father enrolled him in the high school section of the Jesuits' St. Francis Xavier College on West Sixteenth Street in Lower Manhattan. Despite the long daily problem of commuting on the noisy New York Central, Dick managed to pull down second prize in class standing at the end of his first year, as well as honorable mention in all subjects save mathematics and penmanship (a fact which would in later years perhaps prove lugubrious to the local typesetters).

Classmates remembered him as a tall, slim, industrious student, quiet, retiring, with a bit of the bashful about him, and yet not without an encouraging sense of humor. At times first in his class and always among the honor students, his forte was English. Like the rest of the Tierneys he was an inveterate reader, and if one looked closely at his style one could discern even then the writer of power to come.

The seven-year course of high school and college the Jesuits served at Xavier's was a more hearty educational menu than most boys could consume, and of the more than a hundred students who began with Tierney, only twelve graduated. Fourth in merit, his overall average was high but not brilliant. It might have been otherwise had he not had the long daily traintrips and the out-of-doors extra-curriculars that life in the country provides, for he did combine industry with a huge amount of talent. But school grades are at best a precarious prophecy of later achievement, and in any case young Mr. Tierney now stood ready to take the biggest step on the stairway of his career.

Graduation just over, he and his classmen made a three-day retreat under Father Frank Smith, S.J. Under the benevolent magic of grace long and half hoped-for thoughts slowly matured into unshakable convictions and Dick Tierney applied for admission into the Society of Jesus.

No one seemed surprised.

Not that he had talked it over with others of his class. He had said little even to his family. Dick Tierney was always one for battering out his own decisions. But priestly and religious vocations were anything but surprising at Xavier's in those years. Of the students who had entered the College with him, thirteen had already left for the seminary or novitiate. And of his own graduating class of twelve, eight were eventually to be ordained. If the Sixteenth Street campus was not covered with venerable ivy, it was clearly charged with apostolicity.

What happened to Richard Tierney in those first seven years of training in the long journey to Jesuithood was simply what happens to any and all. There were the two years of novitiate with their deep growth in fundamental asceticism, the two years of humanistic studies that expanded his already well oriented familiarity with classical and English literature, and the three horizon-widening years of philosophy and the sciences. Throughout he was a pre-eminent student and an increasingly able writer. To his teachers and fellow students alike it was clear that his future would lie along some rewarding phase of the intellectual apostolate.

Philosophy at an end, his opportunity to trade the student's side of the desk for the teacher's came in 1899 with his appointment to Gonzaga College, Washington, D. C., as an instructor in science. It was during his stay at Gonzaga that he became acquainted with the young Italian priests attached to the household of the Apostolic Delegate. Guiding them through the terrors of idiomatic English, Tierney made deep and lasting friendships with such high-destined men as Cerretti, later Cardinal and Papal Ambassador to France, and Marchetti-Selvaggiani, to become Archbishop of Seleucia, Secretary to the Congregation for the Propagation of the Faith, and finally Cardinal.

After three years in the capital city, Tierney was assigned to the larger Holy Cross College of Worcester, Massachusetts, and given the somewhat uneasy opportunity to demonstrate his pedagogical versatility by teaching this time, not science, but Greek and Latin literature.

The three years at Gonzaga and the two at Holy Cross had the intended effect of weathering the young seminarian; and when he journeyed back to Woodstock, Maryland, to begin his four-year course in theology, it was with rich experiences no amount of mere book grubbing could have supplied. There was much ahead that would draw hard on the wealth of those days.

At Woodstock again there was the old easy excellence in his studies. Coaching others, defending theses in the public disputations, lecturing on phases of ecclesiastical history and canon law, it was the same story of driving industry wedded to high talent. Top honors arrived in his fourth year when he was chosen for the public disputation of the treatise *De Deo Uno et Trino*. Before an auditorium filled with distinguished ecclesiastics, including James Cardinal Gibbons, and Diomed Falconio, the Apostolic Delegate, flanked by professors of philosophy and theology from various seminaries, he took the rostrum for two fluent hours of lucid (and Latin) defense. To cap the occasion off academically, there were four guest objectors to ply him roundly with a long range of objections. But opponents would always be Richard Henry Tierney's meat.

The genuinely important fact of those four years at Woodstock was, of course, his ordination to the priesthood in June of 1907. He was thirty-seven years old; twenty-seven remained to him. Whatever else he was to become, he would be first and last the priest. "Forever," the archbishop had whispered. It would be so.

Theology finished, one last leg of Jesuit basic training remained: the third year of novitiate, tertianship. Instead of the usual assignment to the Novitiate of St. Andrew-on-Hudson, Poughkeepsie, superiors decided that year to send Tierney and three other Americans to Linz, Austria, for the ten months. The four young priests found the community stimulatingly cosmopolitan. Jesuits from England, Belgium, France, Germany, Holland, Switzerland, Hungary, and Ecuador flavored the Austrian group, and Tierney built many friendships that were to flower in Europe's dark days after World War I.

Back in New York in August of 1909, his seventeen years of formal Jesuit initiation completed, he was assigned to return to Woodstock College, this time in the difficult, if dignified, role of professor of philosophy. The appointment made sense: there were few posts in the province where his high talent could command a wider usefulness. Here he would be teaching his own Jesuit brethren, men who in their own turn were to become scholars and educators. Influence at Woodstock would clearly take on the proportions of a logarithmic progression.

An index of Dick Tierney's success as a professor is sharply defined in a series of essays he published on pedagogical problems while at Woodstock, later brought out in book form under the title *Teacher and Teaching*. Discussing "Mental Stimulus in Education" he sketches what turns out to be an accurate self-portrait:

> All good teachng is intensely alive with a commanding personality. To be successful, a live, noble man must put himself into words. He must strip his subject matter clear of the useless accretions of centuries—modernize it, assimilate it, vitalize it, electrify it into life and send it from his heart vibrant, palpitating, enriched with life, his life, his individuality.

His fulminations against the stale teacher whose "jokes and illustrations hoary with years and feeble through constant use will be read from yellow margins of ragged note books," evidently were not self-accusatory. His classroom so often roared with laughter that the professor in the neighboring classroom muttered a mild complaint.

The fact is that the Jesuit students, intellectually a highly critical group, found the young Father Tierney a rather curious combination of qualities. On the plus side were his obvious intellectual abilities and his refreshing drive. The perennial wall that tends to loom between pupil and professor was in his case lightly leapt over. Not above engineering practical jokes on the professors as well as on the students, he was fond of recreating with the younger men and as a brilliant conversationalist and inveterate teaser could always command a crowd.

But like many intensely vigorous personalities, it was his portion either violently to attract or violently to repel, and the same was true of his own preferences. A certain frigidity of manner and abrupt aloofness, wholly surface traits, necessarily narrowed his approachability; and he was largely guided in his attitude toward new acquaintances by instinctive first impressions. With those he did not like he was courteous and painfully polite. But the finer points of social graciousness did not come easy.

"He had a heart, big, kind, and true," remembered a friend, "although he manifested a few cold and odd traits, such as are but too often incident to higher intellectual ability. He overshadowed and overawed; not infrequently, those who did not know him well or who lacked the power to discriminate between the expression and the soul behind that expression, were embarrassed and even depressed in his presence. And yet, Father Tierney was considerate." Volunteered another: "He was the kindest man I have ever known."

This was the man superiors named to the editorial board of *America* in the winter of 1913. Ostensibly he was joining the staff in the capacity of an associate editor; but suspicion ran high that he was being primed for the uneasy chair of editor-in-chief. A month and a half after his arrival a formal announcement made the rumor right: he would succeed Father Campbell, the man who twenty-one years before had as Provincial accepted his application to become a Jesuit.

America was a unique tissue of headaches even for a professionally trained journalist. Editors are normally an aspirin-consuming race of men peculiarly adroit at keeping eighteen things in the front of their mind at once. The editorship of *America* was all that, of course, but because of its position as a national voice of Catholic thought, the man responsible for the speaking had to be a kind of Thomas Aquinas, Leonardo da Vinci, Francis of Assisi, Socrates, and Council of Trent rolled into one errorless genius.

Journalistically, Tierney's direct preparation was slight. His contributions to *America* and other magazines, though well received, had been only occasional. Businesswise, it was anything but the more usual case of the starving newspaperman learning the trade from the bottom up. Tierney was practically starting at the top. But closer inspection uncovered much in his background that could count for indirect preparation.

His training, rich in literature, science, philosophy, and theology, had included a wide familiarity with biography and history, a keen appreciation of fine art, a successful contribution in the literature of pedagogy, and an amateur's interest in nature since the exploring days of Spuyten Duyvil. Beyond this, he brought to the job a prodigious memory that carefully filed away the facts it wanted and could serve them up when requested with IBM efficiency.

What was even more, his stern logical mind had that rare, almost clairvoyant, quality of sensing the undertones and overtones of affairs, of viewing an event not only in its full range of color but also at the infra and ultra ends of the spectrum where inner significance often lies. "Positively uncanny," once commented Cardinal Bonzano, speaking of Tierney's quick and accurate insight. What the Cardinal perhaps forgot was that uncanny shrewdness was the mere ABC's of success in a position so potentially inflammable. In *America's* office, kegs of dynamite were the ordinary furniture.

With the issue of March 7, 1914, the first to appear under his aegis, there were marked changes in make-up and editorial policy. After a tighter, more meaty magazine, Tierney reorganized the duties of the associate editors, shuffled the order of departments, increased the number of signed articles, and geared the editorial machinery to a new tempo of efficiency.

Within a year he had gathered about him a brilliant group of Jesuit associates: Paul Blakely, easily one of *America's* greatest, himself the son of a belligerent Southern editor, one whose encyclopedic interests and crisp pungent style were to pour out an incredible avalanche of first rate journalism for the next twenty-eight years; J. Harding Fisher, a learned observer of world affairs whose keen and balanced judgment Tierney came to respect immensely; John C. Reville, a polished classicist with a Newman-like style who was so much the Southern gentleman that he would not answer the telephone without his immaculate starched cuffs on; Walter Dwight, a suave and soft-spoken New Englander who oversaw the literary sections; and Joseph C. Husslein, specialist in economics and sociology whose perennially mild, smiling manners could climb to a sharp crescendo of indignation in the face of error.

The tone that Tierney intended to set is marked in one of his earliest editorials. Under the lead *The Power of Catholics* he writes in the sharp staccato style that was to stamp his work as unmistakably as his name:

> Boasting is childish, offensive, unprofitable, easy. There is nothing easier except, perhaps, eating, drinking, and sleeping. No great gift or power of any kind is required for boasting. A glib tongue, a wild imagination, a shallow intellect are quite sufficient to accomplish it. There is a great deal of boasting at present amongst a certain class of Catholics. The occasion for it is the "Catholic Directory" for 1914, wherein the faithful are numbered at 16,000,000. The statement of this huge throng has been greeted with dissertations about the sublimity of the faith, the power of Catholics in civil life, and so on. But what power have Catholics in civil life? Is it in proportion to their number or worth? Can they redress wrongs? Have they done so? There are wrongs by the score unredressed. The country is flooded by subsidized papers too vile for the eyes of

decent people, wherein all that Catholics hold dear is reviled shamefully. Sons of Catholic fathers and mothers, who have given themselves to God in a life that is a daily martyrdom of work and prayer, are held up to the American public as lecherous rascals whose one desire in life is to ruin innocent souls by a base use of the confessional. Their very names are mentioned calumniously; the Master Whom they serve is blasphemed; the Sacraments that they administer are ridiculed; their Protestant fellow-citizens are called upon to prepare "for a coming revolution" which is to sweep priests and "the pagan dragon of the Tiber" from the world. What are the 16,000,000 Catholics doing? Sighing in easy chairs and exclaiming over their tea: "How dreadful!" At least visible effects would lead to this or a similar conclusion.

. . . American Catholics . . . lack power because they lack union. They lack union because they lack spirit. Lacking spirit, they either take their thrashing lying down or stand up under it, mistaking it for an affectionate embrace. . . . But then, we are 16,000,000 strong. This is so consoling.

That Tierney was not mistaking a thrashing for an affectionate embrace became dramatically evident in the first few months of his editorship. In early 1914 the political badminton in Mexico was reaching more than mere serio-comic proportions. The Tampico incident followed by the forced occupation of Vera Cruz put the U. S. squarely at the center of the confusion.

Washington, under Woodrow Wilson, favored the Constitutionalists led by Carranza and Villa. In May of 1914 Tierney began gathering verified reports of the Constitutionalists' persecution of religion. Affidavits and sworn testimonies from a wide selection of sources chronicled a brutal story of atrocities. By early summer he began to lay the evidence before an astonished public.

Life, virtue, religion are held cheaper than dross; they are the sport of carnal, brutal men, who respect nothing, not even God, nor their country's honor, nor themselves.

Interchangeable Terms

A leader of the northern rebels, who is held up to us as a liberator, has six concubines; his men have ravished the women of a captured city on two successive days; they have outraged priests; they have treated nuns as things of shame; they have desecrated and robbed churches, breaking open the doors of the tabernacles to seize the sacred vessels; they have been promised riot and loot in abundance on reaching Mexico City. Lust has ruled them; carnage has accompanied them, ruin and despair are left in their wake. Never in the history of modern times have worse scenes been witnessed.

. . . The facts are true. Our part then—what is it? Has this war been brought on by American lust for gold? Has it been prolonged for gold? Who will explain our conduct in regard to the munitions of war? What part have we had in the construction and management of wireless stations for the rebels? Who will explain other acts which await revelation? What is the reason of them? It is hard to say; but one thing is clear: God lives and reigns and in His own good time He will heed the cries of the dying men, the wails of starving children, the shrieks of ruined women. In the meantime let those who can take consolation from the fact that "Though Villa is a Romanist, yet he does not use tobacco nor drink."

It was with this vivid, smouldering indignation that Tierney was for years to continue his blast against the Mexican persecution. Nor was it mere inflated rhetoric. His office became a kind of central depository for information on the Church's martyrdom. Bundles of eye-witnessed facts from below the border mounted into overwhelming evidence. Some of the stories, though fully authenticated, were too lurid to print, but the fighting editor left no one in doubt of the sickening brutality of what was going on.

With Americans who applauded Villa's banditry he could be scathing:

The Guardians of Liberty, a collection of bilious ministers, henpecked husbands and a lone general who wears gold braid even on his bathing suit, congratulated the wretch on the work against the Catholic Church and actually sent him money to help on his cause. So it ever was: low-browed, slant-eyed men, a disgrace to their race and their religion, have never hesitated to join hands with our country's enemies, when they thought that by so doing they could destroy Catholicism. They would run with the devil, if that would ruin the Church. This is not rhetoric: it is sober fact. It has happened every time an attack has been made on Catholicism.

Week after week he published affidavits, documents, reports, and letters that spelled out the revolting truth. Headings were reprinted from an article in a Mexican paper:

No more Roman Catholic Churches.
No more priests.
We need no more churches, only schools.
It is not necessary for people to believe in God, Whom no one can see.
We shall not permit churches to be opened.

The Vicar-General of the Diocese of Tamaulipas, while in Tampico, receives a note from the local commander:

The day after tomorrow (Shrove Tuesday) I shall come for you to wash my feet, after which I shall demand of you all the money the late bishop left you. In default of the gold I shall hang you to the highest tree in the plaza.

While Carranza's representative in Washington cooed that the Constitutionalists "guarantee individual freedom of worship according to everyone's conscience," the tragedy played savagely on. Not content to battle in print alone, Tierney ranged the country delivering fiery lectures, kindling mass meetings to indignation, inveighing against the Wilson—Bryan Administration for espousing the Constitutionalists, and turning over to the press photostatic copies of affidavits detailing atrocities against priests and nuns.

During the crisis members of the Mexican hierarchy leaned heavily on the two-fisted editor for advice and help. Refugees flocked to his office for aid. In early 1915 he initiated a Mexican Fund, appealing to his readers and listeners for financial help. So tireless and effective were his efforts for the Catholic cause in crucified Mexico that Benedict XV was to commend him by name as pre-eminent in the work.

But Mexico, as much as it meant to Tierney, was only one fight in a multi-fronted battle. His editorship was not six months old before Europe's nervous security caved into the havoc of World War I. His response was to throw the full force of his editorial weight behind American neutrality. Readerwise, it was a hazardous stand for the magazine to take. Most of its readers were probably only one or two generations removed from Europe, and sympathies were briskly divided. The war's progress was written with scrupulous efforts at sifting fact from propaganda, but the mailbag fumed daily with the load of letters irately accusing the editor of bias on both sides:

> The pro-German bias of last week's Chronicle is the last straw. I will read your paper no longer.—The insensate hostility to Austria you display shocks and pains me. Drop my name from your subscription list.—Permit me to say that your manifest bias for France comes with bad grace from a paper of your antecedents. Please discontinue my subscription.—Had you not better transfer the place of publication from New York to Berlin and rename the paper *Germany?*—Your recent editorial on "Heroic Belgium" is indefensible. Please stop my subscription at once. —Your account of Ireland's attitude toward the war could not be further from the truth. Stop my paper.

But if the readers liked it or not, Tierney remained for the early years of the war, in his own phrase, "positively aggressive in his neutrality." Only when the U. S. had formally declared war on Germany did he vary his position. Then, with well measured loyalty, he sided with his country's decision. "War is not our choice," he editorialized; "strife has been thrust upon us by repeated and wanton violations of our rights. For a long time the American people bore these outrages with a patience that was heroic, and when at last they spoke through their Chief Executive, their message was a calm, noble document inspired by an elemental and honorable desire for justice."

The paper's patriotism indeed could at times sweep the lyre:

> English and Scotch, German and Irish, French and Italian, Greek and Russian, were our forefathers who sought in this country the opportunities which persecution and political turmoil had denied them in the motherland.
>
> Today, whatever strains may mingle in our veins, at whatever altars we may worship, we admit but one political allegiance. We are not Irish, not German, not English. We are Americans.
>
> . . . We offer no hypocritical lip service, no mechanical loyalty, but a devotion founded on our loyalty to God Himself, and we draw from that high loyalty the firm purpose to dedicate ourselves with all that we are and have to the service of our beloved country. That is the devotion which she rightly expects of us, and the devotion which every Catholic who is not basely recreant to the teachings of the Church will gladly give her.

It is characteristic of the intelligent impartiality of Tierney, who had in the Mexican question damned Wilson so fearlessly, to find him editorializing on the duty of citizens to stand by the President in war time:

> In a Republic such as ours there is always place for criticism, incisive criticism, destructive criticism in certain crises, and criticism of every kind, except dishonest, malevolent criticism. It is only reasonable to assume that Congress and the courts may be relied on to preserve unimpaired the system of checks and balances, characteristic of the American form of government, leaving to the citizen the duty

and privilege of omitting nothing which may strengthen the hands of our civil superiors. Criticism is useful, but obedience comes first, and the first and plain duty of every American citizen is to stand by the President.

Throughout the war he interested himself in all the phases of Catholic participation. He argued for more chaplains, kept an editorial eye on spiritual conditions in the camps, called for the proper religious facilities in the proposed war-prisoner barracks, and widely publicized the Chaplains Aid Association.

But far and away the most notable chapter in the career of Editor Tierney remained to be written. On the face of things, it might not have been expected. For a man who surfaced so anvil-like a personality, his towering charity might have seemed a surprise. Commented an associate:

> To the stupid, he might be irritable or unkind; to the vain he would be sarcastic and even cruel; but to anyone whom he even suspected of not telling the truth or of not acting squarely, he was ruthlessly insulting.—His lordly mannerisms, an air of superciliousness and disdainfulness, his self-confidence and independence of thinking and acting, his intolerance in matters that affected him closely, his indifference to what opinion others might hold of him, all seemed to mark him off as a proud man. To an extent, he was proud, but without being vain. . . . But despite his natural pride and his native stubbornness and strong will, he could force himself to a childlike obedience and resignation. He could tell one in command that the order was a mistake; but he would manfully carry out the order to the best of his ability. There was real humility in him, but it was of the supernatural order and so was more potent than his pride. His manner was apt to belie his spirit.

"Apt to belie his spirit," puts it mildly. Tierney was of that strong cast of religious men whose Christianity is of a peculiarly bold and blunt sort. *Raw Christianity* it might without irreverence be called: deep essential virtues that structure sanctity;

without careful polishing, without delicate refining; rough gold ingots rather than filigreed jewelry. The point is saliently illustrated in the case of his charitableness. He simply could not stop giving things away. It might be his overcoat to a tramp. It might be a quarter of a million dollars to war-rubbled Europe. It might be sums to missions in Uganda or Dutch Guiana. It might be help to Japan, the Philippines, or China. It might be keeping Austrian nuns from starvation, French children from homelessness, or Belgian girls from the life of the streets. Charity with Tierney was not a quality. It was a passion.

Austria was the central case. Mangled by peace treaties, its economy crumbled, literally thousands of its people dying of disease, malnutrition, and rank starvation (more than 1200 a day in Vienna alone), the nation faced a hollow-eyed hell of postwar suffering that tore at Tierney's sympathies. He had studied there, had many friends among the gay Bavarians of a better day, and could appreciate in a particular way the terror that faced them. In 1922 he returned to Europe and had the opportunity to appraise conditions on the scene. His graphic appeals for funds were astonishingly effective. Years later it was computed that *America* had collected $365,000 from its readers alone, a sum that was distributed with practically no administrative expenses. A staff correspondent overseas at the time could recall:

> I was there in Europe, on the ground, in the midst of it all. . . . I doubt if ever, in all the world, there has been anything quite like it. Millions there were, literally *millions*, who died of disease or hunger, or a combination of both, and the world moved serenely on. Outside the stricken areas nobody seemed to care very much about it. . . . And it was into this that Father Tierney plunged. His great heart had been touched with the pity of it all. . . . And how well he succeeded God only knows. But succeed he did. Of this I can bear testimony for I was there and saw with my own eyes the work that he did. And this, specifically, is what I saw: thousands of persons of all classes and

castes saved from what looked to me like certain death by the prompt aid which came from the readers of AMERICA through Father Tierney.

Without doubt the Austria case was one of his finest hours. "He was the great almoner of his generation," so went an appraisal, "and while his achievements in other fields, like journalism and education, may mark his name high up above, I think he would prefer to be remembered as a friend of the poor." It is safe to assume heaven did not forget.

But in the meanwhile there was the usual cauldron of boiling issues to be stirred. There was Ireland, for example. Through the first two years of his editorship the campaign for Home Rule was moving to an explosive head. In the beginning he was content to record events with strict neutrality, feeling it was a problem to be solved by the two nations themselves. But with the blood bath of Easter week in 1916, his hatred of oppression began to flame out editorially:

> An act of rebellion is an act against God. The hand that is raised against lawful authority in State or Church is a hand raised against the Almighty Himself, from whom all well-ordered authority receives its final sanction. No ebullition of patriotism can take from rebellion its true character as an act derogatory to the majesty of the God of men and nations. . . . With all this said, who shall undertake to judge the motives of any man who gives his life that his country may live? The beginner in philosophy or law can define the nature of rebellion. But who will say that an attempt to free one's country prompted by present wrong and the recollection of centuries of dishonoring oppression implies in those who make it the moral iniquity of rebellion? The crumbling walls and blackened ruins of Dublin tell why Pearse and his followers died; but from them at whose hands they fell, the world may look for no truthful story of their motives or of their deeds. For the history of conquered Ireland and oppressing England is ever the same: a narrative of savagery and blood, met by intrepid patriot-

ism and unswerving fidelity to the teachings of Jesus Christ. This is no assertion, inherited from an ancestry springing from the little Isle, set like an emerald in the gray silver of the northern seas. It is a fact which all whose eyes are not held by the red mist of hatred, plainly see.

What Tierney continued to see plainly was that England was saying one thing and doing quite another. British statesmen crowed heroically that they were fighting Imperial Germany over the right of small nations to govern themselves. "What about the right of Ireland?" the editor asked. His coming out for nothing less than complete and absolute independence was, for the times, a bold stand. It is unlikely that he was much disturbed over being blacklisted in British circles, held suspect, called dangerous and incendiary. Tierney was as ready to attack the policies of Britain as he was of Mexico, or Germany, or his own United States. The chips might fall where they may. What mattered was Dame Justice with sword and her scales.

That blindfolded Lady always seems to have half a hundred affairs that need looking after. There was the New York Charities Investigation, a political rotten egg lobbed at the Catholic child-caring institutions in the state. Tierney's twin weapons of flawless logic and devastating sarcasm cut the case wide open, letting in some badly needed fresh air, and vindicating the priests and nuns under attack.

There was the Eighteenth Amendment, Prohibition, which the editor, himself an abstainer, battled vigorously as an invasion of personal and State rights as well as a legislative danger to the Holy Sacrifice of the Mass.

There was federal education legislation threatening the existence of private schools; the French anti-clericalism of Herriot; the fight to get the scurrilous *Menace* out of the mails; and of course the perennial round of anti-Christian heads to crack: birth control, Darwinism, euthanasia, Masonry, divorce, Bolshevism, and all their bedfellows.

There were even such howlers as the proposed Amendment to the Constitution which included such delicately democratic proposals as expelling all Jesuits from the United States, its Territories, and Possessions; the abolishment of all convents and nunneries; and the final payoff: that "every priest, bishop, cardinal or archbishop, officiating as such, and any who in future may be ordained as priests of the Roman Catholic Church and allowed to hear confessions shall either marry or submit to castration!" Whatever else life at *America* was, it was seldom dull.

And for Dick Tierney, life at *America* was furiously more than just the magazine. There was the endless round of lectures on the endless round of topics. There was the gigantic correspondence. There was the chronic stream of callers: the Irish patriots, Italian Cardinals, French Commissioners, and Mexican Bishops, all sandwiched in between the diplomats, lawyers, editors, parish priests, job-seekers, doctors, an Apostolic Delegate looking for confidential information or a hobo looking for a hand-out. Tierney had time to chat with them all.

There were the offices he held in such groups as the Catholic Educational Association, the United States Catholic Historical Society, the Catholic Press Association, and the American Federation of Catholic Societies. And there was, of course, the enormous amount of contemporary journalism to wade through, digest, and analyze. Tierney had Tom Meehan, his chief editorial assistant, blue-pencil the mountain of newspapers, magazines, clippings, and bulletins that poured into the editorial rooms, and then forward them to his own desk. It was simply a case of being fantastically well informed. If John Wynne had left *America* to print the *Catholic Encyclopedia*, Dick Tierney was staying on to become one.

In a sense, the magazine itself was the least important thing at *America*. In Tierney's mind the project was vastly wider than a mere publication. It was to serve as a clearing house for American Catholicism, a nerve center that could coordinate a nation-wide effort, not a mere counter-punching Catholicism, mildly resisting false accusations and meekly content with a tiny place in the sun, but a vitally aggressive force that would take the initiative and hammer out an impact on the nation worthy of Christianity. It would have been flip, and an abomination to the modesty of the man himself, had his contemporaries of those ten furious years jokingly styled Dick Tierney *Mr. Catholic, U. S. A.* It would have been flip, but not altogether untrue.

When he had joined *America*, he had found it with an anemic circulation and a plaguing debt. When he left it, it had climbed to a larger circulation than any review of its class in the country and was well stabilized financially. Under his leadership it had grown strong and incisive in its expression of policies and principles, provocative and controversial in its content. While it might shock the over-timorous Catholic and needle the Church-baiting Protestant, its straightforward, outspoken vigor appealed strongly to the fair-minded. A leading editorial writer of one of the New York dailies, himself a non-Catholic, put the matter bluntly: "I read *America* every week, because it tells me what the Catholic Church is thinking and doing without any damn pussyfooting." That was the kind of magazine Tierney wanted.

He spared neither himself nor his associates in order to get it. Exacting and even severe in his management, he demanded alert, errorless accuracy down to the last comma. Even unimportant slips could bring on biting reprehensions. Foggy thinking or weak-kneed rhetoric was slashed out ruthlessly. When the magazine went to bed, it had to be *right*.

At times arbitrary and dictatorial, measuring decisions by strong personal likes and dislikes, an imperiously willed executive who could irritate associates, he could still command high affection from those about him. Testified layman Eugene Weare: "After years of work with him and for him I can say in truth that he comes nearer to the approach to my ideal among men than anyone I know."

But dynamos have a way of burning themselves out when the voltage is too high, and Tierney was pushing himself to a dangerous acceleration. As early as 1917 unmistakable signs of illness punctuated his high gear routine. In May of the following year he finally acceded to the pleas of the editors that he consult a doctor. Diagnosis revealed a serious condition, but it took an order from higher superiors to make him even temporarily vacate the office. Two and a half months on the West Coast and he was back at his desk at the old speed. But the next four years only wore harder on his diminishing health. Confidential reports from the physicians made the gravity of the case clear; he was either unimpressed by them or had decided to work his huge frame until it collapsed.

In 1922 superiors sent him as a delegate of the Maryland-New York Province to the International Sodality Conference in Rome. The change was much needed, but had little permanent effect on his declining robustness.

Back in New York, he refused to lighten his work and the illusion that he could carry on at the old pace became almost a fixation. The following summer he was again sent to Rome, this time as one of the province's three elected delegates to the General Congregation of the Society of Jesus. The choice of Tierney for this top level mission reflected the high confidence and honor he enjoyed among his confreres, but the rigors of the Roman winter and the grueling importance of the work brought an exhausted man back to New York. "He has the stamp of death on his face," sadly remarked an intimate.

Stubbornly refusing to admit defeat, he went back to the weekly grind. But the old powers were gone. His memory fogging, his grasp of affairs slipping, he drove determinately on for another year before the inevitable stroke fell. It was February 10, 1925. Three years later to the day he was dead.

What those last three years cost Richard Tierney only heaven could compute. What is certain is that they called for a new and subtle bravery in a man whose career had been monogrammed with courage. The physical pain was costly, but it paled before his mental anguish. God had chosen for him what is perhaps the supreme martyrdom for an intellectual: the conscious decline of his own mind.

Reduced to restless inactivity, it was a heavy road to plod for a man who had had such a high velocity career. Tierney met the challenge bravely, but at a frightening cost.

When the end came, hurried mercifully by pneumonia, he was in New York. Somehow the Big Town, center of the publishing world, was the right place. "*America* and Father Tierney were interchangeable terms," mourned Paul Blakely. It was the kind of personal publicity Dick Tierney would have redpenciled out of the copy.

But in the Book that mattered, the record would stand.

T HE GREAT *tide and flow moved restlessly on. The bobbed hair and derby hat were out of date in no time at all. Luxury sired a profligate and spendthrift generation. Amy Semple Mc-Pherson, Doctor Townsend, and Father Divine were commanding enormous followings. Bertrand Russell and Freud became the rage. Value judgments and morals became prudish, unpopular.*

Men in the 'thirties, matured by calamity, looked back twice at the rousing post-war era. Whenever had so sustained an illusion occupied a people? Perhaps this mass intoxication, the race and riot and hot jazz were refuge from responsibility. And final paradox—a grass roots sense of righteousness had jammed through prohibition upon reluctant manhood, the amendment that abetted crime and mothered the bootlegger. Shades of Carrie Nation's umbrella!

The silent screen became now the new temple where millions worshiped Rudolph Valentino, Mary Pickford, and Clara Bow. Into the fears and laughter of multitudes, Lon Chaney and Charlie Chaplin stole their way. Small boys relived the days of the stagecoach and Indian raids. Behind every bush was a redman with feathers and paint. Tom Mix, Buck Jones, and Jackie Coogan became idols in the American home.

One October day the millennium was abruptly terminated. The low grey clouds of want and disillusionment rolled threateningly across the land. Privation entered the home. Pride stood in the breadline. Miles of unemployed men, angry and hurt, jeered a bewildered President.

But an awakened people challenged despair. Americans had the will to survive. With courage and ringing determination this

chastened country began the long climb back. The poor, trans-
fused with new hope, started the fight to reclaim their self-
respect, their dignity in this overshadowing world.

* * *

His Manual of Arms

Father Joseph Stack, S.J.

by TIMOTHY P. FALLON, S.J.

Down the dank trail that led away from a hidden cave, near
Manresa, a crippled Spanish soldier limped slowly. Shocked by
severe penance, his whole body was lacerated and weary, but
the two years of silence he had just spent almost entirely in
vigorous prayer, vivid contemplation, and real ecstasy, had be-
queathed to his soul a breadth of vision and intensity of enthusiasm such as few men in history had ever possessed.

It was this man's earnest resolve to change the face of the
earth, and to waste no time doing it. And by the look of
things, from a spiritual point of view, the earth badly needed a
facial. The year was 1521, and in another country Luther had
just split the unity of Europe, like an old log, with the axe of
his disbelief. Switzerland, some of France, the Low Countries,
Prussia, most of Sweden, Norway, and finally England swung
out after the ex-priest to the intellectual and religious anarchy of
"private interpretation." The people were easy meat for the verbose and heady Reformers: like sheep, they followed the "new
preachers" to their own unspeakable loss. And in Rome, where
more vigorous steps should have, and could have, been taken to
stop this catastrophic defection from the Catholic faith, there
was temporizing and even among some prelates undignified and
disedifying conduct.

It was into this world that the 30-year-old cavalier trudged. His name was, of course, Ignatius, or Inigo, Loyola, and in his hand he carried a manual of arms for the army he would recruit to take on Luther and his cohorts—a weapon for the fight he was determined to enter. It consisted of a hundred pages of ideas, every one of which had been hammered out on a forge of suffering and penance such as had rarely occurred since the iron-handed austerities of the desert monks in the early Church. He called them "Spiritual Exercises" which would be gone through "in order to . . . dispose the soul to free itself of inordinate affections," and thus order its life according to God's will "for its own salvation." Being a soldier, he knew the value of a strategic retreat, the intrinsic need of every army to fall back and evaluate the situation, to lick its wounds, regroup its forces, renew its equipment, bolster its courage, and plan new attacks. It was either that or be driven into retreat, and that way spelled ruin and rout. So he intended to call Catholics "to come apart into a quiet place and rest awhile." Much like a tough top-sergeant with a flock of recruits, he planned to explain carefully what had to be done and why, and then stand aside while they did it till they had it down cold.

His first attack against the power of evil was a rousing success. Returning late in the evening from a convent, he was nearly clubbed to death by a group of "gentlemen" who had begun to resent his effective spiritual work. Inigo did not retaliate, though as a trained soldier he could have handled himself: he simply muttered "for the honor of Jesus Christ," and dropped unconscious. Carried to a monastery he was in sick-bay two months before he recovered. But the wounds and blood were proof positive that he was on the right track, that with the help of God, he would bind up the wounds of the Church, and bring back to her, through the influence of his Society, the nations that had turned away; there could now be no faltering.

Like a giant rising from his slumbers, he set his face resolutely to the work before him and within the next thirty years, he was personally responsible, under God, for the spirituality of such men as St. Francis Xavier, St. Peter Canisius, St. Francis Borgia, Blessed Peter Faber, and a host of others, famous to any historian of the sixteenth century. He started an Order, which today numbers 30,000 trained men, and set up as one of its greatest works the task of giving the Spiritual Exercises to men and women all over the world.

Four centuries later, though joined in this work by hundreds of other priests and religious, the modern Society of Jesus still pursues the course he laid down. In schools and colleges of every country, in parishes and prisons, in missions and sodalities, convents, retreat houses, barns and gymnasiums, hotels, country estates, and the Vatican Palace, every year over a hundred thousand men of every nationality ponder in seclusion the fundamental question of life and happiness: "Why am I here?" The answer, simple and direct, is the basis and ground-work of all that is to follow: "to praise, reverence, and serve God our Lord, and by this means to save my soul . . . all things else on the face of the earth were created to help me attain this end."

With things in that perspective—God first, me second, and everything else subordinate—the diligent examination of one's past actions becomes a disconcerting revelation. Sin and hell are realities with a red-hot core of meaning. No one may trifle with them lightly! At this point in the retreat, the men usually make a complete reform of morals, and seal their determination by a general confession of their life's sins.

Then, on a sudden, they are taken to Christ, and shown Him in a challenging light. "My will is to conquer the whole world, and all My enemies, and thus to enter into the glory of My Father! Will you come along?" This is the call of the King; the whole retreat, though necessarily shortened,* is a development and organic growth in personal love and service of Christ the King-Friend. "It was," said a retreatant once, "like walking along Galilee's shore with our Lord's arm around your shoulder."

For three days each weekend these thoughts are developed by retreat masters, and listened to by business men, movie stars,

* Ignatius planned it for about 30 days.

policemen, doctors, trainmen, laborers, and members of church societies in hundreds of established retreat-houses or temporary shelters throughout the world. In silence and solitude, with only Christ as companion, these men forget the distractions of radio and newspapers, the noise and chatter of family life, and immerse their souls in the spiritual luxuries of daily rosary, Stations of the Cross, good reading, and deep thought.

Just such an experience has been that of thousands who have attended El Retiro San Inigo. A stucco, three-storied building, in the foothills of Santa Clara's blossomed Valley, every weekend for 25 years has renewed this retreat spirit. The inspired men who planted this house on the hill-slopes of the Santa Clara Valley were certain that, with God's help, it could become the rallying point for interested Catholics of northern California, a center of spiritual formation and influence. Proudly they dubbed the site El Retiro San Inigo, after the author of the Exercises. From the day of its founding it grew fast. The ready organization of Catholic men, formed on the old retreat group with roots at the University of Santa Clara and Villa Maria, has grown and borne fruit. By 1950 its brave vision was almost completely realized—in the quarter century since its founding, El Retiro had experienced a wonderful prosperity.

Last year, El Retiro's twenty-fifth anniversary, well-wishers found it quite a bit more than the pitiful handful of buildings which nestled in the foothills the day of its purchase from the Wellman estate. The original log-cabin had long since disappeared and its traces had been blotted out by the magnificent Pereira Hall—retreatants' dining hall and Fathers' living quarters. The old Wellman house now lay noiseless, abandoned; occasionally it welcomed the overflow crowd. Spacious new buildings dotted the hillside—clustered around Rossi Chapel, the heart of Retreatville. Each retreatant enjoyed the simple luxury of bedroom, private bath, and facilities. Paths wound round the hills and introduced them to the numerous shrines—Manresa, Christ the King, the Sacred Heart, Our Lady of Lourdes, and the open-air Stations of the Cross. The crumbled arm of Simon of Cyrene, worn by the weather, testifies to the years of service they have given. As the fog swept up from San Francisco Bay, El Retiro was busy, in a quiet way, full of meditation and communion with God.

The chapel, a narrow, pink-stucco building which had been erected by a young man in memory of his mother and father before he entered the Society of Jesus, was in the center of El Retiro's latest retreat. From an artistic point of view it wasn't much of a church—an aesthetic wonder would have been out of place. But it was, nonetheless, the heart of this little community. A sanctuary for reflection, a conference room for the many daily retreat exercises, the source of life in the day of the retreatant with its offering of early morning Mass and evening Benediction service.

Its simple square windows, half amber, half stained glass, were a sign that El Retiro was still growing. The stained glass provided meditation's first preludes, with details in brilliant color of St. Ignatius at Manresa, Christ the Good Shepherd, and other scenes from the life of Christ.

One week, behind the simple oak desk at the left of the altar, Father Zacheus Maher began his retreat with the text from *The Imitation of Christ*, "To many persons this may seem a hard saying: 'Deny yourself, take up your cross, and follow me.'"

That evening, as the retreatants gathered around one of the Fathers for an informal smoke, one of the men who had come every year since 1925, spoke earnestly to the visiting priest: "You Jesuits give very remarkable retreats. Every one of them is the same—and every one of them is entirely different. When we hear one Father's talk on hell, we are terrified. When Father Stack gave that same conference, we used to come out crying. His voice, sweet and mellow, seemed to match his character."

El Retiro represents a brilliant accomplishment and was due, under God, to Father Joseph Stack. Like his fellow Jesuits the world over, he owned no worldly goods, no home, no furniture. What he needed was provided for him. He was always ready to pack up in an instant and go to any part of the world at his superior's command. That command had sent him into retreat work; in western America he was the forerunner, the grand-daddy of the lay-retreat movement.

Founder Stack's plain, fatherly, nineteenth-century face was that of a veteran campaigner. Before his death in 1950 he had dedicated himself for almost thirty years to the development of retreat houses.

Joseph Stack began his life in the heart of the Westlands. The oldest, most coddled of five children, he was born (1879) in San Francisco, a city filled with the energy of growth and a burning faith in progress; there was warmth here and spirit.

The Stacks were Easterners. They had come out West to San Francisco not too long after the Gold Rush of '49 to settle in the new community and raise a family. Joseph was born soon after. Young Joe's folks were pious people—church-going and exact observers of church feasts in perennial rotation. Public opinion was more or less on their side. Joe, in later years, re-membered the ban put on public showings of the Passion Play at the theater around the corner on the pretext that it would hurt the sensibilities of the religious-minded population.

Joe's father managed a fair living. He was a man who did his job conscientiously and well. He liked a cigar after his evening meal, but there was little or no drinking allowed in the Stack household. The Stacks were a literary-minded family: evenings, Joe, his brothers and sisters, would cluster around mother as she read Dickens to them. Joe was a frail and quiet child. Often, when friends wanted him for a game of cops and robbers, they found him stretched out on the davenport—reading.

He went to Lincoln Grammar School and here made friends he kept all his life. Later he moved on to St. Ignatius College on Van Ness and Hayes. It was here his talents for classic Greek and Latin shone forth. He did brilliantly in the public exhibitions that the Jesuits of those days delighted in putting on. But the Fathers were not, to young Joe Stack, flawless educators. Years later, in his diary, he blamed his swift rise through the grades for his weak grasp of some of the fundamentals.

At seventeen, Joseph Stack entered the Society of Jesus. Old Father Dominic Giacobbi taught him the spiritual life, how to pray, work, eat, and sleep as a Jesuit should. There was some question because of his ill health whether he would take his vows after his two years' novitiate, but gruff Dr. Fred Gerlach, physician to generations of Jesuits, thought he would probably be able to make the grade, so he got his vows. Father Woods taught him the advanced course in Classics, which he breezed through in three years, and then spent three more years teaching at Santa Clara. Here he got a reputation for strictness which his superiors heard about and which later determined their decision to make him prefect of discipline at various schools in the Rocky Mountain mission.

When Stack was doing his stint of teaching and prefecting the boys at Santa Clara, his life-long friends, Fathers Gleeson and Morrissey gave the first laymen's retreats there. These retreats had a profound influence on him; in his three years at Santa Clara he had got his fill of prefecting and was undergoing the ordinary disillusionment of the average Jesuit Scholastic. A strict disciplinarian, he had been roundly disliked by most, loved by few, and to himself was a complete failure. In spite of all his efforts to improve the manners, morals, and intellectual achievement of his charges, they remained, on the surface at least, untamed, arrogant, supercilious barbarians. But the vivid example of immense improvement in the lives of men in so short a time at the annual retreats was like a tonic. Even granted that his own personal errors of over-severity had brought in ennui too soon, still the contrast of good achieved and proportionate energies expended were not lost upon him.

In his early training Joe Stack had dreamed great things for Christ, had seen himself bringing into the Lord's sheepfold many men, young and old, had planned on marching into heaven at the head of an army of souls he would save from sin and hell. There would be martial music, banners waving, joyous shouts, huzzas for the victory against Satan. But things in reality were unlike his dreams. Instead of a strong, vigorous fighter for the Kingdom of Christ, he had found himself, at twenty-five, a rather battered specimen of manhood. In the novitiate a tall fence, used as a back-stop in baseball, had fallen on him and nearly crushed the life out of him. As it was, he sustained numerous injuries to his nose, eyes, and inner organs. Within the few years following his accident he had suffered three nervous breakdowns from strain and overwork. His years as a prefect of boarders at Santa Clara were happy ones at first, but by this time insomnia began to plague him and the blue-gold banners of his dreams were drooping badly. The shock of this first laymen's retreat was a turning point in his thoughts, a revival of enthusiasm for the apostolate.

Joe Stack, Jesuit, determined to make a life work of giving retreats. He set out at once collecting suitable stories, examples, ideas that would be of use in that chosen field. Hard put to it to study for long periods of time because of his nerve injuries, he developed the pleasant, but frowned-upon, habit of bull-sessions during theology at Woodstock and in these conversations with his fellow religious the constant topic under discussion was the ways and means of starting and financing retreat houses all around the country. At that time not a single house exclusively for that purpose existed in the United States or Canada. But now, thirty years later, practically every large Catholic diocese in the country has a place for visiting retreatants; and on the West Coast, where every year over thirty thousand men make closed retreats, Father Stack has had a hand in developing all those under Jesuit auspices.

In 1925, fresh from his theological studies at Woodstock, Maryland, Father was assigned to a well-established parish in Montana's Bitter Root Mountains. He plunged into the work with the newly-ordained priest's enthusiasm. There, at Missoula, the garden spot of these hills, he helped to guide parish sodalities, young men's clubs, people seeking marriage instruction, and all those in need. And all the time in return for the sympathy and priestly zeal which went out from him he gained, little by little, valuable experience and a deeper insight into the problems which nag at the heart of the common man. The long years of studies might, and often do, result in one's losing contact with people. Clerical life, in fostering and protecting the vocation, often insulates too. So he rejoiced in this chance to deepen and sharpen his own outlook on what confronted the layman in the modern world. In the growth of his parish interest he found a base for those succeeding contacts which moulded him into somewhat of an ideal as the approachable, agreeable father of souls.

When the old pastor was retired, Father stepped up to take over the administrative work. He was now in charge of the nerve center of a real Catholic community. Here he was more forcefully than before brought up against a pure faith which grew only more intense with the wide variety of Catholic activities in which he became involved. Miners, storekeepers, railroadmen, and cattle ranchers brought him their problems.

Down snow-covered streets in winter, or in the still, hot days of July, at any hour of the day or night, he could be found tramping his way to the Catholic hospital or on up to the Railroad Hospital on the hill. He would be carrying the Sacrament to some dying parishioner. It was in these halls of starched whiteness, heavy with the odor of death, that his people so often saw their pastor for the last time. In the final moment when death stripped them of their last pretense they unburdened their soul's guilt into the patient priest's ear and, in return, heard: "I absolve you from your sins in the name of the Father, Son, and Holy Ghost. Go in peace." Perhaps behind that sympathetic face was the memory of hours spent in a hospital, three nervous breakdowns, and his own struggle to readjust a vigorous mind to a broken body.

But all this was a build-up for what was to be his life work. During his years of study and again as a parish priest he had come to realize that something more than the ordinary run of parish duties was necessary to feed the insatiable hunger in the souls of these men and women for the complete message of Christ. The lay retreat movement was certainly an answer to this need. Joe Stack was ready when the call finally came to begin his retreat work in earnest. They were going to move the summer laymen's retreats from Gonzaga, the Jesuits' downtown university in Spokane, up to Mt. St. Michael's, the brand-new philosophate in the hills behind the city. Joe Stack was called upon to give the first of these retreats. He was an instant success—not flashy, but solid.

The first retreat was a pleasure to give: a big, spacious, red-brick building built to accommodate a hundred people. . . . The young scholastics helping with the prayers, spiritual reading, and waiting on table, the perfect silence and seriousness of the men—all left a quite favorable impression. This success definitely put him on the retreat circuit and Joe Stack was glad. This was to be his work, with but one interlude, again as pastor, until he died in 1950.

Joe Stack, retreat master, was now very much in demand after his maiden voyage in this work. The next call came from western Washington. Here on Juan de Fuca Straits, beyond Seattle, where the tides carve a channel from the Pacific to Puget Sound, and fog shrouds the little peninsula most of the year, is Port Townsend. The chimes in the downtown city square still ring on the hour and in the gabled mansion, now used as a Jesuit tertianship, the Fathers had decided to try a laymen's retreat. The Port spread her arms wide in welcome, but the cool blasts of fog and the dampness made the retreat a success—with reservations. This was the first and last laymen's retreat held on the peninsula for a long time.

Two thousand miles to the south, in the land of far horizons, distant blue mountain ranges, and the ancient Saguaro, on the edge of the vast Arizona desert, Phoenix had mushroomed into a modern metropolis. It lay in the center of picturesque Salt River Valley, a haven for snow-bound Easterners in the winter. At this time business was booming.

A few miles out of town in the shadow of Camel Back Ridge is a famous inn of the same name. In 1945 this luxurious desert resort turned retreatants' paradise for three days. Under Father Stack's direction over ninety men of the local Knights of Columbus made the Spiritual Exercises. Father had interrupted his work at El Retiro—planed out of San Francisco Airport to serve the Catholics of Arizona.

He knew what retreats meant to the men. From the time El Retiro was a baby he had listened to them pouring out their thanks, telling about their initial misgivings when the retreat was suggested, the sacrifices made to attend, the quiet inspiration they were bringing away to their workaday world.

There were truck drivers from Oakland, fishermen from the wharves in San Francisco, trolleymen, street cleaners, butchers, grocery boys, soldiers, sailors and marines, captains from the air force, doctors and lawyers, students from the University of San Francisco, and St. Mary's, and Santa Clara, from the high schools in San Jose and Berkeley. They came from all over, from Palo Alto, Los Banos, Santa Cruz, from Burlingame and Saratoga, Stockton and Fresno. Each retreat house became a power-house for the surrounding country.

There was the assemblyman who came to catch a few stray influential votes and who wrote back a year later that what he learned in the retreat was standing him in good stead as he pounded out laws at Sacramento. The high and the low, the rich and poor, all classes of men trooped up the hill week after week to pray and consider life's basic concerns. It was the same way in Detroit and New York, St. Louis and Portland, Philadelphia and Boston.

Many times it was hard. The gay life of Baghdad-by-the-Bay was attractive on a weekend. Men were tired. Frequently they gave up a day or two of wages which they could have used. They gave up the family for a few days, their desire for distraction, to be right up front in the pell-mell American scene.

Old Father Stack knew that the *men* had built the retreat movement. He had sketched and planned and inspired and prodded. But they built it. They built its reputation. Their dollars and dimes built the buildings. God was erecting a great temple out of men's souls here in America.

El Retiro had by now grown healthy and prosperous—but at the cost of its founder's failing years. That precarious health of his had occasioned more than one change of occupation in the past. Father Stack now requested a change of status. He was to return once more to the pastorate in a large Southern parish.

Santa Barbara is a prosperous community in the heart of the citrus belt of Southern California. Palm trees thrive in the semitropical climate. Spanish-style homes speak of early Franciscan influence which is still strong at Mission Santa Barbara, restored to its primitive splendor. Here sandaled Franciscan Brothers still guide tourists through the old Mission, while in the modern monastery students and novices pursue a life of prayer and study.

It was into this atmosphere of leisurely Southern living that Father Stack made his way. He soon became one of the most influential Catholics in Santa Barbara. Always reliable for big issues, he built one of the best parish set-ups in Southern California. His plant included a fine church and house, grammar school and Catholic girls' high school.

A tall, dignified figure in frock coat and clerical collar, Father Stack gave dignity that was not comical to civic gatherings. His keen mind was expert at saying what needed to be said well. His was a familiar and welcome presence at more and more community functions. He was a step forward for religion in an America undergoing rapid secularization, because he gave to the priesthood a proper respectability and in a sense helped set the stage for a secular people to welcome men of God, learned and urbane men who could teach and counsel.

As pastor, he had to see to the good of the souls of his people. One of the damaging effects of the free press which he had to battle in his parish was the sale and distribution of indecent literature. He did what he could to discourage its sale at news-stands and hit at the source of supply. It was a losing battle, but he fought it all the way.

In the spring of '35, the Knights of Columbus asked him to come along as chaplain to the Eucharistic Congress in Manila. During the three months away from home they touched on the shores of China and Japan. This was a great experience for him, but it exacted its toll.

Father Stack, now in his sixties and with his health failing, could no longer carry the burdens of a pastor. A younger man was sent to take his place, and he returned once more to El Retiro. Not long after, his superior, Father Provincial, called him to San Jose. He told him that it had been determined to start a permanent retreat house in Los Angeles and he asked him to take over the job. He said he was willing to give it a try despite his age and failing health.

On the Southern Pacific's crack streamliner, the Daylight, for all his sixty-seven years, Joe Stack headed for Los Angeles and another promotional job. It was to be 1925 all over again, with choice real estate scarcer now, and the old priest beginning to feel the weight of his years.

From his home-base at Loyola University he set out each day driving along Sepulveda, through boomtown, Culver City, over the pass to San Fernando Valley. No luck! Out again the next day to Pasadena, Monrovia, and finally Azusa, where he spied the McNeil estate and called for consultation on the advisability of a purchase. When the consultors arrived, they were treated to the sight of a well-preserved French-chateau-styled summer home once owned by this wealthy family. It was sheltered by acres of orange trees and the speedy Pacific Electric's "red-reaper" passed almost at the door. The spacious interior with its well-appointed kitchen and paneled study all recommended the spot as ideal for retreat work. The study would make an ideal chapel, the rooms could accommodate two retreatants apiece and would still leave some to take care of the Fathers and Brothers. It was tentatively decided to secure the place if possible.

Weeks of negotiating passed before Joe Stack could call the place his own. After the final papers had been signed, the moving operations began. Furniture which he had begged, borrowed, or stolen from all the houses of the Province was taken out to Azusa in trucks owned by a firm interested in the success of the project. The retreat master guided the entire operation-transport to set up his fledgling house of retreats in the South. It was the same weary task over again, but Father Stack was willing to do it if it meant a repetition of the good work already well under way in the North.

Manresa, as the retreat house in the South is called, stands today well-established. Several new cottages have been built to accommodate the growing number of retreatants. A new chapel is in the making. What Joe Stack visualized and, in a very real sense, gave his life to establish is slowly being realized.

* * *

It was the fall of 1950. Golden fruit hung temptingly from the green trees in the grove. A dull haze hung over the hot valley. The "red-reaper" screamed by on its early morning run. In the French-chateau, quiet with the silence of twenty-five men on retreat, Father Superior sat at the desk of his cool, shuttered room going over the morning mail. As he slowly sifted through the pile, his eyes were caught by the yellow envelope of a Western Union telegram. Hastily he tore it open:

AUG. 16   FR JOE STACK DIED   O'CONNOR SANITARIUM   SAN JOSE

In a sense Joe Stack represented the passing of an epoch. He had seen the Church in the booming West a rather tolerated and suspected minority. Most of its members were immigrants without too much education.

Every two or three years they got their shot in the arm from a roving missionary who could curdle the blood of the bravest man with his thundering discourses on death, hell, and damnation. With the rank and file, though, there was neither the time nor the opportunity to think about Christian perfection on any more than basic terms.

As is always the case with a culture that mushrooms, there comes a lag, slowdown, a steadier tempo. The blustering raw communities pave their streets, build libraries, read, begin to think and reflect. And there is born then the desire to know more about the qualitative aspects of life. Men want to be perfect, that's what it amounts to.

And as is always the case also, God raises up instruments to do His work, not necessarily extraordinary men, but good men. Joe Stack was one of those good men. Sickness and frailty shaped him to be a pioneer in a work which year by year in America unfolds greater and greater promise.

When many another fellow Jesuit was perhaps temporarily

intrigued by the largeness and ever expansive nature of secular universities, even the football team and the screaming crowds as a medium of good, and hence entered into an all-out effort to match them with Jesuit schools, Father Stack kept plugging for his dream.

The schools would do a lot of good, he knew. But the work of the Order was broader than just schools. He knew that knowledge was not virtue. That's where Plato had been wrong. That's where many modern sociologists in America were wrong. Perfection required discipline, effort over the years, sacrifice— more than philosophy or college religion courses, clean homes and a balanced diet.

So the priest, whom some of his fellow Jesuits thought a little hard to live with and whom most people that were not Jesuits thought was wonderful to live with, faded out of the picture. He had been the man God sent forth to sow the seed. It was growing into a great tree. Father Stack died with no illusions of immense personal worth. The Jesuits had trained him; God had helped him; people had responded. His name would be forgotten. But what a work this man had begun. What a spark he had enkindled in his quiet-steady way. The pattern of redemption was always repeating itself.

The superior drifted back from his reverie. And the quick scream of a jet filled the air as it jumped electrically across the warm sky. The bell was late for the conference; he must call Brother as the men would be waiting.

SOMEONE *would have to pay for the blazing imperialism of the nineteenth century. For a long while Europe held the sprawling dominions together with uncanny statesmanship, a show of force when needed, a succession of useful coalitions. Germany was growing prodigiously and wanted room. Tensions mounted, and inevitably war came.*

Indignation swept America at the violation of sacred boundaries, the iron heel of the Kaiser crushing the flower of Belgian manhood. But there were many who saw deeper causes, thought that England had sown the seeds, before her France and Spain. No one's hands were guiltless of this blood. Each had taught the other well.

Swarms of agitators fanned the fires. There were great demonstrations for and against the war. Wilson tried desperately to steer America clear of the struggle. U. S. ships were going down; gangsterism began to gain the upper hand. Reluctantly but firmly the doughboys went Over There.

It was a costly conflict exacting the combined energies of the republic, but somehow also helping cement the dissident factors which separated one community from another. Brotherhood prevailed and barriers of nationality and strata made less difference than before. One gray November day America went mad with victory.

Then short-sighted men turned off the vision of a faltering Wilson, broke the brotherhood sealed by blood and graves in France, fathered the insulated mentality, the culmination of unbridled self-emphasis. The League died of American apathy. The armistice of twenty years ended with the screams of a Munich maniac. Europe lay enslaved once more from the Rus-

sian Steppes to the Pyrenees. And a fearful peril coiled itself around the heart of Asia. America's dream had turned into a nightmare. How long would it take her to learn?

* * *

So Proudly We Hail

Father Carl Hausmann, S.J.

by JAMES B. REUTER, S.J.

He died in the hold, half-naked, lying on the floor in the darkness and filth, among men who were too exhausted, too sick, too accustomed to death and too near death themselves to make any fuss over him. When he was dead, they stripped the body, giving what clothes he had to the living, and then they dragged the corpse into the patch of light underneath the hatchway. They left it there until the bodies numbered six.

Then the boatswain, whose duty it was, tied a running bowline around the knees and a half-hitch round the neck, looked up at the hatchway, and called: "All right. Take it away." The rope tightened and the body of Carl Hausmann rose slowly up the shaft of sunlight, gaunt and bronzed and naked, while in the darkness the men watched, dully, wondering when they would go up that way too. The body bumped against the side of the hatch and slid out of sight on to the deck. They could hear the shuffle of feet and the jabber of Japanese as it was dragged across the deck and stacked near the railing with the rest of the American dead.

A sailor said: "It's tough. He was a good man. He knew Japanese."

Carl Hausmann died as an officer in the United States Army— the citation which the government eventually sent to his mother never mentioned the fact that he was a chaplain, a priest—but he had come down into the tropics as a missionary. He had once been pastor to the lepers on the Island of Culion in the Philippines. And it was not only Japanese he knew—he could speak in ten different tongues. He was a linguist almost of necessity, because he had lived and worked on three continents, in a whole litter of languages.

He was born at Weisenburg in Alsace-Lorraine, in 1898, while his mother and father were visiting there, and the nurse who cradled him sang him to sleep in German. When he started school in Weehawken, New Jersey, the teacher talked to him in beautiful English that rippled with an Irish brogue, saying: "Oh now child, you must always write with your right hand!" Carl explained cheerfully that he could do it better with his left —that he threw a ball with his left hand, he drew pictures with his left hand, he carved wood and tied knots and *ate* with his left hand; in short, he was *left*-handed!—but she smiled gently and folded the fingers of his right hand around the pencil. A man cannot win in the first grade. Carl bowed his curly head, gripped the pencil hard like a weapon, and went through the rest of his life left-handed, but writing with his right. His hand is neat, strong, carefully controlled, as if whenever he wrote he sat up straight and concentrated.

The fact that he really knew French was impressed upon Carl years later when he was studying in Canada. One afternoon after a public defense of a proposition, the little professor of philosophy blew up like a boiler and told him in fifteen minutes of violent and idiomatic French that he must spend less time on the Latin and Greek classics and more time on ontology! The language hissed and crackled and spluttered and steamed, and Carl was amazed that he could understand every word. When the man's wrath had simmered down, Carl apologized softly and told him in one minute of very gentle French that he loved the classics, while he had no particular affection for ontology, but if the professor wished, he would modify the schedule by which he lived. That night the teacher approved the new schedule, was a little surprised that any philosopher should really have a schedule, and they became fast friends.

When he organized the Lepers' Glee Club on Culion, the singers could not always understand each other because they came from different islands and spoke different languages, but they all understood Carl. He was their bond of union. In him they were united. He taught the tenors in Tagalog and the basses in Visayan, the very old in Spanish and the very young in English. He had a natural gift of tongues, but it was not only that. It was his youth and strength, held out to them like a gift, his deep affection for them, the beauty of his music, his priesthood—these were fundamental things which every leper could understand.

In the prison camps of Mindanao, merely by listening to the guards and asking them questions, he learned a little Japanese. He was quiet most of the time, with his eyes and ears open, and he absorbed a great many things which others missed. With a Japanese grammar he learned swiftly, because his mind was calm, orderly, peaceful. If ever you met his family, you would understand him better.

His father is a gentle old man whose memories would delight the heart of Hilaire Belloc. Julius Hausmann remembers his own father, Franz, who was born in 1789, who fought in the French Army under Napoleon, was wounded in the march on Moscow and for that became a member of the French Légion d'Honneur. Julius was born when his father was sixty years old; he was fifteen when Abraham Lincoln was shot; his brother Fritz was killed in the battle of Antietam; his brother Otto was a colonel in the Prussian Army in the war of 1870; he himself has seen the United States survive one civil and three foreign wars; he is now ninety-seven years old, clear-headed and contemplative, managing his own affairs at Weehawken in New Jersey.

Of Carl's three brothers Adolay graduated from Princeton and is now a teacher; Hudson graduated from Notre Dame and is a certified accountant; Otto is a pillar of industry who has worked steadily with the same firm since high school. All three are married.

Adolay was the eldest boy and Carl was next. His big brother's precedence must have been painfully obvious to Carl, who mentioned in one of his letters that he graduated from Union Hill Public High School "deep in the recesses of Adolay's old suit," but he worshiped Adolay as a kind of a hero. On the local sand-lot football teams Adolay punted and carried the ball; he was fast and clever at fullback. Carl put his head down and bucked in the line.

In baseball, partly because of their rugged builds, both of the boys were catchers. Adolay caught for a team in Ramsey, New Jersey, and Carl succeeded to his position when Adolay went off to college. Carl's throw to second was a thing of beauty and a joy forever; the ball whistled low over the infield in a dead line, fast and hard and accurate; but a left-handed catcher is a nightmare to right-handed batters. In the summer before he entered the Society, Carl hit two men at the plate. Both were carried off the field. Carl confided to Adolay later that this discouraged him a good deal. At the end of the inning after the second injury, he unbuckled his chest-protector and sat on the bench and brooded. He thought that he should give up catching before he killed somebody. Because the team had no substitutes on hand, he had to go back into the game, and he played until the end of the season, but there is no record that he ever caught in the Society.

All four brothers swam in the Hudson River. The baby boy was named after it, Hudson, because he was born on the tercentenary of its discovery. Here in the swift water Carl was in his glory. Deep-chested and heavily muscled, something of a lone wolf, he liked swimming more than any other sport. He would swim far out, through the roll and swell of the liners and tugs, fighting the current, all the way across to the New York side.

Grown up, the four brothers in their pictures are lean, tall, somber-looking men—soldiers, scholars, teachers of Greek and coaches of basketball, natural warriors, like their ancestors. All of them went bald. Adolay, Hudson, and Carl accepted it philosophically, but Otto was handsome. He fought it. He fought it fiercely, savagely, with brushes and ointments and massages and tonics that burned. But he went bald too. Julius Hausmann chuckles in his chair and says: "The women blame it on me, because I have no hair either. But could I help that?"

Of Carl's three sisters Elsa studied in Europe and settled down as a business woman; only Madeline married; Maria is a nun. The nun is the baby among the girls, an artist and a missionary to the Negroes. Once she sent home a series of pencil sketches, portraits of the children in her class. She drew them during study periods, when she had time to watch them. Paging through the pictures, the casual observer comes to the conclusion that either the children in her class are extraordinarily attractive, or else she loves them very much. Mrs. Hausmann says: "Both. But especially she loves them. She is like Carl in that. He loved the students in his class. He loved the people in his mountain parish. He loved the lepers."

Unlike Carl, his little sister is vivacious, effervescent, openly affectionate. Both brother and sister were deeply in love with life, but she shows it. If Carl is a still stream, his little sister is a rapids. Her letters sparkle; they dance; they run as swiftly as a waterfall in the sunlight, bouncing on the rocks. Carl's letters flow deep and smooth and deliberate, like a clear, slow river winding inexorably to the sea. Carl was a violinist and in his pictures looks somber, like Hamlet. His little sister is a painter and in her pictures she is always smiling. She wears her coif tilted slightly sideways, just enough to remind you of a young sailor going out on leave.

Carl is a legend in her convent because of what happened at the time of his ordination. In preparation for his visit, the nuns had put up the prettiest curtains in the guest room; they had got out the good silverware, had decorated the altar, the choir was rehearsing a new Mass—and Carl missed his train. He arrived at the convent shortly after midnight, in the glow of ordination, with the oils still fresh on his hands, in a new suit, with a new black bag. He walked around the silent building, looking for lights. There were no lights. Carl was always gentle, always reserved, unwilling to inconvenience anyone. He would not even ring the doorbell. He would not disturb the sleep of the good Sisters. He settled down on the porch, quietly, and tried to read his office in the moonlight. At dawn when the nuns came out for the milk they found him there, their guest, sound asleep and all curled up in a rocking chair.

At Woodstock in Maryland, where he studied, it was said that he kept silence in seven languages. This is more remarkable in view of the fact that superiors have been trying to get a little silence at Woodstock for years. Woodstock rectors are forever waving the tomahawk and beating the war drums for silence. It is a big house, sheltering three hundred men, and so it is bound to be a little bit like a barracks. An occasional roar in the corridor, after five classes in one day and a *casus conscientiae;* a sudden spasm of horseplay and a banging door; a knot of disgruntled students around the water-fountain on the fourth floor, discussing the virtues and vices of professors—these things are almost inevitable, even among good men. Perhaps they are a sign of life.

Please don't misunderstand. Silence is really kept at Woodstock, about ninety-seven per cent of the time. To outsiders the place seems to be as peaceful as a monastery garden, as hushed as a library, as quiet as a church. But the difference between Carl and everybody else lay in that last human three per cent. Carl was consistent. He was always quiet.

Now keeping silence is different from being silent. A man may be silent, with his chin on his chest and a vacant stare, because he has no thoughts. Keeping silence implies that you have thoughts, which circle through your mind and heart and are stored in your memory; you harbor and treasure these thoughts; you may laugh or weep over them; only you do not speak. This is what Carl did. The finest linguist in the house, at that time he could think in Latin, in Greek, in English, in French, in Spanish, in Italian, in German, but he only voiced his thoughts at recreation. He kept silence in all his seven languages.

What did he think about? Well, strangely enough, his letters are a mirror of the Constitutions. Carl believed in the rules of the Society of Jesus with a peculiar personal conviction. When, for instance, during the First World War his father was suffering persecution because of his German birth and name, Carl, in a beautifully mature letter, written from Saint Andrew's, explained to him that those who hated German-Americans were an irrational minority; they did not represent the nation. He quoted the speeches of the president and editorials in large newspapers, where the real voice of the people could be found. Then he praised the tolerance of the Society, and the wisdom of Saint Ignatius when he wrote the rule: "All must beware of that feeling through which those of one nation are wont to think or speak unfavorably of another; rather they must both think well of, and bear in the Lord peculiar love for those of other countries. . . ."

During the quiet years of his formation he wrote long letters, laying down the principles by which he lived and died. "Elsie seems to be taking a good deal of pains, and I suppose expense, for Mrs. ———" he wrote to his mother in 1922, "which the poor old lady seems not to appreciate at all. Too bad! And yet it is only one of the many things in this world that we must expect. Really, generosity of the truest kind doesn't look for reward here, and the fact that it operates without appreciation shows clearly enough that it is sterling."

There the principle is put badly, but years later Father Duffy (who was a chaplain with Father Hausmann) sat in an armchair at Woodstock and said: "Carl died partly because he gave his food away. We were getting two spoonfuls of rice every third day and he gave his away. And the shame of it was that the men he gave it to weren't worthy of it. He gave it to the whiners, the weaklings. When they complained, he'd lean over and dump his ration into their cup, without a word. The real men wouldn't take it! They kept their mouths shut, like Carl."

Twenty-seven years of letters in the Society, with never a line of cynicism, never a page that was bitter or harsh, but the most important of all his letters he wrote to his father in 1916, when he was graduating from high school.

"Dear Papa,

The time has now come for me to let you know what my ambition is for the future. So far, I have probably led you to believe that it was my desire to enter business. The truth is I lost my idea for a future in business some time ago, for I have finally resolved upon that vocation which, I wrote you, I would talk over with Adolay.

It will probably not come up to your expectations of me, and, I fear, will not please you at first. It is for this reason that I have neglected and even been afraid to tell you, although I have had it in my mind for over a half year. Now I believe the sooner you know the better. It is the priesthood.

You may think perhaps that I am not fit or capable of becoming a priest but there have been many people much worse than I who have changed to the good. I realize my faults of the past and know how much I must improve.

There seems to be a natural instinct in this family to teach. Adolay has become a teacher and I intend to become one too, except that my ambition is to teach the difference between right and wrong.

With the sincere hope that this letter may make a favorable impression on you, believe me, I am

Your loving son,

Carl."

It is a formal little letter, on lined paper, written carefully in the clear young hand, filled with the fear of how his father will take it, but the thought is dynamite. The desire is so simple—to be a priest and to work for men—he could have conceived it in a moment. Its realization took the rest of his life—two years at Saint Peter's Prep in Jersey City to learn Latin, because he was a public school boy; four years at Saint Andrew's on the Hudson where he worked on the grounds and built benches and practiced his violin in the woodshed and sent his previous savings to Central Europe for the relief of the poor who had been struck by the war; bad days at Saint Andrew's during the flu epidemic, when he nursed the sick and buried the dead; his philosophy at Montreal in Canada; his regency, teaching French at Fordham in New York; his theology at Woodstock; thirteen years at a desk, through all his youth, while his hair grew thin and the study lines grew deep around his eyes; then ordination, the *ad grad* (his final exam), tertianship at Saint Andrew's, and the tropics.

The tropics, the work he had dreamed of—and his first job was procurator and teacher of Greek in a Philippine novitiate. It was not quite the way he had dreamed it—studying native dialects at night by the light of a kerosene lamp, stripped to the waist, with a towel around his neck to soak up the sweat . . . balancing books and checking over bills before he went to bed, waking in the night to stare at the white mosquito net and wonder where the money would come from to keep the novitiate going . . . listening to the lizards on the wall calling "Gecko! Gecko!" . . . Mass before daylight amid a buzzing of bugs, pronouncing the words of consecration with one hand over the chalice to prevent the insects from falling into it . . . watching the roaches at breakfast crawling across the table, climbing up the coffee pot . . . walking in the morning sun in the white dust of a road, his cassock wet with perspiration and plastered against his back, to teach catechism to children in a village . . . chopping down the cogon grass with the native laborers, grass that grew to be twelve feet high; blushing when he paid the men fifty cents a day . . . reading his Office on his knees in the chapel in the early afternoon—regularly, every day for two years—while the bright sun beat down on the tin roof and the white heat stood still around him . . . immersed in heat, bathed in it, breathing it . . . then the darkness and the coolness of the rain . . . teaching Greek in the evening to bright-eyed young Filipinos while the rain washed the windows and drummed on the bamboo walls—that was nice . . . waking to the rain for six months on end; the constant sound and smell of it as it fell steadily night and day, dripping from the roof.

Carl liked the tropics, and the Filipinos liked him—his calmness, the humor in his eyes, his patient grin, his willingness to work and learn, the breadth of his shoulders, his gentleness in the classroom. He was a big lean man, and strong, but in class he was as understanding as a mother, blaming himself if ever his pupils did not get the matter.

The priests who lived with him, who taught in the juniorate or philosophate, sometimes sank into chairs in the recreation room and damned the world in general, grumbling about the meals, the monotony, their schedule, the rain, the heat—this is the privilege of men who are working hard. They don't really mean it and it seems to make them feel better. But in these sessions Carl Hausmann would say nothing at all. He would sit in silence, memorizing Tagalog or Visayan words from little slips of paper which he carried in all his pockets. Or else he would walk down the cloistered corridor to admire the beauty of the sunset on Manila Bay. The men noticed this after a while: he never protested about anything. The only thing he did not like about his job was that it was too easy.

He volunteered for Culion.

Once he had read an article by a woman-traveler who had paid a flying visit to a leper colony in China. She reported in a gush of fervor that lepers were the happiest people in the world, because—having nothing else to live for—they turned completely to God. He arrived at the island and it was not true. Lepers are like everybody else.

Years later, his memories of the colony were not all beautiful —the eyes of the old sick ones as they watched a new shipload of patients coming into the harbor; the shrewdness and greed in their high shrill voices as they tried to establish some distant relationship with a small strong boy, so that they could take him to their hut and have him work for them . . . the anger of the young men when the nuns set up a protective dormitory for girls; the sallow faces peering in through the bars, cursing the Sisters . . . the lepers on their beds who laughed at him and said: "If there is a God, then why do we suffer so?" . . . the leper sitting on the edge of his bed in the early morning, receiving Communion; the later startling discovery that he had not been to confession in years; his indifferent shrug, saying:

"Well, why not? You give. I take" . . . the sullen lepers who went out on the sea in tiny fishing boats, working savagely in the sun, so that the fever would take them and they would die.

But there were sweet things, too—his glee club, and the orchestra . . . the young lepers who wept for their sins and begged for a great penance, because they wanted to be good . . . giving Communion to little children who were so small that they could not receive on their knees—their heads would not come up above the altar rail—they stood with their hands folded across their breasts, with the leprosy in their faces and innocence in their eyes . . . the gratitude of the bad cases in the hospital when he came to them each day; the smile of the sick when he spoke to them in their own tongue; the quiet tears when he anointed them; the last pressure of their hands on his just before they died . . . the eyes that followed him in the wards, worshiping eyes, so grateful that there were still good men in the world . . . the sudden deep resolve to pray more, and to work harder, in order to be worthy of these lepers who loved him . . . back home, repairing the roof of his chapel as the sun went down; the little shiver of satisfaction, the feeling of strength and power that comes from working with your own hands . . . writing the history of the colony in the evening; writing to his mother in German; reading the *De Corona* in Greek, because he liked it . . . the moonlit nights by the sea, when the children of lepers, born on the island but born clean, took his hand and asked him questions about Manila and New York and the lands that were not Culion.

He felt when he went to bed that the work was good, that he was doing something. Just as his little sister loved the Negroes in her class, so Carl loved the lepers. He probably would have felt the same toward any souls that came under his care; it just happened that the lepers were assigned to him; still, his heart-strings were all wound around Culion when finally his transfer came. Gaunt and drawn and sick, he did not want to go. Superiors sent him, and superiors took him away. He stood in the back of the boat, and the children sang for him on the shore, and he watched the island until it was a line on the face of the sea, until it was gone.

Mindanao is not the largest tropical island in the world, but it is very big. It has an area of 36,000 square miles and a population of nearly half a million; its southern tip lies about five and a half degrees north of the equator; it contains Mohammedan Moros who are famous for head-hunting and wild black dwarfs called negritos who are famous for poisonous blowpipes. The island has cities, of course, and schools, and colleges, and thousands of good Filipino Catholics, but large chunks of Mindanao are marked on the map as unexplored. Most of the people live in tiny towns and villages called barrios, buried in the hills, and it is the priest's job to get to them. Some priests rattle cheerfully over the mountains in flivvers which civilization has long since abandoned; some ride through the passes on horseback; Belgians go by bicycle. Carl walked.

His new parish was all mountains and jungle, with swamps springing up in the rainy season. He could get to the villages much faster on foot through the forest paths than by the circuitous route of the roads. It was here that the war closed in on him. The first real signs that he saw and heard were Japanese planes, roaring low over the trees. Then his licorice sticks stopped coming. These licorice sticks were not the kind you would buy in a candy store. They were thick and solid, brittle and hard, foul-tasting, an evil German concoction that his mother had used on him as a boy and still mailed to him in the jungle. Carl liked them. When he came back from a barrio to his cottage on the mountainside, out from under the dripping trees, muddy and feverish and soaked with the rains, he chewed on these and the bitterness did something peculiar to his insides which prevented him from getting pneumonia. Missionaries have been known to use other methods for staving off a cold, but this was Carl's way.

There was another thing which he liked very much and was forever trying to grow in the tropics—watermelons. He planted American watermelon seeds in Luzon, in Culion, and in Mindanao, but they never grew. Too much sun or too much rain, washed out or burned up. Each year he would analyze his failure, discover a new way to correct it, write to his sister Elsie for more seeds, and try again. His hope sprang eternal, but the experiments stopped when the Japanese cut off the mails.

For months our army fought on the coasts of Mindanao without air support, without artillery; then they began a slow and bloody retreat back into the interior, back into the hills. In a town called Impulatao they set up a base hospital, to which they carried the wounded from Digos, from Davao, from Zamboanga. The chief surgeon was Doctor Davis, newly enlisted in the army. He had been a civilian, practicing in Negros, until the war swept over the islands. The hospital had no chaplain at all until one morning as he was driving in toward the town the doctor saw a tall lean figure striding along the road ahead of him, dressed in a white cassock. The doctor pulled up alongside of him, stopped the car, and said: "Where to?"

"Hospital," said Carl.

He was sweat-soaked and grateful for the ride. The doctor liked him because he was relaxed. His face was hard, strong, lined with the years. It was a man's face. There was too much asceticism, the doctor thought, in the grim jaw, in the hollow cheeks, in his eyes; but there was ease in his manner, gentleness in the things he said, beauty in his thoughts. He had the deep sense of humor which is God's gift to missionaries. He looked as if time had toughened him, but had enriched him too. By far the most noticeable part of him was his eyes: patient, dreamy, sad, austere, at rare intervals dark and blazing, as if he wanted to rip up the world and change it at its roots—but then he would smile, the fire in his eyes would drop down to a twinkle, his whole face would soften, and he seemed content to bear with the world as it was. He was a dreamer in a practical world, an artist in the wilderness, a man who loved God very much working among men who didn't. But that's why he was there. As he sat in the doctor's car on the way to Impulatao, he was forty-four years old, in the full strength of his manhood, brown with the sun, content with his work, at peace.

"What do you want to go to the hospital for?" asked the doctor.

"I thought that they might need a priest."

They did need him badly, because we were losing on all fronts; more wounded were pouring into the hospital than the staff could handle, and he was the only priest. Eventually, at the request of the commanding officer of the hospital and with the permission of his own superior, he became a regular military chaplain. As Davis had enlisted on Negros, because there was need of a doctor, so Carl enlisted at Impulatao, because there was need of a priest. They inducted him formally into the army. Two days later the army surrendered, the Japanese came in, and he was a prisoner of war.

Carl's career as a captive began when the stocky, confident, slant-eyed little guards marched all the Americans into a barbed wire pen at Impulatao in Mindanao, and locked the gate. The guards all seemed to be heavy in the middle, slogging along on their heels in soft canvas two-toed shoes, Oriental shoes. Through the years, as they stood outside the wire, they were all bow legs, long bayonets, tin helmets, and white teeth.

It wasn't so bad, at first. Carl had never set much stock on food, so he didn't mind the rice. He built a wooden altar in the barracks, and a tabernacle, and said Mass for the men every morning.

But then they were transferred to the penal colony at Davao to work in the rice fields. This was not so good. Rations down to rice and greens, constant hunger, long days in the sun, no water to bathe in, not enough water to drink, skin disease and dysentery: dysentery—the curse of every prison camp in the tropics, wasting big men down to bony frames with yellow skin and sunken eyes; hundreds of sweating men sleeping close together like galley slaves; roll call in the morning, the burial of the dead. Here Carl began to put wine into his chalice with an eye-dropper, pronouncing the words of consecration over a small host, giving the men tiny fragments for Communion. He tried to stretch the hosts, stretch the wine, because no one knew how long the war would last. It was two years already. Then the altar breads ran out and Mass stopped altogether.

The labor crews went into the rice fields in orderly rotation at Davao, so that each man would have regular days to rest. But after a while the major in charge of Carl's barracks, who later died with him on the boat, noticed that Carl was always in the fields. On his rest-days he was substituting for other men. The major didn't like it. He was himself in charge of assigning men to work details, because the Japanese merely demanded a certain amount of work from each barracks and they didn't care who did it. The major thought that he had made a just distribution of labor, so he questioned Carl about those whose place he was taking. "They're sick," said Carl, "and they can't stand the hours in the sun."

"He said they were sick," the major repeated, months later, in the hold of the ship, "and my God, you should have seen *him!* His body was a mass of festering scabs from rice rash."

Sometimes the prisoners were allowed to send word home on printed Japanese cards. This privilege was granted through the courtesy of the Emperor on rare festive occasions: on his birthday, for instance; on the anniversary of the Japanese victory over the Russians in 1905, a victory which the Japanese army remembered with relish as Russia held the Germans; on the day when Japan gave independence to the Philippines. On these days Carl joined in the general joy of the Greater East Asia Co-Prosperity Sphere by writing home. They were not exactly letters. The blank printed cards as they came to the prisoners looked like this:

Imperial Japanese Army

1. I am interned at Philippine Military Prison Camp #——.
2. My health is ——— excellent; good; fair; poor.
3. I am ——— injured; sick in hospital under treatment; not under treatment.
4. I am ——— improving; not improving; better; well.
5. Please see that ——— is taken care of.
6. (Re: Family) ———.
7. Please give my best regards to ———.

The Japanese did not leave much room for poetical inspiration. Carl's mother received four of these cards, all the same, all of them non-committal. Carl said:

Imperial Japanese Army

1. I am interned at Philippine Military Prison Camp #2.
2. My health is *good*.
3. I am *not under treatment*.
4. I am *well*.
5. Please see that *nobody worries*.
6. (Re: Family) ————
7. Please give my regards to *all*.

In three of four cards he left *No. 6 Re: Family* blank. In the fourth, which was probably the first one written, he typed a message: *Am well hope you are the same. Please notify Father Provincial. Love to all. Carl.*

Only once did he really try to say something, and then the card did not get through the Japanese censors. Our army found it in Japan when the war was over and Carl was dead.

Imperial Japanese Army

1. I am interned at Philippine Military Prison Camp #2.
2. My health is *fair*.
3. Message (50 words limit)
   Haven't yet rec'd word from anybody at home. Priests are allowed to say Mass but can't get altar bread and have not been able to contact any Red Cross representative. Climate here bearable enough best regards to all. Carl.

The card is dated June 10, 1944. It was written when he was down with amoebic dysentery at Davao. The only part of prison life which pained him was the absence of the Mass.

Late in June of 1944 the Davao prisoners were shipped north to the island of Luzon, to a camp called Cabanatuan. It was a big camp, filled with the survivors of Bataan and Corregidor. They worked on a Japanese airdrome. Carl was bearded and as bronze as a native now, indistinguishable in the truckloads of half-naked men who were carried at dawn each day from the camp to the airfield. He was just another laborer in a crowd of laborers, pushing a wheelbarrow in the sun. He was just another bent back, shoveling shale; one more month in the rice line; one more hungry American soldier climbing back into the Japanese truck at night, standing, waiting while the others packed in too, until the truck was filled, their bodies pressed close together; jolting back to the barracks in the darkness with his arms thrown across the shoulders of his fellow prisoners, too tired to talk. At night he was like everyone else too: he prayed for freedom and dreamt of food.

But there was an altar at Cabanatuan, and hosts and wine, and every morning by candle-light he said Mass. That made him different. It left a glow within him which lasted through the day. He said Mass so reverently that even the other priests were impressed and non-Catholics came to watch him.

He had always looked holy—so much so that an old Irish scrubwoman in New York City, after hearing him preach once, began immediately to pray to him, while he was still alive, saying: "Glory be to God, the man's a saint!"—but now, gaunt and weather-beaten, with his quiet dignity, his eyes sunken and the golden skin drawn tight over his cheek bones, he looked when he was still like a statue in a church. Catholics called him Saint Joseph. Non-Catholics called him the Holy Ghost. They did not mean to be irreverent. It was merely their way of indicating that to them he stood for the whole of Christianity, for religion in general, for God.

As his body wasted and the years of suffering rolled on, there was something deeply spiritual in the personality of Father Hausmann which came to the fore. It became obvious at first sight even to strangers. Perhaps it was only the peace in his eyes when everyone else was desperate, or his stark simplicity; but when men met him they began immediately to think of heaven and hell and their own private sins. This was not the mere subjective impression of one man; it happened to too many in that camp to be accidental. They could not quite analyze it, but it was something real in Carl Hausmann which they could see and feel. One survivor who knew him only slightly says: "Maybe he was too much at home with God. He was so thoroughly in the state of grace that it made the rest of us feel unclean, uncomfortable. It's not natural for a man to give away his food when he is starving, to work for someone else when he himself can hardly stand up. Holiness is an easy thing to hate, and he was holy, but . . . we liked him."

Through nearly three years of captivity, the characteristic note of Carl Hausmann was meekness. He never complained, never fought back, never cursed his captors. He never even lost his temper with the kleptomaniac in the camp who stole his Mass kit and offered to sell it back to him piece by piece. He obeyed superior officers immediately and without question; even General Sharp testifies that he was a splendid soldier. He was so generous that men were ashamed to take advantage of him. He trusted everybody, even the Japanese—when he shifted from Cabanatuan to Old Bilibid he wrapped up all his possessions in a newspaper, put his name on the bundle, and gave it to a guard, asking him to please see that it was delivered. The guard smiled and disappeared with the package, while Carl's friends groaned. He was definitely gentle, but he was that way on principle. He had a clear, strong, definite mind on what he should and should not do.

Once he resisted the guards.

It was a gray morning late in November of 1944, in the stone courtyard of Old Bilibid Penitentiary in Manila, when he was saying Mass. It was his fourth prison camp and his thirty-first month as a prisoner. He had no shoes any more, but he still had vestments and a missal, and a Filipino woman had sent wine and hosts into Bilibid through a Japanese colonel. Barefoot, bearded, with the men kneeling behind him on the stones and his corporal spread out on a packing box, he had just begun the consecration when the siren sounded. It meant that they were under air raid, that American planes were over the city, that the prisoners should clear the yard and get back to their cells. The men scattered, reluctantly, while Carl went on with the Mass. A guard barked at him, but he stood with his eyes on the Host and did not move. The guard came up on the altar, barked again, and struck him with the butt of his rifle. Carl would not move. A seaman who saw the thing says that the guard flew into a sudden wild rage and began to club the priest, beating him with the butt of his gun for ten full minutes. The sailor's estimate of time at a crisis like that is probably not reliable; a ten-minute beating with a gun butt should have killed him. Other prisoners ran shouting into the courtyard, and the angry guard left the altar to drive them back. When he had gone, Carl finished the consecration of the chalice, consumed the Body and Blood, and went back to his cell.

Toward mid-December of 1944 the Japanese shipped 1619 prisoners of war out of Manila Bay, out into the China Sea, in a liner called the *Oroyku Maru*. It was bound for Japan, but American submarines sighted it before it had cleared the mouth of the harbor. American planes bombed and strafed it for a night and day, driving it in toward shore, until it ran aground off Olongapo in Subic Bay. There the planes came in low and planted three bombs squarely in the rear hold. There was panic below decks and the prisoners made a mad bolt for the ladders, swarming one over the other up to the hatchway. The terrified Japanese turned machine-guns on them, firing point blank, forcing them back into the bowels of the ship.

Then the *Oroyku Maru* caught fire, the ammunition exploded, and the Japanese began to push off in life boats. When most of the guards had gone, the prisoners were allowed to abandon ship too and they poured up into the morning sunlight, wild-eyed and half-starved and most of them wounded. They went over the side into the sea. The water was cool, calm, green in the tropic sun, and Carl Hausmann swam easily through the oil and wreckage, feeling the smart of the salt water in his wounds, cheering as the American planes dived and fountains of flame sprang up from the *Oroyku Maru*.

It was only a swim of five hundred yards, and some of the men as they swam dreamed of an escape into the hinterland, but a division of Japanese infantry was encamped on the shore. When Carl crawled up on the beach, they had already set up a perimeter around the strip of white sand; wherever he looked, little yellow men sat silently behind their machine-guns, waiting for someone to make a break. It was sinister and dramatic, like a moving picture, only it was real.

After a while they were lined up and marched off to a tennis court, where they stayed for a week without cover, roasting in the sun by day and shivering on the cement by night, in the swift change of temperature which is common in the tropics. This heat and cold seems only a little thing, but it is what those who went through it remember most. It was worse than the hunger and thirst. Four times during the seven days each man received one tablespoon of raw rice. There was no other food, very little water. They buried their dead in the soft dirt beside the court.

One day, over in a corner in back of the base line, in the shade of a piece of canvas, Colonel Schwartz amputated the arm of a young marine. He did it without anesthesia, without sterilization, with a cauterized razor. The boy fought to live for five days, as the prisoners went overland in freight cars to a port called San Fernando, but there he died, on the stage of the town's theater, where the prisoners were kept.

The rest were packed into another ship, a freighter; Carl was assigned to a spot low in the stern of it, on top of the propeller shaft. It was a lucky position.

Of the seventeen chaplains on this journey, the most spectacular was Father Cummings. He was a strong, courageous warrior of a man, a religious spark plug, dynamic, a natural leader. He was the man who at Bataan had said: "There are no atheists in fox-holes." Now he stood in the center of the hold and prayed for all of them, saying: "O God, tomorrow please spare us from being bombed."

Nothing spectacular was ever recorded about Father Hausmann. In the lurid tales which are told of the trip he appears only incidentally, in quiet passages like this:

> Late in the afternoon, with 200 others, I climbed down a steel ladder into this small hold. It's three decks down.

Along the forward wall a shelf has been built so that the men can sit in two layers. We can sit on our blanket rolls, or lie back on our neighbor's lap. We have organized ourselves into groups of 20 men. Father Hausmann, Bill, Jack, Fred and I are together in a group of 20. At Cabanatuan I had learned to say the Rosary in Spanish. Father Hausmann, who has been a missionary priest in Mindanao for 18 years and speaks Spanish perfectly, has taught me to say the 15 mysteries in idiomatic Spanish. The Japs sent down one gallon of hot water of which our group received three-fourths of a cup. When Father Hausmann declined his share, he was told, 'Don't be a fool! Water may mean life or death! Take your share!' He meekly took his two spoonfuls.

This is from the diary of Roy L. Bodine, Jr., which was published in *The Catholic World*.

Off Takao in Formosa the bombers came again and scored a direct hit in the forward hold. The Japanese looked down at the bloody mess, at the welter of wounded and dying and dead in the hold; then they locked the hatch and kept it locked for forty-eight hours as the ship limped into port. The forward hold was filled with agony. At night it was pitch black, with the living pinned beneath the corpses, and the blood of the dead running down over them, and the wounded crying for help, and no one able to help anyone else. At dawn the light trickled through cracks in the deck, but with it came the sight of the bodies, the sight of the open wounds and the faces of the dying; with the sun came the heat, and the stench of death. Men wept with pain and crept up the steel ladder and beat on the cover of the hatch, begging to be released. That is why the papers called this a hell ship.

There was no relief for two days. Then in the harbor a barge came alongside with a boom and tackle and a cargo net, and the Japanese opened the hatch. Of the five hundred men who were in that hold, only seven were still alive.

Carl lay on the deck in the sunlight and watched the wire

net rise out of the hold, filled with the naked bodies of his friends. The net swung over the side of the ship and down to the barge, dumping its load in a tangle of arms and legs and up-turned faces. It came back empty, throwing its shadow across the deck, and dropped down again into the hold. The barge was overloaded when finally it made for shore, where the prisoners who were living tied ropes around the ankles of the dead and dragged them up on the beach, leaving them there for Japanese cremation.

Actually, the rest of the voyage was so ghastly that solid sober citizens have to read four accounts of it by independent witnesses before they begin to believe it: the deliberate starva-tion, each man receiving every three days half a cup of rice and a quarter of a cup of water . . . naked men sleeping in a sitting posture, all doubled up, with their heads down and their arms around their knees like Indian fakirs praying; the boatswain making the rounds in the gray light of morning, putting his hand on each man to see if he were alive or dead . . . the bodies being hauled out of the hold . . . old grudges coming to the fore in the darkness; suicide and murder. . . . A young phar-macist's mate crept over to a cluster of warrant officers and said: "Look. I've lost my nerve. The fellows in my bay are plotting to kill me." They told him that it was his imagination, a case of nerves, that he must follow the general order and go back to his bay.

He shook his head and said: "It's not my imagination," but he went back; and in the morning they found him dead, with his stomach slit open . . . a navy chaplain kept reading aloud from his Bible; if ever you have had this done to you when you were under strain, hour after hour, you know what a torture it is; the men around him cursed and gritted their teeth and stopped their ears; but suddenly the chaplain screamed, began to tear the pages out of the book and throw them around the hold, wildly; he bolted for the ladder and got half-way up it before the men pulled him back and tied him down, whimpering . . . a sailor tried to slip up that ladder at night; there were three quick shots from the guard and the body slumped back into the hold . . .

flies and stench and festering wounds . . . the four cans which the Japanese had given them to use as latrines filled and flowing over; dysentery and diarrhea and filth everywhere . . . Father Cummings standing up in the hold, straight and strong, praying; Father Cummings too weak to pray any more; Father Cummings dead . . . the body being hauled out of the hold, up into the light . . . Father Duffy delirious in a corner, demanding that they bring him ham and eggs . . . heat, suffocation, fever . . . a man going mad with thirst and knifing his neighbor, slashing his wrists and sucking his blood before the boy was dead . . . the bodies being hauled out of the hold . . . hunger and thirst, madness and despair.

It was in this dark hold, where he had absolved so many sinners, that Father Hausmann made his own last confession, was sorry for all his sins, blessed himself, and died. He had no last words. He didn't even ask that they give his love to Nussie. On the journey he had done nothing extraordinary, except give his food to those who in his opinion needed it more than he; and he stopped doing this two weeks before he died, on orders from his commanding officer. He was not spectacular.

The men among whom he suffered and died were not religious. It is not true that there are no atheists in foxholes, if by it you mean that all men turn to God when they are in danger of death. They don't. All through the war men died as they had lived: in hatred, in selfishness, in lust, in heroic sanctity. The soldiers and sailors who watched the dying Hausmann, locked in a dungeon below the surface of the sea and face to face with death, were still hardened sinners and hidden saints, like men in a city. There is no sensible wave of grace which comes with danger and death. Bearded and sick and dirty, and some of them sunk in sin, they watched him. And some were touched by the way he died.

Close to him lay an officer, an educated agnostic, with an army jaw and a deep conviction that religion was a lady's game. He despised all ministers of religion because he believed that they were all of them personally hypocritical. Carl, lying beside him in the darkness, had once speculated on the potential corrective value of punching him in the nose because of his brutal language about the Church. He liked Carl for that. One year later he wrote to a priest:

> Father Hausmann died like the saint that he was. His death was actually a beautiful thing. There is no question as to what happened to his soul. Yes, Padre, we lost some wonderful men out there and I'm inclined to believe that the Almighty left us here for some reason. It seems that we are obligated to do something for the good of humanity. Padre, I attend church every Sunday now.

Perhaps it was only a little thing—giving edification like that. Perhaps he was totally unconscious that he was influencing anyone. At any rate, he kept that last rule which reads: "As in the whole of life, so also and much more in death, every one of the Society must make it his effort and care that God our Lord be glorified and served in him, and that those around be edified at least by the example of his patience and fortitude. . . ."

It was a little unusual that this agnostic officer, brutalized by pain, should have seen something beautiful in that quiet death in the hold. But the beauty was really there, because other prisoners saw it too, even in the filth and slime. His death was as quiet and as peaceful as the chime of a clock in the darkness, as if his soul had dwelt within his body like a great prince in a stone castle and the enemy had done nothing but beat in rage against the iron gates and howl around the walls; it was as if his soul left gracefully, serene and handsome and unsoiled, leaving the castle empty. He died as if the pain had never touched him, as if he had not suffered at all.

In the pocket of his ragged shorts, after the body had been hauled up on deck, they found his rosary and his stole—the only things that he had saved through the weeks of torture.

It is not certain that he was buried in the Japanese Sea. At one moment the corpses were stacked near the railing; a little later, when one of the men was brought up on deck, they were gone. There was no sign of them, not even in the sea. Some of the bodies were long dead and should have floated. The man saw streaks on the deck from the spot near the railing to the hatch which led to the boiler room. Perhaps the Japanese, who needed fuel badly, used the bodies to stoke the ship on toward Japan.

It was a strange ending for such a gentle, quiet priest, but Saint Francis of Assisi, another very gentle soul, would love to have died that way.

Epilogue

An officer who survived, telling his story to an American rescue party after Japan had surrendered, listened in silence as his hearers expressed their opinions of the Japanese. When they had finished, he said: "Yes, the Japanese were as bad as you say. But we, the two hundred or so who are still alive, we were devils, too. If we had not been devils, we could not have survived. When you speak of the good and the heroic, don't talk about us. The generous men, the brave men, the unselfish men, are the men we left behind."

This conversation was held when the man was emotionally moved; his words obviously mean to suggest a situation; they do not state a scientific fact. The speaker was humble; at least he was contrite; probably he was a much better man than many of those who died. For not only the good men perished, and not only the bad survived. God seems to have no such simple, obvious formula for death in a war. God does not consistently kill off the good and preserve the evil. Still, most of the survivors speak that way, as if they were ashamed of their survival, as if all the dead were noble. Perhaps, really, they are. Perhaps any man is dignified by dying for his country. He could not have given more than his life, even if he gave it unwillingly. It is a great sacrifice and perhaps we should salute the real glory of it.

Father Hausmann died for his country, but only incidentally. He died for it in passing, while he was trying to do something else. However, his death was more heroic than the average, and this placard hangs in the home of his parents at Weehawken.

So Proudly We Hail

In grateful memory of
First Lieutenant Carl W. Hausmann

Who died in the service of his country
In the Pacific Area, January 20, 1945

He stands in the unbroken line of patriots who have
dared to die
That freedom might live, and grow, and increase its
blessings.
    Freedom lives, and through it, he lives—
In a way that humbles the undertakings of most men.

(Signed) Harry Truman
President of the United States of America

THIS *twentieth century, only half spent, was an era of suffering and cataclysm. Whole peoples were uprooted, minorities wiped out, nations erased. Not for ages had such brutality and barbarism been let loose on defenseless men. The gas chamber, the machine gun, the concentration camp, the air armada: all these had shattered the ramparts of human dignity.*

Tragedy forced men back upon themselves; hurt and fear clamored for more certain solutions to life's basic concerns—man's origin and destiny, how best to use this human span of years. Lawyers began to shift away from their judicial gods, Hobbes and Holmes. Educators started ferreting out contradictions in their Messias—Dewey, in James, and in Horace Mann.

People were losing their faith in vaunted science; they paid less heed when Einstein pontificated from the throne of theology or practical politics. One by one the myths were being exploded. Darwin and evolution, Marx and Communism, Hitler and Aryan superiority, Freud and sex perversion, Adam Smith and inhuman economics, Ricardo and the iron law of wages, Margaret Sanger and "Planned Parenthood." God was the only panacea. That became increasingly clear.

The world had little choice now as it tottered perilously on the brink of ruin. Law and reason and truth were vindicating themselves more and more clearly. The desertion of values could terminate only in chaos. The times themselves preached eloquently of the need for spiritual reclamation.

Out of these gaping wounds, from the slaughter and bloodshed there might be born now a deeper vision. Perhaps in a broken and shattered world the Father would discern less resistance to the gentle suasion of His grace. The awareness of a close-knit solidarity was beginning to grip men, tear down the barriers, make philosophers of fools; and of wayward men, saints. No one could tell about the future, but man was filled with a sense of prospect as he struggled to recapture the spirit which once had made him great.

* * *

The Unbroken Phalanx

Father James Shannon, S.J.

by Thomas J. Flynn, S.J.

Learned men are anxious to be held in great esteem and to be called wise. There are many things the knowledge of which is of little advantage to the soul. And he is very unwise who busies himself with anything save God and the things which may serve him for salvation.
—*The Imitation of Christ.*

On September 11, 1950, the following telegram was received in California:

FATHER SHANNON ONE OF OUR GREATEST MEN HAD GALL BLADDER OPERATION. PROGRESSED REMARKABLY WELL AT FIRST. COMPLICATIONS SET IN WHICH HIS WEAKENED CONDITION COULD NOT STAND. GREAT AT THE END AS IN HEALTH. NEVER COMPLAINED NEVER REQUESTED RELIEF FROM GREAT PAIN. TRULY IGNATIAN.

VAL K ROCHE SJ
(Minister, St. Louis University)

The St. Louis papers made the following brief chronicle:

The Unbroken Phalanx

Father Shannon was a widely known physicist and geologist who had been on the University Faculty since 1909 and had been Head of the Department of Physics since 1912. He had also developed the department of geology, and apart from the scientific field was, at times, dean of the School of Philosophy and Science, vice-dean and regent. It was he who had been instrumental in inducing Father James B. Macelwane, the present dean of the University's Institute of Technology, to enter the field of geophysics in which he had attained distinction as a seismologist.

They had collaborated in the publication of a manual of physics laboratory experiments in 1917 which was employed in many institutions. They had also, in 1934, directed a field camp near Canon City, Colorado, in which methods of geological mapping were applied to the embayment there. Father Shannon's many years of service on the council of regents and deans and as secretary of the board of graduate studies had made him influential in shaping the policies of the university. In a few weeks he was to have celebrated his 60th year as a Jesuit. He had taught mathematics at Xavier College in Cincinnati and Marquette University prior to obtaining his master's degree from St. Louis University. Surviving him were five brothers and five sisters, all Canadians.

Such was the public account of Father Shannon's death. But what was significant in this full life the newspapers, perforce, left quite unsaid.

Of middle size, with a strong and well-shaped head and features, Father Shannon was a markedly earnest and simple man, devoid of eccentricities. It would be excessive to style him a first-rate physicist, although his list of publications runs to more than thirty titles, the most important being his book, *The Amazing Electron*, published in 1946. He was not a pioneer of genius, but a masterful and diligent collator of the best new discoveries in his field. No one denies that as a teacher of physics and geology he was first-rate, and many of his students estimate him the best teacher they encountered in this field.

He was extremely plain: clear and methodical, short on brilliance, but long on thoroughness and lucidity. To uncounted students at the University he was a familiar figure, regular as clockwork, pacing up and down "the Tar Patch" saying his Office, often serenely ignoring spiraling footballs from adjacent games of touch-tackle.

A month and a half before his death Father Shannon made a trip to California. Plagued by intermittent attacks of gall-bladder, he was anxious to visit the huge cyclotron at Berkeley and the California Institute of Technology, and he seemed glad to pay discomfort in order to go there. Much younger men were astonished and discomfited by his vital interest in all about him: terrain, crops, irrigation, and a stream of new faces. He was living very much in the present, as a series of postcards to newly-won friends warmly testified. Superiors, half his age, were struck by the care of this visitor to obtain small permissions. Obviously it was a precaution, so that if death should find him at such a dinner, or at a stop-over in Salinas, it would be because obedience put him there.

A month before his death Father Shannon remarked that he was "hopelessly old-fashioned." And indeed there was about him a marked gentility and courtesy not usually associated with the mid-twentieth-century man. His choice in literature was Victorian (Tennyson seems the favorite); his judgments on persons and events were mild and reticent, and the constant moderation of language, the grave, curiously-inflected speech, the dominant air of gentleness and kindness were continually in danger of betraying him as "a nice old man." Further acquaintance revealed that Father Shannon was somewhat more than a nice old man; long years of discipline and prayer and the care of souls had taught him what was in human nature. Yet he was content to forget it and rather reflect on what lay within the power of grace.

Fortunately, he kept a number of diaries during the last forty years of his life. Some are detailed observations of weather conditions; others carefully chronicled botanical discoveries; others cover Missouri Province Jesuit affairs (even in the last days his knowledge of the recent status, appointments and achievements of a host of younger Jesuits was admirable). The longest diaries, however, concern the births, deaths, marriages, hospitalizations, and movements of his many relatives. Himself the fourth child in a family of seventeen, it was his hobby to record the vital statistics of his family. His mother, Bridget Hanley, had died at the age of 38 after bearing nine children. His father, James Shannon, had married again, and by his second wife, Mary Cowan, had eight more children. All this Irish-Canadian stock was notable for both longevity and fecundity, and it was a formidable task to trace the multiple proliferations of the Shannons, Hanleys, Conveys, Butlers, Brunelles, and Lees.

There is no evidence that he ever faltered at this cataloguing, as page after page of his diaries testifies. It may be said, though, that to an outsider these family diaries are prodigiously dull: there is never any personal comment on the soberly recorded entries, never a striking phrase, never a flashing turn of thought. He neither praises, nor blames, nor interprets. He records. It is, of course, a carry-over from the scientific habit. But the same habit does damage to the spiritual diaries, which too often are unattractively skeletal. At the best we find 60 repeated year's resolutions to exact fidelity to spiritual exercises, to harder work, to less despondency, to greater love.

When we turn to the sermons and conferences of Father Shannon, another side is revealed. They are orderly, doctrinally solid, almost painfully explicit, and distressingly unoriginal. The style is semi-hypnotic Victorian, and the doctrine is almost an anthology from "approved" spiritual writers. Yet, curiously enough, one had only to listen to the earnest, pedantic tones of the preacher to realize that it was doctrine he himself literally lived by and in whom it had undoubted results.

From 1919–1922 Father Shannon was superior of the scholastics at St. Louis, and there is no doubt that his extreme conscientiousness made this a heavy burden to him. In a notebook he kept account of each permission he gave, and his instructions to the philosophers and theologians are unalterably insistent upon the exact and complete observance of religious rules and customs. It was his way, and the literal way, and the approved way, and he was at a loss to understand anything else. The forbearance and kindness of his character made this duty acutely painful for him, and he was much relieved to be freed of its responsibility.

During his last decade Father Shannon's hearing failed, to the impairment of his classroom technique, since he made considerable use of oral questioning. A man singularly devoid of crotchets, he was called "Rod" by his students from his peculiar inflection of this word as "rawed," e.g., "Now I take this glass rod, and I rub it with this cloth . . ."

It was his practice to get to the classroom early and write a summary of the whole lecture on the blackboard. This was used for prelection, explanatory reference, and as a capitulation. His most distinguished pupil, Father Macelwane, writes:

> I consider him the best teacher I ever had. He was thorough and painstaking. In addition to that he was a scholar. . . . At the end of third year philosophy I was assigned, with seven Jesuit scholastics, to a summer school in field geology in Colorado under Father John J. Coony, as our superior, and Father Shannon as our professor. They had taught a previous summer field course in Colorado to a group of scholastics in the summer of 1910 and we had the advantage of Father Shannon's observations on that occasion together with his wide reading and study of the literature in preparation for his teaching and guidance. We had regular lectures and we had also to prepare reports on the various phases of the localities in which we did the field work, which were primarily Canon City, Leadville, and Manitou, and the Pike's Peak Region.
>
> In addition to the geological training which he gave us, he awakened in several of us a lively interest in botany, in which he was quite expert. It all started one afternoon when Father Coony decided that we needed a little rest from the strenuous field work and declared a half holiday. Father Shannon called Father Joseph S. Joliat and myself and asked if we did not want to take a little walk. He did

not go very far. He pulled out a botany book in the midst of a patch of wild flowers and started trying to interest us in the means of identifying the various plants and flowers.

At first I was not very enthusiastic. I would have preferred to rest, naturally, but it was not very long before he had awakened my curiosity and then enthusiasm so that we took every opportunity we had on the side to gain more information of the Rocky Mountain flora and when, on our return to St. Louis, we were assigned to special studies, we arranged a regular course of geological field work on Thursdays (the vacation day) under Father Shannon's direction; and he often came along with his botany book and before the year was over we knew most of the flora in the St. Louis region, in addition to having a rather thorough field course in geology.

Father Shannon was born on a homestead near Hastings, Ontario, Canada. He attended the little frame Catholic grammar school at Campbellford. At the age of 15 he secured the highest marks in the second-class non-professional examination at Campbellford High School. He then passed the third-class professional examination and obtained a teacher's certificate at the age of 17. The following three years he taught at Campbellford, spending his summers working on the harvest. At the age of 20 he entered the Normal School at Ottawa and after passing with honors the second-class professional examination and teaching one semester in the Senior Division of the Model School at Forest, he was appointed principal in Belleville, Ontario, in January, 1889.

He had progressed rapidly, and his career already seemed secured. But two boyhood friends had three years before entered the Jesuit Novitiate at Sault-au-Recollet, Quebec. One of them, Thomas Gorman, gave him a little book entitled *The Choice of a State of Life*, by Father Rossignoli, S.J., which made a deep impression upon him. A month after becoming principal at Belleville, a startlingly vivid dream of the last judgment impelled him to make a retreat. At its end he wrote to

Father John Pierre Frieden, S.J., the Provincial of the Missouri Province, and asked admission to the Society. Missouri seemed to attract the Irish-Canadian more than the French customs of the Canadian Jesuits. After an examination in Detroit he received a letter dated February 15, 1890, from Father Frieden:

> My dear Mr. Shannon,
>   I write to let you know that the result of the examination is satisfactory, so that you can present yourself at Florissant [the Jesuit Novitiate] at any time. Please let me know when we may expect you.
>   I remain
>   Yours faithfully in Christ,
>   J. P. Frieden, S.J.

The following September he began novitiate. But a week after the long retreat he was struck with typhoid fever. It was the beginning of a series of illnesses that were to plague him intermittently throughout his career.

Testimony from his years of study shows that as a religious his conduct was exemplary, and that as a student he was competent and industrious. It was during these years, too, that he developed an interest in the physical sciences that were to be his life's avocation. In 1900 he again returned to Cincinnati, this time teaching physics and mathematics. In 1902 he went back to St. Louis for four years of theology in which he was "eminently successful." In his diary of this period he has an account of the Jesuit "Grand Act" (a defense of the whole course of scholastic philosophy and theology), in St. Louis on April 29, 1903, at which President Roosevelt, Cardinal Gibbons, Archbishop Kain, and a host of visiting professors witnessed and quizzed the defendant, Father Gabriel Vilallonga. It was Vilallonga, later a Provincial in Spain, Superior and Visitor of the Philippine Mission, who remarked some years afterwards that he had found two very holy Jesuits in the United States: Father Shannon and Father Furay.

In the midst of a botanical diary kept during these years we come across the following entry, perhaps the unique subjective note in such chronicles:

Nov. 14 (1903) Felt dispirited and lonely at 4 P.M. and went outside by myself to walk in the fresh clear air of the moderately cool November day, fresh breezes blowing from the West. Felt almost immediately cheered and after a time exhilarated by the subtle influences of the air and bright light and by thinking of fresh grass, trees and brisk autumn wind blowing over pasture lands and of all kindred scenes called up by these. How good God is to provide us in our loneliness and sense of helplessness and despondency with these lovely and gentle monitors of His providence . . .

The spiritual diaries kept during these years find him always urging himself to the practice of fundamental virtues: "to practice most carefully the virtue of chastity," "to be exact and fervent in spiritual exercises and to continue my particular examen on these" (Dec. 7, 1897). On June 19, 1900, he writes:

O surely I have enough to answer for in my past life. Let me strive heroically day by day to make my succeeding life more *true*, more *pure*.

He was ordained in 1905 at the age of 37. In 1906 he was sent on to graduate studies in physics at Johns Hopkins University. Before beginning these studies we find the following retreat entry:

Sept. 22. I feel within me and have always felt an ambition to distinguish myself, to do something good and noble, not to go through life without having a strong influence on my fellow men. . . . Of myself I am qualified neither physically nor morally nor intellectually to distinguish myself and do what I desire. Whatever I accomplish will have to be done through Him. If then I wish to realize my ambitions, I must make myself a perfectly pliable instrument in His hands.

The same passage gives the clue to his life-long interest in his relatives:

> I feel that I have a strong influence over my relatives and friends and others with whom I come in contact; that my relatives in particular look to me to obtain spiritual favors for them, to plead their cause with God. What a powerful motive this is for striving to make myself a man of prayer, a man of God. What a shame for me to be no better than they who have had none of my opportunities.

During the following two years at Johns Hopkins he did well. But his undergraduate training was deficient and the effort to make it up together with the advanced work wore down his never-too-strong physique; and superiors, fearing a breakdown, called him home for a rest. After the conclusion of tertianship (a final year of spiritual training for Jesuits) in Cleveland in 1908, he was assigned to teach a group of 24 Jesuit scholastics field geology on the shore of Lake Erie, near Vermilion, Ohio. In addition to lectures, he conducted field work on the stratigraphy and glacial geology of northern Ohio and the islands in the lake, and ended with a longer excursion to Niagara Falls and the Niagara Gorge.

Instead of returning to Johns Hopkins, he was then sent to St. Louis University as Associate Professor of Physics. This began his 37 years' work at that University. His effectiveness as a teacher caused rapid promotion, so that in 1912 he was made Head of the Department, which he remained till his death.

Father James Macelwane tells something of those years:

> The following year, 1912, I was assigned to his Department of Physics to teach both high school and sophomore college physics and the physics course of the premedical students. That was a very strenuous regime with much laboratory and I found myself the first morning faced with some eighty students in the laboratory, all needing help at once. However, when I saw what I was up against, I walked out of the laboratory and went directly over to

Father Shannon's room and said, 'This is impossible. I cannot give attention to those eighty students all at once. What can we do about it?' Father Shannon's answer was characteristic:—'I shall be right over and take half of them.' —and within ten minutes he was in charge of one-half of the laboratory. It was not long before we began to collaborate on the *Loose-Leaf Manual of Laboratory Experiments in College Physics.*

. . . I returned to St. Louis University in 1925 with a commission to organize a department of geophysics, the first in the Western Hemisphere. In this I was helped very much by Father Shannon who was Dean of the School of Philosophy and Science as well as head of the Department of Physics.

. . . I was often edified when Father Shannon would be over in the Physics Department laboratory writing out on the blackboard the detailed outline for his eight o'clock class the following morning and would break off when the Litany bell rang, would go all the way down to Litanies, come back up again and continue with his writing on the blackboard. I must confess that I often found an excuse, which perhaps was not so edifying, for having to remain up there. Father Shannon did not say a word although his classroom was across the corridor from the one in which I was writing my outline.

Following this began the long years of an unceasing round of classes and study, broken only by short intervals in the hospital. The botanical diaries, which were an occasion of much pleasure to him, disappear, and with them entries of such charm as these:

July, 1907. Made the distinguished acquaintance of the Sweet Fern *Myrica asplenifolia* so abundant in the Massachusetts woods but never noticed by me before. Its fragrance is quite pronounced but delicate. It has long fern-like linear-lanceolate fragrant leaves, but is not a real fern, belonging instead to the sweet-gale family (*Myricaceae*).

May 15, 1909. Made an identification of a plant which had

puzzled me on two or three different occasions and which I had been unable to refer with certainty to any particular family. *Caulophyllum thalictroides* . . .

June 14 (1907). Took a walk in afternoon through Roland Park and country N.E., returning by Charles St. extended. Admired in Embla Park the great number of fine chestnut trees—large, with ridged and furrowed trunks. I noticed that they were preparing to flower. The long naked cylindrical calkins of the sterile flowers were conspicuous but had not yet opened out the individual blossoms. *Castanea sativa var. Americana.*

He had now become a specialist in physics, and to this end was to forego much that he had enjoyed before. As he noted in an instruction to the scholastics under him in 1920:

The specialist in any line of human learning, precisely because he is a specialist, must sacrifice much, must concentrate his effort and his intentions, must forego many pleasures and distractions, must make up his mind to remain ignorant of many things of common interest. And this precisely because human energy is limited, his time on earth is measured by years and not by centuries . . . Now, the religious is a specialist in the spiritual life.

It was during this long round of years in the classroom (it is estimated that Father Shannon spent 20 years behind the desk as a student, and 50 years in front of the desks as a teacher) that articles began to appear in scientific periodicals on the *Quantum Theory, The Foundation of Physics and the Structure of Matter, The Nature of Light and Radiation,* which were lucid assessments of the most significant modern findings. More significant, however, was the interior spirit that animated this unremitting work. The spiritual diaries, especially the annual retreat, unfold the picture: in 1915 he finds himself at middle-age and reproaches his tepidity "in the autumn of the spiritual life." In 1916 he resolves "not to buy during the coming year any newspapers, magazines, etc., without permission. I must be strict with myself on this point." In 1918 he writes:

> Be on your guard to avoid *unnecessary* work, i.e., work not imposed by obedience or duty, so as to have strength for the necessary. Have spiritual holidays and bodily and mental holidays. Refuse to be an everlasting grind. Let no cent of money come to you which is not turned over to the treasurer to be entered on books and accounted for.

King Arthur and the Table Round still fire his imagination as in boyhood long ago. There are no subtleties in the diaries; they are an ascetic's notebook, and the straightforward indices of a chosen soul. In 1920 he resolves again to "make every meditation well," "for I must at all costs advance in perfection, must love my blessed Saviour more . . ." In 1922 he determines "to go through my belongings, papers, etc. to see if there are not many things I could dispense with." And he notes, "I have only to make one day's spiritual exercise at a time. Let me see to it that nothing shall come between me and these duties." In 1923 he is much heartened by the doctrine of St. Therese of Lisieux, and remarks simply, "Let me cultivate the love of suffering."

Classes are repeated year after year; each semester brings a new wave of faces whose anonymity wears off just before the course is finished. He must avoid the rut; he must bring into his classes new matter, new methods; he must try to get into each student's mind and beckon him toward the light. It is a long grind, certainly, an everlasting routine. He bestirs himself ceaselessly to greater love of Our Lord. In 1925 he notes, "Surely deliberate venial sin should be a thing of the past with me." In 1926 he ponders "the extremely great need of keeping close to the demands of obedience. God wants not our *work* but our *service*." And, he is getting old. In 1931 he resolves "to celebrate each Mass as if it were to be the very last. Any one Mass *may* be my last." In 1932 he is underlining "affective prayer" and he warns himself at the age of 64: "I must perfect my observance of chastity and strengthen my guard against all dangers that threaten it. . . . They are about us on every side making their appeal to our eyes and other senses. No one, least of all myself, can hope to be unaffected by them. In particular I must guard against one source of danger." And here he quotes a favorite maxim from St. John Berchmans: "If thou wishest to be a child of Mary, be a zealot for thy chastity."

In 1934 he was superior of a group of Jesuit graduate students at Canon City, Colorado. Father Macelwane writes again:

> All through the field work he kept along with us younger people, climbing steep mountain sides and tracing formations in a way that commanded our admiration. It was nearly too strenuous for him and on the way back to St. Louis he was obviously ill. After his arrival he took to his bed and was transferred to a hospital with a serious case of thrombosis in the leg which eventually necessitated an operation and kept him in the hospital for months.

The following year he urges himself to find time to write:

> I am now in a position to write a book on electron physics; the Society has a right to expect that I shall publish something . . . .

And again there appears the lifetime theme of absolute exactitude in spiritual exercise:

> Meditation—preparing for it the night before; making the preparatory prayer, preludes, etc. carefully.

On the seventh day of his retreat in 1937 he asks:

> Why have I not been more fervent, more exact, more earnest? Is there not in me a deep vein of triviality . . . ?

Three years later occurs his golden jubilee in the Society. St. Louis University tries to honor him. His diary breaks a pattern and he allows himself a cryptic two-word comment:

> Mon. Sept. 11. Golden Jubilee Day. Solemn High Mass in church at 8:30; Father W. J. Ryan Deacon; Father R. R. Rooney Subd., Father Macelwane preached. Bishop Don-

nelly attended the dinner at 6:15 and at the end gave a short speech.

The scholastics put on an entertainment at 7:15; very fine.

What of infused contemplation? What of mystical graces? There is no written evidence for or against them. His attention is always upon the lowly and unspectacular virtues: more work, more faith, more hope, more love. In the midst of the war, in 1942, he is teaching a full schedule. He notes:

> I must cultivate the virtue of *gratitude*. Every breath I draw, every impulse of grace, every power of mind and body is a new incentive to gratitude.

In 1947 he reminds himself "of the shortness of time that is left to me and the great work still to be accomplished." His book *The Amazing Electron* has by this time attracted favorable attention. A lifetime's work in science and religion weights the book's final remarks:

> As we look at most of the discoveries and inventions connected with the subject of this book—at the X-ray tube, the photoelectric tube, vacuum tubes of all kinds, the electron microscope—we see clearly that their use for laudable or at least indifferent purposes vastly outweighs the wrong or unlawful use. . . .

He has something to say to his fellow-scientists:

> Those sad abuses that we see about us are a proof clear as noonday that man needs something more than mere knowledge and learning if he is to use the gifts of God rationally at all times. He needs more than mere intellectual training and information. He needs a training of the will and of the moral sense, and these can be secured fully only through the help of sound philosophy and religion. For it is only philosophy and religion that can show him his true relation to his fellow men and to God and his obligations to them, and can give him strength to act accordingly. While we love all knowledge and all science, we must in honesty

acknowledge that for the consistently proper use of it, man needs the guidance of a higher power.

Who loves not Knowledge? Who shall rail
Against her beauty? May she mix
With men and prosper! Who shall fix
Her pillars? Let her work prevail. . . . .

A higher hand must make her mild
If all be not in vain. . . .

In 1948, at the age of 80, he is still pegging away at his meditation, still resolving fervent recitation of the Divine Office, is stirred by Fatima:

I must strive to do more in the way of intercessory prayer for sinners and making sacrifice for them and for "the freedom and exaltation of Holy Mother the Church."

He writes out for himself an appealing "Visit to Nazareth" and ends:

I must make a great deal of the recitation of the Rosary. There are rich treasures here which I must do my utmost to secure.

In 1949 he is carrying on some ministry, is attending some scientific conventions (he was a member and officer in the St. Louis Academy of Science, the American Physical Society, the American Association for the Advancement of Science, and a number of Jesuit scientific organizations), and is quite busy in the classroom. He notes:

First Semester 1949–50. Taught the following classes: Ph 170—11 students; Ph 9—3 students; Ph 141—two students (Mr. Harris; Father Andrack, C. R.)

In June, 1950, he receives word from the Provincial that he is to go to California for the First Solemn Mass of a Jesuit cousin and he is happy at the prospect of visiting the Coast, especially the huge cyclotron at Berkeley. A diary account of new people met and places visited is faithfully recorded; an expense account is exactly entered. Painful gall bladder attacks throw him somewhat off schedule, but he has time, even, to check the rock formations on the beach at Santa Cruz before spending a few days there in the hospital. His gall bladder trouble forbids him taking a cocktail with his relatives, and a few days later he quietly urges an apology on his host lest he should have been offended. The painful attacks increase alarmingly and he decides to cut short his trip and return to St. Louis where there are doctors who know his case well. But he gambles that the attacks will hold off long enough to get a look at rich Southern California and do a little business there. From Phoenix he sends gracious cards to new friends, and from Kansas City writes, "Shall be glad to get back home."

It was, he realized, toward evening. He was closing sixty years of incessant response to bells for spiritual exercises and class, of the humdrum of scholastic life and long research. On the one hand, he would like a few more years of teaching, on the other . . . as always, he would let Another decide.

"As in the whole of life," runs the Jesuit rule, "so also and much more in death, everyone of the Society must make it his effort and care that God our Lord be glorified and served in him. . . ." Father Shannon, who loved these rules, knew that no single one of them was more important than this. In early August he underwent a critical operation at St. John's Hospital in St. Louis. He sent optimistic postcards: "Patient progressing favorably." He was even up and saying Mass and the Office. But courage was not enough. A disastrous relapse brought with it new and excruciating pain. It was the end and so he received the Last Sacraments and in peace awaited his final "status."

The fine features of the dying man became more sharply etched and luminous. Over and over, visitors to the sick room heard a grave and cheerful "Thank you, nurse," "Thank you, Father." His pain increased; and then, on the happy Feast of the Birth of Our Lady, September 8, he died.

* * *

Autumn had just come to St. Louis. The Chronicler wants to step in at this point and take the reader by the hand. He wants to lead him back over those years—more than half a century of them, and to go with him through the thousands of hours he spent before his classes explaining the beautiful mysteries hidden in whirling electrons, in rock and granite and the petal of a flower.

The onlooker wants to remind his hearer how unending the toil of teaching can become, how inexorable the schedule, the problem of transmission to such various capacities, the finishing and starting all over again, how routine wears the spirit down, and what a stern mother monotony is.

And beneath all Father Shannon's uncompromising love of duty and his determination to make himself a better teacher, scientist, and writer, there lay his even more adamant resolve to better himself spiritually. After all, there have been great teachers down the ages who had been just as vitally absorbed in their work as he, just as stimulating, just as young because they lived with the young, men who continued to grow mentally long after their bodies and nerves had begun to decline.

But this Jesuit pieced the prodigious years of intellectual work into an even fuller and more laborious task of Christian perfection. No one probably gave much thought to that as the decades marched by, at what faith in God is needed to teach for more than 50 years, study, write, pray, offer Mass with relatively little in the line of tangible returns.

That is why the man, Shannon, typifies perhaps best of all the modern American Jesuit. For most of the approximately 7000 American Jesuits are teachers; usually, too, they are mild-mannered, and not given to needless expenditure of energy, realizing as Father Shannon remarked, that God wants "our service more than our work," that we can't do it all anyhow. Outwardly, perhaps, inconspicuous, they are quite successful in the classroom, and known and admired by a growing segment of alumni who recall their thoroughness, their discipline, their way of saying things or, at times, "sounding off."

Gradually the Jesuit teacher grows old; but there is no compromise with his work: he is up for his hour of communion with God every morning, his Holy Mass, his breviary, his beads, and he becomes more deeply aware of how important the interior life is, the one thing that ultimately matters. Toward the Society which took him in as a young man and has cared for him ever since he manifests a quiet and unshakable affection. His brother Jesuits with whom he labors and laughs and even quarrels at times are very dear to him. He loves his work because he is convinced of its cumulative impact.

Then some autumn morning, it may be, a simple piece of paper is placed on the Mass board in the cloister and as the priests hurry by in the dim light they read that Father so-and-so died last night, R.I.P. (May he rest in peace). But always, it seems, there is someone who will step up and fill the empty space. The ranks close together again. The swift mobile corps of Loyola is moving over the battlefield prepared for combat.

A NOTE ON THE TYPE

IN WHICH THIS BOOK IS SET

This book is set in Janson, a Linotype face, created from the early punches of Anton Janson, who settled in Leipzig around 1670. This type is not an historic revival, but rather a letter of fine ancestry, remodelled and brought up to date to satisfy present day taste. It carries a feeling of being quite compact and sturdy. It has good color and displays a pleasing proportion of ascenders and descenders as compared to the height of the lower case letters. The book was composed and printed by The York Composition Company, Inc., of York, Pa., and bound by Moore and Company of Baltimore. The typography and design are by Howard N. King.

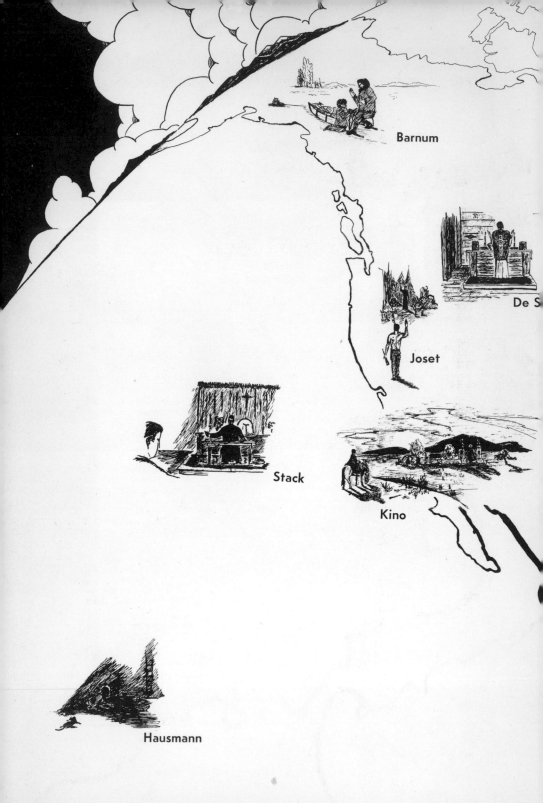

Barnum

De S

Joset

Stack

Kino

Hausmann